WITHDRAWN

HARVARD LIBRARY

WITHDRAWN

CHURCH AND REFORM

STUDIES IN MEDIEVAL AND REFORMATION TRADITIONS

History, Culture, Religion, Ideas

FOUNDED BY HEIKO A. OBERMAN †

EDITED BY

ANDREW COLIN GOW, Edmonton, Alberta

IN COOPERATION WITH

THOMAS A. BRADY, Jr., Berkeley, California
JOHANNES FRIED, Frankfurt
BRAD GREGORY, University of Notre Dame, Indiana
BERNDT HAMM, Erlangen
GUSTAV HENNINGSEN, Copenhagen
SUSAN C. KARANT-NUNN, Tucson, Arizona
JÜRGEN MIETHKE, Heidelberg
M. E. H. NICOLETTE MOUT, Leiden

VOLUME CV

LOUIS B. PASCOE, S.J.

CHURCH AND REFORM

Pierre d'Ailly Kneeling in Prayer before the Virgin and Christ Child
Bibliothèque Municipale de Cambrai, Ms. 954, f. 1

CHURCH AND REFORM

BISHOPS, THEOLOGIANS, AND CANON LAWYERS
IN THE THOUGHT OF PIERRE D'AILLY (1351-1420)

BY

LOUIS B. PASCOE, S.J.

BRILL
LEIDEN · BOSTON
2005

Cover illustration: Coat of Arms: Cardinal Pierre d'Ailly
Bibliothèque Municipale de Cambrai, Ms. 926, f.1

Frontispiece: Pierre d'Ailly Kneeling in Prayer before the Virgin and Christ Child.
Bibliothèque Municipale de Cambrai, Ms. 954, f.1

This book is printed on acid-free paper.

Library of Congress Cataloging-in-Publication Data

A C.I.P. record for this book is available from the Library of Congress.

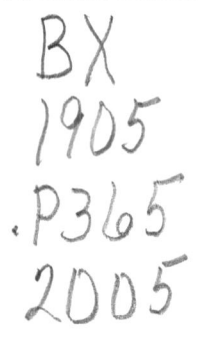

ISSN 1573-4188
ISBN 90 04 14062 X

© *Copyright 2005 by Koninklijke Brill NV, Leiden, The Netherlands*
Koninklijke Brill NV incorporates the imprints Brill Academic Publishers,
Martinus Nijhoff Publishers and VSP.

All rights reserved. No part of this publication may be reproduced, translated, stored in
a retrieval system, or transmitted in any form or by any means, electronic,
mechanical, photocopying, recording or otherwise, without prior written
permission from the publisher.

Authorization to photocopy items for internal or personal
use is granted by Brill provided that
the appropriate fees are paid directly to The Copyright
Clearance Center, 222 Rosewood Drive, Suite 910
Danvers, MA 01923, USA.
Fees are subject to change

PRINTED IN THE NETHERLANDS

In memory of my mother and father

CONTENTS

Preface ix
Abbreviations xi

Introduction... 1

Chapter One. Church and Reform: The Apocalyptic Context 11
   1. Church History as Series of Persecutions 12
   2. Schism, Antichrist, Knowledge of Arrival 28
   3. Antichrist and Post-Apostolic Prophetic Revelation 37
   4. Reform: The Gospel and the Apostolic Ideal 44

Chapter Two. Bishops: Status, Office, Authority.................... 53
   1. Prelates: Terminology, Evolution, Categories................. 53
   2. Status: Apostolic Succession 55
   3. Apostolic Mission and Authority 69

Chapter Three. Bishops: Pastoral Reform, and the Apostolic
   Life 93
   1. Dimensions of Reform Program 93
   2. Pastoral Reform and the Apostolic Ideal 95
   3. Specific Areas of Pastoral Reform............................ 102

Chapter Four. Bishops: Personal Reform, and the Apostolic Life .. 137
   1. Personal Reform: Nature and Goals 137
   2. Specific Aspects of Personal Reform 140
   3. Episcopal Models of the Apostolic Life 157

Chapter Five. Theologians: Status, Office, Authority............... 165
   1. Status: Order, Hierarchy and Corporation 165
   2. Office: Apostolic Mission: Teaching and Preaching........... 181
   3. Authority: Corporate and Individual 192

Chapter Six. Theologians: Theology, Science, Method 207
   1. The Question of Influences 207
   2. Theology: Definition, Unity, and Subject..................... 208
   3. The Scientific Status of Theology............................ 216
   4. Method: Theological Discourse and Apologetics 225

Chapter Seven. Canon Lawyers: Law, Critique, Authority......... 235
   1. Attitude towards Canon Lawyers 237
   2. Law: Nature, Varieties, Relationships 241
   3. Canon Law: Characteristics and Relationships 250
   4. Relationship of Canon Law to Theology 257

Conclusion 277

Bibliography 289

Index of Subjects and Terms...................................... 311
Index of Persons and Places...................................... 319
Index of Modern Scholars 323

PREFACE

After the completion of my work on Jean Gerson many years ago, I envisioned as my next research project a comprehensive study of the ecclesiological and reform thought of several major personalities associated with him at the University of Paris, namely, Pierre d'Ailly, Nicolas of Clamanges, Jean Courtecuisse, and Gerard Machet. Such an extensive study, I hoped, would show the diverse approaches toward the problems of ecclesiology and church reform operative at Paris at the time of the Great Schism and the Council of Constance. With the passage of time, the enormity of such a project gradually dawned on me and I eventually came to the realistic decision to concentrate on only one of the above personalities. Because of the close association of Pierre d'Ailly with Gerson as both mentor and personal friend, I decided to center my research on him. Given the extensiveness of d'Ailly's ecclesiological and reform thought, I further restricted my research to three major dimensions of that thought, namely, his views on bishops, theologians, and canon lawyers. Although I eventually realized that each of these topics could easily merit a separate monograph, advancing age and increasing prudence strongly dictated that I remain with my previous goal.

Any project that has taken so much time to bring to completion is naturally indebted to a large number of institutions and persons. While it is impossible to enumerate all of these, I would like to thank the academic administrators at Fordham University for providing me with the series of faculty fellowships that made much of the research for and writing of the present work possible. I am also very much indebted to the Fordham University Library whose strength in the medieval field is such that I rarely lacked for anything in the realm of printed primary and secondary sources. To my fellow medievalists at Fordham and to Fordham's Center for Medieval Studies, I also extend my gratitude for their support and interest in my work as well as for the highly personal and professional companionship which they have provided over these many years. To my graduate students I also owe much but I am especially grateful to Christopher Bellitto, Daniel La Corte, and

Elizabeth Lowe. Outside of Fordham there are the many libraries and their staff to whom I am indebted for the manuscript and incunabular aspects of my research, especially the Bibliothèque Nationale, the Bibliothèque Mazarine, and the Bibliothèque de l'Arsenal at Paris, the Biblioteca Apostolica Vaticana in Rome, the British Library in London, the Emmanuel College Library at Cambridge University, and the Bibliothèque Municipale in Cambrai.

Finally, I would like to conclude by listing three medievalists to whom, over these many years, I owe a special debt of gratitude for their inspiration, encouragement, and scholarly guidance. The first is the late Gerhart B. Ladner, my doctoral mentor at UCLA, who introduced me to the realm of reform thought and whose scholarly model I have tried to imitate but only at a distance. Secondly, the late Heiko A. Oberman who, while at the University of Tübingen and later at the University of Arizona at Tucson, continually encouraged me in my research on Gerson and d'Ailly. Thirdly, Gilbert Ouy, at the Centre National de la Recherche Scientifique in Paris, whose extensive knowledge of the manuscript tradition of the works of Gerson and d'Ailly has always been at my disposal in both a warmly personal and professional manner.

It is something of a cliché in the writing of prefaces to assume personal responsibility for all errors and shortcomings in the work being presented, and I do so now knowing well that in all clichés there is also much truth.

Louis B. Pascoe, S.J.
New York City
September, 2004

ABBREVIATIONS

AC	L'Année Canonique
ACC	Acta Concilii Constanciensis
AFH	Archivum Franciscanum Historicum
AHC	Annuarium Historiae Conciliorum
AHDLM	Archives d'Histoire Doctrinale et Littéraire du Moyen Age
AKG	Archiv für Kulturgeschichte
BEC	Bibliothèque de l'Ecole des Chartes
CBQ	The Catholic Biblical Quarterly
CCCM	Corpus Christianorum Continuatio Medievalis
CF	Cahiers de Fanjeux
CH	Church History
CHR	The Catholic Historical Review
CS	Chicago Studies
CUP	Chartularium Universitatis Parisiensis
DDC	Dictionnaire de Droit Canonique
DEC	Decrees of the Ecumenical Councils
DMA	Dictionary of the Middle Ages
DSAM	Dictionnaire de Spiritualité Ascétique et Mystique
DTC	Dictionanaire de Théologie Catholique
FS	Franciscan Studies
FZThPh	Freiburger Zeitschrift für Theologie und Philosophie
HPT	History of Political Thought
HTR	Harvard Theological Review
IPQ	International Philosophical Quarterly
JES	Journal of Ecumenical Studies
JHI	Journal of the History of Ideas
MEFr-MA	Mélanges de l'Ecole Française de Rome, Moyen Age
MPT	Medieval Philosophy and Theology
MS	Medieval Studies
MSR	Mélanges de Science Religieuse
NLF	Natrual Law Forum
NRT	Nouvelle Revue Théologique

PBA	Proceedings of the British Academy
PG	Patrologia Greca
PL	Patrologia Latina
PLut	Positions Lutheriennes
PP	Past and Present
RB	Revue Benedictine
RDC	Revue de Droit Canonique
RFN	Rivista di Filosofia Neoscholastica
RHDF	Revue Historique de Droit Français et Etranger
RHE	Revue d'Histoire Ecclésiastique
RHPR	Revue d'Histoire et de Philosophie Religieuse
RL	Revue de Lille
RNP	Revue Néoscholastique de Philosophie
RQH	Revue des Questions Historiques
RSE	Revue des Sciences Ecclésiastiques
RSPT	Revue des Sciences Philosophiques et Théologiques
RSR	Revue des Sciences Religieuses
RT	Revue Thomiste
RTAM	Recherches de Théologie Ancienne et Médiévale
SGrat	Studia Gratiana
SGreg	Studi Gregoriani
ST	Summa Theologiae
TS	Theological Studies
TTQ	Tübinger Theologische Quartalschrift

INTRODUCTION

Pierre d'Ailly (1351–1420) has long been regarded as one of the leading intellectual, ecclesiastical, and political figures of the late Middle Ages. His reputation rests primarily upon the important role that he played within the University of Paris, the Church, and French politics. This role began in his early years as a student and member of the arts and theological faculties (1364–1384), and continued throughout his later life as rector of the Collège de Navarre (1384–1389), University Chancellor and Royal Chaplain (1389–1395), Bishop of Le Puy (1395–1397) and Cambrai (1397–1411), and, finally, as Cardinal (1411–1420). While his teaching and administrative duties at the University of Paris necessarily immersed him in the internal affairs of the university, they also involved him in its external relationships, especially in the complex diplomacy between the University of Paris, the French Crown, and the Avignon Papacy in their many attempts to resolve the impasse created by the Great Schism. D'Ailly's participation in these negotiations continued, in varying degrees, while Bishop of Cambrai and intensified after his elevation to the cardinalate. As cardinal, he played a major role at the Council of Constance (1414–1418) which finally resolved the ecclesiastical division caused by the Schism through the restoration of a unified papacy in the person of Martin V (1417–1431).

Given this threefold dimension of his life, namely, university, church, and country, it is not surprising that research into the thought of Pierre d'Ailly up to the present has concentrated heavily upon its philosophical, theological, and political dimensions. From that research over the past seventy years a slow but steady series of monographs has emerged.[1] Among the earliest of these works was the primarily biographical study of Louis Salembier published posthumously in 1932

---

[1] The following brief survey of the major scholarly publications on d'Ailly consists primarily of monographs. A reasonable number of articles have also appeared which also fall within the same areas of concentration. Such articles will be discussed in detail at appropriate places in the present work and fully listed in the footnotes and bibliography.

but which was heavily based on his doctoral dissertation of 1886.[2] Having long served as a broad introduction to the life, thought, and writings of d'Ailly, Salembier's work has recently been superceded by the detailed biographical study of d'Ailly by Bernard Guenée, a study which skillfully synthesizes the latest research not only on d'Ailly's life but also on the persons and events closely associated with that life.[3]

One of the earliest monographs on d'Ailly's philosophical interests was that of Bernhard Meller who emphasized the epistemological foundations of d'Ailly's thought.[4] More recently, Olaf Pluta and Marguerite Chappuis have published monographs on several of d'Ailly's early philosophical works, namely, his commentaries on Aristotle's *De anima* and Boethius' *De consolatione philosophiae*.[5] Finally, d'Ailly's cosmological interests, especially in the realm of astronomy and astrology have been studied by Laura Ackerman Smoller. While these interests began during his academic years at Paris, they continued throughout his entire life and indeed influenced his interpretation of the Church's history, especially with regard to the period in which he lived and worked.[6]

Within the theological realm, the emphasis has been primarily upon d'Ailly's ecclesiology and especially its conciliar dimensions. In this domain, the work of Francis Oakley far surpasses the much earlier work of Paul Tschackert and is still the most comprehensive analysis

---

[2] Louis Salembier, *Le Cardinal Pierre d'Ailly: Chancelier de l'Université de Paris, Evêque du Puy et de Cambrai, 1350–1420* (Tourcoing: Georges Frère, 1932). Salembier's doctoral thesis was entitled: *Petrus ab Aliaco. Theses Insulenses ad Magisterium in Sacra Theologia*, 4 (Archigymnasium Catholicum Insulense, 1886).

[3] Bernard Guenée, *Between Church and State: The Lives of Four French Prelates in the Late Middle Ages* (Chicago: The University of Chicago Press, 1991). The lengthy chapter dedicated to the life of d'Ailly can be found on pp. 102–258. For a detailed survey of the diocese of Cambrai during the period of the Great Schism see Monique Maillard-Luypaert, *Paupauté, clercs et laïcs: Le diocèse de Cambrai à l'épreuve du Grand Schisme d'Occident (1378–1417)* (Bruxelles: Publications des Facultés Universitaires Saint Louis, 2001). This work is a mine of information on the geographical, institutional, and operational dimensions of that diocese not only internally but also in relationship to the various political authorities and papal allegiances that characterized the period.

[4] Bernhard Meller, *Studien zur Erkenntnislehre des Peter von Ailly* (Freiburg: Herder, 1954).

[5] Olaf Pluta, *Die Philosophische Psychologie des Peter von Ailly* (Amsterdam: B.R. Grüner, 1987), and Marguerite Chappuis, *Le Traité de Pierre d'Ailly sur la Consolation de Boèce, Qu. 1* (Amsterdam: B.R. Grüner, 1993).

[6] Laura Ackerman Smoller, *History, Prophecy, and the Stars: The Christian Astrology of Pierre d'Ailly, 1350–1420* (Princeton: Princeton University Press, 1994).

of d'Ailly's conciliar ecclesiology available.[7] Oakley's study also remains the best analysis of d'Ailly's political thought. While the immediate goal of his work was to analyze d'Ailly's conciliar ideology, his ultimate goal was to ascertain in that ideology the more fundamental principles of d'Ailly's political theory, such as the nature of law and its various forms, the repository, functions, and limits of authority in a body politic, and the distinctions between absolute and constitutional forms of government. In a series of subsequent articles, Oakley has continued his study of these aspects of political thought not only in d'Ailly but also in other major thinkers of the late Middle Ages.[8]

D'Ailly's involvement in university politics is seen in Alan Bernstein's study of d'Ailly's participation in the Blanchard Controversy (1384–1386). This controversy involved the successful efforts of the university to remove its chancellor because of his demand for financial remuneration for granting the licentiate and for the performance of other academic functions associated with his office. In addition to shedding light on the medieval attitude toward knowledge and teaching, the controversy also provides a window into the structure and government of the University of Paris as well as its relationships with the Avignon Papacy and the French Crown during the early years of the Great Schism.[9]

In the present work, I intend to concentrate primarily on the theological dimensions of d'Ailly's thought and especially upon his ecclesiology. Since, as indicated earlier, scholarly research on his ecclesiology has concentrated primarily on its conciliar dimensions, my work will deal with areas which have been relatively neglected by previous scholarship. The areas selected for our study relate to bishops, theologians, and canon lawyers, and, more specifically, to their status, office, and authority. While there is no doubt that in d'Ailly's thought these aspects had a conciliar dimension, it is upon their broader, non-conciliar dimensions that our attention will be primarily focused. I also

---

[7] Francis Oakley, *The Political Thought of Pierre d'Ailly: The Voluntarist Tradition* (New Haven: Yale University Press, 1964); Paul Tschackert, *Peter von Ailli: Zur Geschichte des grossen abendländischen Schisma und der Reformconcilien von Pisa und Constanz* (Gotha: Friedrich Andreas Perthes, 1877).

[8] See his *Natural Law, Conciliarism, and Consent in the Late Middle Ages: Studies in Ecclesiastical and Intellectual History* (London: Variorum, 1984). For an overall evaluation of Oakley's political and ecclesiological views see Constantin Fasolt, 'Voluntarism and Conciliarism in the Work of Francis Oakley,' *HPT*, 22 (2001), 41–52.

[9] Alan E. Bernstein, *Pierre d'Ailly and the Blanchard Affair: University and Chancellor of Paris at the Beginning of the Great Schism*, Studies in Medieval and Reformation Thought, 24 (Leiden: E.J. Brill, 1978).

hope to show that d'Ailly's thought on the status, office and authority of bishops, theologians, and canon lawyers unfolds, in varying degrees, within an apocalyptic, reformative and apostolic or pastoral context.

Before beginning our study, however, some mention should be made about the status of d'Ailly's writings, and, more specifically, the existing catalogues of his works, the various editions, and the quality of those editions. Of the several attempts to identify and catalogue the works of d'Ailly during the nineteenth century, that of Louis Salembier has been the most extensive. In his doctoral dissertation of 1886, Salembier identified some one hundred and fifty three works of d'Ailly and catalogued them in a twofold manner. The first catalogue listed his works according to their date of composition and the second according to their subject or literary genre, e.g. philosophy, theology, sermons, hagiography, letters etc. In the latter catalogue, Salembier also cited the major manuscripts for each work, their location and incipits, as well as existing editions and their dates.[10] In 1908 he published a revised list of d'Ailly works.[11] By the time of his death in 1913, Salembier had expanded his catalogue of d'Ailly's works to include some one hundred and seventy four titles but unfortunately listed them only according to their chronological order. This catalogue was the one used in his monograph on d'Ailly which was published posthumously in 1932.[12]

Salembier's catalogues of d'Ailly's writings were brought up to date in the latter part of the twentieth century by a series of additions, annotations, qualifications, and deletions made in 1965 by Palémon Glorieux.[13] His contributions were the result of long years of manuscript studies related to the history of the University of Paris, especially its faculties of arts and theology, and to the writings of individual theologians such as Gerson and d'Ailly.[14] While Glorieux left intact Salembier's division of d'Ailly's works according to subject and literary genre,

---

[10] Salembier, *Petrus ab Alliaco*, xiii–xlix. An earlier but far less detailed index of d'Ailly's works can be found in Tschackert's *Peter von Ailli*, 348–366.

[11] Salembier, 'Bibliographie des oeuvres du Cardinal Pierre d'Ailly, évêque de Cambrai (1350–1420),' *Le bibliographie moderne*, 12 (1908) 160–170.

[12] Salembier, *Le Cardinal Pierre d'Ailly*, 366–374.

[13] Palémon Glorieux, 'L'oeuvre littéraire de Pierre d'Ailly: Remarques et précisions,' *MSR*, 22 (1965), 61–78.

[14] On the arts and theology faculties of the University of Paris see the following works of Glorieux, *La faculté des arts et ses maîtres au xiiie siècle* (Paris: J. Vrin, 1971), *Aux origines de la Sorbonne*, 2 vols. (Paris: J. Vrin, 1966) and *Repertoire des maîtres en théologie de Paris aux xiiie siècle*. 2 vols. (Paris: J. Vrin, 1933–1934). For Glorieux's edition of the works of Gerson, see his *Jean Gerson: Oeuvres complètes*, 10 vols. (Paris: Desclée, 1960–1973).

he did provide much new information about many of d'Ailly's individual works, especially with regard to authenticity, manuscripts, editions, and dating.

More recently, Gilbert Ouy has further expanded our knowledge about the works of d'Ailly, especially with regard to their manuscript tradition. As a result of many years of codicological research, Ouy has shown that d'Ailly was very much concerned with personally rereading, correcting, recopying, and republishing his earlier works. Because of d'Ailly's preoccupation with such matters, Ouy has been able to identify many more autograph and personally annotated manuscripts of d'Ailly's works than earlier realized. He has also has called our attention to d'Ailly's varying styles of calligraphy and to his use of a dual form of orthography. As a result of his extensive study of d'Ailly's autograph and annotated manuscripts, Ouy has also identified some sixty-five manuscripts that once belonged to d'Ailly's personal library. While we do not know the exact number of volumes in d'Ailly's library at the time of his death, Ouy is convinced that it was one of the most extensive private libraries in fifteenth-century France.[15]

There are no complete editions, either critical or pre-critical, of d'Ailly's works. A complete critical edition, therefore, remains a desideratum but given the monumental size of the endeavor, such an edition remains unlikely at the present time. The form in which individual works of d'Ailly are currently available to the reader, therefore, varies considerably. A small number of his individual works can be found in critical editions published during the twentieth century. A much larger portion of his works is available in pre-critical editions of the seventeenth, eighteenth, and nineteenth centuries. Many of d'Ailly's works are to be found only in incunabula of the late fifteenth century, some of which have been recently reprinted in facsimile format. Finally, a few works are available only in manuscript form. The exact textual status of each work of d'Ailly used in this study will be indicated in full when that work is first cited.

---

[15] Among the many works in which Ouy refers to the writings of Pierre d'Ailly see especially the following: *Le recueil épistolaire autographe de Pierre d'Ailly et les notes d'Italie de Jean de Montreuil*, Umbrae codicum occidentalium, 9 (Amsterdam: North-Holland Publishing Company, 1966), 'De Pierre d'Ailly à Jean Antoine de Baïf: Un exemple de double orthographe à la fin du xive siècle,' *Romania*, 97 (1976), 218–248, and 'Autographes d'auteurs français des xive et xve siècles: Leur utilité pour l'histoire intellectuelle,' *Commentationes*, 28 (1983), 67–103.

Works which have been attributed to d'Ailly but whose authenticity has been seriously challenged have naturally not been relied upon in this study. In this category, special mention must be made of the *Capitula agendorum in Generali Concilio Constantiensi*, a document containing some twenty-six proposals related to a wide range of ecclesiastical reforms. This document exercised considerable influence on many of the reform proposals and decrees later discussed and issued by the Council or incorporated into the various concordats later concluded by Martin V with individual nations. Neither the precise date nor the authorship of the document is indicated in the manuscripts.

Since the latter half of the nineteenth century, the authorship of the *Capitula agendorum* has been attributed to several prominent ecclesiastical leaders active before and during the Council of Constance. Many scholars of the conciliar period and its ecclesiological and reform theories have ascribed the document to the authorship or general editorship of d'Ailly and, until recently, their judgement remained predominant. Some twenty years ago, however, Francis Oakley reviewed the complex history of the controversy over the authorship of the *Capitula agendorum* and conducted his own detailed analysis of the document's dating, content, and sources. As a result of his study, Oakley firmly concluded against both the authorship and the editorship of the work by d'Ailly.[16] While more recent scholarship has not established d'Ailly's authorship, it has reasserted his strong influence upon and even possible editorship of the work since its provenance is clearly related to university circles closely associated with d'Ailly.[17] The arguments and conclusions of Oakley, however, still appear to me as more persuasive and explain my reasons for not including the work among those of d'Ailly.

In the presentation of d'Ailly's thoughts on bishops, theologians, and canon lawyers in the main body of this study, technical Latin terms or phrases used by d'Ailly will either be translated into English with the Latin in parentheses or they will be preceded or followed by an explanatory sentence or sentences. Once so treated, such Latin terms or phrases will then be used freely without further explanation. In certain cases, the meaning of the Latin term or phrase is so clearly

---

[16] Francis Oakley, 'Pseudo-Zabarella's "Capitula Agendorum": An Old Case Reopened,' *AHC*, 14, (1982), 111–123.

[17] See Jürgen Miethke and Lorenz Weinrich, eds. *Quellen zur Kirchengeschichte im Zeitalter der Grossen Konzilien des 15 Jahrhundert*, 2 vols. (Darmstadt: Wissenschaftliche Buchgesellshaft, 1995–2002), 1:25–27. An improved edition of the *Capitula agendorum*, together with a German translation, is included in this work at 1:186–245.

obvious that no translation or explanation is really needed. In the transcription of Latin passages from d'Ailly's works in the footnotes, all abbreviations of and within words are spelled out in full. Contracted case endings are also transcribed in their more recognizable form.[18]

Finally, since d'Ailly spent so many years of his life at the University of Paris as student, teacher, and chancellor and since many of his works date back to that period (1364–1395), a review of the various stages in his studies, the curricula involved, as well as the diverse academic functions and ceremonies associated with each stage is in order. Many of d'Ailly's works composed during his university years, moreover, are often referred to in primary and secondary sources in terms of the specific academic context, function, or ceremony for which they were composed.[19]

Upon his arrival in Paris in 1364, d'Ailly took up residence at the prestigious Collège de Navarre which had been founded in 1305 by Jeanne de Navarre, the wife of Philip the Fair (1285–1314), for students from the county of Champagne. Shortly after his arrival, d'Ailly matriculated in the arts faculty at the university. At Paris, the completion of the full program leading to the master's degree in the arts faculty during d'Ailly's time usually required six years with the first four of these years generally spent in attending lectures and disputations. During these four years, students were designated as auditors (*auditores*). By

---

[18] First declension endings of genitive and dative singulars and nominative plurals (e) are transcribed in more recognizable forms (ae). Where applicable, c's are transcribed as t's.

[19] The sources upon which the following description has depended are: H. Rashdall, *The Universities of Europe in the Middle Ages*, ed. F.M. Powicke and A.B. Emden, 3 vols. (Oxford: Oxford University Press, 1936), 1:439–496; H. DeRidder-Symoens, ed., *Universities in the Middle Ages*, Vol 1 of *A History of the University in Europe*, ed. Walter Rüegg (Cambridge: Cambridge University Press, 1992), 307–359, 409–441; Olaf Pedersen, *The First Universities: Studium Generale and the Origins of University Education in Europe* (Cambridge: Cambridge University Press, 1997), 242–301; Jacques Verger, *Les universités françaises au Moyen Age*, Education and Society in the Middle Ages and Renaissance, 11 (Leiden: E.J. Brill, 1995); Charles Thurot, *De l'organisation et de l'enseignement dans l'Université de Paris au moyen-âge*, (Paris: Dezobry, 1850); Palémon Glorieux, 'L'enseignement au moyen âge: Techniques et méthodes en usage à la faculté de théologie de Paris au xiiie siècle,' *AHDL*, 35 (1968), 65–186, 'Les années d'études de Pierre d'Ailly,' *RTAM*, 44 (1977), 127–149. For the history and intellectual life at the Collège de Navarre see Nathalie Gorochov, *Le Collège de Navarre de sa foundation (1305) au début du xve siècle (1418)* (Paris: Honoré Champion, 1997). For the university vocabulary and terminology see Olga Weijers, *Terminologie des universités au xiiie siècle* (Rome: Edizioni dell'Ateneo, 1987), 283–424, and Mariken Teeuwen, *The Vocabulary of the Intellectual Life in the Middle Ages*, Etudes sur le vocabulaire intellectual du moyen âge, 10 (Turnhout: Brepols, 2003).

d'Ailly's time, the subject matter of the arts curriculum at Paris consisted primarily of philosophy, which essentially meant Aristotle and his Arabic commentators. The traditional subject matter of the arts curriculum, namely, the trivium and the quadrivium, had been considerably marginalized and the teaching thereof increasingly relegated to the colleges. Upon completion of his required course work and disputations in the arts faculty, the student underwent a series of qualifying examinations and disputations after which he received the bachelor's degree.

After attending further lectures and participating in additional disputations for two more years, the student received from the chancellor the licentiate (*licentia*) which involved the right to teach the arts subjects (*jus docendi*). Paris was one of the few medieval universities where, as a result of papal concessions, that right extended to the whole of Christendom (*jus ubique docendi*). The formal recognition of the student as a master took place shortly after the reception of the licentiate and was primarily the prerogative of the faculty. In a series of actions known as the inception ceremonies, the candidate for the master's degree participated in and presided over disputations and was then invested by the faculty with his magisterial insignia, that is, the biretta, the ring, and the book. These ceremonies were then followed by a formal lecture given by the new master in his discipline. The reception of the master's degree in the arts faculty was generally followed by an obligatory two year teaching period in that faculty which was designated as the regency.

While, as indicated earlier, the completion of the full program leading to the master's degree in the arts faculty at Paris generally required six years, D'Ailly appears to have attained his master's degree in the arts faculty in record time. Although we have considerable information as to d'Ailly's years in the theological faculty, precise data with regard to his time in the arts faculty is considerably less, especially as to the specific stages involved in securing his arts degree. Despite this paucity of information, it seems clear that d'Ailly completed all his course work and disputation requirements within four years for he received the licentiate in 1367 and the master's degree in 1368. For d'Ailly's regency in the arts faculty, the situation again is not very clear. Some authorities have maintained that he performed his regency teaching the arts to students at the Collège de Navarre during his first two years as a student in the faculty of theology; others are silent on the subject.

After the reception of the master's degree in the arts faculty, the student could then proceed to matriculate in one of the higher faculties, namely, theology, law, or medicine. Since d'Ailly was a theologian, it is the theology faculty that is of primary interest here. The program of theological studies at the University of Paris involved six years of lectures and disputations during which the student was also designated as an *auditor*. After this period and upon due examination the student received the bachelor's degree in theology. For d'Ailly, this period lasted from 1368 to 1374. Upon reception of his bachelor's degree, the student then embarked upon three years of combined teaching and study. In the first two of these years, he taught basic courses in the Scriptures and was known as a *baccalarius biblicus*. The last of these three years involved teaching the *Sentences* of Peter Lombard and during this time the candidate bore the title of *baccalarius sententiarius*. D'Ailly completed these stages of his studies from 1374 to 1377. After four more years of study and disputations, which in d'Ailly's case ran from 1377 to 1381 and during which time the student was designated as a *baccalarius formatus*, he then received the licentiate in theology, again from the university chancellor. As in the case of the licentiate in arts, the recipient of the licentiate in theology at Paris was authorized to teach that discipline not only at Paris but throughout the Christian world as well.

The final inception ceremonies leading to the granting of the master's degree in theology were, like the inception ceremonies in the arts faculty, the prerogative of the faculty, and designated as the *Vesperiae*, the *Aulica*, and the *Resumptio*. The *Vesperiae* consisted of a lecture and disputations before the faculty and student body and took place, as the name implies, in the late afternoon. This ceremony was followed the next morning by the *Aulica* which, as indicated by its title, was held in the bishop's hall and involved the formal investiture of the candidate by the faculty with his academic insignia and rights, the delivery of an inaugural lecture, as well as several additional disputations over which the new master presided. In d'Ailly's case, his *Vesperies* took place on April 10, 1381 and was followed on the next day by the *Aulica*. The *Resumptio* generally fell on the first teaching day in the fall term. As its name implies, in this ceremony, the young master took up for further disputation and determination issues which had been neglected in the previous disputations. Finally, as in the arts faculty, the new master was obliged to undergo a two year regency which involved teaching in the theology faculty at Paris. With the completion of all the requirements for his theology degree, d'Ailly was now able to formally begin his multifaceted career as university professor, chancellor, bishop, and cardinal.

CHAPTER ONE

CHURCH AND REFORM:
THE APOCALYPTIC CONTEXT

While the goal of the present work is to extend our understanding of d'Ailly's ecclesiological thought beyond the realm of his conciliarism, especially as that thought relates to the offices of bishops, theologians, and canonists, it is important to realize that there is a broader context in which his views on those offices unfold and which in great measure has escaped the attention of many scholars. That context relates to the extent to which it shared in the apocalyptic spirit and reform ideologies that permeated so much of the late Middle Ages.[1] Marjorie Reeves and Heiko Oberman have made brief references to the apocalyptic dimensions of d'Ailly's thought but neither has investigated these aspects in any detail.[2] While the more recent work of Laura Ackerman Smoller has deepened our knowledge of the astrological dimensions of his apocalyptic views, the more extensive biblical, theological, and historical dimensions those views have remained relatively unexplored.[3] None of the above works, moreover, have delved deeply into the relationship between his apocalyptic thought and his views on church reform.[4] A deeper analysis of the apocalyptic dimensions of d'Ailly's thought,

---

[1] For recent studies of late medieval apocalyptic thought see Marjorie Reeves, *The Influence of Prophecy in the Later Middle Ages* (Oxford: Clarendon Press, 1969), *Joachim of Fiore and the Prophetic Future* (London: SPCK, 1976), and Roberto Rusconi, *L'Attesa della fine: crisi della società, profezia et apocalisse in Italia al tempo del grande scisma d'Occidente (1378–1417)* (Rome: Istituto storico italiano per il medio evo, 1979), *L'Attesa dell' età nuova nella spiritualità della fine del medioevo*, Convegni del centro di studi sulla spiritualità medievale, 3 (Todi, 1962).

[2] Marjorie Reeves, *The Influence of Prophecy*, 422–423; Heiko A. Oberman, 'The Shape of Late Medieval Thought: The Birth-pangs of the Modern Era,' in *The Pursuit of Holiness in Late Medieval and Renaissance Religion*, ed. Charles Trinkaus (Leiden: E.J.Brill, 1974), 16.

[3] Laura Ackerman Smoller, *History, Prophecy, and the Stars: The Christian Astrology of Pierre d'Ailly, 1350–1420* (Princeton: Princeton University Press, 1994).

[4] An initial but very brief attempt to study the apocalyptic and reform dimensions of d'Ailly's thought was made in my article, 'Pierre d'Ailly: Histoire, Schisme et Antéchrist,' in *Genèse du Grande Schisme d'Occident (1362–1394)*, ed. Michel Hayez (Paris: Centre National de la Recherche Scientifique, 1980), 615–622.

therefore, will not only enrich and contextualize our understanding of his ecclesiological views on the offices of bishops, theologians, and canonists but also add to our understanding of his views on the reform and renewal of those offices.

1. *Church History as Series of Persecutions*

Like many of his contemporaries, d'Ailly viewed the situation in which the Church found itself during the period of the Great Schism with deep anxiety and foreboding. This spiritual and psychological distress engendered within him an increasingly apocalyptic view of the Church's history which manifested itself early in his ecclesiastical career and remained integral to his thought throughout his life. Most of his major writings reveal traces of this apocalyptic tendency. The sincerity, intensity, and consistency with which this tendency was manifested in his works rules out any attempt to dismiss it simply as a passing concern or mere rhetorical device. Prolonged and extensive study of his writings during different stages of his career provides convincing proof of the genuineness with which the apocalyptic spirit permeated the thought of this prominent late medieval theologian and ecclesiastical statesman throughout his life.

As was common to most medieval exegetes of Revelation, especially those from the mendicant orders, d'Ailly viewed the Church's history as a series of persecutions which would eventually terminate in the coming of the Antichrist.[5] Persecution, according to him, was the hallmark of Christ's life on earth, and the Church, if it was to be truly the mystical body of Christ, must also undergo the same experience. D'Ailly often speaks about the persecution of the Church only in a generic context, but on several occasions in his life he describes in detail the various persecutions which the Church has undergone in its history. While the chronological divisions according to which he explains these persecutions vary, his apocalyptic view of ecclesiastical history in terms of a continual succession of persecutions remains constant.

---

[5] For a brief survey of the Parisian exegetical tradition with regard to Revelation in the twelfth and thirteenth centuries see David Burr, *Olivi's Peaceable Kingdom: A Reading of the Apocalypse Commentary* (Philadelphia: University of Pennsylvania Press, 1993), 27–62.

Although the earliest expression of his view of the Church's history in terms of successive persecutions was made in a sermon on the feast of St. Dominic given on August 4, 1379, a fuller expression of his thought on this matter is to be had in a sermon which he preached before the faculty and students of the University of Paris on October 4, 1380, the feast of St. Francis of Assisi. Although d'Ailly was still a student in the faculty of theology at the time of this sermon, the apocalyptic context in which he conceived the history of the Church was already clearly evident. In this sermon, D'Ailly casts the Church's history in the context of the persecutions predicted by the seven angels in Rev. 8:2–11:19. The first three, he asserts, have already occurred, the fourth is presently occurring, and the final three will follow in the near future.[6]

In accordance with the predictions of the first three angels, d'Ailly describes what he regards as the first three persecutions in the Church's history. The first period of persecution occurred during the lifetime of Christ and the Apostles and was perpetrated by the Jews. The second period took place during the time of the early martyrs who suffered so intensely at the hands of their pagan persecutors. A third stage was initiated by the ever-increasing number of heretics. The victims of this period were the confessors. D'Ailly assigns precise chronological periods to each of these persecutions. The first lasts from the time of Christ to the destruction of the Temple under Titus and Vespasian in 70 A.D., the second from the destruction of the Temple until the ascension of Constantine in 312. The period of the third persecution spans from the age of Constantine until the year eleven hundred.[7] D'Ailly is of the opinion, however, that despite continual oppression at the hands of Jews, pagans, and heretics, the Church during these periods preserved

---

[6] *Sermo de Sancto Francisco*, *TS*, 6. 'Ad cuius declarationem considerandam nobis est quod septem leguntur persecutiones ecclesiae. Quarum tres ut opinor precesserunt et tres in proxime futura sunt, sed quarta est et media prochdolor quae nunc viget.' The edition used for this sermon is that found in *Petrus de Ailliaco: Tractatus et Sermones* (Strassburg, 1490; repr., Frankfurt: Minerva, 1971). The Strasburg edition was based on the edition published in Brussels by the Brethren of the Common Life in 1483. The reprint of the Strassburg edition is used in the present work because it is more readily available. Since, however, this edition is unpaginated, reference to specific works contained in it will be cited according to the title of the work, the abbreviation of the edition (*TS*), and the respective column within the work on which the citation can be found. For the dating of this sermon, I have followed that of Palémon Glorieux, 'L'oeuvre litteraire de Pierre d'Ailly: Remarques et précisions,' *MSR*, 22 (1965), 70.

[7] *Sermo de Sancto Francisco*, *TS*, 6–7.

its moral integrity and firm commitment to the evangelical spirit of Christ which he identified with the life of poverty, chastity, and humility.[8]

Such was not to be the case in the future, however, for the Church would soon slacken in its commitment to the evangelical ideal. Decline, indeed, characterized the fourth period of its history, a period which, according to d'Ailly, began around eleven hundred and continued until the time of the Great Schism. These years were also marked by persecution, but a persecution inflicted upon the Church not by external enemies but by the internal forces of moral decline. Clerics in ever increasing numbers abandoned their earlier commitment to the gospel ideal. Cupidity replaced poverty, lust followed upon chastity, and pride triumphed over obedience.

D'Ailly asserts, moreover, that the persecution of this period was predicted by the fourth angel in Rev. 8:12 for when that angel sounded its trumpet, the light of the sun, the moon, and the stars was lessened by one-third. Throughout d'Ailly's writings, the sun, the moon, and the stars symbolize the major officials of Christendom, namely, ecclesiastical prelates, secular princes, and the lower clergy. The lessening of the light of the sun, moon, and stars is interpreted by d'Ailly as indicating the diminution of moral integrity within all the leaders of Christendom.[9]

D'Ailly does not, however, paint an overly bleak picture of this period of the Church's history, for he recognizes that despite its many weaknesses, this era has provided medieval Christendom with some of its most prominent saints. In France there appeared Bernard of Clairvaux (1090–1153), in England, Thomas of Canterbury (1118–1170), in Germany, Hildegard of Bingen (1098–1179), and in Spain, Dominic (1170–1221). During this period there also flourished in Italy such prominent holy men as Joachim of Fiore (c. 1135–1202) and Francis of Assisi (c. 1182–1226).[10] Although d'Ailly primarily singles out the great monas-

---

[8] *Sermo de Sancto Francisco*, TS, 7. 'Nam licet tribus prioribus temporibus multas persecutiones passa est ecclesia ... tamen pacem habuit cum vitiis quia evangelicam Christi regulam sequens ... et per viam consiliorum evangelicorum, id est, paupertatis, castitatis, et humilitatis.'

[9] *Sermo de Sancto Francisco*, TS, 7. 'Cum illa priora felicia tempora pertransissent et hoc quartum muliebre ac infelicissimum tempus advenisset percussa est iusto Dei iudicio tertia pars solis, id est, prelati et rectores spirituales, et tertia pars lunae, id est prepositi et rectores seculares, et tertia pars stellarum, id est clerici et spiritales inferiores, ita ut obscuraretur tertia pars earum.'

[10] *Sermo de Sancto Francisco*, TS, 8.

tic and mendicant leaders of this period, it appears that his concern over the decline of the evangelical ideal in the Church is directed more towards the prelates and members of the diocesan clergy than the monastic and mendicant orders, most of which, at least until the beginning of the fourteenth century, were still in the fervor of their early years. Within the context of the diocesan clergy, however, d'Ailly shows little awareness of the reform of the canonical life which played an important role in the Gregorian Reform.[11]

Among the saints cited by d'Ailly, Francis plays a major role in his view of history, for he compares him to the eagle in Rev. 8:13 which, after the persecutions predicted by the first four angels, pronounces the triple woe introducing the remaining three persecutions. In D'Ailly's view, the eagle symbolizes the evangelist John and the evangelical ideal associated with his Gospel. Francis is compared to John and the eagle because he surpassed all others in his imitation of the evangelical ideal. He alone, moreover, bore in his body the signs of the suffering and persecuted Christ. By his espousal of the spirit of poverty, chastity, and humility, Francis countered the proclivity of his age toward avarice, lust, and vanity.[12] D'Ailly also believed that as a result of his dedication to the evangelical life Francis was favored with a special vision from God which revealed the further persecutions which the Church would undergo because of its abandonment of the spirit of the Gospel.[13]

The fifth persecution in the Church's history follows upon the pronouncement of the first woe by the eagle in Rev. 8:13 and is clearly identified by d'Ailly with the Great Western Schism which from 1378 to 1418 divided the Church in his time.[14] He regards the Schism as a form of divine punishment meted out upon the Church for its aban-

---

[11] On the reform of the canonical life during the period of the Gregorian Reform see G. Bardy, 'Saint Gregoire VII et la reforme canoniale au xie siècle,' *SGreg*, 1 (1947), 47–64, Jean Becquet, *Vie canonial en France aux xe–xiie siécles* (London: Ashgate Variorum, 1985), Jean Chatillon, *Le mouvement canonial au moyen age: reform de l'Eglise, spiritualité et culture* (Paris: Brepols, 1992), and Charles Dereine, 'Vie commune, régle de saint Augustin et chanoines réguliers au xie siècle,' *RHE*, 41 (1947), 365–406.

[12] *Sermo de Sancto Francisco*, *TS*, 8. 'Nam sicut beatus evangelista Johannes per aquilam figuratur ... sic iste convenienter aquilae comparatur quia evangelicae regulae perfectionem prae ceteris sui temporis artius observavit.'

[13] *Sermo de Sancto Francisco*, *TS*, 8.

[14] *Sermo de Sancto Francisco*, *TS*, 9. 'Tamen ex scripturis sanctis et dictis propheticis ac etiam ex malis quae experimentaliter vidimus et verisimiliter provenire speramus ex turbatione presentis scismatis primum vae, hoc est persecutionem, imminentis temporis convenienter coniecturare possumus.'

donment of the evangelical rule of Christ. By deviating from the counsels of poverty, chastity, and humility, the ecclesiastical hierarchy from the pope down to the lowest cleric has incurred the divine wrath which has manifested itself in the Schism presently ravaging the Church. By their sins, these prelates have merited the title of pseudo-pastors, for their actions have resulted in the desolation and almost near destruction of the Church.[15]

D'Ailly concludes his sermon on St. Francis with his analysis of the fifth persecution. Nothing is said about the time and nature of the sixth and seventh persecutions. Perhaps as a young theologian d'Ailly thought it prudent to terminate his historical analysis with the present and not to venture, at this stage in his career, into the more dangerous realm of prophecy. A similar prudential judgement may also explain his reluctance to speculate on the role of the Antichrist in his concept of history. A more likely explanation, however, is that at the time of this sermon the Schism had only just begun. While the Schism was clearly viewed by d'Ailly in an eschatological context, there is no evidence that as of yet he saw it as a precursor to the Antichrist. As will be seen, the prolongation of the Schism increasingly caused d'Ailly, in his later writings, to regard the Schism as antecedent to the arrival of the Antichrist. Indeed in his sermon on St. Bernard which most likely was written after the sermon on St. Francis, there is clear evidence that he saw the Schism as a precursor to the arrival of the Antichrist.[16]

Before passing on to other manifestations of the apocalyptic dimensions of d'Ailly's thought, some mention should be made of the sources he used in constructing his sermon on St. Francis. Obviously, Revelation played a most important role in the evolution of his thinking. In the western Church from the time of Tyconius and Augustine in the fourth century the persecutions of the Church described in Revelation were seen primarily in a spiritual and moral context, that is in the context of the struggle between the forces of good and evil within the Church as a whole and within the souls of individual Christians. This approach

---

[15] *Sermo de Sancto Francisco*, TS, 6. 'Quantum ad tertium articulum sciendum est quod viri ecclesiastici hanc evangelicam regulam Ihesu Christi iam diu minime secuti fuerunt, sed ab eius observantia plurimum oberraverunt. Ideo diversa persecutionum mala Christianae paci contraria hiis temporibus patitur ecclesia.'

[16] Glorieux dates the sermon on St. Bernard as written sometime between 1378 and 1393. While Smoller holds for the same chronological period, she maintains that it was written after the sermon on St. Francis. Cf. Smoller, *History, Prophecy, and the Stars*, 97, n. 71.

to the interpretations of the persecutions described in Revelation was especially manifested by Augustine. While he was famous for his teaching on the six ages of the world which he built upon the Old Testament typology of the six days of creation, he was especially careful in his explanation of the sixth age, namely the period of the Church, not to identify the persecutions in Revelation with concrete historical circumstances, events, or personalities.[17]

Augustine's spiritual and moralistic interpretation of the persecutions in Revelation continued to prevail in the realm of apocalyptic exegesis throughout the early Middle Ages and into the High Middle Ages. This Augustinian exegetical heritage can be seen in the biblical commentaries of Primasius (†c. 560), Bede (†735), Ambrose Autpert (†c. 784), Haimo of Auxerre (†c. 875), Bruno of Segni (†1123), Rupert of Deutz (†1131), and Richard of St. Victor (†1173). There was, however, among many of these authors an increasing tendency to interpret the seven letters, seals and trumpets of Revelation in a more historical context. In describing the seven stages in the Church's historical journey from the first to the second advent of Christ, the persecutions associated with most of these stages were increasingly identified with the historical opposition that the Church experienced in its mission during the different periods of its history. This tendency reached its peak in the writings of Joachim of Fiore (c. 1132–1202) and remained the predominant interpretation of Revelation throughout the later Middle Ages.[18]

While the identification of each period of the Church's history with specific persecutions differed somewhat with each writer, there gradually emerged a relatively common tradition of identifying the agents of the first four persecutions in terms of Jews, pagans, heretics, and hyp-

---

[17] An analysis of Tyconius' and Augustine's exegesis of Revelation can be found in Paula Fredriksen, 'Tyconius and Augustine on the Apocalypse,' in *The Apocalypse in the Middle Ages*, ed. Richard K. Emmerson and Bernard McGinn (Ithaca: Cornell University Press, 1992), 20–37. For an excellent synthesis of Augustine's views on the seven ages of the world see Gerhart Ladner, *The Idea of Reform: Its Impact on Christian Thought and Action in the Age of the Fathers* (Cambridge, Mass.: Harvard University Press, 1959), 222–238. See also Elizabeth Sears, *The Ages of Man: Medieval Interpretations of the Life Cycle* (Princeton: Princeton University Press, 1986), 55–58, and J.A. Burrow, *The Ages of Man: A Study in Medieval Writing and Thought* (Oxford: Clarendon Press, 1986), 80–82.

[18] For an excellent survey of the history of the exegesis of *Revelation* in the early and high Middle Ages up to the time of Joachim of Fiore see E. Ann Matter, 'The Apocalypse in Early Medieval Exegesis,' in *The Apocalypse in the Middle Ages*, 38–50, and Bernard McGinn, *The Calabrian Abbot: Joachim of Fiore in the History of Western Thought* (New York: Macmillan, 1985), 74–97.

ocrites. This exegetical tradition was gradually incorporated into the *Glossa Ordinaria*, which by the middle of the twelfth century covered all books of the Bible.[19] Once incorporated into the *Glossa*, this tradition entered into the mainstream of medieval apocalyptic thought. It frequently appeared in the mendicants' exegesis of Revelation in the thirteenth and fourteenth centuries and its presence in d'Ailly's thought indicates its continued influence in the exegetical tradition of the secular masters at Paris in the late Middle Ages.[20]

In his description of the fourth chronological period of the Church's history and its accompanying persecutions d'Ailly was also strongly influenced by Hildegard of Bingen (1098–1179). As will be recalled this period was frequently described as one of internal moral decline occasioned by the forces of hypocrisy. The dating of the fourth period as beginning about eleven hundred was clearly borrowed from Hildegard. A strong supporter of the Gregorian reform movement, Hildegard saw the reign of Henry IV (1056–1106) as one which had contributed greatly to the decline of the Church's moral integrity by its continued insistence upon maintaining the traditions and privileges of the Imperial Church (*Reichskirche*), especially its subordination of ecclesiastical authority to the temporal authority, and its failure to stamp out simony and concubinage among the clergy. Hildegard frequently described this period of internal moral decline in the Church as a 'womanish time' (*tempus muliebre*).[21]

---

[19] For a brief analysis of the complex historical development of the biblical *Glossa Ordinaria* see Beryl Smalley, *The Study of the Bible in the Middle Ages* (Notre Dame: Notre Dame University Press, 1964). See also Smalley's contribution, 'The Bible in the Medieval Schools,' in *The Cambridge History of the Bible*, Vol 2: *The West from the Fathers to the Reformation*, ed. G.W.H. Lampe (Cambridge: Cambridge University Press, 1969), 197–220, as well as Jean Châtillon, 'La Bible dans les écoles du xiie siècle,' in *Le Moyen Age et la Bible*, ed. Pierre Riché and Guy Lobrichon (Paris: Beauchesne, 1984), 163–197.

[20] The mendicants' approach toward the exegesis of Revelation is treated by David Burr, 'Mendicants' Reading of the Apocalypse,' *The Apocalypse in the Middle Ages*, 89–102.

[21] *Sermo de Sancto Francisco*, TS, 7. 'Propter haec ergo mala sicut dicit Hyldegardis ... in hoc quarto muliebri et infami tempore omnia ecclesiastica instituta sive spiritualia sive secularia in deterius descenderunt.' The works of Hildegard which d'Ailly cites are the *Liber divinorum operum* and the letters to Emperor Conrad III (1137–1152) and to the Archbishops of Cologne and Trier. Critical editions of her letters by L. Van Acker and of her *Liber divinorum opera* by A. Derolez and P. Dronke can be found in *CCCM*, 91, 91A, 91B, and *CCCM*, 92 respectively. With regard to Hildegard's letters to the Archbishops of Cologne and Trier, d'Ailly is not very specific. Hildegard had written several letters to each but d'Ailly does not refer to any specific letter. Those to the Archbishop of Cologne are indicated in Van Acker's edition as letters XIV^r, XV^r, and XVII. Those to the Archbishop of Trier can be identified as XXVI^r, XXVII^r, and

While d'Ailly borrowed Hildegardian apocalyptic chronology to delineate the moral decline associated with the fourth period of the Church's history, he carefully bypassed the more radical dimensions of her apocalyptic thought such as the disendowment of the Church and the birth of the Antichrist within the Church. In the fourteenth and early fifteenth centuries, such themes were often extracted from her writings by radical reformers, enlarged upon, and disseminated in their writings. This was especially the case with the Wyclilffite and Lollard reformers and their writings in late medieval England. Some of these reformers further radicalized her thought in the above areas through the creation of pseudonymous apocalyptic texts.[22]

While maintaining the chronological parameters and general context of Hildegard's views concerning the fourth period in the Church's history, d'Ailly transformed their essentially Gregorian emphasis upon moral decline, especially in terms of simony and concubinage, into a more Franciscan context of moral decline as a deviation from the evangelical teaching of Christ. While Hildegard placed her hope for reform on Gregory VII and his followers, d'Ailly saw Francis as the model for the renewal of the Church. All this is not to say that d'Ailly's hope for ecclesiastical renewal rested upon the Franciscan Order as many Spiritual Franciscans maintained. As has been seen, this was clearly not the case. Such a view, moreover, would hardly be consonant with the tradition of the secular clergy which d'Ailly so prominently represented and defended. Nevertheless, as will be seen, it was the evangelical ideal so nobly represented by the Francis and the application of that ideal to the secular clergy in a manner consonant with their lifestyle which provided him with such high hopes for the renewal of the Church.

XXVIII. For Hildegard's frequent use of the phrase 'tempus muliebre' see the following letters in Van Acker's edition: XXIII, XXVI[r], LXXVII[r] and CCXIII[r]. The translation of '*tempus muliebre*' as 'womanish times' is taken from Smoller, *History, Prophecy, and the Stars*, 97. Smoller, however, tends to overemphasize Hildegard's influence upon d'Ailly. As in most cases, d'Ailly draws from a diversity of sources in the construction of his apocalyptic views. For a succinct analysis of Hildegard's reform ideology as well as her apocalyptic views see Barbara Newman's introduction to the translation of Hildegard's *Scivias* by Columba Hart and Jane Bishop, Classics of Western Spirituality (New York: Paulist Press, 1990).

[22] For the Hildegardian apocalyptic legacy in late medieval England, see Kathryn Kerby-Fulton, 'Prophecy and Suspicion: Closet Radicalism, Reformist Politics, and the vogue for Hildegardiana in Riccardian England,' *Speculum*, 75 (2002), 318–341, and her earlier *Reformist Apocalypticism and Piers Plowman* (Cambridge: Cambridge University Press, 1990).

Another major source to which d'Ailly frequently refers is in his sermon on St. Francis is Joachim of Fiore. It is extremely difficult to ascertain whether d'Ailly actually read Joachim since the only work he cites by direct title is the pseudo-Joachite treatise *Super Hieremiam Prophetam*.[23] All other references to Joachim are very general and give no indication of the precise work drawn upon. As with Hildegard of Bingen, d'Ailly normally utilizes Joachim as support for his interpretation of the Church's history in terms of successive persecutions but he expands that interpretation by incorporating the period of the Schism. He does not, however, adopt the Joachimite tripartite division of the Church's history in terms of the ages of the Father, Son, and Holy Spirit. The more radical and revolutionary views of this tripartite division which characterized the thought of some of Joachim's followers, especially the Spiritual Franciscans, are also absent from D'Ailly's sermon.[24]

A somewhat later work which indicates d'Ailly's continued emphasis on the Church's history in terms of persecutions is his treatise, *De falsis prophetis, II*, written sometime before 1397 when he became bishop of Cambrai.[25] The chronological framework which he uses in this work to describe the various persecutions in the Church's history is less complex than in his sermon on St. Francis. In the *De falsis prophetis, II*, D'Ailly maintains that the Church has undergone four major persecutions in its history. The first persecution occurred at the hands of tyrannical rulers and extended from the time of the apostles and martyrs up to the rule of Constantine. The second came in the period after Constantine, when the Church suffered the attacks of various heretics who by falsely interpreting the scriptures taught doctrines contrary to the Christian faith. D'Ailly does not mention any of these heretics by name but he is obviously thinking of those associated with the Trinitarian and Christological controversies from the fourth to the eighth centuries.

---

[23] On the controversial issue of the authorship of the *Super Hieremiam Prophetam*, see Reeves, *The Influence of Prophecy*, 151–158, and, more recently, Robert Moynihan, 'The Development of the Pseudo-Joachim Commentary "Super Hieremiam:" New Manuscript Evidence,' MEFr-MA, 98 (1986), 109–142.

[24] For Joachim of Fiore's views on the ages of the world and the Church's history in terms of successive persecutions see McGinn, *The Calabrian Abbot*, 152–153.

[25] With regard to the dating of this treatise, I have followed Max Lieberman, 'Chronologie Gersonienne, VIII', *Romania*, 81 (1960), 82–84. Smoller dates the composition of this work as occurring between 1378 and 1388, but she follows Lieberman in maintaining that the *De falsis prophetis, II* was actually written before *De falsis prophetis, I*, Cf. Smoller, *History, Prophecy, and the Stars*, 191, n. 92, 207, n. 7.

The third persecution which the Church experienced in its history came at the hands of hypocrites, a multifaceted term which d'Ailly uses in this treatise to describe all those whose lives were contrary to the spirit of the Scriptures which they outwardly professed to observe. When applied to bishops and priests, d'Ailly uses the term in the context of pseudo-pastors who are not only forerunners of the next stage of persecution but also precursors of the Antichrist, since during this period their hypocrisy intensifies to such a degree that the arrival of the Antichrist becomes ever more imminent. D'Ailly does not give any clear chronological boundaries for this third period but from the context of his treatise it would appear to extend from the eighth century up to the period of the contemporary Church.[26] The fourth persecution of the Church is identified by d'Ailly with the contemporary Church which was experiencing the division unleashed by the Great Schism of 1378.

The theme of the Schism as the precursor of the Antichrist, absent in d'Ailly's earlier sermon on St. Francis but which began to manifest itself in his sermon on St. Bernard is now much more clearly in evidence. D'Ailly's thought on the Antichrist follows in the Pauline tradition as embodied in 2 Thess. 2:3–4 where he is described as 'the man of sin' (*homo peccati*) and 'the son of destruction' (*filius perditionis*). In that same passage, the phrase 'unless the defection comes first' (*nisi venerit discessio primum*) is interpreted by d'Ailly as indicating that the arrival of the Antichrist will be preceded by a general separation of many churches from the Roman Church.[27] There is no doubt in d'Ailly's mind that this defection has been realized in the Great Schism of 1378 which splintered the Church into two and later three papal allegiances. D'Ailly

---

[26] *De falsis prophetis, II*, Dupin, 1:515–516. 'Pro quo sciendum est quod tres generales persecutiones passura est ecclesia ... Prima facta est per tyrannos, tempore apostolorum et martyrum, Christianos generaliter occidentes. Secunda sequuta est per apertos haereticos, fraudulenta scripturae expositione, Christianum populum decipientes sed post istas duas sequutura est tertia per falsos ypocritas ... ipsi ypocritae sunt praecursores seu preambuli illius antichristi famosi ... Et ideo multitudo talium ypocritarum sibi invicem adhaerentium in magno et potenti numero, est signum seu praesagium propinquitatis adventu antichristi et preparatio sedes ejus.' The edition used for the *De falsis prophetis II* is that found in L. Ellies Dupin, *Opera omnia Joannis Gersonii*, 5 vols. (Antwerp, 1706). This edition of the works of Jean Gerson also contains many other treatises of d'Ailly which will be used in this study. References to Dupin's edition will be cited as Dupin and will be followed by volume and column number.

[27] *De falsis prophetis, II*, Dupin 1:516. 'Quae divisio erit via seu preparatio antichristo venturo de qua prophetavit Apostolus 2 Thessa.ii.'

strongly fears, therefore, that the Great Schism is but the preamble to the coming of the Antichrist.[28]

While the chronological divisions of the Church's history and persecutions in the *De falsis prophetis, II*, are broader than those in his sermon on St. Francis, there are, nonetheless, some clearly recognizable similarities. The experience of persecution remains central to his view of the Church's history as does the role of the apostles, martyrs, and confessors in that experience. With regard to the agents of the persecution, there is the same gradual transition from external enemies to internal enemies as causes for the moral and spiritual decline within the individual members of the Church, especially its clerical members. In the *De falsis prophetis, II*, however, even greater emphasis is placed upon the hypocritical dimensions of the lives of the Church's pastors.

In seeking to explain why persecution was such an integral part of the Church's historical experience, d'Ailly has recourse to an argument already used in his sermon on St. Francis. He continues to maintain that if persecution plays such an important role in the Church's history, the reason lies in the fact that persecution was of central importance in the life of Christ. The persecutions of the Church, therefore, were prefigured in the life of Christ.[29] Christ's life, according to d'Ailly, reveals a threefold period of persecution. The first, he declares, came early when Herod sought to find the newly-born child of Bethlehem in order to kill him. The second came during the years of Christ's ministry when the scribes and doctors of the Law unceasingly charged him with acting contrary to the true spirit of the Law. The Pharisees, finally, represent the third persecuting force in Christ's life, for their hypocritical opposition to him eventually resulted in his betrayal and crucifixion. As his mystical body, therefore, the Church must endure all that Christ experienced in his life on earth, and persecution was indeed foremost among these experiences. He finds added scriptural support

---

[28] *De falsis prophetis, II*, Dupin, 1:517. 'Cum jam appareat hujusmodi discessio in ecclesia, id est divisio schismatica ... timendum est ne sit antichristi praeambula ...' For a brief analysis of the biblical texts related to the Antichrist see Emmerson, *Antichrist in the Middle Ages*, 34–46. For a brief survey of the Antichrist theme in the late Middle Ages especially within the context of the Great Schism, see Bernard McGinn, *Antichrist: Two Thousand Years of the Human Fascination with Evil* (San Francisco: Harper, 1994), 173–199.

[29] *De falsis prophetis, II*, Dupin, 1:516. 'Harum vero persecutionum figura fuit Christus.'

for his position in 2 Tim. 3:12, where Paul states that 'all who desire to live a godly life in Christ Jesus will be persecuted.'[30]

With regard to the sources used by d'Ailly in the development of the apocalyptic views expressed in the *De falsis prophetis, II*, it is clear that he uses sources different than those utilized in his sermon on St. Francis. In the area of Scripture, little use is made of Revelation. As seen earlier, he draws more upon Pauline thought as expressed in 2 Thess. 2:3–4, a classical medieval source for the biblical teaching on the Antichrist. In his exegesis of this important biblical text, d'Ailly also gives evidence of following closely the interpretation of the biblical *Glossa Ordinaria*.[31] With regard to his interpretation of the Church's history in terms of persecution, he may well have been influenced by Franciscan apocalyptic writings, but he makes no clear references to such sources. What is striking then about d'Ailly's apocalyptic teaching in the *De falsis prophetis, II* is its highly biblical orientation and its lack of reference to traditional medieval prophecies such as those Hildegard of Bingen and Joachim of Fiore, prophecies of which d'Ailly availed himself in his sermon on St. Francis. In his later apocalyptic writings, however, d'Ailly returns to these and other medieval sources.

That d'Ailly maintained an apocalyptic view of the Church's history in terms of persecution throughout his life is seen in the fact that he again emphasized that theme in a small treatise written in 1418, just two years before his death. This treatise is the *De persecutionibus ecclesiae*.[32] Here again, as in the Sermon on St. Francis, D'Ailly has recourse to Revelation to discover the inner meaning of the Church's history and its major chronological divisions, and again he finds that meaning in terms of persecution. D'Ailly continued insistence on the importance of persecution in understanding the Church's history is especially noteworthy since the *De persecutionibus* was most likely written after the resolution of the Schism by the Council of Constance earlier that year.[33] The Church's life, he asserts, is essentially one of persecution. Persecu-

---

[30] *De falsis prophetis, II*, Dupin, l, 516. '... sicut Christus in hac vita continue persecutionem passus est, ita ecclesia sua nunquam est sine persecutione.'

[31] The edition of the *Glossa Ordinaria* used here is that of A. Rusch, *Biblia Latina cum Glossa Ordinaria*. 4 vols. (Strasbourg, 1480, repr. Turnhout: Brepols, 1992). The glosses on 2 Thess. 2:3–4 can be found at 4:403.

[32] The edition of the *De persecutionibus ecclesiae* used is that of Noël Valois which is contained in his 'Un ouvrage inédit de Pierre d'Ailly: Le *De Persecutionibus Ecclesiae*,' *BEC*, 55 (1904), 557–574. This, however, is an extensive but not complete edition of the work.

[33] Smoller, *History, Prophecy, and the Stars*, 47.

tion, indeed, has beset the Church at all stages of its history and will greatly intensify with the appearance of the forces of Antichrist which are to precede the final coming and judgement of Christ.

Relying upon the series of the six visions described in Rev. 1:10–3:22, d'Ailly delineates six ages of the Church with each age characterized by a distinctive form of persecution.[34] According to d'Ailly, the visions in Revelation to which these ages correspond are those of the seven seals (4:1–8:1), the seven angels (8:2–11:19), the woman and the dragon (12:1–14:10), the seven plagues (15:1–16:21), the whore of Babylon (17:1–19:10), and Antichrist, the Last Judgement, and the New Jerusalem (19:11–22:5). With regard to the corresponding ages of the Church, the first age dates from the foundation of the Church to the reign of Julian the Apostate (361–363) and was marked by persecutions initiated by the pagan emperors. The second age spans from the death of Julian to the reign of Maurice (582–602). Persecution at this time came at the hands of numerous heretics whose false teachings plagued the Church. With Phocas (602–610), the successor of Maurice, began the third age, which lasts until the death of Constantine VI (780–797). During this period, the Church suffered persecution at the hands of the Mohammedans.

The reign of Charlemagne (768–814) inaugurates the fourth stage in the Church's historical evolution and lasts until the time of Henry IV (1056–1106). D'Ailly, however, does not describe clearly the nature of the persecution which the Church underwent at this period. The fifth age, according to d'Ailly, lasts from the time of Henry IV through the period of the Great Schism. During the first part of this period, persecution of the Church came primarily at the hands of the emperors who strove to reduce its freedom by asserting the privileges of the Imperial Church (*Reichskirche*). These tribulations were followed in later years by the difficulties occasioned by the Great Schism.[35]

In the *De persecutionibus ecclesiae*, d'Ailly does not elaborate on the specific afflictions that beset the Church during the period of the Schism. For clarification on this point, we must turn to a slightly earlier work, his famous letter to Pope John XXIII, written in June, 1414, and therefore between the convocation of the Council of Constance in Decem-

---

[34] *De persecutionibus ecclesiae*, Valois, 570. 'Sicut haec prophetia in vi visiones divisa est, sic proportionaliter status Ecclesiae secundum descriptionem historiarum dividi potest in sex etates.'

[35] *De persecutionibus ecclesiae*, Valois, 570–571.

ber, 1413 and its solemn opening on November 5, 1414. At the very beginning of his letter, d'Ailly reaffirms his apocalyptic view of the Church's history in terms of successive persecutions. Scripture is so clear on this point, he asserts, that there is no need to belabor the issue.[36] There is, moreover, no doubt in d'Ailly's mind that the Schism constituted a major period in the history of the Church's tribulations and he dedicates a considerable portion of his letter to the precise nature of these tribulations.

First among the tribulations enumerated by d'Ailly is the defection of churches from the Roman Church. Here again he refers back 2 Thess. 2:3–4. On this point, however, he deals not only with the divisions within the Church occasioned by the Great Schism but also with the division caused by the Schism of 1054 which separated the Eastern and Western Churches. Like many conciliarists of his day, he was firmly convinced that the unity of the Church could never be fully restored until all traces of schism were removed. Another source of tribulation was the prevalence of simony in areas relating to the sacraments and ecclesiastical office. A further cause for disturbance was the unequal distribution of ecclesiastical wealth. Some ecclesiastics follow a lifestyle that surpasses even that of prominent secular princes while others are poorer than the lowest levels of society. A fourth area of tribulation was that caused by the arrogance of prelates as manifested in the lavishness of their retinues and dress. The Church, he maintained, suffers from the tyranny of its pastors who seek the aggrandizement of their own power and neglect the pastoral needs of their flocks.[37]

There are many other tribulations that d'Ailly saw as affecting the Church of his day, but the above mentioned suffice to indicate his general frame of mind. While there is little new in such complaints, for they indeed follow the classical pattern of late medieval ecclesiastical gravamina, it is important to recognize that d'Ailly saw these tribulations in an apocalyptic context, namely, as so many preambula to the imminent appearance of the Antichrist. In his estimation, no previous age could equal his own in its spirit of rebellion, its advocacy of evil, and its adherence to heretical beliefs. Looking at the vast panorama of tribulations that beset the Church of the late Middle Ages, d'Ailly could

---

[36] *Epistola I ad Joannem XXIII*, Dupin, 2:876. 'Sciendum est igitur quod exercitatis in sacra Scriptura ita notorium est quod Ecclesia patietur, quod ad hoc allegare superfluum videtur ...'
[37] *Epistola I ad Joannem XXIII*, Dupin, 2:877–878.

only conclude that the stage was well set for the arrival of the Antichrist and the beginning of the sixth and final stage of persecution.

When we look at the sources which d'Ailly drew upon for the apocalyptic context of his *De persecutionibus ecclesiae*, we find that, in addition to the traditional biblical sources, the Franciscan influence so prominent in his early apocalyptic writings is again in evidence and with even greater emphasis. D'Ailly draws heavily upon the writings of the Franciscan Peter Aureoli (1280–1322), especially his *Commentary on Revelation*. It was from Aureoli's commentary that d'Ailly borrowed his chronological division of the six ages of the world and their associated persecutions. These historical divisions were taken in turn by Aureoli from the biblical commentaries of his fellow Franciscan, Nicholas of Lyra (c. 1270–1340).[38] Yet as he did with Hildegard of Bingen, d'Ailly modified the chronological parameters of Aureoli's fifth age in order to incorporate events associated with the Great Schism.

In adopting the chronological categories of Aureoli and Lyra, d'Ailly indicates clearly that he is following the more moderate school of Franciscan apocalyptic thought. As was the case with his earlier works, the *De persecutionibus ecclesiae* is singularly free of the more radical views of Franciscan groups such as the Spirituals who transformed Joachim of Fiore's apocalyptic views on the Church's history into a more revolutionary ecclesiology. Although he utilized Franciscan authorities with regard to the six ages of the Church's history, he did not adopt the tripartite and Trinitarian teachings of radical Franciscanism with its controversial views on the nature of the Church in the third state. Indeed, while bishop of Cambrai, d'Ailly in 1411 censured a certain sect in his diocese known as the *Homines intelligentiae* for maintaining a Joachite interpretation of history in trinitarian terms and for viewing themselves as the embodiment of the age of the Holy Spirit.[39]

---

[38] *De persecutionibus ecclesiae*, Valois, 570–572. The *Compendium Bibliorum* of Peter Aureoli has been edited by Philibert Seeboeck (Quaracchi, 1896). The most recent edition of Nicholas of Lyra's *Postilla litteralis super totam Bibliam* is the Antwerp edition of 1634. The earlier Strasbourg edition of 1492 by J. Mentelin has been reprinted in four volumes (Frankfurt: Minerva, 1971). On Nicholas of Lyra as a biblical commentator see Philip D.W. Krey, 'Nicholas of Lyra: Apocalypse Commentator, Historian, and Critic,' *FS*, 52 (1992) 53–84, and Philip D.W. Krey and L. Smith, eds., *Nicholas of Lyra: The Senses of Scripure*, Studies in the History of Christian Thought, 90 (Leiden: E.J. Brill, 2000). For the English translation of Lyra's Apocalypse Commentary see Krey, *Nicholas of Lyra's Apocalyptic Commentary* (Kalamazoo: Medieval Institute Publications, 1997).

[39] *Errores sectae hominum intelligentiae*, ed. Etienne Baluze, *Miscellanea nova ordine digesta*, 4 vols. (Lucca: Junctinius, 1761–1764), 2:288–292.

Analysis of d'Ailly's *Sermon on St. Francis*, the *De falsis prophetis, II* and the *De persecutionibus ecclesiae*, as well as his first letter to John XXIII reveals the centrality of d'Ailly's view of the Church's history in terms of persecution. The fact that these works were composed at different periods of his academic and ecclesiastical career also demonstrates that this interpretation of the Church's history was constant throughout all his life. The fact that while at the Council of Constance, d'Ailly, in the early months of 1417 had his 1380 *Sermon on St. Francis* made available again to the members of the Council without any revisions or retractions in the hope that it would be of value to the Council as it dealt with the issue of reform within the Church further substantiates the consistency of his views on the nature of the Church's history in terms of persecution.[40]

The above mentioned writings of d'Ailly and the chronological periods of his life that they represent do, however, reveal a gradual development in his views with regard to the apocalyptic context of the Schism. While he initially saw the Schism as representing the most recent period of persecution in the history of the Church, he increasingly came to regard it as prefiguring the arrival of the Antichrist. In fact, he gradually came to believe that the period in which he was living, the period of the Schism, represented the final stage of the Church's persecution before the advent of the Antichrist. Further persecution would follow upon the arrival of the Antichrist after which the Church would experience the second coming of Christ.

The variety of apocalyptic sources upon which d'Ailly drew in his different writings might at first give the appearance of a highly eclectic outlook, but it is important to note that he carefully adapted his sources so as to fit the specific circumstances in which the Church of his time found itself. Proceeding in this manner, he created a relatively unified and personal synthesis with its strong belief that the Church's history is essentially one of persecution and that these persecutions will reach their climax with the arrival of the Antichrist. Another constant element in his apocalyptic thought was his strong premonition that the period in which he was living, the period of the Great Western Schism, represented the semifinal stage in the Church's persecution before the advent of the Antichrist.

---

[40] D'Ailly refers to the republication of his sermon on St. Francis in his *Ad laudem Christi*, ed. Heinrich Finke, *ACC*, 4 vols (Münster: Regensbergschen Buchhandlung,

2. *Schism, Antichrist, Knowledge of Arrival*

Given d'Ailly's increasing preoccupation with the idea of the Antichrist, it is not surprising to find that he was very much concerned with the question of whether or not it was possible to predict accurately the arrival of the Antichrist. In his *Sermon on St. Dominic*, delivered in 1379, he strongly rejected all claims to such knowledge. His arguments to this effect were heavily based on the classic passage in Acts, 1:6–7 where the Apostles asked Christ if the time had come to restore the Kingdom to Israel and Christ replied that it was not for them to know the times and periods set by the Father.[41] As will later be seen, this passage from Acts was the major biblical source that patristic authorities such as Jerome and Augustine had used to reject strongly any attempts to ascertain the arrival of the Antichrist and the End-Times. Thus in his early years, d'Ailly followed the essentially agnostic attitude of Jerome and Augustine with regard to the knowability of the arrival of the Antichrist.

While d'Ailly makes no mention of the Antichrist in his *Sermon on St. Francis* in 1380, in his *Sermon on St. Bernard*, most likely written sometime after 1380, he began to entertain the opinion that some knowledge of the Antichrist was available to the Church of his day. Such knowledge, he argued, could be attained through a close reading of the Scriptures as well as through a detailed analysis of the contemporary experiences of the Church. While not challenging the prevailing Augustinian exegesis of Acts, 1:6–7, d'Ailly preferred to base his position upon 2 Thess. 2:3 where Paul warns the Thessalonians not to be deceived as to the day of the coming of the Lord for it will not occur until a 'dissension' or 'division' has occurred within the Church and the 'Man of Sin,' or the 'Son of Perdition' has appeared. Clearly for d'Ailly that dissension or division became increasingly identified with the Schism. Concerning the contemporary experiences of the Church over and above the experiences of the Schism, d'Ailly enumerated the increased iniquity in the world and the continued decline in the practice of charity.[42]

While in his *Sermon on St. Bernard* d'Ailly clearly began to move away from his earlier negative stance with regard to knowledge of the arrival of the Antichrist, it is important to note that he strongly maintained

---

1896–1928), 4:730–733. The *Ad Laudem* is essentially a defense of his position against the Dominicans in the secular-mendicant controversies at the Council.

[41] *Sermo de Sancto Dominico*, TS, 8.
[42] *Sermo de sancto Bernardo*, B.N. Lat. 3122, fols 97^r–97^v.

that the scriptural sources and the experiences of the Church upon which he based his arguments could not provide certitude on the matter but only a degree of probability. His cautious response in this regard, however, must be seen within the nominalistic context of his thought. Given the more stringent norms for certitude required by nominalism, it is not surprising that he would take such a stand with regard to his sources. As will be seen, however, in the analysis of d'Ailly's views on theology and theological method, his concept of probability often approaches the level of high probability and in some cases even the level of moral certitude.[43]

By the time of his *Advent Sermon* of 1385, d'Ailly's reflections on the knowability of the time for the arrival of the Antichrist and the End-Times had become more positive. His increasing tendency to see the Schism as the forerunner to the arrival of the Antichrist as well as the prolonged failure to resolve the Schism no doubt intensified his speculations on the date of the Antichrist's appearance. The liturgical season of Advent with its emphasis upon the different modes of Christ's coming, moreover, provided d'Ailly with a most suitable context in which to expand upon his apocalyptic speculations. The scriptural text upon which he constructed his advent sermon was Lk. 21:5–36, which contains Christ's famous discourse on the destruction of Jerusalem and the coming of the Son of Man. Early in his sermon, d'Ailly makes clear his belief that some knowledge of the final times was possible and gives a variety of reasons in support of his position.

D'Ailly begins his argumentation with a series of *a minori* arguments based primarily upon scriptural sources. The first of such arguments is based on the Old Testament. The fathers of the Old Testament, he argues, were able to know clearly the time of the first coming of Christ. As an example of such knowledge, d'Ailly cites Dan. 9:24–27, where it is stated that 'seventy weeks of years' would precede the arrival of the messianic kingdom. D'Ailly concludes, therefore, that if God provided

---

[43] *Sermo de sancto Bernardo*, B.N. Lat. 3122, fols 97ʳ–97ᵛ. 'Et ideo de tempore determinato nec possumus nec debemus certidinaliter [sic] diffinire. Sed tamen ex scripturis quas legimus et experientiis quas videmus antichristi propinquitatem et finis mundi vicinitatem probabilibus conjecturis valemus.' Epistemologically, the operative phrases in this text are 'certidinaliter diffinire,' and 'probabilibus conjecturis.' Smoller's translation of 'probabilibus conjecturis' as 'plausible conjectures' misses the philosophical context of this term in d'Ailly's thought and considerably weakens his assertion as to knowledge of the arrival of the Antichrist and the End Times. See Smoller, *History, Prophecy, and the Stars*, 97.

such information in the Old Testament concerning the first advent of Christ, how much more reasonable is it to believe that he would provide similar information in the New Testament concerning Christ's second advent.[44]

In his second *a minori* argument in support of the predictability of the arrival of the Antichrist, d'Ailly maintains that the first advent of Christ and the advent of the Antichrist are two contraries. The goal of the former is the building up of the Christian polity, while the end of the latter is to work towards its destruction. If it was fitting and useful for man to know the time of the first advent of Christ, then, he asserts, it is clearly more appropriate that he should be able to ascertain the time for the coming of the Antichrist, for only in this way can he successfully withstand the persecutions associated with this coming. Such knowledge would also provide the Church with greater assurance as to the time of the second advent of Christ since Christ himself said in Mt. 24:29–30 that shortly after such tribulations the Son of Man would appear in the heavens.[45]

A third *a minori* argument that d'Ailly proposes in support of the Church's capacity to ascertain the time of the arrival of the Antichrist is based primarily upon the letters of Paul and John. In 1 Cor. 10:11, Paul states that the Corinthians will witness the end of the ages. 1 Jn. 2:18 also states that the last hour has come and that many antichrists have appeared. As a result of these texts, d'Ailly argues that both Paul and John clearly felt that they were in the final stages of history. D'Ailly realizes, however, that these apocalyptic expectations never materialized in their time, but, he argues, that if such expectations prevailed in the early years of the Church's history, then the expectations of the contemporary Church are more realistic because so much time has elapsed between the time of Paul and John and the fourteenth century.[46]

The second major line of argumentation employed by d'Ailly's on behalf of the Church's ability to determine an approximate date for

---

[44] *Sermo tertius de adventu Domini*, TS, 5. 'Ergo videtur quod nobis non debeat esse ignotum sed determinate praecognitum tempus ultimi adventus quo Christus ad iudicium est venturus.'

[45] *Sermo tertius de adventu Domini*, TS, 8. 'Scito autem tempore Antichristi satis precognoscitur tempus futuri iudicii ... cum statim sequeretur signa consummationis seculi et adventus filii hominis.'

[46] *Sermo tertius de adventu Domini*, TS, 6. 'Cum ergo iam longum tempus transierit postquam haec dicta sunt, sequitur quod modicum tempus superest usque ad finem mundi, quare videtur quod saltem nunc illud tempus residuum possit scire.'

the second coming of Christ rests upon patristic authorities. Many patristic writers, he asserts, believed firmly in man's ability to know when the final advent of Christ would occur.[47] In this context d'Ailly singles out Augustine who, he maintains, in his *De civitate Dei*, 20:2–7 asserted that the End-Times could be ascertained with reasonably accuracy. D'Ailly argues that Augustine's belief in the predictability of the coming of the Antichrist rests upon his interpretation of Rev. 20:1–4 where the angel is said to bind the dragon for a thousand years. As seen earlier, Augustine's theory of the six ages of the world was built upon the Old Testament typology in Gen. 1:1–3 of God's creation of the world in six days as well as the New Testament passage in 2 Pet. 3:8 where it is said that 'with the Lord one day is as a thousand years.' D'Ailly maintained, therefore, that Augustine argued that world history would unfold according to a sixfold pattern with each period lasting a thousand years. Augustine, d'Ailly continues, identified the thousand years of Rev. 20:1–4 during which the dragon remained bound with the sixth age of the world, namely the period of the Church. At the end of this period, the dragon, representing the Antichrist, would be released. The ensuing persecution by the Antichrist would then be followed by a final millennium which would be some form of an earthly paradise, a sabbath rest of the saints, which would end with the second coming of Christ.[48]

D'Ailly's use of Augustine as an authority on the predictability of the arrival of the Antichrist is rather surprising. As seen earlier, Augustine eschewed any attempt to identify the persecutions described in *Revelation* with precise historical events or personalities. Augustine also refused to see the 'thousand years' of Rev. 20:1–4 as designating a precise historical number of years. A closer reading of *De civitate Dei*, 20:2–7 reveals that Augustine maintained that the thousand years in which Satan was to be held in chains can be interpreted in two ways. The first is the one described above by d'Ailly. But Augustine himself makes clear in this same passage that while in his early years he adopted this essentially

---

[47] *Sermo tertius de adventu Domini*, TS, 6–7. '… quia multi doctores sancti quos non est credendum obviasse catholicae veritati determinata tempora consummationis seculi tradiderunt.'

[48] On Augustine's teaching on all these points see Ladner, *The Idea of Reform*, 222–238. Augustine identified the seventh age of the world with the meta-historical context of the soul's rest in God before the time of the resurrection of their bodies and their entrance into the peace of eternity.

millenarian interpretation of the Church's history and the role of Satan within it, he soon broke with that tradition.

The second interpretation of the thousand years, therefore, reflects Augustine's more mature position, namely that the thousand years in which Satan was to be bound were no longer to be seen in terms of a precise historical number of years but more as referring to the totality of time, that is, the entire period of the Church's history, the termination of which Augustine steadfastly refused to predict.[49] D'Ailly's selection of Augustine's early views and his neglect of Augustine's more mature position on the subject, therefore, represent a highly opportunistic mode of exegesis, especially since later on in the same sermon he gives clear evidence of being aware of Augustine's essentially agnostic position as to the knowability of the End-Times.

Augustine's negative view as to the knowability of the End-Times was also revealed in his strictly literal interpretation of Acts, 1:7 where, when the Apostles asked the resurrected Christ whether the time to restore the kingdom to Israel had arrived, Christ replied that such knowledge was not to be theirs but belonged solely to his Father in heaven. Since Augustine's time many medieval thinkers had used this passage as well as Augustine's exegesis thereof as a strong argument against the predictability of the End-Times. Finally Augustine, while identifying the dragon of Rev. 20:2–6 with Satan did not designate him in terms of the Antichrist. In general, following closely upon his primarily moralistic interpretation of the persecutions in Revelation, Augustine saw the Antichrist in a corporate and moral context, namely, comprising all those whose beliefs and actions were contrary to those of Christ.[50]

The third major line of argumentation that d'Ailly employs on behalf of the Church's ability to determine the arrival of the Antichrist and the final coming of Christ, draws heavily upon the well known medieval legal principle of utility (*utilitas*).[51] First he argues that armed with such knowledge the Church will be better able to recognize the forces of

---

[49] *Sermo tertius de adventu Domini*, *TS*, 7. For the development of Augustine's views on the millennial context of Rev. 20:1–4, see Ladner, *The Idea of Reform*, 222–231, Burrow, *The Ages of Man*, 55–94 and Sears, *The Ages of Man*, 54–79.

[50] For Augustine's views on the Antichrist, see Emmerson, *Antichrist in the Middle Ages*, 65–66, and Bernard McGinn, *Antichrist*, 74–77.

[51] On the legal notion of *utilitas* and its various divisions see Walter Ullmann, *Law and Politics in the Middle Ages: An Introduction to the Sources of Medieval Political Ideas* (Ithaca: Cornell University Press, 1975), 110, 115, 240, and 256.

deception which will be so prevalent at the time of the Antichrist. Unless protected against these forces, many will become confused in the last days and will abandon their commitment to Christ. Knowledge that their tribulations were in fact the work of the Antichrist would allow many to remain more steadfast in their loyalty to Christ and his Church.[52] An additional advantage of being able to recognize the arrival of the final days is that it permits one to endure better the tribulations of those days. In Mt. 24:3–34, Christ describes vividly the many trials that will beset Christians at the end of time and 2 Tim. 3:1 designates the last days as times of stress. Foreknowledge that the time for such tribulations has arrived or will soon arrive enables one to sustain them better.[53]

A third advantage which d'Ailly sees in knowing the arrival of the last times is that such knowledge would move obstinate sinners to conversion. He humorously compares hardened sinners to horses and asses. Such animals, he states, are rarely moved by the melodious and soothing sounds of a lyre. Only loud blasts of music from instruments such as trumpets spur them into action. With hardened sinners, therefore, the ordinary preaching and exhortations of the Church to conversion serve to no avail. What is needed to stir up the spirit of repentance in such souls is the frightening revelation that the final times are at hand. D'Ailly felt that the author of Job recognized this problem when he wrote that the ears of the wicked must always be filled with terrifying sounds. The Church, therefore, must continually imitate the prophet Ezekiel who proclaimed that 'the end has come upon the four corners of the land.' Only then will obstinate sinners take note and change their way of life.[54]

The final advantage that d'Ailly sees in the Church's ability to know the time of the final appearance of Christ is that such knowledge would prevent the Church from becoming an object of derision. For the Church to believe in and continually proclaim the end of the world and yet not to be able to know with relative accuracy when the final stage of human history will occur, is to expose itself to the ridicule of its enemies. Of what value is it for the Church to preach assiduously the

---

[52] *Sermo tertius de adventu Domini*, TS, 8. 'Nam huius scientiae prima utilitas est, ut ecclesia armis Christi premunita cautius vitet deceptionis periculum.'

[53] *Sermo tertius de adventu Domini*, TS, 8. 'Secunda ut levius toleret persecutionis flagellum, quia ut dici solet, iacula previsa minus feriunt.'

[54] *Sermo tertius de adventu Domini*, TS, 8–9. The references to Job and Ezekiel are Jb. 15:21 and Ez. 7:2.

advent of the Antichrist unless it is able to ascertain when the forces of Antichrist will begin their reign upon the earth?[55]

After having argued extensively for the Church's ability to attain some knowledge of the time of Antichrist's arrival and the End-Times, d'Ailly nuances his thought on the above matter by stating that while the Church can attain and benefit greatly from such knowledge, it cannot gain that knowledge through mere human industry. He bases his argumentation to this effect upon an analogy with creation. Just as the human mind, without the aid of revelation, cannot arrive at a knowledge of creation, so too the knowledge of the last days cannot be ascertained by natural reason but requires a special revelation on the part of God. D'Ailly firmly maintains, therefore, that with regard to the knowledge of the final times all the arguments of philosophers are useless since they are based purely on human reason.[56] D'Ailly also maintains that the calculations of astrologers are incapable of ascertaining the time of the arrival of the Antichrist and the End-Times.[57] The speculations of astrologers on these issues are also constructed upon human efforts and consequently can never attain to a knowledge that transcends the capacities of human reason.[58] His argument with regard to astrologers, therefore, is essentially the same as that used against philosophers.

With regard to d'Ailly's attitude toward astrology and its capacity to predict the final days, Smoller's recent study of d'Ailly's astrological writings and interests has shown that there were three stages in the

---

[55] *Sermo tertius de adventu Domini*, TS, 9. 'Quarta utilitas est ut ecclesia apparentius evitet irrisionis opprobrium. Nam ridiculum videretur ecclesiam evangelizare quotidie consummationem seculi et tamen circa finem mundi non precognoscere tempus appropinquationis ipsius.'

[56] *Sermo tertius de adventu Domini*, TS, 9. '… scientia huiusmodi non est acquisibilis per naturalem acquisitionem industriae humanae.'

[57] Since the days of Isidore of Seville (c. 560–636), the Middle Ages distinguished between astronomy (*astronomia*) and astrology (*astrologia*) with the former referring to the study of the motions of the heavens and the latter to the study of their effects upon the human condition and history. Isidore also distinguished between natural and superstitious astrology. Smoller has wisely pointed out that these 'neat distinctions' were not always maintained, for the meaning of the terms were often reversed, interchanged, or equated. D'Ailly's own use of the terms varied considerably. For a detailed analysis of the medieval debate about the nature and value of astrology in all its various meanings, see Smoller, *History, Prophecy, and the Stars*, 25–42. These pages also contain an excellent summary of d'Ailly's position in the debate.

[58] *Sermo tertius de adventu Domini*, TS, 9. '… nec per philosophorum rationes aut astrologorum speculationes, seu quascunque alias humanae industriae vel naturalis inquisitionis considerationes presciri.'

development of his thought. The first period extends from 1375 to 1380, the period covered by his Sermons on St. Dominic and St. Francis. During this period, d'Ailly, like most of his university confreres, showed a considerable knowledge of astronomical theory and even produced a popular commentary on John of Sacrobosco's *De sphera*, which was in essence, a synthesis of Ptolomey's *Almagest*, the basic textbook in astronomy for young students in the arts faculty at Paris. Despite his interest in and knowledge of astronomy and its relationship to astrology, d'Ailly strongly denied the ability of the latter to predict the arrival of the Antichrist and the End-Times.[59]

The second period delineated by Smoller in the development of d'Ailly's astrological interests and their influence upon his apocalyptic thought covers the years from 1381 to 1409, the period essentially covered by his Advent Sermon and his *De falsis prophetis, II*. This period, she maintains, gives evidence of an increased interest in and knowledge of astrology. While at times there is also some evidence of d'Ailly's willingness to accept astrology's capability to predict the time of the arrival of the Antichrist, d'Ailly's final judgement in this matter remained essentially negative. Nonetheless, Smoller feels that d'Ailly remained intrigued by the possible role of astrology in the realm of apocalyptic predictions.[60] The third and more positive phase in the development of d'Ailly's attitude toward the value of astrology in the realm of apocalyptic predictions and which covers the period from 1410 to his death in 1420, will be taken up later in this chapter.

Despite his earlier emphasis upon the Scriptures as the most reliable source for determining the arrival of the Antichrist and the End-Times, d'Ailly cautions that such knowledge is not to be had from a literal interpretation of the Scriptures.[61] He does not deny that Scripture can reveal some knowledge of these events, but the knowledge it yields is extremely general and at times even confusing. One would think, he asserts, that the New Testament would be more explicit than the Old in

---

[59] Smoller, *History, Prophecy, and the Stars*, 44–47, 95–98. As Smoller shows, d'Ailly's position during this period essentially represents the viewpoint characteristic of the major intellectual figures at the University of Paris during his time, especially after the Condemnations of 1277. Among the most notable of these figures were Henry of Langenstein, Nicholas of Oresme, and d'Ailly's own student, Jean Gerson.

[60] Smoller, *History, Prophecy, and the Stars*, 46–52, 98–101.

[61] *Sermo tertius de adventu Domini*, TS, 9–10. '… scientia de tempore determinato persecutionis Antichristi vel consummationis seculi non est deducibilis per litteralem expositionem divinae scripturae.'

this regard since the revelation contained therein is obviously closer chronologically to the final times, yet such is not the case. As seen earlier in his sermon, he admits that there are indications in 1 Cor. 10:11 and 1 Jn. 2:18 that the Church is in the final age but he now maintains that these indications are too general. While they point out that the Church has entered upon the final stage of its existence, they do not indicate the precise duration of that stage.[62]

Continuing his argumentation, d'Ailly affirms that although a strictly literal interpretation of Scripture cannot reveal specific information as to the persecutions to be unleashed by the Antichrist and to the time of the second advent of Christ, such knowledge is available to the Church through the special inspiration of prophecy.[63] While d'Ailly does not make clear to what extent such prophecy follows upon a close study and analysis of the Scriptural texts related to matters apocalyptic, it seems reasonable to suppose that given the general orientation of his apocalyptic teaching such is generally the case. Prophetic inspiration based upon the Scripture, therefore, can make more specific the general and even confusing teaching of the Scriptures as to the nature and time of the final age. In this respect, d'Ailly would seem to be following closely Joachim of Fiore's teaching on the role of the '*intellectus spiritualis*' in the reading and interpretation of the Scriptures.[64]

At first glance, it may seem surprising that a prominent theologian such as d'Ailly would be so open to the role of prophetic inspiration and predictions. This impression is also enforced by his great concern in his *De falsis prophetis, II* to identify and distinguish true from false prophets and by his condemnation of William of Hildernissen and his followers. Yet as Millet has shown, during the period of the Schism, a period in which apocalyptic and prophetic fervor intensified considerably, many ecclesiastical prelates, whether of the Roman, Avignon, or Pisan allegiances, had recourse to apocalyptic prophets, especially those whose prophecies supported the cause of their respective allegiances. While this recourse to prophetic authorities was very

---

[62] *Sermo tertius de adventu Domini, TS*, 10. 'Haec enim dicta sunt ... ad significandum novissimum statum mundi qui est ultima etas, de qua non est diffinitum quanto ipsa sit temporis duratura.'

[63] *Sermo tertius de adventu Domini, TS*, 13. '... scientia de tempore Antichristi vel futuri iudicii est nobis revelabilis per specialem inspirationem prophetiae futurae.'

[64] On Joachim's understanding of '*intellectus spiritualis*,' see McGinn, *The Calabrian Abbot*, 123–144.

widespread among prelates trained in canon law, d'Ailly adds further evidence to Millet's contention that such recourse was, although to a lesser degree, also characteristic of prelates trained in theology.[65]

3. *Antichrist and Post-Apostolic Revelation*

From the tenor of d'Ailly's arguments in his *Advent Sermon* of 1385 concerning the role of prophecy in ascertaining the time of the arrival of the Antichrist, it is clear that he regards such prophetic knowledge as a form of post-apostolic revelation. In this context, d'Ailly's position is extremely interesting since most of the theologians of his day maintained that revelation terminated with the New Testament. D'Ailly himself admits that his position on the possibility of future revelation is indeed contrary to that held by Thomas Aquinas in his *Scriptum super libros Sententiarum*. D'Ailly further maintains that his argument on behalf of prophetic revelation after the New Testament is not based upon the idea of God's *potentia absoluta*. All would readily admit that by his use of that power God could allow post-apostolic inspiration to occur. D'Ailly's position is much more specific, for he maintains that it is by his *potentia ordinata* that God has provided for prophetic revelation after the apostolic age.[66] For d'Ailly, therefore post-apostolic revelation has been and continues to be part of the present dispensation and it is through such revelation that the Church can acquire more definite knowledge as to the final stages of its history.

In explaining why prophetic revelation is or will be available to the Church in its search to ascertain more accurately the time of the coming of the Antichrist and the final advent of Christ, d'Ailly returns to a previously used argument, namely, the argument from utility. He categorically states that God will not fail his Church *in utilibus*.[67] There

---

[65] Hélène Millet, 'Ecoute et usage des prophéties par les prélats pendant le Grand Schisme d'Occident,' *MEFr-MA*, 102 (1990), 425–455. On the relation of prophets and prophecy to the ecclesiastical hierarchy see also P. Alphandéry, 'Prophètes et ministère prophétique dans le Moyen Age latin,' *RHPR*, 12 (1932), 334–359. For the attitude of theologians towards prophets and prophecy during the period of the Avignon papacy and the Great Schism see also André Vauchez, 'Les théologiens face aux prophètes à l'époque des papes d'Avignon et du Grand Schisme,' *MEFr-MA*, 102 (1990), 577–588.

[66] *Sermo tertius de adventu Domini*, TS, 13. '... non solum de potentia Dei absoluta, quia hoc clarum est, sed etiam de potentia ordinata.'

[67] *Sermo tertius de adventu Domini*, TS, 13. '... cum scientia huiusmodi sit vel aliquando erit utilis ecclesiae Dei maxime circa finem mundi ... sequitur quod Deus qui ecclesiae

is, consequently, no doubt in d'Ailly's mind that God will provide prophets for his Church who will enlighten it as to the time and nature of the final days, especially since such knowledge is so useful to the Church in the fulfillment of its evangelical mission. As examples of such revelations in the past, he singles out the Angelic Oracle of Cyril, Hildegard of Bingen, and Joachim of Fiore.[68]

While d'Ailly stands firmly in his belief that the Church can have some knowledge about the final days of its existence, especially through the revelations of new prophets within the Church, he recognizes that there are scriptural arguments against his position. The major scriptural passage which he sees as possibly contrary to his views is the classic passage in Acts 1:7, where Christ, when asked by his apostles whether he will restore the kingdom of Israel at that time, replies: 'It is not for you to know the times or seasons which the Father has fixed by his own authority.'[69] As seen earlier, Augustine used this passage as the primary basis for his agnostic stance as to the possibility of knowing the End-Times. While d'Ailly had referred to Augustine's earlier and more positive attitude towards the availability of such knowledge, he now faces up to the full force of Augustine's later view. He readily acknowledges that Augustine in his *De civitate Dei* used Acts 1:7 to argue against the possibility of knowing when the sixth age of human history, the period of the Church's history, would come to a close. Augustine maintained that if God had intended man to have clear knowledge about the arrival of the Antichrist and the second advent of Christ, what better way to reveal it to him than through the instrumentality of Christ himself. When asked by the apostles, Christ could easily have informed them about the end of time, but such was not the will of God. Augustine concluded, therefore, that it was useless to speculate on the amount of time left to the world since we have it on the authority of Christ himself that such knowledge is not to be ours.[70]

D'Ailly responds to Augustine's literal interpretation of Acts 1:7 by offering his own highly nuanced exegesis of that passage. He first asserts

---

suae in suis utilibus non deficit, tunc huiusmodi scientiam per specialem inspirationem propheticam revelari disposuit.'

[68] *Sermo tertius de adventu Domini*, TS, 13–14. 'Sic enim beatus Cirillus, Abbas Joachim et Sancta Hyldegardis de temporibus novissimis multa prophetasse creduntur.'

[69] *Sermo tertius de adventu Domini*, TS, 14. 'Sed contra hanc et simul contra primam conclusionem esse videtur illud dictum Christi Actuum I, Non est vestrum nosse tempora vel momenta que pater posuit in sua potestate.'

[70] *De civitate Dei*, 18:53

that when Christ said to the apostles that it was not for them to know the time and the season he used the present (*est*) not the future tense (*erit*) of the verb (*esse*). By this subtle choice of tenses, d'Ailly argues, Christ would seem to have indicated that at the time he was speaking it was not appropriate for the apostles to have such knowledge, but that at some future date, when they are better prepared, the revelation of such knowledge was a distinct possibility. For this part of his argument d'Ailly relies heavily upon the interpretation of the *Glossa Ordinaria*.[71] D'Ailly asserts that Augustine himself espoused a similar view in his *De Trinitate* when he exegeted Mt. 24:36. In that passage Christ states: 'But of that day and hour no one knows, not even the angels of heaven, nor the Son, but the Father only.' Augustine, according to d'Ailly, maintained that by those words Christ affirms that he was not free to reveal any information with regard to the final times, but that he would do so at some future and more opportune moment.[72]

D'Ailly's exegesis of Acts 1:7 continues with an analysis of the word '*vestrum*'. He states that when Christ said in that passage that 'It is not for *you* to know the times or the season,' he implied that they could not obtain such knowledge through the use of human reason. In his exegesis of the word '*vestrum*' d'Ailly departs from that of the *Glossa Ordinaria* which, following in the tradition of Augustine, states that in Christ's view it was not expedient that the apostles have such knowledge. Christ's manner of speaking here is similar to that in Lk. 21:14–15, where he states that when his disciples suffer persecution he will teach them how to respond, for on such occasions it will not be they who respond but the spirit of the Father who speaks in them. According to d'Ailly, however, what Christ is denying in Acts 1:7 is the apostles' capacity to know the final days through mere human initiative; he does not deny that such knowledge could be made known to them through divine inspiration.[73] On this latter point, d'Ailly is fairly consistent with his earlier views on the roles of human reason and prophecy as to the knowledge of the End-Times.

---

[71] *Sermo tertius de adventu Domini*, TS, 14. 'Prima ergo consideratio est quod ibi Christus loquitur per verbum de presenti, dicens non est vestrum ubi ait glossa, non dicit non erit sed non est.' Cf. *Glossa Ordinaria*, 4:452.

[72] *Sermo tertius de adventu Domini*, TS, 14. The reference in Augustine's *De Trinitate* is at 1:12.

[73] *Sermo tertius de adventu Domini*, TS, 14. 'Unde cum hoc pronomen vestrum ex sua significatione referatur ad vires humanas per hoc voluit innuere quod propriis viribus non poterant nosse tempora de quibus interrogabant.'

D'Ailly concludes his textual exegesis of Acts 1:7 by stating that the use of the past infinitive 'to have known' (*nosse*) in that passage indicates that Christ meant that up to that time such knowledge was not available to the apostles but that it could be theirs or their successors in the future. Christ, he argues, was most likely implying that such knowledge was not useful to the Church at the present time but that if it later became useful it would be revealed.[74] On this third point, d'Ailly also deviates from the *Glossa Ordinaria* which states that the reason the apostles were not given such knowledge was that it might lead to a certain complacency and that it was better for them to lead their lives in a state of continued anticipation and preparedness.[75]

Adding a final touch to his highly complex and at times tortuous exegesis of Acts 1:7, d'Ailly states that in that passage the apostles were really not asking about the coming of the Antichrist or the second advent of Christ. The precise question which the apostles posed to Christ, he asserts, was whether he would at that time restore the kingdom to Israel.[76] Once Christ had undergone his passion and death and had triumphed in the resurrection, it was logical, d'Ailly maintained, that his followers would ask him such a question. D'Ailly therefore regards the use of Acts 1:7 against his position regarding the possibility of knowing about the End-Times as an inappropriate argument. Indeed, of all his exegetical arguments in relationship to Acts 1:7 this last argument is probably the most sound since it is clear from the text that the Apostles still viewed the messianic kingdom in terms of a political restoration of the kingdom of David.

With his exegesis of Acts 1:7 d'Ailly brings to a close the first and major portion of his *Advent Sermon* of 1385. In the remaining part of this sermon he turns his attention to an analysis of the apocalyptic signs in Lk. 21:5–28 and Mt. 24:4–44 that were traditionally associated with the final days. As seen above, d'Ailly did maintain that the Church could attain some knowledge of the final days through a prophetic reading of the Scriptures in terms of the contemporary experiences of the Church. These experiences, therefore, are to be seen as the fulfillment

---

[74] *Sermo tertius de adventu Domini*, TS, 15. 'Innuens quod hujusmodi noticia, licet non fuisset aut pro tunc non esset utilis suis discipulis, tamen aliquando foret utilis eis aut successoribus eorum futuris.'

[75] Cf. *Glossa Ordinaria*, 4:452.

[76] *Sermo tertius de adventu Domini*, TS, 15. 'Nec etiam de hujusmodi tempore adventus Antichristi vel consummationis seculi quarebant discipuli sed interrogabant dominae si in tempore hoc restitues regnum Israel …'

of the scriptural signs, and if interpreted correctly through prophecy can yield considerable knowledge as to the arrival of Antichrist and the End-Times. In discussing these signs, however, d'Ailly makes no personal claim to the charism of prophecy, nor does he designate any contemporary figure or figures as prophets regarding the prediction of Antichrist's arrival and the End-Times. Yet there is no doubt that at this point in his sermon d'Ailly seems unable to resist the temptation to assume the prophetic mantle himself.

The cosmic signs utilized by Luke and Matthew in their eschatological discourses are those common to the prophetic and apocalyptic traditions of the Old Testament and include earthquakes, famines, pestilences, betrayals, as well as signs in the sun, moon, and the stars. As he begins his analysis of these signs in Matthew and Luke, d'Ailly recognizes that many prominent figures in the Church's history have analyzed such signs but were unable to render any accurate knowledge of the End-Times. The sayings of the Sibyl which d'Ailly found recounted in Lactantius and Augustine were very much concerned with signs of the last judgement yet that prominent oracle predicted no determined time for its realization.[77] Jerome had spoken of signs that would precede the last days but arrived at no certain conclusions as to the time of their fulfillment. As seen earlier, Augustine himself in his *De civitate Dei* had denied the possibility of such knowledge. In a letter to Hesychius, bishop of Salona in Dalmatia, Augustine asserted that many of the apocalyptic signs in Luke and Matthew were concerned not with the arrival of the End-Times but with the future destruction of Jerusalem. Even with regard to those signs more closely associated with the coming of the Son of Man, Augustine concluded that one could not arrive at an approximate determination of the time of the final days. In that same letter, he firmly asserts that man can determine neither the week, month, year, or even decade when the final advent of Christ will occur.[78]

While recognizing the hesitations of outstanding doctors of the early Church such as Jerome and Augustine, d'Ailly nevertheless maintains

---

[77] *Sermo tertius de adventu Domini*, TS, 16. '… licet illa praememorata sibilla de signis iudicii multa scripserit sicut testatur Lactantius et prout recitat Augustinus, tamen ipsa ut supradictum est nullum tempus determinatum predixit …'

[78] *Sermo tertius de adventu Domini*, TS, 16. '… quod nec de mense nec de anno aut ebdomada vel decada seu quovis alio numero consummationis seculi potest haberi certitudo.' For Aquinas's views on the role of apocalyptic signs in Luke and Matthew see his *ST, Sup*, q. 73, a. 1.

that such signs can be a valuable aid in determining the time of the final age. He was of the opinion that Lk. 21:5–28 and Mt. 24:4–44 provided three types of signs which he classifies according to their degree of proximity to the second coming of Christ, namely, signs that are proximate (*signa propinqua*), those which are more proximate (*signa propinquiora*), and those that are most proximate (*signa propinquissima*).[79] Proximate signs are understood in terms of years; more proximate signs in terms of months, and most proximate signs in terms of days or even hours. Following in the patristic tradition, d'Ailly identifies this threefold sequence of signs respectively with the appearance of the crucified Son of Man in the heavens, the cosmological disturbances discussed earlier, and the coming of the Antichrist and the persecutions associated with that arrival.

When he turns his attention to a further analysis of these signs, d'Ailly surprisingly says practically nothing about the proximate and most proximate signs but concentrates his comments on the more proximate signs, which as indicated above, related to the cosmological disturbances which will precede the appearance of the Son of Man in the heavens. While this choice may at first seem surprising, it is more understandable in view of the fact that Lk. 21:5–28 was the gospel for the Sunday in Advent on which d'Ailly preached. In the specifics of these cosmological events, d'Ailly identifies four signs. The first of these is the darkening of the sun, the moon, and the stars. The second concerns the distress of nations caused by the uncontrolled waves of the ocean. The third sign is seen in the fear of men as they await the outcome of these developments. The fourth and final sign indicates that the powers of heaven will be shaken. In this sign, d'Ailly refers primarily to the consternation of the angelic hosts resulting from these cosmic upheavals.[80]

While d'Ailly believes that these cosmological events will occur as described literally in the texts of Luke and Matthew, he also maintained that for a fuller understanding of these biblical texts one must transcend their literal content and have recourse to their mystical sense which d'Ailly understood primarily in the broader context of the allegorical or

---

[79] *Sermo tertius de adventu Domini*, *TS*, 16. '… tres gradus signorum propinquitatem futuri iudicii significantium distinguere possumus. Nam quaedam sunt propinqua, quaedam propinquiora et quaedam propinquissima.'

[80] *Sermo tertius de adventu Domini*, *TS*, 17. 'Inter signa igitur propinquiora quae sub secundo gradu contineri praediximus, Christus in evangelio hodierno quattuor enumerat que merito considerare debemus.'

symbolical.[81] This recourse to the mystical sense in the interpretation of the eschatological signs follows logically upon his previous teaching that the knowledge of the final days of human history could not be fully obtained through a literal interpretation of the Scriptures.

As he proceeds to unravel the various allegorical meanings of these more proximate signs as found in Lk. 21:5–28 and Mt. 24:4–36, d'Ailly turns first to the darkening of the sun, the moon, and the stars. As seen earlier, throughout d'Ailly's writings, the sun, the moon, and the stars symbolized the major officials of Christendom, and refer respectively to ecclesiastical prelates, secular princes, and the clergy. The darkening of these celestial bodies, therefore, symbolized for him the decline of moral integrity among the leaders of Christendom.[82] For ecclesiastical prelates, this darkening is described in terms of a decline in wisdom (*sapientia*); for secular princes it is synonymous with a lessening of justice (*justitia*) in their actions, and for the clergy it is associated with a decline in grace (*gratia*).[83]

The second of the more proximate signs as narrated by d'Ailly was the distress of the peoples on earth caused by the roaring waves of the sea. The loud sounds of the ocean are interpreted allegorically by d'Ailly to signify the vast displeasure of the Christian people with their ecclesiastical leaders. This displeasure, he asserts, may indeed at some future date break out into open opposition to the Church.[84] The third sign, the fear of men as they observe the events of the final days, symbolizes the fear that Christians have when they see the moral degradation which characterized the Church of their day. This fear is intensified by the realization that the situation will probably become worse with the passage of time.[85] The fourth and final sign, that of the

---

[81] *Sermo tertius de adventu Domini*, TS, 17. 'Ideoque litterali sensu praesupposito … ad sensum mysticum transeamus.'

[82] *Sermo tertius de adventu Domini*, TS, 17. 'Quid est enim erunt signa in sole et luna et stellis, nisi quod ecclesiae luminari tenebrescent, quod utique, iam prodolor, factum esse conspicimus.'

[83] *Sermo tertius de adventu Domini*, TS, 17–18. 'Iam certe solem, lunam, et stellas tenebrescere percipimus, dum in prelatis lucem sapientiae, in principibus lumen iustitiae, in inferioribus autem et fere in omnibus splendorem gratiae pene deficere videamus.'

[84] *Sermo tertius de adventu Domini*, TS, 18. '… in sonitu maris et fluctuum murmur popularium convenienter intelligitur, quod hodie adversus ecclesiasticos tantum esse dinoscitur, ut ex eo pressura gentium, id est, oppressio ecclesiae a ceteris gentibus verisimiliter futura credatur.'

[85] *Sermo tertius de adventu Domini*, TS, 18. 'Cur ergo non arescerent homines prae timore et expectatione quae supervenient universo orbi, cum ex tot et tantis malis quae presentia vident plura et maiora universaliter ventura presumant.'

shaking of the powers of heaven, interpreted allegorically, means that even those confirmed in grace might be tempted and led into error.[86]

In d'Ailly's mind, all the above signs were especially recognizable in the Great Western Schism which so gravely afflicted the Church of his times. As seen earlier, d'Ailly regarded the Schism as the more recent and intensive of the persecutions which the Church experienced throughout its history, and, therefore, as a form of divine punishment inflicted upon the Church because of its abandonment of the evangelical ideal. This abandonment was especially evident in the intellectual and moral decline among the Church's prelates and clergy, the prevalence of simony in the administration of the sacraments and in the pursuit of ecclesiastical office, and, finally, in the uneven distribution of ecclesiastical wealth. These factors, when added to the great scandal caused by the Schism, had considerably contributed to the spiritual anguish and distress of the Christian people. As the Schism dragged on, therefore, d'Ailly became increasingly convinced that it was the last harbinger of the coming of the Antichrist and the final judgement by Christ.

4. *Reform: The Gospel and the Apostolic Ideal*

The question that now arises for d'Ailly is what attitude the Church should take in the face of these apocalyptic signs. He strongly believed that the Church could postpone the appearance of the Antichrist if it adopted the proper measures to resolve the difficulties with which it was beset. In a letter written to John XXIII early in 1414, d'Ailly delineated four possible attitudes towards the apocalyptic signs so evident within the Church and gave his reaction to each. The first attitude he described as a spirit of overoptimism which was characteristic of many prelates who rely too heavily upon Christ's promise to his disciples in Mt. 28:20 that he would be with them until the end of time. A second attitude was that of procrastination. The Church, many argued, has survived periods of tribulation before and will survive the present one as well. A third attitude adopted by many towards the problems of the time was best characterized by the classical notion of 'seize the day'

---

[86] *Sermo tertius de adventu Domini*, *TS*, 18. 'Sed quid est virtutes celorum movebuntur, nisi quia virtuosi ac celestes viri propter persecutionem malorum de boni propositi mutatione temptantur adeo ut ... inducantur in errorem, si fieri posset etiam electi.'

(*carpe diem*). According to this view, prelates should continue to enjoy the benefits of ecclesiastical life and let the deluge come when it may. D'Ailly finds this view the most pernicious. The fourth attitude was that of pessimism and despair. Advocates of this position, he asserted, have resigned themselves to the decline of the Church and the inevitable triumph of the forces of the Antichrist.[87]

Although he was most sensitive to the apocalyptic signs of his day with regard to the immanent arrival of the Antichrist and indeed feared that the tribulations which afflicted the Church during the Great Schism were forewarnings of that arrival, d'Ailly adopted a moderate position which avoided the overly optimistic and procrastinating dimensions of the first two attitudes as well as the negative and fatalistic outlook of the latter two. As seen earlier in his view of the Church's history, he preferred to see the tribulations afflicting the Church of his day as God's way of punishing the Church for its sins, a view of historical causality very common to the patristic and medieval tradition. Despite this view of God as a determined avenger, d'Ailly also asserts that God is ultimately a consoler and will gradually bring peace to his people.

This moderately optimistic outlook of d'Ailly with regard to the Church's ability to postpone the arrival of the Antichrist and the End-Times contrasts with the more pessimistic interpretation by Smoller. As seen earlier, Smoller delineates three periods in the development of d'Ailly's attitude towards astrology's ability to predict the arrival of the Antichrist and the End-Times. The first two periods, namely, from 1375–1380 and 1381–1409 reflect an essentially negative reaction to astrology's claims. As Smoller sees it, the third period, from 1410 to 1420, the period covered by d'Ailly's letter to John XXIII, represents a more positive attitude on d'Ailly's part with regard to such astrological claims. This more positive attitude, she argues, results ironically from d'Ailly's increasing pessimism regarding the tribulations facing the Church of his day, especially as successive attempts to resolve the Schism failed. In this context, Smoller argues that the failure of the Council of Pisa to resolve the controversy between the Roman and Avignon claimants to the papacy, the emergence of the newly elected Pisan pope, Alexander V (1409–1410), and the continuation of the Pisan claims by his successor, John XXIII (1410–1415) intensified d'Ailly's

---

[87] *Epistola prima ad Joannem XXIII*, Dupin, 2:878–879.

fears as to the imminence of Antichrist's arrival. Nor did the convocation of the Council of Constance in 1414 help to alleviate d'Ailly's concerns and fear.[88]

The effect of all these concerns, according to Smoller, was that during the period 1410–1420 d'Ailly began to search for new resources which might better enable him to predict the arrival of Antichrist's arrival. According to Smoller, these years represented for d'Ailly a period of intensified study as well as increasing confidence in the field of astrology. It was during this period that he composed most of his major astrological treatises. In contrast to his earlier astrological writings, these treatises reflect a considerable change for the positive in d'Ailly's attitude towards astrology as a science and its capabilities to predict the arrival of the Antichrist.[89]

D'Ailly's renewed and intensified study of astrology, according to Smoller, led him to the conclusion that the appearance of the Antichrist was not as imminent as he had previously believed. Indeed, these studies led d'Ailly to believe that the Antichrist would not appear in his lifetime but sometime much later in the following centuries. The most common dates of which he spoke were 1518 and 1789, dates which nineteenth and early twentieth-century readers of d'Ailly's astrological writings readily associated with the Lutheran Reformation and the French Revolution. With the resolution of the Schism in 1417, Smoller maintains that d'Ailly's fear of the immediacy of Antichrist's arrival further diminished and by the end of his life had almost completely disappeared.[90]

There is no doubt that Smoller's study of d'Ailly's changing attitude toward astrology's potentialities in the realm of apocalyptic predictions has highlighted important and neglected dimensions of his apocalyptic thought. She has indeed pointed out the importance of astrological as well as biblical, historical, and prophetic influences in the evolution of his apocalyptic thought. Her study has also served to emphasize d'Ailly's concern that all these sources be seen as essentially complementary and ultimately capable of harmonization (*concordantia*). D'Ailly's, optimism about the Church's ability to delay the arrival of the Antichrist, however, was not restricted to the 1410–1420 period of his life. While his astrological studies during this period certainly pro-

---

[88] Smoller, *History, Prophecy, and the Stars*, 44–54.
[89] Smoller, *History, Prophecy, and the Stars*, 57–60.
[90] Smoller, *History, Prophecy, and the Stars*, 102–121.

vided him with added reasons for hope, an essentially optimistic attitude regarding the possibility of postponing the End-Times characterized his apocalyptic thought from his early years.

This viewpoint was clearly evident in his *Sermon on St. Francis* of 1380 where he insisted that the punishments inflicted upon the schismatic Church must be seen not as a sign of its ultimate destruction but more as a process of purification and an opportunity for renewal. In emphasizing the purifying effects of persecution, d'Ailly has recourse to the classical passage in Isa. 1:24–25, where the prophet compares the purification of Israel to the process of purifying metal in a furnace. Even though he increasingly saw the Schism as the precursor of the Antichrist, he still remained optimistic as to the Church's ability to stave off that arrival if it could achieve its internal reform and renewal. In his letter to John XXIII on the eve of the Council of Constance in 1414, he evinced a moderately optimistic attitude towards the problems afflicting the Church during the Great Schism provided that it took the proper path to reform. Such a course of action could indeed postpone the arrival of the Antichrist and the End-Times.

When he turns to the nature of the reform which the Church must undergo if it is to postpone the advent of the Antichrist, d'Ailly manifests again his basic tendency to regard the process of decline and renewal in the Church within an evangelical context. As seen in his 1380 *Sermon on St. Francis*, d'Ailly regarded the numerous problems afflicting the contemporary Church as rooted in its abandonment of the evangelical teaching of Christ. It is not surprising, therefore, to discover that he views the reformation of the Church in terms of a return to its evangelical roots. As will be recalled, when he signaled out Francis as having realized the fullness of the evangelical ideal, it was his spirit of poverty, chastity, and humility that he so greatly emphasized. D'Ailly therefore maintained that only by fostering these evangelical virtues within the entire Church can the proclivity of his age towards avarice, lust, and vanity be countered. The exercise of these virtues, he felt, will provide protection against future tribulations and contribute toward the Church's realization of the true peace of Christ.[91]

---

[91] *Sermo de Sancto Francisco*, *TS*, 12. '… ut per ea contra previsa persecutionum iacula cautiores reddamur et inter futura perturbationum mala per evangelicae regulae observationem pacem Christi veram finaliter consequamur.'

The same evangelical emphasis is seen in d'Ailly's *De materia concilii*, written in 1402/1403, wherein he cites a passage in Peter the Chanter's *Verbum Abbreviatum* which narrates how John of Salisbury as bishop of Chartres strongly advised the Third Lateral Council (1179) that it not pass a multitude of laws in its efforts to reform the Church but that it direct all its efforts to insure that the spirit of the Gospel be understood and fully integrated into the lives of all Christians.[92] As will also be recalled, d'Ailly, without making any changes or additions, had his 1380 *Sermon on St. Francis* recirculated at the Council of Constance in 1417, a convincing sign of his continued emphasis upon the evangelical ideal as the basis for all Church reform.

This evangelical orientation of d'Ailly's thought provides us not only with a much richer and heretofore neglected dimension of his views on church reform but also allows us to place him in the long tradition of evangelical reformers, which, as Chenu has so masterfully shown, goes back to the twelfth century.[93] We are also able to situate him more accurately within the evangelical movements of his own time. The general tenor of his *Sermon on St. Francis* clearly shows his sympathy with the essentially evangelical spirit of the Franciscan movement without however embracing the more extreme manifestations of that movement as represented by the Spiritual Franciscans. His emphasis on evangelical values in the reform of the Church also serves to emphasize his close affiliation and affection for the Brethren of the Common Life, whose staunch defender he proved to be at the Council of Constance. At Constance the Dominican Matthew Grabow had sought to condemn the claim of the Brethren of the Common Life that their form of life was essentially identical with that of the recognized religious orders, namely the pursuit of Christian perfection in terms of the evangelical ideal. Grabow sought to restrict such a claim only to those recognized religious orders whose members professed the vows of poverty, chastity, and obedience. Since the Brethren of the Common Life did not formally profess such vows, Grabow argued, they could not make such a claim. Together with Gerson, d'Ailly strongly opposed the position of

---

[92] *De materia concilii*, Oakley, 255. The edition used for this work is that of Francis Oakley as contained in his *The Political Thought of Pierre* d'Ailly, 252–342. The reference to the *Verbum Abbreviatum* is at c. 79:206, *PL*, 205:235.

[93] M.D. Chenu, *Man, Nature, and Society in the Twelfth Century* (Chicago: University of Chicago Press, 1968). See especially the essays 'Monks, Canons, and Laymen in Search of the Apostolic Life,' 202–238, and 'The Evangelical Awakening,' 239–269.

Grabow and defended the right of the Brethren to describe their mode of life as the pursuit of Christian perfection in terms of the evangelical life.[94]

Yet despite his close association and affection for these major manifestations of the evangelical spirit in the late Middle Ages, d'Ailly remained essentially within the episcopal tradition. In a very true sense, his goal was the renewal of that tradition through a revival of the evangelical ideal among its members. This goal was first seen in his *Sermon on St. Francis* when d'Ailly raises the question of who will initiate and bring to fulfillment the reform of the Church according to the evangelical ideal. In his response to this question, d'Ailly has recourse to Isa. 1:24–26 wherein the prophet speaks of the purifying and reformative dimensions of the punishment that God had inflicted upon his people. The prophet then predicts that God will restore Israel's judges and that Israel will again be noted for its justice and faithfulness. In his exegesis of this passage, D'Ailly sees an analogy between Israel and the contemporary Church. As in the case with Israel, the Church of his day was also afflicted by a series of tribulations primarily identified with the Schism. These tribulations, he maintained, had their purifying and reformative dimensions. There was, finally, every reason to believe that, as he did with Israel, God would again raise up 'new judges' (*judices novi*) who would lead the Church back to the observance of its ancient evangelical ideal.[95]

D'Ailly's concept of 'new judges' shows a striking parallel with the theme of new 'spiritual men' (*viri spirituales*) characteristic of the reform thought of Joachim of Fiore and the Spiritual Franciscans. As will be recalled, it is such men who were to bring about the reform and renewal of the Church in the third stage of its history. D'Ailly indeed makes clear that his notion of the 'new judges' was rooted in the Joachite tradition for he cites the Joachite *Super Hieremiam Prophetam* as

---

[94] On the controversy at Constance over the claims of the Brethren of the Common Life, see R.R. Post, *The Modern Devotion: Confrontation with Reformation and Humanism*, Studies in Medieval and Reformation Thought, 3 (Leiden: E.J. Brill, 1968), 289–292, and John van Engen, ed. *Devotio Moderna: Basic Writings* (New York: Paulist Press, 1988), 39–40. D'Ailly's attack was based heavily upon Jean Gerson's report on the claims of Grabow, namely, his *Contra conclusiones Matthaei Graben*, Glorieux, 10:70–72. For Gerson's views and role in the controversy see Pascoe, *Jean Gerson: Principles of Church Reform*, Studies in Medieval and Reformation Thought, 7 (Leiden: E.J. Brill, 1973), 165–167.

[95] *Sermo de Sancto Francisco*, TS, 10. '... et instituentur iudices novi, per quos ecclesia ad antiquam evangelicae regulae iusticiam dei gratia reducetur.'

his source.[96] This association of 'new judges' with new 'spiritual men' is especially interesting since, as seen earlier in his apocalyptic thought, d'Ailly generally did not adopt Joachim of Fiore's tripartite division of the Church's history, nor the particularly controversial interpretation of the third stage as espoused by the more radical Spiritual Franciscans. With regard to Joachim's teaching on the new 'spiritual men,' it should be remembered that he essentially identified them with two groups, the first dedicated to the apostolic life of preaching and the second to the contemplative life. Both groups, according to Joachim, were to prepare the way for the transition into the third stage of the Church's history, namely, a spiritually reformed and renewed Church. Joachim's Franciscan interpreters, however, especially the Spiritual Franciscans, increasingly interpreted the concept of the new 'spiritual men' in terms of the mendicant orders, especially their own order.[97]

D'Ailly, however, rejects the prevailing Franciscan interpretation of Joachim's new 'spiritual men' and this rejection is especially seen in his reaction to Nicholas of Lyra's commentary on Rev. 20:1–3 wherein is described how the angel seized and bound Satan for a thousand years. In his reflections on that passage, Lyra saw the angel as symbolizing Innocent III (1198–1216) who approved the foundation of the Franciscan and Dominican Orders which, Lyra maintained, by their teaching and preaching of the Gospel, had proven to be the major restraining force within the Church against the threatening power of the Antichrist and indeed had become the principle agents in the renewal of the Church.[98]

D'Ailly's rejection of Nicholas of Lyra's exegesis of Rev. 20:1–3 is not surprising. Given the long and intense controversies between the secular and mendicant masters at the University of Paris, it would indeed be surprising if he granted them a leading role in the reform

---

[96] *Sermo de Sancto Francisco*, TS, 10–11. 'Hii namque secundum sententiam abbatis Ioachim super Hieremiam erunt fideles in doctrina, spirituales in vita, obedientes in pressura, electi scilicet ad predicandum evangelium …'

[97] For Joachim's thoughts on the 'spiritual men' see McGinn, *The Calabrian Abbot*, 112–113. For an illuminating survey of the diverse manners in which later religious groups, especially the mendicants, sought to identify themselves with Joachim's notion of 'the spiritual men' see Reeves, *Joachim of Fiore and the Prophetic Future*, 29–58. For a comprehensive survey of the Spiritual Franciscans see David Burr, *The Spiritual Franciscans: From Protest to Persecution in the Century After Saint Francis* (University Park: Penn State University Press, 2001).

[98] *De persecutionibus ecclesiae*, Valois, 572. For Nicholas of Lyra's exegesis of Rev. 20:1–3 see his *Postilla litteralis super totam Bibliam*, 4.

and renewal of the Church. D'Ailly, moreover, felt that the mendicant orders of his day had radically departed from the spirit and ideals of their founders.[99] A vast majority of mendicant theologians and canonists were also supporters of the papal cause in the many ecclesiological controversies related to the resolution of the Schism. D'Ailly felt that by their writings and actions the mendicant orders had contributed greatly to the prolongation of the Schism.

If d'Ailly refuses to identify the mendicants with the new 'spiritual men' who are to reform the Church according to the evangelical spirit of Christ, with whom, then, does he identify them? D'Ailly provides no clear answer to this question but since he rejected the mendicant orders as their embodiment and since, as will be seen, he saw the Church's evangelical decline and renewal primarily in terms of its prelates, it seems reasonable to maintain that it is from the ranks of the Church's prelates, especially the episcopacy, that God would raise up a new group of reformers who would lead the Church back again to the spirit of the Gospel. For d'Ailly, therefore, an evangelically renewed episcopacy is to replace the monastic and mendicant orders as the primary agent in the reformation of the Church in the late Middle Ages. The great emphasis which d'Ailly places throughout his writings upon bishops as agents of reform within the Church further substantiates this conclusion. D'Ailly's decision at the Council of Constance in 1417 to recirculate an unrevised version of his 1380 *Sermon on St. Francis*, wherein he first proposed this dimension of his reform thought, provides added evidence of the continuity and prominence of his ideas on this point. This stress on the evangelical nature of episcopal office also places d'Ailly in the context of those late medieval currents of episcopal reform that found their eventual fulfillment in the Catholic Reformation of the sixteenth century.

---

[99] *De persecutionibus ecclesiae*, Valois, 573. '… cum iam a primitiva sua perfectione atque puritate et suorum primorum fundatorum sanctitate multum cecidisse videantur.'

CHAPTER TWO

BISHOPS: STATUS, OFFICE, AUTHORITY

Given the important role that d'Ailly assigns to the episcopal office in the reform and renewal of the Church according to its evangelical foundations, it will help, first of all, to study his views on the nature and authority of the episcopal office before investigating the specific manner in which that office was to participate in and advance that reform and renewal. In order to achieve this task more effectively, however, it is important to understand the general medieval concept of ecclesiastical office as well as d'Ailly's own views on this topic. This study, therefore, will begin with an analysis of the major ecclesiastical offices in the Middle Ages as well as with a description of their historical evolution. It will then proceed to analyze these offices in terms of their respective rank (*status*), duties (*officia*), and authority (*auctoritas*) within the Church.[1] The specific emphasis in this chapter will be upon the status, office, and authority of bishops. The succeeding chapter will then study the specific manner in which bishops participate in the reform and renewal of the Church according to its evangelical foundations.

1. *Prelates: Terminology, Evolution, Categories*

The technical terms generally used to describe ecclesiastical officials within the ancient and early medieval Church were *praepositus*, *rector*, and *praelatus*. All three terms have their origins in classical and post-

---

[1] For a deeper analysis of the understanding of these terms in the theologians of the Middle Ages, see A.J. Robilliard, 'Sur la notion de condition (status) in St. Thomas,' *RSPT*, 29 (1936), 104–107, and M.D. Chenu, 'Officium: Théologiens et canonists,' in *Etudes d'histoire du droit canonique dediées à Gabriel Le Bras*, 2 vols. (Paris: Sirey, 1965), 2:835–839. The varying meanings attached to the term *status* in the deliberations and documents of the Council of Constance have been described in detail by Phillip H. Stump, *The Reforms of the Council of Constance, 1414–1418*, Studies in the History of Christian Thought, 53 (Leiden: E.J. Brill, 1994), 256–263.

classical Latin where they were first used of military and political officials. While these terms continued to describe such officials, they were also gradually adopted by the early Church to designate its own officials. During the high Middle Ages, especially during the latter half of the twelfth century, the term *praelatus* was used with greater frequency and eventually gained predominance over the use of *praepositus* and *rector*.[2]

The intensified use of *praelatus* in the high Middle Ages to describe major ecclesiastical officials is closely associated with the efforts of the newly emerging sciences of theology and canon law to clarify the nature of ecclesiastical jurisdiction. The need for such clarification had been occasioned by the increasing clericalization of the monastic orders, their increased pastoral activities and their consequent conflicts with the diocesan clergy over the question of pastoral jurisdiction. As a result of these conflicts, the term *praelatus* was increasingly applied to those members of the diocesan clergy who were entrusted with the pastoral care of a geographically determined number of people and who, accordingly, had the requisite jurisdiction over them. Understood in this more restricted context, the term was used to designate not only cardinals, archbishops, bishops and priests, but also archdeacons, and deans of cathedral chapters. In an extended application of the term, *praelatus* was also applied to heads of houses of both secular and religious canons, abbots of monastic orders, and ministers general and provincials of the mendicant orders since they exercised jurisdiction over the members of their respective groups.[3] While d'Ailly uses *praelatus* in all these senses, his primary use and understanding of the term is clearly related to the offices of cardinal, bishop, and priest. In this respect, he also reflects the principal medieval understanding and application of the term.

---

[2] For an historical study of the terms *praepositus*, *rector*, and *praelatus* as used in the ancient and early medieval Church see Yves Congar, 'Quelques expressions traditionnelles du service chrétien,' in *L'épiscopat et l'Eglise universelle*, ed. Yves Congar et al., (Paris: Editions du Cerf, 1962), 124–132.

[3] The different senses in which the term *praelatus* was used within the ecclesiastical realm during the Middle Ages are clearly enumerated in J.F. Niermeyer, *Mediae Latinitatis Lexicon Minus* (Leiden, 1976), 834–835. For the conflicts between the monastic orders and diocesan clergy over the pastoral care of and jurisdiction over the laity see M. Peuchmaurd, 'Le prêtre ministre de la parole dans le théologie du xiie siècle: canonistes, moines et chanoines,' *RTAM*, 29 (1962), 52–76.

2. *Status: Apostolic Succession*

While the primary intent of this chapter is to study d'Ailly's views on the status, office, and authority of the episcopacy, it is necessary to begin our analysis with his teaching on the cardinalate since the historical origins and evolution of the episcopal office, in d'Ailly's view, was closely associated with those of the cardinals. D'Ailly's most extensive analysis of the status of the cardinalate is to be found in his *De potestate ecclesiastica*, a treatise written while he was a member of the Council of Constance and presented to the Council on October 1, 1416, five years after his own elevation to the cardinalate by Benedict XIII.[4] D'Ailly divides his treatise into three parts which deal respectively with the origins and development of ecclesiastical office, the rights of ecclesiastical ministers, especially with regard to property, and the nature and limitations of the papal plenitude of power. Only the first part of this treatise is pertinent to the topic at hand. It should be noted, however, that while this part of the treatise promises to deal with the origins of the entire ecclesiastical hierarchy it concentrates primarily upon the papacy and the cardinalate.

In his analysis of the origin and development of the Church's hierarchical structures, d'Ailly delineates three historical stages. The first period is identified with Christ's life before the Ascension and includes not only the missionary years of his life but also his passion, death, and resurrection. In describing this stage, d'Ailly emphasizes primarily Christ's calling of the apostles and his relationship to them. During this period, according to d'Ailly, Christ is both physically and spiritually head of the Church. All the apostles are equal with one another and no distinctive authority was exercised even by Peter. The function of all the apostles at this time was to serve as Christ's assistants in the work of establishing the Kingdom of God on earth.[5]

---

[4] The text of this treatise can be found in Dupin, 2:925–960. The full title of this treatise as given by Dupin is *Tractatus de potestate ecclesiastica seu de Ecclesiae, Concilii Generalis et Summi Pontificis auctoritate*. Although this work is frequently referred to as d'Ailly's *De Ecclesia*, subsequent reference to this treatise will be made under the title *De potestate ecclesiastica*.

[5] *De potestate ecclesiastica*, Dupin 2:934. 'Pro cujus declaratione sciendum est quod apostoli possunt tripliciter considerari: primo, ut Christo praesentialiter astiterunt ante ejus Ascensionem ... In primo statu, apostoles pares, nec Petrus eis praeerat.' D'Ailly's analysis of the apostolic college at this stage neglects the prominent role played by

The Ascension in d'Ailly's view marks the transition from the first to the second stage in the development of the cardinalate. Unfortunately, d'Ailly gives no precise date as to the end of this second stage. Since he indicates, however, that it ends with the separation of the apostles from Peter and their dispersal throughout the world, i.e. their mission to the Gentiles, it seems most likely that d'Ailly identifies this period with the time of the apostolic mission of Peter and the apostles to the Jews in Galilee, Judea, and Samaria as described in Acts 2:14–9:43.[6]

According to d'Ailly, what characterizes this stage first of all is that as a result of the promises made to him in Mt. 16:18–19 and the special commission given to him in Jn. 22:17, Peter emerges as head of the universal Church.[7] It is also during this stage that the Church's diverse ministerial orders evolve according to the offices described in Eph. 4:1–16. In this passage, after speaking of the essential unity of the Church in terms of one Lord, one faith, and one baptism, Paul describes the different ministerial charisms which the ascended Christ bestowed upon his Church, namely, the offices of apostles, prophets, evangelists, pastors, and teachers.[8] D'Ailly sees this action as marking the further delineation of the Church's ministerial structure.[9] According to d'Ailly, these offices are also hierarchically structured under the headship of Peter for the maintenance of their proper beauty and order.[10] Because

---

Peter in that college, even before the promises made to him in Mt. 16:18–17 and Jn. 22:17. For an analysis of this role see Raymond Brown, et al., *Peter in the New Testament* (Minneapolis: Augsburg Publishing House, 1973), 159–168.

[6] In the first part of his *De potestate ecclesiastica* on the origins and development of the Church's hierarchical order, d'Ailly occasionally mentions that he is following the historical order presented in the Acts of the Apostles, other ecclesiastical histories, and the decrees of the holy Fathers. An example of such references can be found at Dupin, 2:928–929.

[7] *De potestate ecclesiastica*, Dupin 2:934. '... secundo ut astiterunt Petro tanquam primo pastori ante divisionem apostolorum et separationem a Petro ... In secundo ... statu praeerat eis Petrus.'

[8] *De potestate ecclesiastica*, Dupin 2:934. 'Ubi primo supponendum est quod Christus Ecclesiam suam instituit statibus, officiis, et gradibus variis hierarchice distinctam.'

[9] *De potestate ecclesiastica*, Dupin 2:934. 'Et haec perfecta et completa statuum distinctio maxime in die Ascensionis instituta est, ut notant praemissa verba Apostoli allegantis illud Psal. lxvii.19, Ascendens in altum dedit dona, etc.'

[10] *De potestate ecclesiastica*, Dupin 2:934. 'Ulterius supponitur quod praemissa officiorum varietas ad sui pulchritudinem et ordinem requirit quod inter authoritates Ecclesiae regitivas sit hierarchica subordinatio, et quod una, scilicet papalis authoritas, sit suprema, ex Christi institutione et non tantum humana authoritate sed divina.'

of their scriptural foundation these offices are regarded by d'Ailly as established in divine law and thereby enjoying a permanence which human or positive law cannot provide.[11]

With regard to the apostles, moreover, this stage is seen essentially as a continuation of their earlier collegial relationship with Christ, now represented by Peter. This relationship is characterized first of all by their close physical and geographical contact with Peter and with each other. Secondly, neither they nor Peter are permanently associated with any one particular local church. They are, as d'Ailly describes them, 'apostles of the world' (*apostoli orbis*) rather than 'apostles of the city' (*apostoli urbis*).[12] Thirdly, although Peter is described during this period as principle minister and hierarch as well as supreme pontiff, the apostles are presented as his principle assessors, counselors, and co-workers in the governance of the entire Church.[13] As such, they are also frequently described in the distinctly Roman context of a *senatus* or *collegium*.[14] D'Ailly, indeed, goes so far as to assert that during this second stage of the Church's hierarchical development, the apostles, because of their collegial association with Peter in the governance of the whole Church, should be regarded more as prototypes of the cardinals than of the bishops[15] In this context, d'Ailly states that just as Peter was pope of the universal Church before he became bishop of Rome, so too the apostles were first cardinals of the universal Church before becoming cardinals of the Roman Church.[16]

---

[11] *De potestate ecclesiastica*, Dupin 2:934. 'Ex quo sequitur quod varietas officiorum, statuum, graduum et dignitatum in Ecclesia non principaliter est ex institutione Ecclesiae aut cujuscumque puri hominis auctoritate processit, quare nec eam destitere potest sive destituere.'

[12] *De potestate ecclesiastica*, Dupin 2:929. 'Ex quo iterum sequitur quod prius fuerunt cardinales orbis quam urbis.'

[13] The titles given to Peter can be found in the *De potestate ecclesiastica*, Dupin 2:928. ' ... tamen nihilominus Petrus et quilibet ejus vicarius Pontifex Summus potuit dici caput Ecclesiae inquantum principalis est inter ministros, a quo tamen, tanquam a principali hierarcha et architecto, aliquo modo dependet totus ministrorum ecclesiasticus ordo.' For references to the apostles and their functions see 2:929: 'Petro ... assistebant ... tanquam ejus principales assessores et conciliarii atque cooperatores in regimine universalis ecclesiae.'

[14] *De potestate ecclesiastica*, Dupin 2:930. 'sacro collegio vel senatui apostolorum.'

[15] *De potestate ecclesiastica*, Dupin, 2:929. '... apostoli Petro tanquam papale officium gerenti assistebant tanquam cardinalatus ministerium exercentes, sicut nunc papae assistunt cardinales.'

[16] *De potestate ecclesiastica*, Dupin, 2:929. 'Nam sicut Petrus prius fuit papa orbis, id

As a result of his historical views, there is no doubt that d'Ailly regarded the cardinals of his day as the direct successors of the apostles, especially with regard to their relationship with the pope as the successor of Peter.[17] As was the case with Peter and the Apostles, this relationship was also described by d'Ailly in a collegial context by the use of phrases that depicted the cardinals as 'part of the body of the pope (*pars corporis papae*), coworkers (*coadjutors*), assessors (*assessores*), counselors (*conciliarii*), cooperators (*cooperatores*) of the pope, and as an integral part of the apostolic see (*sedes apostolica*).[18] While d'Ailly's emphasis on the collegial nature of the cardinalate certainly intensified when he himself was elected to that rank, his conviction on this matter predated that elevation. In his *Epistola ad novos Hebraeos*, written in 1378, three years before his reception of the doctorate, he describes both pope and cardinals as a single *collegium*.[19]

In his description of the origins and collegial nature of the cardinalate, d'Ailly showed great concern to base his arguments on canon and divine law. With regard to canon law, he cites Innocent III as his source for the notion of the cardinals as *pars corporis papae* and *coadjutores papae*, and Guido of Baysio as his authority for the senatorial analogies.[20] Similar views, he maintained, were also shared by such promi-

---

est universalis ecclesiae antequam episcopus Eclesiae Romanae, ut dictum est, sic et apostoli prius fuerunt cardinales orbis quam aliqui fierent cardinales Romanae Urbis.'

[17] *De potestate ecclesiastica*, Dupin 2:934. 'Ex praemissis infertur quod sicut status papae sic et post eum status cardinalium ad ordinem hierarchicum ecclesiae ex Christi institutione pertinet. Nam ipsi, quantum ad hunc statum, statui apostolico immediate succedunt.'

[18] For reference to the cardinals as *pars corporis papae* and *coadjutores papae* see *De potestate ecclesiastica*, Dupin 2, 946. Reference to them as part of the *sedes apostolica* can be found in the same work, Dupin 2:935. For their identification as *assessores, conciliarii*, and *cooperatores papae* see Dupin 2:929.

[19] *Epistola ad novos Hebraeos*, Salembier, 258. The edition of this work used in the present study is that of Louis Salembier as published in his article, 'Une page inédite de l'histoire de la Vulgate,' *RSE*, 60 (1889), 23–28, 97–108, 257–267, 369–382 and will be cited as above.

[20] *De potestate ecclesiastica*, Dupin 2:946. The reference to Innocent III is to his decretal *Per venerabilem*, X, 4, 17, 13. In addition to Innocent's decretal, d'Ailly also cites X, 2, 24, 4 which is essentially an oath taken by bishops to the pope and which in its essential form goes back to Gregory VII. An additional reference is also made by d'Ailly to Boniface VIII's decretal *Fundamenta*, VI, 1, 6, 17. For the canonical development of the teaching on the cardinals as *collegium, senatus, pars corporis papae*, and *coadjutores papae*, see J.A. Watt, 'The Constitutional Law of the College of Cardinals from Hostiensis to Johannes Andreae,' *MS*, 33 (1971), 127–157, 'Hostiensis on *Per Venerabilem*: The Role of the College of Cardinals,' in *Authority and Power: Studies on Medieval Law and Government*

nent canonists as Hostiensis and Johannes Monachus.[21] While d'Ailly used canon law to establish the origin and development of the cardinalate, he was even more concerned with establishing the cardinalate in divine law.[22] By arguing from Acts 2:14–9:43 wherein the apostolic mission of Peter and the Apostles to the Jewish world had been described and by showing that the pope and cardinals were the direct successors of Peter and the Apostles, d'Ailly felt that he had established the cardinalate in divine law.

D'Ailly's arguments for the establishment of the cardinalate in divine law represent a strengthening of his views on the origins of the cardinalate. In his *De materia concilii*, written in 1402/1403, d'Ailly, while discussing many of the abuses rampant in the College of Cardinals, entertained the opinion of some that the cardinalate might not be of divine origin and could therefore possibly be abolished as was the case earlier with the institution of chorbishops.[23] While he indicates his disapproval of this opinion, his rejection of it was even stronger in his *De reformatione*, which was a revision of the *De materia concilii* and was presented to the Council of Constance in November of 1416.[24] Earlier that same month and with equal vigor, he had condemned that opinion in his *De postestate ecclesiastica*.[25] The intensification of d'Ailly's views on the establishment of the cardinalate in divine law no doubt is reflected in the fact that by the time he composed the *De reformatione* he had already been a cardinal for five years. Since there was no essential change in d'Ailly's views on

---

Presented to Walter Ullmann, ed. Brian Tierney and Peter Linehan (Cambridge: Cambridge University Press, 1980) 99–113.

[21] *De potestate ecclesiastica*, Dupin 2:933. For an analysis of Hostiensis' and Johannes Monachus' teaching on the cardinalate see Brian Tierney, *Foundations of the Conciliar Theory* (Cambridge: Cambridge University Press, 1955), 149–153, 179–190. As Tierney indicates the description of the College of Cardinals in terms of a Senate was widely used by canonists in the thirteenth and fourteenth century, especially John of Paris, Guido of Baysio, and Johannes Monachus. This description, moreover, was not an honorific title since in Roman Law the senators acted on behalf of the whole Roman People.

[22] *De potestate ecclesiastica*, Dupin, 2:934. 'Sed ultra jura praemissa, humana et positiva, restat in jure divino fundare statum hierarchicum cardinalium et eorum authoritatem.'

[23] *De materia concilii*, Oakley, 328.

[24] *De reformatione*, Miethke-Weinrich, 1:354. 'Hunc autem errorem in hac synodo Constantiensi quodammodo resuscitare aliqui praesumpserunt.' The edition used for this treatise is that contained in Miethke-Weinrich, *Quellen zur Kirchenreform*, 1:338–377, and will be cited as above.

[25] *De potestate ecclesiastica*, Dupin, 2:925–926. In his *De reformatione*, Miethke-Weinrich, 1:352–254, D'Ailly refers directly to his earlier rejection of this opinion in his *De potestatate ecclesiastica*.

the divine law origin of the cardinalate as the successor of the apostolic college, charges of self-interest and personal opportunism seem exaggerated. Oakley's explanation in terms of d'Ailly's growing realization of the importance of the college of cardinals better represents his primary motivation.[26]

The notion of the college of cardinals as the successors of the apostolic college began in the latter part of the eleventh century with the Gregorian reformers, especially Peter Damian (1007–1072) and Deusdedit (c. 1030–1100), as they sought to enhance the role of the cardinals in the governance and reform of the Church. The reference to apostolic succession emerged again in the decretals of Gregory IX (1227–1241), especially those related to his conflicts with Frederick II (1194–1250). The chancery of Frederick II, under Piero della Vigna, had earlier described the cardinals as the successors of the apostolic college and sought to use that theme as a means of weakening papal authority. The attribution of apostolic succession to the college of cardinals, subsequently, became popular not only among canonists but also with theologians and was modified according to the specific purpose of each writer.[27] That attribution came under considerable attack during the Great Schism because of the disfavor in which the cardinals fell as a result of their role in the schism. Indeed, as indicated earlier, there was a movement at Constance to abolish the cardinalate which d'Ailly strongly opposed. In opposition to this movement, d'Ailly intensified his association of the college of cardinals with the apostolic college.

The third stage in d'Ailly's interpretation of the development of the Church's hierarchical order begins with the geographical separation of the apostles from Peter and their dispersal throughout the world to carry out Christ's mandate to preach the Gospel to the Gentiles. While d'Ailly does not identify the scriptural beginnings of this chronological period, it would appear to coincide with the conversion of the Roman centurion, Cornelius, in Acts 10. In this period, according to d'Ailly,

---

[26] Oakley, *The Political Thought of Pierre d'Ailly*, 251.

[27] For a masterful study of the origins and development of the cardinalate in the ancient and early medieval Church see Stephan Kuttner, 'Cardinalis: The History of a Canonical Concept,' *Traditio*, 3 (1945), 129–214. A similar study for the high and later Middle Ages but with greater emphasis upon the ecclesiology of the cardinalate can be found in Giuseppe Alberigo's *Cardinalato e collegialità: Studi sull' ecclesiologia tra l'xi e il xiv secolo* (Florence: Vallechi Editore, 1969). The history of the cardinalate during the Avignon Papacy and the Great Schism is treated by G. Mollat, 'Contribution à l'histoire du sacré college de Clemente V à Eugene IV,' *RHE*, 46 (1951), 22–112, 566–594.

the apostles began to exercise their ministry within more restricted geographical boundaries which eventually became dioceses, archdioceses and provinces. As a result of these more geographically localized ministries, the ecclesiastical titles of bishop, archbishop, and primate began to be increasing used.[28] Despite its universal dimensions, even the Petrine office became more geographically identified at first with Antioch and then with Rome. With regard to the other apostles, d'Ailly does not associate any of them with a specific local church but merely affirms that association in general.[29]

According to d'Ailly, the difference between the apostles in the second and third historical stages of the Church's hierarchical development is seen in the fact that in the latter stages they held not only an apostolic rank (*status apostolicus)* but also a pastoral rank (*status pastoralis*), with the former state involving primarily the governance of the universal Church and the latter the governance of a particular local church.[30] In the third stage, therefore, the apostles effectively began to exercise the episcopal office in the New Testament sense of a bishop as superintendent or overseer of a local church.[31]

This distinction between a *status apostolicus* and a *status pastoralis*, while raising many questions, must not be taken in the sense that a pastoral dimension was absent from the apostles' *status apostolicus*. When speaking of the apostles in the context of the *status apostolicus*, d'Ailly makes clear that he regards them primarily as *pastores* and even when he speaks of the *status apostolicus* in the sense of the governance of the entire church, he clearly understands that government as essentially pastoral.[32] The distinction he draws, therefore between the two states is really based more on the difference between the exercise of pastoral care on a universal level and on the more geographically limited level of a local church.

---

[28] *De potestate ecclesiastica*, Dupin, 2:929. 'Licet nomina papatus et cardinalatus tempore Petri et aliorum apostolorum non fuerunt in usu Ecclesiae sed postea, crescente Ecclesia, in titulum honoris ex devotione fidelium haec nomina, sicut nomina patriarcharum, primatuum, archiepiscoporum, et episcoporum, in usum venerint a sanctis patribus allegatum seu approbatum ...'

[29] *De potestate ecclesiastica*, Dupin, 2:929. 'Postquam vero apostoli a Petro separati in opus praedicationis diversa mundi loca perlustrantes, speciales sibi dioceses sortiti sunt.'

[30] *De potestate ecclesiastica*, Dupin, 2:934. 'Et hoc notavit apostolus distinguens statum Ecclesiae, cum distinguit statum pastoralem cui incumbit cura animarum particulariter a statu apostolico ad quem spectat regimen et ordinatio totius Ecclesiae generaliter.'

[31] *De potestate ecclesiastica*, Dupin 2:929. '... ex tunc episcopale officium exercuerunt.'

[32] *De potestate ecclesiastica*, Dupin 2:934.

From the analysis of d'Ailly's thought with regard to the third stage in the historical development of the Church's hierarchical order, it is clear that he envisions a dual apostolic succession with the cardinals as the successors to the apostles in the context of their concern for the governance and needs of the Universal Church and the bishops as the successors to the apostles in the context of the *cura animarum* of a particular local church. Although d'Ailly's explanation of the development of the cardinalate and the episcopate within the context of three historical periods appears to be original to him, the notion of a dual apostolic succession was reasonably well developed in the thought of some theologians of the thirteenth and fourteenth centuries. Among these are to be numbered the Franciscan Guibert of Tournai (c. 1210–1284), and the Augustinians Giles of Rome (c. 1243–1316) and Augustine of Ancona (c. 1275–1378).[33] While d'Ailly makes no specific references to the sources upon which he relied for his views on a dual apostolic succession, he is clearly following in this earlier medieval tradition.

There is another characteristic which d'Ailly attributes to cardinals and bishops, and that is of their being in the 'state of perfection' (*status perfectionis*). This status relates not so much to the evolution of their ecclesiastical rank but more to the degree of Christian perfection that should characterize their lives. The biblical, patristic, and medieval tradition, summarized so succinctly by Thomas Aquinas, had described Christian perfection in terms of charity, i.e. love of God and neighbor. While always recognizing that the life of charity was an integral dimension of every Christian's life, that tradition especially recognized those who by formal religious vows dedicated themselves in a special way to the pursuit of a life dedicated to charity and attributed to them a special status in Christian society designated formally as a state of perfection (*status perfectionis*). This status, moreover, was recognized as manifesting itself in a twofold manner, namely, in terms of 'acquiring perfection' (*status perfectionis acquirendae*) and 'exercising perfection' (*status perfectionis exercendae*). The former was identified with members of religious orders who were primarily concerned with their own personal growth in Christian charity while the latter was associated with the episcopal and priestly orders whose members were to be principally concerned with fostering the growth of Christian charity in the lives of those committed to their pastoral care.[34]

---

[33] Alberigo, *Cardinalato e collegialità*, 92, 112, 126.
[34] For Aquinas' analysis of the nature of Christian perfection, the *status perfectionis*,

Unlike Aquinas who restricted the *status perfectionis exercendae* to the episcopacy alone, d'Ailly not only extended that status to the cardinals but also attributed to them a level within this *status* higher than that of the episcopate. His reasons for so doing follow closely upon his analysis of the evolution and nature of the cardinalate as a distinct status within the Church. Since, as seen above, the cardinals exercise their pastoral office on the level of the universal Church, their *status perfectionis* is of a higher nature than that of bishops whose primary pastoral concerns were restricted to the particular local churches committed to their care. In support of his position, d'Ailly cites Aristotle's dictum that the more something pertains to the common good, the greater its dignity.[35]

At first glance, d'Ailly's teaching in the *De potestate ecclesiastica* on a dual apostolic succession in terms of the cardinalate and the episcopacy and their respective pastoral jurisdiction in terms of the Church universal and its particular churches might seem to have lessened the authority of the bishops not only in relationship to the papacy but also within the universal Church. It is important, however, to remember that d'Ailly's views on the episcopacy which, as will be seen, were essentially developed before the writing of his *De potestate ecclesiastica*, were conceived of primarily in terms of the pastoral care of the local churches and did not manifest a sense of episcopal collegiality in relationship to the papacy or to a pastoral concern for the universal Church.

D'Ailly's views on the cardinalate and the episcopacy, their historical origins, development, and specific roles within the Church, therefore, remained essentially within the mainstream of high and late medieval ecclesiology. Such an ecclesiology allowed little opportunity for the development of the idea of an episcopal collegiality in relationship to the pastoral concerns of the universal Church, such as that expressed in the documents of Vatican II. Even during the late medieval conciliar period, when one would expect to find greater awareness of the status and office of the episcopacy, the theology of episcopal collegiality did not fully emerge. Most theologians at Constance when reflecting upon

---

and its division into *status perfectionis acquirendae* and *status perfectionis exercendae*, see *ST*, 2, 2, q. 184, a. 1–5. Aquinas frequently describes these two states in terms of *status religiosorum* and *status praelatorum*.

[35] *De potestate ecclesiastica*, Dupin, 2:935. '... cardinales sunt in statu perfectionis altioris quam sit generaliter status pastoralis quia inferiores pastores tenentur se exponere pro grege particulari, sed cardinales tenentur se exponere pro universali Ecclesia, quod est perfectius, quia bonum quanto communis tanto dignior, ut dicit Philosophus.'

the ecclesiology of the council formed that ecclesiology more on the basis of the council as representing the entire congregation of the faithful than on the council as a gathering of the episcopacy acting collegially.[36]

Because of his emphasis upon establishing the apostolic succession and divine foundation of the cardinalate in his *De potestate ecclesiastica*, it is not surprising that d'Ailly says little in that treatise with regard to the status of bishops and priests within the Church. For a more detailed analysis of their status within the hierarchical order of the Church, one has to turn to d'Ailly's earlier works especially those written during the years when he served as bishop of Cambrai and later cardinal. As will be recalled, d'Ailly had been named bishop of LePuy by Benedict XIII in 1395 but he never took up residence there. In 1397, Benedict appointed him bishop of Cambrai and in 1411 elevated him to the rank of cardinal. During his stay in Cambrai, d'Ailly devoted himself earnestly to his episcopal duties. In this context, we have three important addresses delivered by him on the occasion of diocesan synods at Cambrai. While Salembier tentatively dates these sermons in terms of the years 1398–1400, it is very difficult to determine their exact date.[37] In these works, as might be expected, considerable attention is given to the status of both bishops and priests within the hierarchical order of the Church. That d'Ailly's views on the status of bishops and priests as expressed in these sermons were not essentially modified after becoming a cardinal in 1411 can be seen in the fact that he repeated many of these same views in his 1417 Pentecost Sermon at the Council of Constance.[38]

In one of these synodal addresses delivered in 1398 at Cambrai, d'Ailly presents a detailed explanation of the status of bishops and priests in the ecclesiastical hierarchy, especially in terms of their being

---

[36] For an excellent survey of the fate of the notion of episcopal collegiality in the Middle Ages see Yves Congar, 'Notes sur le destin de l'idée de collégialité épiscopale en occident au moyen age (viie–xvie siècles),' and Charles Moeller, 'La collégialité au concile de Constance' in *La collégialité épiscopale: histoire et théologie*, ed. Yves Congar (Paris: Editions du Cerf, 1965), 99–129; 131–149.

[37] Salembier, *Le cardinal Pierre d'Ailly*, 370–371. These sermons can be found in D'Ailly's *Tractatus et Sermones*. In this edition, the first two of these sermons are listed as *Sermo primus in synodo cameracensi* and *Sermo secundus in synodo cameracensi*, while the third bears the title *Homelia facta in synodo cameracensi*.

[38] *Sermo in die Pentecostes, II*. An earlier Pentecost sermon was delivered by d'Ailly while at the University of Paris and before he became bishop of Cambrai. The text for both sermons can be found in the *Tractatus et Sermones* edition.

successors of the apostles and disciples. In that sermon, with only a general reference to the Gospel of St. Matthew as his source, d'Ailly expostulates first on the theme of Christ's selection of the twelve apostles and seventy two disciples.[39] After the development of this theme comes his identification of the bishops and priests respectively as the successors of the apostles and disciples. He describes the latter, furthermore, as being in the second order of the presbyterate with the clear implication that bishops belonged to the first order. As support for his distinction of bishops and priests in terms of first and second orders of the presbyterate, d'Ailly cites the *Glossa Ordinaria*.[40] He also expressed this distinction between bishops and priests in terms of *praelati maiores* and *praelati minores*.[41]

---

[39] *Homelia facta in synodo Cameracensi*, TS, 1–2. 'Primum enim ut in matheo legitur Christus duodecim apostolos elegerat, postea vero hos alios discipulos designavit.' If d'Ailly is correct in citing Matthew as his scriptural source, his reference most likely is to Mt. 10:1–15 but reference might have been made more appropriately to Lk. 9:1–6 and 10:1–12 since Matthew does not distinguish between apostles and disciples. Luke, however, not only distinguishes between apostles and disciples but also narrates separately the mission given by Christ to each group. The possibility that d'Ailly erred in citing Matthew instead of Luke is strengthened by the fact that in his *De potestate ecclesiastica* when speaking about the selection of the disciples, he cites Lk. 10:1 and the *Glossa Ordinaria* on this text.

[40] *Homelia facta in synodo Cameracensi*, TS, 8–9. 'Apostolis enim succedunt episcopi, discipulis vero minores presbyteri et parochiales curati. Nam ut hic dicitur glosa, sicut in apostolis forma est episcoporum, sic in septuaginta duobus discipulis forma est presbiterorum secundi ordinis.' For the *Glossa Ordinaria*'s commentary on Lk. 10:1–12, see 4:177. The medieval textual tradition that saw bishops and priests as successors of the apostles and disciples is treated in detail by Congar, 'Aspects ecclésiologiques de la querelle entre mendiants et séculiers dans la seconde moitié du xiiie siècle et le début du xive siècle,' *AHDL*, 28 (1961), 59–63. For the history of the development of ecclesiastical offices within the early Church see A.M. Farrer, 'The Ministry in the New Testament,' and Gregory Dix, 'The Ministry in the Early Church,' in *The Apostolic Ministry: Essays on the History and Doctrine of the Episcopacy*, ed. Kenneth E. Kirk (London: Hodder and Stoughton, 1946), 113–182, 185–303; Jean Colson, *L'évêque dans les communautés primitives* (Paris: Editions du Cerf, 1951), *Les fonctions ecclésiales aux deux premiers siècles* (Bruges: Desclée de Brouwer, 1956), *L'épiscopat catholique: collégialité et primauté dans les trois premiers siècles de l'église* (Paris: Editions du Cerf, 1963), *Ministre de Jésus-Christ ou le sacerdoce de l'Evangile* (Paris: Beauchesne, 1965); M.M. Bourke, 'Reflection on Church Order in the New Testament,' *CBQ*, 30 (1968), 493–511, Hans von Campenhausen, *Ecclesiastical Authority and Spiritual Power in the Church of the First Three Centuries* (Stanford: Stanford University Press, 1969), and Raymond E. Brown, *Priest and Bishop* (Paramus, N.J.: Paulist Press, 1971). See also Albert Vanhoye, 'Le ministère dans l'Eglise: les donnés du Nouveau Testament,' *NRT*, 104 (1982), 722–738 and Henri Crouzel, 'Le ministère dans l'Eglise: temoignages de l'Eglise ancienne,' *NRT*, 104 (1982), 738–748.

[41] For d'Ailly's use of this terminology see his *Homelia facta in synodo Cameracensi*, TS, 9, and his *Sermo in die Pentecostes, II*, TS, 4.

The theme of bishops and priests as the respective successors of the twelve apostles and the seventy-two disciples first appeared in the writings of Jerome (c. 340–420). It was further developed by Caesarius of Arles (c. 472–542), and reached its fullest formulation with Bede (c. 673–735). In identifying bishops and priests respectively as the successors of the apostles and disciples, Bede, however, emphasized neither strict historical nor numerical sequence. Through its incorporation in the *Glossa Ordinaria*, Bede's teaching made its way into the mainstream of medieval theology.

His interpretation also influenced the medieval canonical tradition, for in the ninth century it was employed by the compilers of the *Pseudo-Isidorian Decretals*. Desirous of abolishing the office of the chorbishop, these compilers availed themselves of Bede's teaching on bishops and priests as successors of the apostles and disciples to argue that chorbishops were not part of the apostolic tradition and therefore enjoyed no validity in the Church of their day. In order to enlist the authority of the primitive Church, canons embodying Bede's teaching were fabricated and attributed to popes Clement, Anacletus, and Damasus. In the tenth and eleventh centuries these texts were included in canonical collections such as that of Burchard of Worms (c. 965–1025). They were also incorporated into the canonical collections of the Gregorian reformers, especially the collection of Ivo of Chartres (c. 1040–1115). From these collections, they found their way during the first half of the twelfth century into Gratian's *Decretum* and thereby became an integral part of the medieval canonical teaching.[42]

An especially important period in the development of the idea of bishops and priests as successors of the apostles and disciples came in the thirteenth century with the controversy between the secular clergy and the mendicant orders. This controversy not only centered on the role of each group in the pastoral care of the laity but also included issues related to the role of poverty in all forms of the clerical life as well as the compatibility of university teaching with the secular and mendicant vocations. As was to be expected, the tradition of bishops and priests as successors of the apostles and disciples played a central role in the arguments of the secular clergy and attained its fullest formulation in the polemical writings of William of St. Amour (1200–1272). Defenders of the mendicant orders such as Gerard of Borgo San

---

[42] Congar, 'Aspects ecclésiologiques,' 61–63.

Donnino († 1276), Thomas Aquinas (c. 1225–1274), and Bonaventure (c. 1217–1274) sought not to deny this tradition but to qualify it so as to allow a role for the mendicant orders in the pastoral as well as in the academic realms. As will be seen in later chapters, this controversy continued in diverse forms throughout the later Middle Ages and involved both canonists and theologians.[43]

D'Ailly's distinction between the apostles and disciples in terms of *prelati maiores* and *prelati minores*, and the gradation in status, office, and authority that that distinction entailed also owed much to Jerome and Bede. In this context, Jerome clearly described the status of the disciples as a *gradus minor*, while Bede saw them in terms of an *ordo secundus*. Through Bede, these distinctions also entered the scriptural *Glossa Ordinaria* and by the time of Aquinas and Bonaventure had become an integral part of the medieval theological tradition.[44]

In the realm of canon law, however, the adoption of these distinctions proceeded more slowly. In the early Middle Ages such distinctions were not universally employed. The *Pseudo-Isidorian Decretals*, while embodying Bede's teaching on the bishops and priests as the successors of the apostles and disciples, did not emphasize the distinction between bishops and priests in terms of either *gradus* or *ordo*. Such distinctions, indeed, would have weakened their arguments against the existence of chorbishops as well as against the extensive authority of metropolitans. As would be expected, however, Archbishop Hincmar of Rheims (c. 806–882), one of the chief defenders of the prerogatives of metropolitans, did utilize Bede's distinction and described priests, in contrast to bishops, as exercising a *secundi ordinis sacerdotium*.[45] By Gratian's time, however, not only are the differences between bishops and priests in terms of *gradus* and *ordo* strongly affirmed but the designation of bishops and priests respectively as *maiores* and *minores sacerdotes* had clearly emerged. The decretalists and theologians of the thirteenth century continued in this same tradition.[46]

---

[43] Congar, 'Aspects ecclésiologiques,' 63–64. For a comprehensive study of the early conflicts between the seculars and the mendicant orders at the University of Paris, see Michel Dufeil, *Guillaume de Saint Amour et la polémique universitaire parisienne, 1250–1259* (Paris: Picard, 1972).

[44] Congar, 'Aspects ecclésiologiques,' 60.

[45] For Hincmar's use of the term *praelatus* and its various gradations see Congar, 'Aspects ecclésiologiques,' 61.

[46] Congar, 'Aspects ecclésiologiques,' 62. It should be noted that Gratian's distinction between *sacerdotes maiores* and *minores* is to be found in the *dicta ante* of D. 21 which in the

In speaking of bishops and priests as successors of the apostles and disciples, d'Ailly, relying on the Scriptures, recognizes that in the life of the early Church the terms *episcopus* and *presbyter* were not always clearly distinguished. In Paul and in the Acts of the Apostles these terms were often used interchangeably and the functions performed by each were not always fully differentiated.[47] Despite this terminological and functional imprecision, d'Ailly maintains that sufficient differences did exist in the real order between bishops and priests even during the time of the early Church. The source he cites for his position is the *De ecclesiastica hierarchia* of Dionysius, the Pseudo-Areopagite, whom he, like most medieval thinkers, mistakenly regarded as the disciple of St. Paul.[48] Although d'Ailly cites Dionysius as his authority, he does not describe the functional differences between bishops and priests according to the categories of hierarchical activity normally associated with Dionysian ideology, namely, purgation, illumination, and perfection, but uses the more scriptural description of bishops as overseers or superintendents of the local churches and presbyters as the elders within those churches.[49]

---

subsequent canon draws support from Isidore of Seville's *Etymologiae*, 7, 12 wherein is contained Isidore's teaching on the gradations and names of the various ecclesiastical offices.

[47] *Homelia facta in synodo Cameracensi*, *TS*, 9. 'Sciendum quippe est quod olim quantum ad nomen non distinguebantur episcopi et presbyteri ... Unde et apostolus hoc nomine quantum ad utrosque utitur.' For a similar but later expression of the same idea see *Sermo in die Pentecostes, II, TS*, 4.

[48] *Homelia facta in Synodo Cameracensi*, *TS*, 9. 'Sed semper secundum rem inter episcopos et presbyteros fuit distinctio etiam tempore apostolorum ut patet per Dionysium, v.c. ecclesiasticae heirarchiae.' For a similar assertion see his *Sermo in die Pentecostes II, TS*, 4. The specific reference in both these texts to Dionysius' *De ecclesiastica hierarchia* is at 5:1–6, wherein the orders and functions of bishops, priests, and deacons are described. The Greek text of this work can be found in *PG*, 3:369–584. In the West some fifteen translations of Dionysius' works were made into Latin. For the Latin texts of Dionysius in use at the University of Paris, see H.F. Dondaine, *Le corpus dionysien de l'Université de Paris au xiiie siècle* (Rome: Edizione di storia e letteratura, 1953). The most recent English translation of the complete works of Dionysius is that of Colm Luibheid, *Pseudo Dionysius: The Complete Works* (Paramus, N.J.: The Paulist Press, 1987). The most recent English translation of and commentary on the *De ecclesiastica hierarchia* is that of Thomas Campbell, *Dionysius the Pseudo-Areopagite: The Ecclesiastical Hierarchy* (Lanham, Md.: University Press of America, 1981).

[49] *Homelia facta in Synodo Cameracensi*, *TS*, 9. '... nam episcopi dicuntur ex eo quod superintendunt, ut dicit Augustinus, presbyteri autem grece dicuntur quasi seniores.' Pseudo-Dionysius's hierarchical thought, especially its concepts of hierarchical activity, never played as important a role in d'Ailly's ecclesiology as it did in that of his close friend, student, and successor as chancellor of the University of Paris, Jean Gerson

As a result of his views on the differences between bishops and priests in the early Church, d'Ailly rejects the position of Jerome that these differences were not of divine foundation but more a matter of historical development resulting from the practical needs of the Church, especially its need for order in the pastoral care and governance of its people.[50] According to d'Ailly, however, the increasing terminological differentiation between bishops and priests resulted from the desire to better reflect differences in the actual functions characteristic of each group and to avoid the many internal conflicts that resulted from earlier and imprecise language.[51] As such, therefore, these differences remain grounded in divine law. D'Ailly also asserts that Augustine was so convinced of the differences between the episcopal and priestly ranks within the Church that he regarded opposing arguments as heretical.[52]

3. *Apostolic Mission and Authority*

Closely allied to the notion of the prelate's status are the notions of office and authority. Here again, d'Ailly's synodal talks given at Cambrai between 1397 and 1411 are extremely rich sources. As in his discussion of ecclesiastical status, d'Ailly's analysis of ecclesiastical office and authority takes place first of all in the broader and more general context of ecclesiastical prelates. In analyzing and discussing d'Ailly's views on the office of prelates, both major and minor, it is important to remember that he sees these offices and their holders primarily in the general context of an apostolic calling and mission. By emphasizing these dimensions of ecclesiastical office, d'Ailly illustrates again

---

(1363–1429). As recent scholarship has shown, Gerson's ecclesiological thought was heavily influenced by Pseudo-Dionysius. On this point see Pascoe, *Jean Gerson*, 17–48.

[50] *Homelia facta in Synodo Camercensi, TS,* 9. 'Nec contra hanc sententiam movere debent verba Hieronymi super epistolam ad Tytum ubi postquam dixerat olim idem presbyter qui et episcopus postea subdit: Sicut ergo presbyteri sciunt se ecclesiae consuetudine ei qui sibi propositus fuerit esse subiectos ita episcopi noverint se magis consuetudine quam dispensationis dominice veritate presbyteris esse maiores et in communi debere ecclesiam regere.' The passage referred to is from Jerome's *Commentarium super epistolam ad Tytum.*

[51] *Homelia facta in Synodo Cameracensi, TS,* 9. 'Unde postea ad vitandum scisma necesse fuit ut etiam nomina distinguerentur, ut sicut maiores dicerentur episcopi, minores autem vocarentur presbyteri.'

[52] *Homelia facta in Synodo Cameracensi, TS,* 9. 'Ideo presbyteros ab episcopis non differe Augustinus libro de heresibus inter dogmata heretica connumerat.'

the highly biblical framework of his views on ecclesiastical prelates and their respective offices. This calling and mission, however, are described not in the broad biblical terms of salvation history reaching back through the pages of the Old Testament but in the context of the New Testament.

D'Ailly begins his analysis of ecclesiastical vocation by affirming the biblical basis of that vocation and its threefold dimension.[53] The primary scriptural text which he cites is Rom. 8:28–30 wherein Paul portrays the broad outline of the Christian vocation in terms of predestination, justification, and glorification. The first calling is to eternal beatitude and is described by d'Ailly primarily in terms of predestination.[54] The Pauline sense of predetermination, however, does not primarily imply an arbitrary selectivity on God's part but more a sign of his care and planning for all. D'Ailly's views on pedestination, however, follow more in the late medieval scholastic tradition, especially the school of thought that saw predestination in terms of divine foreknowledge, that is, *post praevisa merita*. This emphasis, however, while clearly a development of Paul's thought, remains fundamentally consonant with it.[55]

The second calling to which d'Ailly refers is that of justification by grace.[56] The scriptural source he relies on here is again Rom. 8:28–30, where after indicating the call to eternal beatitude through predestination, Paul add that those whom God has thus called, he has also justified. In addition to Rom. 8:28–30, d'Ailly finds added scriptural support for this calling in terms of justification in Eph. 1:4, wherein Paul affirms that those whom God has chosen, he has chosen to be holy and without blemish.[57] In his description of the third calling, d'Ailly deviates considerably from the context of glorification and describes it

---

[53] *Sermo in Synodo Cameracensi, I, TS*, 1. 'Qua in re illud nobis in primis notandum est quod in sacris eloquiis divinisque scripturis triplex legitur vocatio.'

[54] *Sermo in Synodo Cameracensi, I, TS*, 1. 'Prima est ad beatificam retributionem … Prima ergo vocatio est eternalis predestinationis, de qua dicit apostolus: Quos predestinavit hos et vocavit …'

[55] For the varying schools of thought in the late Middle Ages with regard to predestination, especially the views of Scotus, Ockham, Gregory of Rimini, Pierre d'Ailly, and Gabriel Biel, see Oberman, *The Harvest of Medieval Theology* (Cambridge, Mass.: Harvard University Press, 1963), 185–217.

[56] *Sermo in Synodo Cameracensi, I, TS*, 1. 'Secunda (vocatio) est ad gratificam iustificationem.'

[57] *Sermo in Synodo Cameracensi, I, TS*, 2. The precise passage in Rom. 8:28–30 upon which d'Ailly depends is the concluding phrase: 'Quos predestinavit hos et vocavit, et quos vocavit hos et iustificavit.' The reference from Eph. 2:4 is: 'Eligit nos ad mundi constitutionem ut essemus sancti et immaculati conspectu eius.'

essentially in terms of pastoral care and as such restricted to prelates[58] This calling is essentially a continuation of and participation in Christ's call to his apostles and disciples. Since, as in all callings, the initiative is primarily divine, this call can never be reduced to the level of private choice.[59] The pastoral context of this calling also serves as the guideline by which the quality of one's apostolic life is continually measured. Medieval ecclesiastical reformers such as d'Ailly never tired of appealing to the Pauline norm that the conduct of one's life should closely accord with one's chosen vocation.[60]

Closely associated with the notion of calling in the case of ecclesiastical prelates is that of mission. While d'Ailly understands mission in the general context of fostering the growth of the Kingdom of God on earth, he prefers to concentrate on the specific pastoral activities that promote that growth. He describes these activities as preaching the basic beliefs of Christianity, teaching proper moral values and actions, and absolving the people from their sins. These activities also include working for the conversion of those who have wandered from their beliefs, correcting those who remain firm in their error, consoling the weak and the hesitant, and providing for the needy.[61]

In his *De potestate ecclesiastica*, written in 1416 at the Council of Constance and five years after he had become a cardinal, d'Ailly's description of the activities associated with the office of prelates remained essentially pastoral but involved administrative and financial dimensions as well. In this work, d'Ailly enumerates these activities as six-

---

[58] *Sermo in Synodo Cameracensi, I, TS*, 1–2. 'Tertia (vocatio) est ad ecclesiasticam administrationem.' It is clear from the following line in this passage that d'Ailly understands that administration primarily in a pastoral context: 'Tertia est vocatio pastoralis prelationis.' Further evidence for this conclusion is to be had in his reference in this passage to Jn. 15:16 where the work of the apostles is called upon to bear fruit.

[59] *Homelia in Synodo Cameracensi, I, TS*, 2. In speaking of Christ's selection of his apostles, d'Ailly states that 'ut per hoc ostenderet quod nullus propria auctoritate intrusus sed solum divina approbatione vocatus ecclesiasticum officium assumere debeat.' He finds added support for emphasizing the divine initiative in the realm of ecclesiastical vocations in Heb. 5:4 where it is stated that with regard to the office of high priest no one is to take this honor upon himself unless specifically called by God as was Aaron.

[60] *Sermo in Synodo Cameracensi, I, TS*, 3. The precise Pauline text is Eph. 4:1: 'Obsecro vos ut digne ambuletis vocatione qua vocati estis.' While the Pauline call is directed to all Christians, d'Ailly cited it primarily in a clerical context.

[61] *Homelia in Synodo Cameracensi, TS*, 4. 'Quippe mittuntur enim ad predicandum credenda, ad docendum facienda, ad venandum peccatorum occulta, ad absolvendum penitentium delicta. Mittuntur ad reducendum errantes, ad corrigendum pertinaces, ad consolandum pusillanimes, ad reficiendum indigentes.'

fold and rooted them essentially in the mission which Christ entrusted to his apostles and disciples. These activities included confection of the Eucharist, administration of the sacraments, especially penance, preaching the Gospel, fraternal correction, the deposition of ministers, i.e. the assignment of bishops to specific dioceses, and, finally, the reception of necessary material sustenance from those to whom they spiritually ministered. With the exception of the disposition of ministers, which is reserved to the pope, these powers were shared in by cardinals, bishops, and priests.[62]

Having seen the specific types of activities associated with the notion of mission in d'Ailly's thought on the office of prelates, it now remains to analyze the manner in which these activities were to be realized by the various types of ecclesiastical prelates. This analysis begins first with the cardinalate. As seen earlier, most of d'Ailly's views on the status and office of the cardinalate were developed after he was elevated to that office in 1411 and were described in his *De potestate ecclesiastica*. As will be recalled, in that work d'Ailly described the cardinals' office primarily in terms of their collegiate relationship with the papacy in the governance of the Church.[63] Since in d'Ailly's description of the third stage in the development of the Church's hierarchical order the pope maintained both a universal and a local dimension as Bishop of Rome, the cardinals because of their close association and cooperation with the him were therefore regarded by d'Ailly as both cardinals of the universal Church as well as cardinals of the Roman Church. The cardinals, consequently, were to cooperate with the pope in the governance of both the Universal Church and the Roman Church.[64]

---

[62] *De potestate ecclesiastica*, Dupin, 2:928. This description of the pastoral activities associated with ecclesiastical office was not original to d'Ailly, but was borrowed from the Dominican John of Paris (c. 1250–1306). The reference to John of Paris is from his *De potestate regia et papali*, 12. The most recent Latin edition of this treatise is that of F. Bleienstein, *Johannes Quidort von Paris: Über königliche und päpstliche Gewalt* (Stuttgart: Ernst Klett Verlag, 1969). Earlier editions are those of Jean Leclercq, *Jean de Paris et l'écclesiologie du xiiie siècle* (Paris, 1942), and Melchior Goldast, *Monarchia Sancti Romani Imperii*, 3 vols. (Hanover, 1611–1614), 2:108–147.

[63] *De potestate ecclesiastica*, Dupin, 2:935. 'Unde ulterius sequitur quod ad statum cardinalium tanquam ad statum apostolicum primo pertinet, una cum papa, regimen et ordinatio totius Ecclesiae.'

[64] *De potestate ecclesiastica*, Dupin, 2:929. 'In utraque vero tam urbis quam orbis praesidentia, coassistunt Papae cardinales tamquam speciales ipsius coadjutores, vice et nomine tam Romanae quam Universalis Ecclesiae.'

The specific ways in which that cooperative activity is manifested are also clearly delineated by d'Ailly. The first specific function which d'Ailly attributes to the cardinals as a collegial body is the election of the pope. He hesitates to state categorically that this right is established in divine and natural law, but cautiously concludes that it is somehow rooted in these laws. The reason for his qualified response is his belief that strictly speaking divine and natural law place this right with the Roman people, for in a true sense the pope is their bishop. Canon law, he asserts, has traditionally maintained that the choice of a prelate rests with those over whom he is to exercise his office. Since, however, with the passage of time considerable conflicts and confusion resulted from such elections, d'Ailly affirms that the Roman people turned over their right of election to the Roman clergy because of their preeminence in learning and holiness.[65]

Eventually, d'Ailly argues, the Roman clergy transferred that right to the pope himself, in the sense that he could designate a single elector or group of electors to select his successor. In this context, he argues, Pope Hadrian I (772–795) and the Roman Synod granted Charlemagne the right to elect the pope. Pope Leo VIII (963–965), also in conjunction with the Roman clergy and people, bestowed a similar privilege upon the emperor Otto I (962–973). Finally it was Nicholas II (1058–1061) who, with the consent of the Roman people and clergy gathered in synod in 1059 transferred the right of papal elections to the cardinals since they were the most prominent representatives of the Roman clergy and people.[66]

While willing to accept the premise that the right of the Roman people to elect their bishop rests on divine law, d'Ailly admits that the prevailing tradition in which the cardinals alone have the right to elect the pope rests completely on positive or canon law which by its very nature can be revoked or modified.[67] By so restricting the nature of the cardinals' rights with regard to papal elections, d'Ailly preserves for the pope, the Roman clergy, and the Roman people their fundamental

---

[65] *De potestate ecclesiastica*, Dupin 2:930–931.

[66] *De potestate ecclesiastica*, Dupin 2:931. In this historical analysis, d'Ailly constantly affirms that he has obtained his historical data from Gratian's *Decretum*. While he does not indicate what precise canons he is drawing upon, it seems certain the he is relying upon D. 63, c. 22 and c. 23; and D. 23, c. 1.

[67] *De potestate ecclesiastica*, Dupin, 2:930. '... sed quod ad eos totaliter pertineat, hoc est de jure positivo, in quo ex causa rationabili cadere potest justa dispensatio.'

right to revise electoral procedures in the future in accordance with the needs and common good of the Church.

Continuing his analysis of the role of the cardinals in papal elections, d'Ailly cites another position that holds that since the pope is also pastor of the Universal Church the right to his election devolves directly upon the Church or upon its representative, the General Council, rather than upon the Roman people or clergy.[68] This argument would appear to rest upon the same canonical principle that he used to establish the right of the Roman people and clergy in his previous argument, namely, the right of a people to select those who are to govern them. D'Ailly prefers this line of argumentation and later in his treatise regards it as closer to the truth and better supported by reason.[69]

Since, however, d'Ailly also espoused the earlier position that the right to elect the pope rested with the Roman clergy and people and eventually with the cardinals as their representatives, he appears to be faced with the dilemma of two different rights both grounded in divine and natural law. Merely stating, as he does, that the right of the Roman people and clergy and the cardinals as their representatives relates to the election of the pope as Bishop of Rome while the right of the Universal Church and General Council relates to the pope as Supreme Pontiff of the Universal Church may provide some logical clarification, but it does little to resolve the problem in the real order. D'Ailly recognizes this difficulty and attempts to resolve it by asserting that the right of the Roman people, clergy, and cardinals, founded somehow though it is in divine and natural law, is essentially rooted in the right of the Universal Church, for the right to elect a pope belongs principally (*principaliter*) and originally (*originaliter*) to the Universal Church or to the Council as its representative.[70] The right of the Roman Church to elect the pope as exercised through the cardinals, rests therefore on the fact that on such occasions the Roman Church acts in the name and place of the Universal Church.[71] In this context, d'Ailly, relying

---

[68] *De potestate ecclesiastica*, Dupin, 2:931. 'Si vero dicatur quod ex praedicta ratione sequitur quod cum Romanus Episcopus in quantum Summus Pontifex praeficiatur Universali Ecclesiae, videtur quod jus eligendi ipsum ad Universalem pertineat Ecclesiam vel ad Generale Concilium ipsam repraesentans potius quam ad Romanos.'

[69] *De potestate ecclesiastica*, Dupin, 2:936. 'Et haec opinio verior reputatur ... .'

[70] *De potestate ecclesiastica*, Dupin, 2:936. 'Hoc tamen jus principaliter et originaliter pertinet ad Universalem Ecclesiam seu General Concilium ipsam representans.'

[71] *De potestate ecclesiastica*, Dupin, 2:936. 'Si universitas Romanorum, naturali aut

upon the canonical principle of utility (*utilitas*), cites first of all that it is often very difficult and time-consuming to summon universal councils each time a pope dies, and, secondly, even if one were called it is often difficult to secure the required consensus as to a suitable person for the office.[72]

A second specific function of the cardinals acting in their collegial capacity is that of providing counsel for the pope in his efforts to govern the universal Church.[73] While d'Ailly does not go into much detail as to the particular form in which this counsel is to be manifested, there is no doubt as to its importance in his thought. This importance, he maintains, is especially brought out in the papal oaths frequently made to the cardinals before election. Employing a concrete example, d'Ailly asserts that Boniface VIII before his election promised the cardinals that he would exercise his papal ministry with the advice, consent, direction, and awareness of the cardinals.[74]

The importance of counsel is also brought out in d'Ailly's earlier historical analysis of the diverse occasions in which the popes entrusted the emperors Charlemagne and Otto I and later the cardinals with the right to elect the pope, for on each of these occasions he maintains that the pope did not act alone but always with the consent of the Roman clergy and people gathered in synod.[75] Although d'Ailly does not give

---

divino jure habeat potestatem in electione Summi Pontificis, hoc est vice et nomine Universalis Ecclesiae, cujus Summus Pontifex est particularis Romanae Ecclesiae episcopus.'

[72] *De potestate ecclesiastica*, Dupin, 2:936. The operative phrase in this passage is 'publicae utilitati magis videtur expedire ...' The canonical sources d'Ailly cites in support of his analysis are drawn from Gratian's *Decretum*, D. 23, c. 1, the famous decree of Nicholas II which in 1059 gave the cardinals the right to elect the pope, D. 79, c. 1, also a decree of Nicholas II, reaffirming the need for election by the cardinals, and D. 65, c. 9. The first two canons, however, do not support d'Ailly's arguments from *utilitas publica*, while the third canon does not even relate to papal elections.

[73] *De potestate ecclesiastica*, Dupin, 2:929. 'Papae assistunt cardinales tanquam ejus principales assessores et consiliarii atque cooperatores in regimine Universalis Ecclesiae.'

[74] *De potestate ecclesiastica*, Dupin, 2:929–930. 'Papa ante suam consecrationem profiteri debet sanctae Romanae Ecclesiae cardinalium consilio, consensu, dilectione, et rememoratione ministerium suum gerere et peragere ut patet in professione quam fecit Bonifacius Octavus.' While the Dupin text uses the term 'dilectione' the text of the oath as given in Baluze, *Miscellanea novo ordine digesta*, 2:418, reads 'directione,' and contextually is a more accurate reading.

[75] *De potestate ecclesiastica*, Dupin, 2:931. Speaking of these concessions, d'Ailly asserts that in the case of Charlemagne, Hadrian acted 'non solus sed ipse et synodus celebrata Romae.' With regard to Otto I, Leo VIII is described as acting 'cum multo clero et

much information as to the specific manner in which the cardinals are to exercise this counsel, he does cite one concrete area, that of ordaining and installing bishops. While d'Ailly asserts that the pope has a right in this area, he also maintains that the pope should exercise that right only with the consent of the cardinals.[76]

A third function which d'Ailly ascribes to the cardinals' office is that of assisting the papacy in declaring and clarifying those truths which are necessary or useful for salvation. These truths, moreover, can pertain directly to matters of belief or to the general administration of the Church. This teaching dimension of the cardinals' office is rooted in the fact that, as seen earlier, the cardinals are regarded as the successors of the apostles in the general care and administration of the Church.[77] As such they also succeed the apostles in the general ministry of the Word of God and therefore must provide for the general instruction of the faithful.[78] Despite the authority which d'Ailly ascribes to the cardinals with regard to the declaration and defense of the truths of the faith, he does not endow the college of cardinals and the pope with the special charism of infallibility. Early on in his theological career, d'Ailly maintained that the teaching of the Scriptures on this point was not sufficiently clear as to justify such an attribution.[79]

The fourth specific function which d'Ailly attributes to the college of cardinals in its relationship to the papacy, and one which follows closely upon the previous ones is that of fraternal correction. Given

---

populo Romano.' In the case of Nicholas II's decree entrusting papal elections to the cardinals, the text reads 'non sine consensu Romanorum in quadam Romana Synodo.'

[76] *De potestate ecclesiastica*, Dupin, 2:930. 'Ad Romanum pontificem, de fratrum suorum cardinalium consilio, pertinet episcopos ordinare et instituere.'

[77] *De potestate ecclesiastica*, Dupin, 2:935. 'Ex eodem fundamento patet quod ad sedem apostolicam, id est ad papam et cardinales, prae caeteris sedibus particularibus, pertinet declaratio veritatum necessariarium aut utilium ad salutem, sive quantum ad fidem, sive quantum ad utile regimen Ecclesiae militantis, quia in hoc succedunt Petro et caeteris apostolis quantum ad statum apostolicum primitivum de quo dictum est prius.'

[78] *De potestate ecclesiastica*, Dupin, 2:935. 'Quia ipsi cardinales succedentes apostolis in ministerio generali verbi Dei et deputati ex statu suo ad instruendum generaliter fideles de his quae pertinent ad salutem.'

[79] *Epistola ad novos Hebraeos*, Salembier, 258. 'Ex quibus omnibus aperte colligitur quod auctoritati universalis Ecclesie tanquam auctoritati Spiritus Sancti seu a Spiritu Sancto revelatae firmiter credendum est de necessitate salutis. Sed an id tenendum sit de auctoritate alicujus particularis Ecclesiae vel collegii, ut esset collegium Papae et cardinalium aut cleri romani, non ita clarum est ex scriptura ...' For d'Ailly's views on papal infallibility, see Francis Oakley, 'Pierre d'Ailly and Papal Infallibility,' *MS*, 26 (1964), 353–358.

the enormous problems that beset the late medieval papacy, especially that of the Great Schism, it is not hard to understand why the biblical notion of correction became so popular in ecclesiological discussions. D'Ailly, however, does not root this corrective authority in the more general principle of fraternal correction expressed in Mt. 18:15–17, but in Gal. 2:11–14 where Paul states that he openly criticized Peter when, under pressure from Jewish converts in Jerusalem, he ceased taking his meals with the Gentiles. Paul also states in this passage that his reason for so acting was that Peter's action was not in accord with the principles of the Gospel.[80] D'Ailly's attribution of corrective powers to the cardinals, therefore, rests not merely on the general notion of apostolic succession but also on the more specific notion that just as the pope succeeds Peter, the cardinals succeed Paul in the office of preaching the Gospel and therefore on matters of belief enjoy the same privileges of correction which he exercised in Gal. 2:11–14. As will be seen in later chapters, in the Middle Ages different groups, especially theologians, claimed a similar right of correction with regard to the papacy on matters related to both doctrine and jurisdiction and used the same passage from Galatians to justify their claims.[81]

As a fifth specific function associated with the cardinals and the collegial nature of their office, d'Ailly cites their obligation to temper

---

[80] *De potestate ecclesiastica*, Dupin, 2:935. After reaffirming that the cardinals inherit from the apostles the obligation to teach the truths necessary for salvation, he states that they '... in illa paritate in qua a sanctis doctoribus Paulus dicitur fuisse par Petro, predicationis officio, scilicet legis evangelicae, succedunt Paulo et exemplo ipsius ad Gal 2, successori Petri, manifeste in praejudicum religionis Christiane oberranti, possunt resistere quia licet sit Vicarius generalis Christi, et officio et authoritate praelationis maximus, tamen in ministerio praedicationis et doctrinae Christiane, connumerare se debet aliis episcopis.' As his authority on this aspect of his teaching, d'Ailly cites Guido de Baysio.

[81] For the history of the use of Gal. 2:11–14 to justify the right to correct papal teaching and actions see G.H.M. Posthumus Meyjes, *De controverse tussen Petrus en Paulus: Galaten 2:11 in de historie*, Inaugural Lecture at the University of Leiden (The Hague: Martinus Nijhoff, 1967), Karlfried Froehlich, 'Fallibility instead of Infallibility? A Brief History of the Interpretation of Galatians 2:11–14,' in *Teaching Authority and Infallibility in the Church*, ed., Paul C. Empie et al. (Minneapolis: Augsburg Press, 1978), 259–269, H. Feld, 'Papst und Apostel in Auseinandersetzung um die rechte Lehre: Die theologische Bedeutung von Gal 2:11–14,' in *Grund und Grenzen des Dogmas*, ed. H. Feld et al. (Freiburg: Herder, 1973), 9–26. While the passage from Galatians played an important role in Gerson's teaching with regard to the theologians' corrective authority vis-a-vis the papacy, he also roots this authority in the more general mandate of correction expressed in Mt. 18:15–17. For his views on the subject of correction, see Pascoe, *Jean Gerson*, 90–91.

or modify when necessary the papal use of the plenitude of power (*plenitudo potestatis*).[82] For d'Ailly, the *plenitudo potestatis* which he ascribes to the papacy relates to jurisdictional authority (*potestas jurisdictionis*) and not to the sacramental power of orders (*potestas ordinis sacramentalis*) which he regards as equal in all the apostles and their successors.[83] D'Ailly's attribution of a plenitude of power to the papacy may seen surprising since he is generally represented as holding that that power resides ultimately not in the pope but in the entire Church or in an ecumenical council as its representative.[84] A closer reading of the *De potestate ecclesiastica*, however, reveals that d'Ailly's thought on this topic is much more nuanced than previously believed.[85]

Following Maurice of Prague, d'Ailly maintains that the *plenitudo potestatis* can be considered in a threefold manner: *separabiliter*, *inseparabiliter*, and *representative*. D'Ailly establishes his argument for this threefold conception of the plenitude of power on what he describes as a threefold mode of inherence, that is, three ways in which something can be said to inhere in something else. In the first mode, something can be said to inhere in something else as in a subject. In this sense, virtue is said to inhere in a person's soul as accidents in a substance. The second mode and third modes of inherence relate to the manner in which something can be in an object. In the second mode, something is said to be in an object in the form of a final cause while according to the third mode something can be in an object in the form of an exem-

---

[82] *De potestate ecclesiastica*, Dupin 2:946. Referring to the role of the cardinals, d'Ailly states: 'qui cum papa et sub eo Ecclesiam regerent et usum plenitudinis potestatis temperarent.' For the historical evolution of the idea of *plenitudo potestatis* see Robert L. Benson, 'Plenitudo Potestatis: Evolution of a Formula from Gregory IV to Gratian,' *SGreg*, 14 (1967), 193–217, and Gerhart B. Ladner, 'The Concepts of "Ecclesia" and "Christianitas" and their Relationship to the Idea of Papal "Plenitudo Potestatis"' in *Sacerdozio e Regno da Gregorio VII a Bonifacio VIII*, Miscellanea Historiae Pontificae, 18 (1954), 49–77.

[83] *De potestate ecclesiastica*, Dupin 2:950. 'Primo dico quod jura quae loquuntur de plentitudine postestatis intelliguntur de potestate jurisdictionis et non de potestate ordinis sacramentalis quia haec fuit aequalis in omnibus apostolis ... .'

[84] For this interpretation see Oakley, *The Political Thought of Pierre d'Ailly*, 238. 'The basic assumption underlying d'Ailly's conciliar arguments is the belief that the community is the ultimate source of political power.' Other passages in Oakley substantially maintaining the same interpretation can be found on pp. 4, 123, 154, 158, and 162.

[85] For a more nuanced interpretation of d'Ailly's views on the *plenitudo potestatis*, see Louis B. Pascoe, 'Theological Dimensions of Pierre d'Ailly's Teaching on the Papal Plenitude of Power,' *AHC*, 11 (1979), 357–366. The following interpretation of d'Ailly's position is, with some modifications, dependent upon this article.

plar. Such is the case when a form is said to be reflected in a mirror or a particular teaching can be found in a book. This is what d'Ailly calls representational inherence.[86]

According to the first mode, that is *separabiliter*, the *plenitudo potestatis*, d'Ailly maintains, resides in the pope alone and not in any community or group of individuals. While he claims that on this point he has the solid support of canon law, he also rests his argument on Aristotle's principle of supposits, namely that actions are predicated only of substances. This principle was interpreted by d'Ailly to mean that the exercise of the plenitude of power pertained to an individual and not to any community or group of persons. D'Ailly, therefore, restricted the exercise of that power to one individual, namely the pope.[87]

In the second mode, namely *inseparabiliter*, the plenitude of power can be said to be in the Universal Church not in the sense that it is the ultimate source of that power but in the Aristotelian sense of a final cause, namely, that toward which the exercise of all papal authority must be directed and according to which it must also be evaluated.[88] This finality is conceived by d'Ailly in the Pauline context of the spiritual edification of all members of the Church. The Universal Church, therefore, has a regulatory role with regard to the papal use of the plenitude of power, that is, it has the power to determine

---

[86] *De potestate ecclesiastica*, Dupin, 2:950–951. 'Pro cujus declaratione sciendum est quod quantum ad propositum pertinet, aliquid dicitur tripliciter esse in alio. Primo, tanquam subjecto, sicut virtus in anima et accidens in substantia subjective. Secundo modo tamquam in objecto, sicut aliquis effectus dicitur esse in sua causa vel in suo fine quia in illum tendit tanquam in suum objectum finale. Tertio modo, tanquam in exemplo, ut res visa dicitur esse in speculo vel aliqua doctrina in libro quia ibi est representative.' From the above text, it is clear that d'Ailly reasoning develops within the context of Aristotle's teaching on the different types of causes, especially efficient, final, and formal causality. For Aristotle's teaching on the four causes see his *Physics*, 2:3 (194b 16–195b 30), and his *Metaphysics* 5:2 (1013a 24–1014a 25).

[87] *De potestate ecclesiastica*, Dupin, 2:950. 'Secundo, dico quod haec plenitudo jurisdictionis, proprie loquendo, solum resident in romano seu summo pontifice Petro succedenti, quia proprie aliqua potestas plene dicitur esse in aliquo qui illam potest generaliter exercere et ministerialiter in omnes dispensare. Hoc autem est in solo papa et non proprie in aliqua communitate, quia, secundum philosophum, actiones sunt suppositorum. For Aristotle's thought on supposits see his *Metaphysics*, 1:2 (981a 17), and the *Nicomachean Ethics*, 3:1 (1110b 6). A good example of Aquinas' understanding and use of this principle can be found in *ST*, 2, 2, 58, 2, c.

[88] *De potestate ecclesiastica*, Dupin, 2:951. 'Secundo est in Universali Ecclesia tanquam in objecto ipsam causaliter et finaliter continente.'

whether the papacy is exercising its authority according to the end for which it was granted, namely, the building up of the Mystical Body of Christ.[89]

The third mode of inherence, namely *representative*, relates more to a General Council. The plenitude of power is said to be *representative* in the General Council since it represents the Universal Church. As such, the General Council exercises a regulatory role with regard to the papal use of the plenitude of power. Indeed, it is the primary agent through which the Universal Church can regulate the papal plenitude of power, especially whenever it feels that the papacy is not exercising that power for the purpose for which it was given, namely, the edification of the Mystical Body.[90] The specific circumstances designated by d'Ailly in which the regulative authority of the General Council can be operative are those in which the pope is accused of heresy, tyrannical use of power, and notorious crime.[91]

In the context of d'Ailly's highly nuanced views on the *plenitudo potestatis*, it is clear that despite his strong emphasis on the cardinals as *pars corporis papae*, and *pars apostolicae sedis*, they do not participate, properly speaking, in the exercise of the papal plenitude of power according to d'Ailly's first mode of inherence. As seen above, according to this mode, the pope alone has received and exercises this power. No community or group within the community can share in its exercise. Consequently, neither the Universal Church, the General Council, nor the Roman Church, as represented by the pope and the cardinals share in the exercise of the papal plenitude of power. The cardinals as a corporate body, moreover, do not participate in the plenitude of power according to the second mode of inherence (*inseparabiliter*) since

---

[89] *De potestate ecclesiastica*, Dupin, 2:951. 'Secundum patet quia plenitudo potestatis non est causaliter propter papam sed papa et ejus potestas propter ecclesiam et ad eam ordinatur sicut ad finem, id est, ad ejus aedificationem.' The Pauline reference d'Ailly cites here is 2 Cor. 10:8.

[90] *De potestate ecclesiastica*, Dupin, 2:951. 'Tertio, est in generali concilio tanquam in exemplo ipsam repraesentante et regulariter dirigente.'

[91] *De potestate ecclesiastica*, Dupin, 2:951. 'Tertium patet ex eodem verbi apostoli, quia si papa uteretur hac potestate ad destructionem Ecclesiae, Generale Concilium est exemplum vel speculum dictam universalem Ecclesiam repraesentans et, ejus vice et nomine, abusus hujusmodi plenitudinis potestatis coercens, regulans, et dirigens.' The concrete references to heresy, tyranny, and notorious crime can be found at Dupin 2:959. These actions were among the principle actions for which a pope could also be deposed according to the medieval canonical tradition. See Brian Tierney, *Foundations of the Conciliar Tradition*, 47–67. The charge of tyranny would generally be interpreted in terms of actions against the common welfare of the Church (*status ecclesiae*).

obviously the finality of all papal activity is directed primarily not to the common good of the college of cardinals but to that of the Universal Church.

The authority which d'Ailly attributes to the cardinals with regard to the papal plenitude of power pertains more to the third mode of inherence (*representative*), that is, together with the pope, they are representative of the *Ecclesia Romana*, which, like the General Council, is representative of the Universal Church.[92] The cardinals, therefore, have the authority to limit the pope's exercise of the plenitude of power whenever it is not used in accordance with its proper finality, namely the building up of the Church as the Mystical Body of Christ. As in the case of the General Council, the circumstances in which they can exercise that prerogative are also similar, namely, heresy, tyranny, and notorious crime. For d'Ailly, therefore, while the papacy alone exercises the *plenituto potestatis* according to the first mode of inherence, cardinals share in that authority according to the third degree of inherence in the sense of overseeing and if necessary in specific cases limiting the papal use of that authority. This is the sense in which d'Ailly asserts that cardinals while not exercising the *plenitudo potestatis* participate in it by showing their concern and oversight of its use (*in partem sollicitudinis*).[93]

Last among the particular functions which d'Ailly ascribes to the cardinals is the right to convoke a General Council in circumstances when the preservation of the faith and the proper administration of the Church become so important that they fall within the canonical realms of necessity (*necessitas*) and utility (*utilitas*). In such situations, this convocation would ordinarily fall to the pope in consultation with the cardinals but in the absence of a pope or the failure of a pope to do so, this obligation devolves upon the cardinals. This right, he further argued, was rooted not in human but divine law. The basis for his assertion is to be found again in one of his central theses with regard to the cardinals, namely, that as the successors of the apostles

---

[92] *De potestate ecclesiastica*, Dupin, 2:951. 'Ex praemisis patet quod sicut plenitudo potestatis est in generali concilio repraesentative, ita aliquo modo, licet non aequaliter, est in Romana Ecclesia, quia ipsam universalem Ecclesiam repraesentat.'

[93] *De potestate ecclesiastica*, Dupin 2:939. 'Romana Ecclesia habet alias in partem sollicitudinis, non in plenitudinem potestatis.' See also Dupin 2:949. 'Canonica jura clamant papam habere plenitudinem potestatis, ceteros autem vocatos in partem sollicitudinis.' For the complex historical development of the understanding of the phrase '*in partem sollicitudinis*,' see Jean Rivière. 'In Partem Sollicitudinis: Evolution d'une formule pontificale,' *RSR*, 5 (1925), 210–231.

in the general ministry of God's Word and as the pope's assistants in governing the *Ecclesia Romana* which represents the Universal Church they can act in the place and in the name of the Universal Church.[94]

D'Ailly's views on the office of ecclesiastical prelates are most fully revealed in his reflections on the episcopacy and priesthood. As is to be expected, these views were primarily developed during the early years of his career when he was at the University of Paris and when he served as bishop of Cambrai. As noted earlier, during the period of his cardinalate, his views remained essentially the same. As in the case of the cardinals, d'Ailly consistently places his teaching on the office of the episcopacy and the priesthood within the broad evangelical context of calling and mission as described earlier. That calling and mission, furthermore, are primarily portrayed in the pastoral context of the *cura animarum*.[95] Although, according to d'Ailly, bishops and priests as *prelati maiores* and *prelati minores* share in the same apostolic calling and mission according to their respective rank within the ecclesiastical hierarchy, it is the bishop who best exemplifies the pastoral ideal and is primarily responsible for its realization in his diocese.

The specific ways in which bishops and priests share in their common calling and mission follow more or less along the lines of the six specific powers which d'Ailly in his *De potestate ecclesiastica* attributed to ecclesiastical prelates. Foremost among these specific functions are those of teaching and preaching. More importantly, these duties relate directly to the Scriptures, for it is the teaching and preaching of the Scriptures, both Old and New Testaments, that most accurately characterize the episcopal office.[96] These functions, indeed, constitute the

---

[94] *De potestate ecclesiasticia*, Dupin 2:935. 'Ex quo ulterius sequitur quod ubi necessitas aut utilitas imminet pro conservanda fide vel bono regimine Ecclesiae, ad papam vel, in ejus defectu, ad cardinales pertinet generale concilium convocare, et hoc eis convenit non tam humana quam divina institutione, vice et nomine totius universalis Ecclesiae, quia ipsi cardinales succedentes apostolis in ministerio generali verbi Dei.'

[95] *Sermo in Synodo Cameracensi, I, TS*, 2–3. 'Ideo reverendi patres et in Christo fratres charissimi vobis in hac sancta synodo congregatis, vobis ad ecclesiasticam administrationem vocatis, vobis domino vocante ad curam pastoralem prelationis electis, non inmerito specialiter diriguntur verba per me vestris praelibata reverentiis.'

[96] *Utrum indoctus in jure divino*, Dupin, 1:653. 'Praelatus debet esse doctus in doctrina sacrae Scripturae, cum ejus praecipuum officium sit sacram Scripturam docere et praedicare.' While there has been considerable debate over the date and circumstances of this *quaestio disputata*, it is no longer regarded as a work associated with d'Ailly's inception ceremonies as a master in theology which occurred in 1381. The more commonly accepted date is 1394 when d'Ailly was still chancellor at the University of Paris. This work, together with others associated with his years at the University, was

primary thrust of the apostolic mission given the Apostles in Mk. 16:15 when they were entrusted with the task of proclaiming the gospel throughout the whole world.[97] In support of this teaching role, d'Ailly cites 1 Pt. 3:15 where the Apostle informs his readers that they should always be ready to explain the reasons for their hope. While this text is primarily addressed to all the members of the Christian churches in Asia Minor, d'Ailly applies it more exclusively to the episcopal and priestly offices. In this context, therefore, bishops and priests are to be always ready to explain the reasons for their faith to all those under their care.[98] In general, however, the activities of teaching and preaching should not be too strictly distinguished for in the New Testament sources they are closely interrelated, and, as will be seen in a later chapter, remained so in the ancient and medieval Church.

Also clear from an analysis of d'Ailly's views on the episcopal activities of teaching and preaching the Scriptures is the fact that he sees these activities very much in a doctrinal context. That he should do so is hardly surprising given d'Ailly's training and interests as a theologian as well as the needs of the Church at that time, beset as it was with numerous heretical movements, especially those inspired by the writings of Wyclif and Hus. This doctrinal emphasis, however, should not be interpreted to mean that he neglects the moral dimensions of the Scriptures, for, as will be seen later, d'Ailly does give considerable attention to the fostering of virtue as an integral part of the episcopal and priestly offices.

Closely associated with the episcopal obligation to teach and preach the faith as reflected in the Scriptures is the consequent obligation to

---

recopied in d'Ailly's own hand after the Council of Pisa, most likely around 1410–1411. For the dating and historical circumstances surrounding this work see Douglass Taber, 'The Theologian and the Schism: A Study of the Political Thought of Jean Gerson (1363–1429)' (Ph.D diss., Stanford University, 1985), 169–171, 196–197.

[97] *Utrum indoctus in jure divino*, Dupin, 1:654. 'Item in persona apostolorum a Christo praelatis dicitur. "Euntes in mundum universum, praedicate Evangelium omni creaturae."'

[98] *Utrum indoctus in jure divino*, Dupin, 1:654. 'Et illud Petri in canonica sua, eis specialter dirigitur. "Parati omni poscenti vos rationem reddere de ea quae in vobis est fide." Et plures aliae authoritates Scripturae sunt, quibus patenter ostenditur quod praelati ex officio specialiter tenentur Evangelium praedicare et fidem docere atque deffendere.' While the text d'Ailly quotes for 1 Pt. 3:15 speaks in terms of explaining the reasons for their 'faith', the text in the critical edition of the Vulgate reads in terms of giving reasons for their 'hope.' See *Biblia Sacra Iuxta Vulgatam Versionem*, 3rd ed., Robert Weber, ed. (Stuttgart: Deutsche Bibelgesellschaft, 1983), 1867.

condemn all doctrinal beliefs which are contrary to or contradict the faith as elaborated in the Scriptures. D'Ailly's principle source for this episcopal function is Titus 1:7–9, where in speaking of the qualities of a bishop, Paul states that a bishop should be able to 'exhort with sound doctrine as well as refute opponents.' In addition to St. Paul, d'Ailly cites Aristotle's dictum that the actions of a wise man are twofold: first, not to lie about those things which he knows to be true and, secondly, to expose the error of those who lie.[99] In this context, it should be remembered that at Constance, d'Ailly was a member of the commission that interrogated and judged John Hus.[100]

While the episcopal functions of teaching and preaching sound doctrine as well as refuting contrary or contradictory beliefs can be carried out in a variety of ways such as preaching, pastoral visitations, and diocesan synods, they are most forcefully expressed in the context of episcopal determinations or definitions which can be doctrinal or disciplinary in nature. In their original context, a *determinatio* or *definitio* referred to the important moment in a disputation when after all sides of a question under debate had been sufficiently argued, the master or bachelor was called upon to render a decisive judgement on the question at issue. Similar action could be undertaken by a whole corporation of masters such as a theological faculty in controversial cases involving important doctrinal matters. In such circumstances, the faculty approved a particular teaching as orthodox or condemned it as erroneous or heretical.[101]

D'Ailly's views on the nature of episcopal and university determinations and their various types were developed in great detail in his *Tractatus contra Johannem de Montesono*. John of Monzón was an Aragonese Dominican who, during his *vesperies*, *aulica*, and *resumpta* ceremonies at the University of Paris in 1387, developed a series of propositions which essentially attacked the doctrine of the Immaculate Conception.[102] The

---

[99] *De potestate ecclesiastica*, Dupin, 2:925.

[100] For d'Ailly's role in the condemnation of John Hus see Tschackert, *Peter von Ailli*, 221–235, Salembier, *Le Cardinal Pierre d'Ailly*, 274–279, and Guenée, *Between Church and State*, 242–244.

[101] For a brief analysis of the university context in which the terms *determinare/determinatio* and *definire/definitio* were used, see Olga Weijers, *Terminologie des universités au xiiie siècle*, 173–174; 404–407. Since these terms were often used interchangeably, especially by d'Ailly, for reasons of economy, *determinare/determinatio* alone will be used in subsequent descriptions.

[102] For a brief history of the Monzón Affair and d'Ailly's role therein see Louis Salembier, *Le cardinal Pierre d'Ailly*, 72–77; Paul Doncoeur, 'La condemnation de Jean

controversial propositions defended by Monzón were brought to the attention of the chancellor of the University of Paris by the faculty of theology. With his approval, the theological faculty appointed a commission of twelve theologians to study these propositions. In its report, the commission enumerated fourteen questionable statements contained in Monzón's propositions. This report, in turn, served as the basis of the theological faculty's debate and was approved by that faculty on July 6, 1387. Monzón was given three days to retract those statements. When he did not do so, the theological faculty presented the case to the Bishop of Paris.

After several failed attempts to get him to appear before the bishop to defend his teaching, Monzón was declared suspect of heresy on August 23, 1388. Before this episcopal decision, however, Monzón, with the support of many prominent fellow Dominicans, had appealed his case to the papal court in Avignon. He based his appeal from the Bishop of Paris to the Pope at Avignon on the fact that his case involved a matter of faith and as such fell canonically within the category of *causae maiores*, that is, eclesiastical matters which because of their importance were regarded by canon law as reserved to the pope alone for final and authoritative judgement.[103] To argue on its behalf, the University of Paris in May or June, 1388 sent a delegation whose spokesman was Pierre d'Ailly. After a private audience with Clement VII, the delegation received papal approval to present its case in a public consistory. Here again d'Ailly served as the University's spokesman[104] Sometime

---

de Monzón par Pierre d'Orgemont, évêque de Paris, le 23 août 1387,' *RQH*, 81 (1907), 176–187, Daniel A. Mortier, *Histoire des maîtres generaux de l'ordre des Frères Prêcheurs*, 8 vols. (Paris: Picard, 1903–1920), 3:616–647; Taber, 'The Theologian and the Schism,' 10–56, and J.M.M.H. Thijssen, *Censure and Heresy at the University of Paris, 1200–1400* (Philadelphia: University of Pennsylvania, 1998), 107–111. With regard to the historical development of the doctrine of the Immaculate Conception see Martin. Jugie, *L'Immaculée Conception dans l'Ecriture et dans la tradition orientale* (Rome: Officium Libri Catholici, 1952); R. Masson, 'De Immaculata Conceptione apud Fratres Praedicatores,' *Angelicum*, 31 (1954), 358–408; Ignatius Brady, 'The Development of the Doctrine on the Immaculate Conception in the Fourteenth Century after Aureoli,' *FS*, 15 (1955), 175–202, and E.D. O'Connor, *The Doctrine of the Immaculate Conception: History and Significance* (Notre Dame: University of Notre Dame Press, 1958).

[103] In medieval canon law, *causae maiores* generally involved matters of doctrine, discipline, or administration, and their number varied considerably. For a general treatment of the historical and canonical development of the concept of *causae maiores*, see s.v. 'causes majeures,' *DTC*, by J. Steiger, and *DDC*, by R. Naz.

[104] D'Ailly's address in the private audience with Clement VII, namely, his *Prima propositio coram papam facta*, can be found in Dupin, 1:697–702. His address before the

after these talks, d'Ailly, on behalf of the University of Paris, published his *Tractatus contra Johannem de Montesono*.[105] The investigation continued under a commission of cardinals but Monzón fled from Avignon in early August and failed to appear personally before the commission. After several attempts to secure his appearance, Clement VII issued a decree of excommunication for contumacy on January 27, 1389.

Since, as has been seen, Monzón based his appeal on papal prerogatives with regard to *causae maiores*, and given the strong canonical tradition supporting those prerogatives, d'Ailly obviously did not think it prudent at Avignon to challenge that tradition, nor is there any evidence that he did not agree with it. What he does strongly object to is Monzón's overly stringent interpretation of that tradition which in effect deprived the bishop of Paris of all authority over matters of faith in his diocese. While not denying the papacy's right to serve as the ultimate adjudicator in matters of faith, d'Ailly's primary concern was to vindicate the rights of bishops in this area by delineating the respective role of popes and bishops in dealing with cases involving matters of faith. Furthermore, he sought to urge upon the papacy the need for exercising more caution before accepting appeals from episcopal courts on matters relating to the faith.

The Monzón Controversy, as is clear from the above description, raised major questions as to the respective role of the university, the bishop, and the pope with regard to doctrinal matters and provided d'Ailly with an excellent opportunity to present his views on the subject. Within the context of the university, especially Paris and its theological faculty, d'Ailly asserts that determinations can be of two types. The approval of a particular teaching as orthodox or its condemnation as erroneous or heretical was described in terms of a *determinatio scholastica* or *doctrinalis*. This activity was regarded as the special prerogative of the members of the theological faculty since it was the theologians who were primarily involved with the study of the Scriptures. As a result of

---

pope and cardinals in public consistory is entitled: *Propositio facta in consistoria* and is printed in Dupin, 1:702–709. Taber argues that this text, even in manuscript form, is incomplete since it does not mention the theological and ecclesiological issues of this controversy. See Taber, 'The Theologian and the Schism,' 49–52.

[105] The text of d'Ailly's *Contra Johannem de Montesono* as it appears in Dupin 1:709–722 is also incomplete. The complete text used here is that found in Charles de Plessis d'Argentré, *Collectio judiciorum de novis erroribus*, 3 vols. (Paris: Lambert Coffin, 1724–1736; repr., Brussels: Culture et Civilisation, 1963), 1:75–129.

this study, it was they who were regarded as best qualified to ascertain the truths of the Catholic faith as contained in the Scriptures and to reject those not so contained.[106]

A theological faculty could also prohibit its own members from teaching doctrines which it regarded as heretical or erroneous and even impose a censure or penalty upon any of its members who refused to observe its decisions. The right to exercise such authority over its members was founded upon the oath which members of that faculty made to the theological faculty as a corporation.[107] In such cases, a theologian could be suspended from the exercise of his magisterial activities and privileges and, in extreme cases, even deprived of them. This type of action on the part of a theological faculty was designated as a *determinatio judicialis* or a*uctoritativa*.[108]

The terminology and distinction between doctrinal and juridical determinations that developed within theological faculties was also used to describe the actions of the ecclesiastical hierarchy, especially popes and bishops, with regard to matters of faith. As the successors of the apostles, popes and bishops received from Christ the authority necessary for the pastoral government of the Church, especially with regard to matters of belief. Their authority, however, varied according to their rank within the ecclesiastical hierarchy. The fullest and most extensive use of such authority was attributed by d'Ailly to the Apostolic See since it was to the holder of that see, Peter, that Christ in Lk. 22:31–33 promised that his faith would never fail.[109] Adherence to such authorita-

---

[106] *Contra Johannem de Montesono*, d'Argentré, 77. 'Quia ad eos pertinent ea quae sunt fidei per modum doctinae determinare et doctrinaliter definire ad quod pertinet Sacram Scripturam docere et ex ea haereticas assertiones et in fide erroneas reprobare ac vertitates catholicas approbare. Sed ad doctores theologos pertinet secundum, ergo et primum.'

[107] *Contra Johannem de Montesono*, d'Argentré, 78. 'Quinta conclusio est quod ad dictam facultatem theologiae contra certas personas, scilicet contra singulares magistros et baccalaureos ejusdem facultatis juratos, quandoque pertinet non solum doctrinaliter sed etiam aliquo modo judicialiter assertiones haereticas aut erroneas condemnare.'

[108] *Contra Johannem de Montesono*, d'Argentré, 83. In distinguishing a *determinatio scholastica* from a *determinatio judicialis*, d'Ailly makes clear that one of the major differences rests on the fact that the latter is generally associated with a punishment (*poena*), a privation (*privatio*), or a suspension (*suspensio*).

[109] *Contra Johannem de Montesono*, d'Argentré, 76. 'Prima ergo conclusio est quod, ad sanctam Sedem Apostolicam pertinet auctoritate judiciali suprema circa ea quae sunt fidei, judicialiter definire. Et haec probatur, quia ad illius tanquam ad supremi judicis auctoritatem pertinent in fide judicialiter definire, cujus fides nunquam deficit. Sed sanctae sedis apostolicae fides nunquam deficit.'

tive papal decisions was obligatory throughout the universal Church.[110] D'Ailly's line of argumentation has occasionally been used to claim him as a supporter of the doctrine of papal infallibility. Recent scholarship, however, has challenged the extension of d'Ailly's argumentation to the realm of infallibility.[111]

According to d'Ailly, moreover, bishops also enjoy a similar authority to issue doctrinal and judicial determinations but to a lesser degree and in subordination to the power of the papacy.[112] By this qualification, he asserts that episcopal determinations, unlike those of the papacy, oblige only the subjects within their own diocese and only to the extent that the pope has not determined otherwise.[113] Although of a subordinate nature, this power of the episcopacy, according to d'Ailly, is not derived from that of the papacy and is established as firmly in divine law as the papal prerogatives in this regard. D'Ailly draws the scriptural authority for his position from Acts 20:28 where Paul addresses the elders at Ephesus and urges them to be on guard for the flock over which the Holy Spirit had made them supervisors.[114]

Given the foundation in divine law of the bishop's authority, especially with regard to determining matters of faith, d'Ailly strongly urges that the papacy show respect for that authority and not too readily accept appeals from persons whose case has been or is being adju-

---

[110] *Contra Johannem de Montesono*, d'Argentré, 85. '… suprema definitio papae catholici, qui est universalis episcopus, ubique obligat; et ideo hujusmodi definitio dicitur summa simpliciter et absolute.'

[111] On these claims see Francis Oakley, 'Pierre d'Ailly and Papal Infallibility,' 353–358. Oakley argues convincingly that such an extension is not consonant with the general context and goal of d'Ailly's treatise as well as with the many other references in his works where he denies infallibility not only to the pope but to the council as well.

[112] *Contra Johannem de Montesono*, d'Argentré, 76. 'Secunda conclusio est, quod ad episcopos catholicos pertinet auctoritate inferiori et subordinata circa ea quae sunt fidei, judicialiter definire. Et haec probatur, quia ad eos pertinet auctoritate judiciali inferiori et subordinata in fide definire, ad quos pertinet consimili auctoritate ecclesiam regere. Sed ad episcopos catholicos pertinet secundum. Ergo et primum.'

[113] *Contra Johannem de Montesono*, d'Argentré, 85. 'Sed subordinata definitio episcoporum catholicorum inferiorum non sic universaliter obligat; et ideo non dicitur definitio vel sententia nisi secundum quid … Circa hoc tamen stat, quod obligat suos subditos secundum quid, scilicet quousque per Sedem Apostolicam vel Summum Pontificem aliter fuerit sententiatum et definitum.'

[114] *Contra Johannem de Montesono*, d'Argentré, 76. 'Unde probatur, quod jure divino et auctoritate Spiritus Sancti, episcopi positi sunt ad regimen Ecclesiae Dei. Regimen autem importat judiciariam auctoritatem. Ergo sequitur quod ad eos pertinet auctoritate judiciali inferiori et subordinata … ecclesiam regere, et per consequens de fide cognoscere et in ea definire.'

dicated in an episcopal court. Before being granted, all such appeals must be seriously evaluated. In this evaluation, moreover, there should be complete access to all previous information related to the case. Only after mature analysis and deliberation have been exercised and serious and compelling reasons established should such an appeal be granted.[115]

When the above cautions are not exercised, appeals from episcopal courts to the papal courts become too numerous and burdensome for bishops. The result of such excessive appeals is that bishops become remiss in carrying out their duties with regard to detecting and uprooting heretical beliefs in their diocese. They become quickly worn down and disheartened by the time consuming efforts, the legal hassles, and the expenses involved in such appeals. Relying upon Bernard of Clairvaux's admonition to Pope Eugene III on the matter of appeals, d'Ailly raises questions as to the motives behind many appeals. Often, he asserts, they are not a recourse (*refugium*) but rather a flight (*diffugium*) from justice.[116]

In relationship to theological faculties, the bishop's authority to issue doctrinal and judicial determinations was more comprehensive. Since his authority extended to all the members of the diocese entrusted to his care, it also extended over the University of Paris, especially its theological faculty. While a more detailed study of the manner in which episcopal and university authority interacted with regard to erroneous and heretical teaching will be developed in a subsequent chapter, suffice it here to refute a common misconception of the nature of that relationship. In much secondary literature the interaction between theological faculties and bishops with regard to heretical or erroneous doctrinal issues is explained by stating that the *determinatio scholastica* lies within the domain of the theological faculty while the *determinatio judicialis* relates primarily to episcopal authority.[117] In the case of Pierre d'Ailly, however, it is clear that bishops have the right to exercise both forms of determinations. It also seems reasonable to believe that, at least until

---

[115] *Contra Johannem de Montesono*, d'Argentré, 79. 'Sexta conclusio est, quod ad superiorem judicem pertinet processum per dictos episcopum et facultatem theologiae factum nec sine magna et notabili causa favorabiliter impedire, nec appellationi contra eos in causa interjecta sine matura deliberatione et praevia informatione deferre.'

[116] *Contra Johannem de Montesono*, d'Argentré, 79. The reference to Bernard of Clairvaux is to his *De consideratione*, 3, 2, 6–12, *Sancti Bernardi Opera*, ed. Jean Leclercq et al., 8 vols. (Rome: Editiones Cistercienses, 1957–1977), 3:435–439.

[117] For this point of view, see Oberman, *Harvest of Medieval Theology*, 375–376.

studies are made of the thought of other late medieval theologians on this subject, that d'Ailly's views remain representative of the theological mainstream.

In discussing the bishop's right to issue judicial determinations, d'Ailly makes clear that the bishop's authority extends not only over matters clearly heretical or erroneous but also to matters which might not be such but whose promotion at a particular time might, in the bishop's view, confuse, disturb, or scandalize the faithful under his care. In such cases the bishop can decide not to allow such teaching to be promulgated or defended. D'Ailly describes such a course of action in terms of *judicialiter inhibere*. The bishop also has the right to determine the extent and length of time in which each prohibition is to be in effect.[118]

The argument that d'Ailly gives to justify the bishop's right to forbid the publication, preaching or teaching of particular propositions, even though they may not be heretical, rests upon the general principle that bishops can licitly inhibit the promulgation of a particular teaching to those under their jurisdiction if that teaching is not essential to the faith of their subjects and if they have a reasonable cause for so acting.[119] D'Ailly gives no further explanation or justification of the principle upon which he constructs his argument and the canonical sources which he cites do not directly relate specifically to the principle itself but more broadly to the obedience owed by priests to their bishops.[120]

In presenting his arguments on behalf of the University of Paris at the papal court in Avignon, d'Ailly makes very clear that, contrary to the assertions of Monzón, the Bishop of Paris did not declare his propositions as false, heretical, or erroneous. What the bishop did do was to

---

[118] *Contra Johannem de Montesono*, d'Argentré, 83. 'Secundo dicendum quod aliud est aliquas propositiones sententialiter et judicialiter condemnare et aliud est eas, seu earum dogmatizationem et defensionem, ex causa rationali inhibere ... Et ideo quandoque licitum est praelatis interdicere aliquas veritates ex causa rationabili, scilicet ad evitandum scandalum vel periculum; et si non omnibus aut pro omni tempore, saltem aliquibus et pro aliquo tempore possunt inhibere ...'

[119] *Contra Johannem de Montesono*, d'Argentré, 83. 'Et hoc probatur, quia omne illud quod potest a subditis licite praetermitti, potest ex causa rationabili a praelatis et aliis jurisdictionem habentibus supra subditos inhiberi, quia in talibus licitis et honestis oportet subditos obedire, sicut colligitur ex sacris canonibus ...'

[120] *Contra Johannem de Montesono*, d'Argentré, 83. In citing his canonical sources, d'Ailly does not give full citations but from the titles of the canons given, the references made to specific questions, and the nature of the subject matter under discussion, it is safe to conclude that he is referring to Gratian's *Decretum*, C. 11, q. 3, c. 2, 5, 6, 7, 11, 13, 14.

prohibit (*judicialiter inhibere*) the publication, preaching, or teaching of those propositions, an action which, as seen above, validly falls within his competence.[121] D'Ailly, moreover, adds that even if the Bishop of Paris had formally condemned Monzón's teachings as heretical, or erroneous, he would still be acting within his competence, provided he recognized the inferior and subordinate nature of that authority with respect to the papacy. Monzón's denial of such an authority to the bishop and his consequent claim that matters of faith, as *causae maiores*, fall under the sole jurisdiction of the papacy, was regarded by d'Ailly as a misinterpretation of canonical legislation and intent.[122]

---

[121] *Contra Johannem de Montesono*, d'Argentré, 83. 'Ad tertium objectum respondetur primo quod nec facultas theologiae nec episcopus praedicti conclusiones praemissas sententialiter seu judicialiter damnaverunt, sed solum earum publicationem et dogmatizationem inhibuerunt.'

[122] *Contra Johannem de Monetsono*, d'Argentré, 84.

CHAPTER THREE

BISHOPS: PASTORAL REFORM, AND THE APOSTOLIC LIFE

D'Ailly's detailed analysis of and high regard for the status, office, and authority of ecclesiastical prelates because of their evangelical origin and mission did not blind him to their actual condition in the late medieval Church. D'Ailly indeed recognized the diminished respect with which prelates were held and treated and he joined the multitude of others in his day who called for their reform. He was also greatly concerned with what would happen to the Church if its prelates failed to answer the call of reform. As will be recalled, this concern often reached apocalyptic dimensions when he stated that unless the ecclesiastical order is reformed inestimable damage will be inflicted upon the Church. In short, if ecclesiastical prelates fail to rise to the challenge of reform, they will have indeed prepared the way for the arrival of the Antichrist. If they do take the path to reform, however, they can indeed postpone that arrival and insure a relative period of peace for the Church.

1. *Dimensions of Reform Program*

While this and the following chapter will be concerned with the reform of ecclesiastical prelates, especially as it relates to bishops, it is important to remember that his plans for the reform of the pastoral and personal dimensions of prelates' lives represent only one aspect of his overall plan of church reform. D'Ailly revealed the extensive nature of his vision of church reform in a variety of treatises, sermons, and letters and the general outline of his program of reform remained essentially unchanged throughout his life. Primary among these treatises were his *De materia concilii*, written sometime between August, 1402 and March, 1403 in response to a proposed council of the Avignon obedience, his *De reformatione*, presented to the Council of Constance on November 1, 1416 at the time when he served as a member of the council's first reform commission but which in effect is essentially a slightly revised version of the third part of *De materia concilii*, and his *Ad laudem Christi* of February 28, 1417 which represents his response to a sermon by the Dominican Leonard Statius which criticized d'Ailly's ideas on the reform of religious orders. His major sermons and letters dealing with reform themes include two sermons on the Nativity written between 1372 and 1395, his three synodal sermons at Cambrai dating sometime between 1397 and 1411, his second Advent sermon of 1414, and his first letter to John XXIII written in 1413 or 1414.

When looked at in their totality, these works, especially his treatises, present a six fold approach to church reform in accordance with the different dimensions of the Church. The first approach deals with the Church in its universal and corporate context. The second relates to the reform of the Church's head which for d'Ailly comprised both the papacy and the cardinals of the Roman Curia. The third relates to ecclesiastical prelates. The reform of religious orders comprises the fourth approach, and the fifth is concerned with the reform of ecclesiastics who did not fall into the ranks of the prelates. Finally, the sixth approach deals with the reform of the laity. In his earliest presentation of his six fold program, namely in the *De materia concilii*, d'Ailly added that in the reform of the laity special attention was to be given to the secular princes. In the later outlines of his reform program, this emphasis was lessened and the goal placed more generally upon the reform of the overall body of the laity.

As indicated earlier, the aspect of church reform to be studied in this and the succeeding chapter will be restricted to the office of prelates and primarily that of the major prelates. This emphasis clearly reflects the emphasis given by d'Ailly himself in his major reform treatises, for in these treatises it is clear that his primary concern was with the major prelates. He even goes so far as to assert that the major prelates represent the principal parts of the Church.[1] Even within the context of the major prelates, it is also clear that d'Ailly's principal emphasis was on the episcopacy. While it is true that d'Ailly often uses the term *prelati* without further qualification and that in such cases the sense intended by d'Ailly must be determined by the context, in most cases the context

---

[1] See especially his *De materia concilii*, Oakley, 317 and the *De reformatione*, Miethke-Weinrich, 1:340–354. Even in his *Ad laudem Christi* wherein d'Ailly reemphasizes his earlier views on the leadership role of prelates in the reform of the Church, it is clear that his primary concern is with the major prelates.

is that of the episcopacy. It can also be asserted that throughout his active life it was the episcopacy upon which he greatly pinned his hopes for the leadership in the reform of the Church.[2]

D'Ailly's stress on the leadership of the episcopacy in the reform of the Church, however, should not be interpreted to mean that some of the reform proposals he advocated would not also be applicable to the cardinalate as well, especially to those enjoying episcopal rank. By the same token, much of what he has to say about episcopal reform was also applicable to the priesthood, especially in the realm of preaching and the administration of the sacraments. Thus while d'Ailly's reform proposals were primarily intended for bishops they are not to be interpreted as applying exclusively to them but are also applicable in appropriate degrees to the cardinalate and the priesthood as well.

2. *Pastoral Reform and the Apostolic Ideal*

Returning now to d'Ailly's concern about the diminished reputation of ecclesiastical prelates, it can be said that he saw their decline within the general context of their failure to follow in the path of their predecessors, namely the apostles and disciples. In d'Ailly's mind, this failure to adhere to ideal of the apostolic life (*vita apostolica*) has manifested itself primarily in the pastoral exercise of their office and in the conduct of their personal lives and it is through the return to the apostolic ideal in both of these areas that the reform and renewal of the episcopacy will take place. D'Ailly grounds his call for such a return on Paul's first letter to the Corinthians in which the apostle implores his followers in Corinth to be imitators of him as he was of Christ. While d'Ailly recognizes that this imitation of the lives of the apostles and disciples will never be a perfect one, he does ask that prelates strive for it in all their actions.[3] With regard to the exercise of their pastoral office, he urges

---

[2] For excellent surveys of the state of the episcopacy in the late Middle Ages, especially in France, see the following articles: Bernard Guillemain, 'L'éxercice du pouvoir épiscopal à la fin du moyen-âge,' and Hélène Millet, 'L'évêque à la fin du Grand Schisme d'Occident: Lucerna supra candelabrum posita,' in *L'Institution et les églises de l'antiquité à nos jours*, Miscellanea Historiae Ecclesiasticae, 8, ed. Bernard Vogler (Bruxelles: Editions Nauwalaerts, 1987), 101–132, and 133–147.

[3] *Homelia facta in Synodo Cameracensi*, TS, 9. 'Et si non in consumata perfectione saltim in studiosa imitatione, dicente apostolo imitatores mei estote, sicut et ego Christi.' The Pauline reference is to 1 Cor. 11:1.

prelates to govern their churches not in the style of a tyrant but in the manner of the apostles.[4]

Given the strong emphasis upon the *vita apostolica* in d'Ailly's reform thought, it is not surprising that d'Ailly describes the prelates of his day who fell short of this apostolic ideal as 'pseudo-pastors,' 'mercenaries,' 'thieves,' and 'bandits.'[5] While the language used by d'Ailly is indeed harsh, it must be remembered that it is essentially the language used in the New Testament by Christ in Jn. 10:1–8 where he contrasts the motives and traits of good and bad shepherds. D'Ailly also has recourse to the shepherd theme as found in the Old Testament, namely in Ezek. 34:1–16 where the prophet roundly criticizes the leaders of Israel who as shepherds of their people should have been caring for them but in fact cared only for themselves. In the symbolic language of the text, the prophet accuses such leaders of feeding off the milk of their sheep, wearing their wool, and slaughtering the fatlings for their own enjoyment.[6] The scriptural model of the good shepherd, as portrayed in the above passages therefore, remained central to the ideal of the episcopal office throughout the patristic and medieval periods and it is from this tradition that d'Ailly draws much of his thought and imagery. While the theme of the good shepherd does not play as important a role in d'Ailly's thought as it did in that of Gerson, it describes, nonetheless, a major aspect of his reform teaching with regard to the office of prelates.[7]

As a result of the failure of prelates to live up to the apostolic ideal as portrayed in the Scriptures, d'Ailly maintains that the entire ecclesiastical order has lost considerable respect within the Church. In his homily at the Synod of Cambrai in 1398, he clearly asserts that

---

[4] *Sermo in die Pentecostes, II, TS*, 4. 'Attendite vos positos ad regendam hanc ecclesiam non modo tyrannico sed modo apostolico …'

[5] For the use of these terms see *Sermo de nativitate, I, TS*, 5; *Invectiva Ezechielis contra pseudopastores*, Tschackert, 13–14; *Homelia facta in Synodo Cameracensi, TS*, 2.

[6] Cf. *Epistola ad Joannem XXIII, II*, Dupin, 2:878; *Invectiva Ezechielis contra pseudopastores*, Tschackert, 13. Jn. 21:15–17, which narrates the commission given to Peter by Christ in terms of feeding his sheep, was also employed by d'Ailly but, given its context, was primarily restricted to the papal office.

[7] In the late Middle Ages, Jean Gerson (1363–1429), d'Ailly's student and close personal friend, wrote extensively on the pastoral duties of bishops and priests and in these writings frequently used the theme of the good shepherd. His famous sermon to the clergy of Rheims during the diocesan synod of 1408 bore this title and had as its central theme the Johannine ideal of the *bonus pastor*. For Gerson's views on the pastoral office see, Pascoe, *Jean Gerson*, 110–174, and D. Catherine Brown, *Pastor and Laity in the Theology of Jean Gerson* (Cambridge: Cambridge University Press, 1987).

the failure of the prelates to cultivate the apostolic virtues so necessary to the exercise of their office has resulted in a serious depreciation of that office on the part of secular rulers and the people.[8] D'Ailly stressed a similar theme much earlier in his career when in 1375, while still a student of theology at Paris, he delivered a sermon before a diocesan synod at Amiens. After describing the luxurious lifestyle of prelates, he asserts that the consequence thereof is that, unlike the other orders in medieval society, the clerical order alone is the one that is without order. The failure, then, of prelates to follow and live up to the apostolic ideal of their office has transformed their state from one of order into one of chaos.[9] D'Ailly's views on the apocalyptic consequences of this failure and subsequent chaos have been detailed in the first chapter of this work where it was also seen that the Church's hope for postponing the arrival of the Antichrist and the End-Times rested primarily upon the reformed leadership of the episcopal office.

D'Ailly's call for the prelates of his day to return to the apostolic ideal in the exercise of their office and in their personal life places him in the long line of medieval reformers who saw reform within the context of a return to the *vita apostolica*. This return was also expressed in terms of the evangelical life (*vita evangelica*), or as a return to the life of the primitive Church, (*ecclesia primitiva*). Many groups used these terms interchangeably.[10] In a sense there is nothing surprising in such calls to emulate the *vita apostolica*, for the Gospel ideal is the fundamental source of all Christian inspiration and a principal norm for all true reform in the Church. Within early and medieval Christianity, however, there were periods when that call became more intense than in other periods and constituted a challenge to the prevailing conditions within

---

[8] *Homelia facta in Synodo Cammeracensi*, TS, 9. '... ut ex hoc status ecclesiasticus a secularibus et popularibus contemnatur et quasi pedibus conculcetur.'

[9] *Sermo in Synodo Ambianis*, Tschackert, 4.

[10] The literature on the apostolic and evangelical renewal movements in the historical summary which follows relies heavily upon the following sources: Ladner, *The Idea of Reform*, 319–424, M.D. Chenu, 'Monks, Canons, and Laymen in Search of the Apostolic Life,' in his *Nature, Man, and Society in the Twelfth Century*, 202–238, Giles Constable, *The Reformation of the Twelfth Century* (Cambridge: Cambridge University Press, 1996), 125–167, Jean Châtillon, *Le movement canonial au moyen age: spiritualité et culture*, J.M. Phelps, 'A Study of Renewal Ideas in the Writings of the Early Franciscans,' (Ph.D. diss., University of California at Los Angeles, 1972), Duane V. Lapsanski, *Evangelical Perfection: An Historical Examination of the Concept in the Early Franciscan Sources* (St. Bonaventure, N.Y.: The Franciscan Institute, 1977), and John Van Engen, trans., *Devotio Moderna: Basic Writings*, 7–35.

the Church. In such cases the ideal of the *vita apostolica* often became a norm for measuring the spiritual vitality of the Church and for delineating those areas in which that vitality was deficient or in which it failed to meet new pastoral needs or challenges within the Church. In these circumstances, the apostolic ideal also became a normative basis for reform and renewal.

Historically the model of the *vita apostolica* has been interpreted in a twofold manner in accordance with the dual context in which the lives of the apostles were presented in the New Testament. It was interpreted, first of all, in terms of the interior life of the early Christian community gathered in Jerusalem as reflected in Acts 4:32–37. This life stressed the internal unity of the community, especially in terms of its shared beliefs, its witness to those beliefs to the outside world, and its espousal of the common life in the terms of common ownership of property and provision for the material needs of all its members. The second way in which the model of the *vita apostolica* has been interpreted relates more to the mission given by Christ to his apostles and disciples in Mt. 10:1–15 and Lk. 10:1–12 to preach the Gospel and to do so in a context of a personal lifestyle distinguished by its material simplicity and dependence. These two modes of interpreting the *vita apostolica* were frequently described in terms of the 'contemplative life' (*vita comtemplativa*) and the 'active life' (*vita activa*). While both of these interpretations of the *vita apostolica* are intimately interrelated, throughout history one or the other has been emphasized by the different reform movements in accordance with their specific nature and goals.

In early Christianity and in the early Middle Ages, when monasticism was the principle agent for reform, the first dimension of the *vita apostolica*, namely the interior and communal life of the Christian community, was emphasized. So close was this association that the *vita apostolica* was frequently identified with the monastic life (*vita monastica*). Such an association was maintained by Pachomius, Basil, Cassian, Benedict, and the Carolingian reformers such as Benedict of Aniane. In the high Middle Ages, especially as a result of the Gregorian Reform, the second dimension, namely, the activity of preaching the Gospel or evangelization, came to be increasingly stressed. This emphasis is first seen in the renewal of the canonical life (*vita canonica*), especially that of the canons regular, who modeled their rule upon that of St. Augustine. Although the renewal of the *vita canonica* naturally involved the internal spiritual and communal life of the canons, its distinguishing characteristics related primarily to its pastoral dimensions, that is, the preaching of the Gospel, teaching, dispensing the sacraments, and the general administration of the cathedral and collegiate churches.

This renewed *vita canonica* also increasingly came to be described in terms of the *vita apostolica* and was especially manifested in the life of the canons of St. Victor in Paris, St.Ruf in Avignon, St. John Lateran in Rome, and the chapters at Rottenbuch and Marbach in Germany. It must be remembered, however, that this renewal of the *vita canonica* took its place alongside a renewed *vita monastica* as manifested in the new foundations of Cluny, Grandmont, Vallombrosa, Citeaux, and La Grande Chartreuse. For Urban II (1088–1099) both monks and canons regular were equally identified with the *vita apostolica*. Both the renewal of the *vita monastica* and the *vita canonica*, therefore, were identified with the model of the *vita apostolica* although each emphasized different dimensions of that model.

The increasing interpretation of the *vita apostolica* in terms of preaching the Gospel was also seen in the high Middle Ages in the rise of numerous itinerant preachers, both lay and clerical. What is to be especially noted in such preachers is the increasing emphasis upon preaching the Gospel in the context of a life of penance and poverty. In this sense, such preachers reflected a fuller interpretation and application of Christ's mission to the apostles and disciples in Mt. 10:1–15 and Lk. 10:1–12 wherein he enjoins them to take up their preaching mission with nothing but the essentials in clothing and travel gear and in a spirit of complete dependence upon their hearers for their material sustenance. Among such preachers are to be numbered Robert of Arbrissel (c. 1060–1117), Bernard of Thiron (1046–1117), Vitalis of Savigny (†1122), and Norbert of Xanten (c. 1082–1134). Peter Waldo and his followers, it will be recalled, also began their work as itinerant preachers of the Gospel but their preaching later took an heretical turn and was condemned. A similar fate befell the Humiliati, an Italian apostolic movement comprised of both lay and clerical elements, but unlike the Waldensians, the Humiliati were reconciled to the Church in 1201 by Innocent III.

The wave of itinerant preachers of the Gospel that characterized the twelfth and thirteenth centuries certainly contributed to and influenced the rise of the mendicant orders such as the Franciscans and the Dominicans. These orders incorporated and enlarged upon the evangelical ideal that motivated the earlier apostolic movements. As such they emphasized evangelical preaching within the context of a personal and communal life of poverty and penance. The preaching mission which was characteristic of these new religious orders was especially directed to the pastoral needs of the new social classes resulting from the revival of trade and commerce and the consequent renewal of urban life. The constitutional structures of the mendicant orders, therefore, reflected new institutional formulations of the *vita apostolica*.

Francis himself, however, did not use the term *vita apostolica* but preferred instead the term *vita Christi* as the model upon which his order was to be founded and governed. This preference, however, must not be seen as representing a radical difference from previous apostolic movements since Francis' own life and that of his order were also primarily concentrated on preaching the Gospel in the context of penance and poverty. What Francis effectively does is to establish his model of poverty more on the poverty of Christ than on that of the apostles and disciples. Even here, however, there is no complete disjunction since the poverty of the apostles and disciples was essentially that mandated by Christ.

Even with regard to his use of the term *vita Christi*, Francis' differences with previous apostolic movements must not be exaggerated but should be seen as representing a different degree of emphasis. As preachers of the Gospel, previous apostolic movements obviously emphasized the person and life of Christ as a model, but with Francis it was the nature, degree and intensity of that imitation, especially its great stress on the concrete historical dimensions and experiences of Christ's life, that distinguished his concept of the mendicant life. Finally, it should be noted that along with the *vita Christi* the term *vita apostolica* reappears in the writings of later Franciscan writers such as Thomas of Celano, Julian of Speyer, Hugh of Digne, and others. In the late Middle Ages, especially with the Spiritual Franciscan movement, the notion of both the *vita apostolica* and the *vita Christi* were more closely associated with a much more rigorous interpretation of poverty. Such an association was especially seen in the writings of Peter Olivi, Angelo of Clareno, and Ubertino of Casale.

Finally, coming even closer to d'Ailly's own time and territory, the movement of the Brethren of the Common Life can also be said to reflect a return to the *vita apostolica* but more in the earlier monastic context of the term with its emphasis on the internal life of the community, that is, a common life lived in the spirit of simplicity, humility, charity, individual and communal poverty, a strict personal asceticism and prayer life, and some form of physical or intellectual labor. Here too, as with the Franciscans, while the *vita apostolica* provided the model for their communal life and endeavors, it was the *vita Christi* which served as the personal model for the spiritual and moral growth and development of its members.

Having seen the varying and detailed manner in which the model of the *vita apostolica* evolved during the early Christian and medieval periods, one naturally asks how precisely d'Ailly's views on the *vita apostolica* fit into this history. While a comparison with regard to the specific dimensions of his understanding of the apostolic model must await the fuller analysis of his program of episcopal reform which will follow, several general conclusions can be advanced at the present time. First of all, it is clear that d'Ailly understands the *vita apostolica* primarily in its more active and pastoral context of preaching, teaching, and the administration of the sacraments. Not being a monk or a canon regular but a member of the secular clergy, d'Ailly would not be personally concerned with the *vita apostolica* in its earlier and more monastic and community-centered context.

What is especially distinctive of d'Ailly's general approach to the renewal of the *vita apostolica* in his time is the fact that he not only was concerned with the reform of the episcopal office but also that he assigned to that office a leading role in the renewal of the Church. Obviously the office of the bishop was always seen as a central feature in the pastoral and administrative running of the Church. The pastoral model of the bishop was clearly established in the writings of the Fathers of the Church and best exemplified in Gregory the Great's *Regula Pastoralis*, which exercised considerable influence throughout the Middle Ages. One of the major goals of the Gregorian Reformers in the eleventh and twelfth centuries was to secure the freedom of the episcopal office from the limitations imposed upon it by its incorporation into the feudal structures of the time, especially its dependency upon the secular authorities. The reforms of Innocent III (1198–1216) and the Fourth Lateran Council (1215) also did much to revive the pastoral ideal and effectiveness of the episcopacy. While all these movements did much to reform, renew, and sustain the episcopal office in its pastoral and administrative dimensions, none of them emphasized the episcopacy as a principle agent in the reform of the Church to the degree that d'Ailly did.

In d'Ailly's own time, it is true that his former student, Jean Gerson, was also greatly concerned with the reform of the episcopacy, but he did not stress as much as d'Ailly did the leadership of the episcopacy in the overall reform of the Church. Gerson also presents his program of episcopal reform primarily within the Platonic ideological context of the triple powers of the soul and the Pseudo-Dionysian notion of hierarchy and hierarchical activity. With its emphasis upon the *vita apostolica*, d'Ailly's thought on the nature of episcopal office and his program of episcopal reform unfolds in a more directly biblical context.

The biblical dimension of d'Ailly's views on the episcopal office is also seen in the fact that he frequently refers to that office in terms of a vocation modeled closely upon Christ's call to his apostles and disciples. In one of his sermons before a synod of his clergy in the diocese of Cambrai, d'Ailly sees the Scriptures as presenting a triple call or vocation for Christians. The first call is to eternal beatitude in heaven. The second he describes in terms of a call to personal justification and sanctification while still on earth. The third vocation is presented in terms of a call to ecclesiastical office. Such an office, according to d'Ailly, has a twofold dimension. It must provide first of all for the pastoral care of those under its jurisdiction and secondly for the efficient administration of the finances and institutions committed to its care.[11] It is therefore the primary function of those called to the office of prelates to so provide for the pastoral care and administrative needs of those under their jurisdiction that they may be aided in effectively responding to their call to personal justification and holiness and in turn realize their ultimate vocation to eternal beatitude. While the immediate context of d'Ailly's synodal sermon would indicate that he is addressing his remarks to the priests of his diocese, there can be no doubt that his reflections on ecclesiastical office are equally applicable to bishops and then even more so.

3. *Specific Areas of Pastoral Reform*

After surveying d'Ailly's general critique of the status of prelates in the Church of his day and his call for their return to the original ideal of their apostolic vocation, it will help to take a closer look at some of the specific areas that were part of that critique as well as the spe-

[11] *Sermo in synodo cameracensi,*, TS, 1. 'Qua in re illud nobis in primis notandum est quod in sacris eloquiis divinisque scripturis triplex legitur vocatio. Prima est ad beatificam retributionem. Secunda est ad gratificam iustificationem. Tertia est ad ecclesiasticam administrationem.'

cific reform proposals advanced by him to correct the problems enumerated. In both instances, those aspects more directly related to the office of bishops will be especially emphasized. In his treatment of the reform of ecclesiastical prelates, d'Ailly generally singled out four specific areas. The first area relates to their appointment, examination, and financial support; the second to the question of their learning; the third to their pastoral training, and the fourth to their personal virtue.[12] D'Ailly does not always follow this fourfold division in his reflection on the reform of ecclesiastical prelates, but it does nonetheless represent the major areas of his thought on this subject. Even when he uses other categories, there are considerable similarities with the above divisions. Since the relationship of personal virtue and the apostolic ideal plays such an important role in d'Ailly's views on the personal reform of ecclesiastical prelates, it will be treated in the following chapter.

With regard to the first specific area of his concern, namely, the appointment, examination, and financial provision for ecclesiastical prelates, d'Ailly concentrates first on the authorities and procedures involved in the appointment of candidates for ecclesiastical office. In this context, the two most corruptive influences d'Ailly cites are what he calls the use of tyrannical power and the closely associated phenomenon of simony. While it is not fully clear what d'Ailly meant by tyrannical power or who were the agents who wielded this power, it seems safe to conclude that he is referring primarily to the intervention of secular princes and the papacy in ecclesiastical appointments. The result of such intervention is the diminution of the apostolic ideal that should serve as the model in such selections. In this context, d'Ailly again has recourse to the passage on the good shepherd in Jn. 10:1–8, especially where Christ distinguishes between the good and bad shepherd according to whether or not one entered the sheepfold through the proper gate. In the case of bishops, the entry through the proper gate is interpreted by d'Ailly in terms of free and proper canonical election by a cathedral chapter. With regard to priests, the mode of proper entry was primarily through episcopal appointment or approval in the

---

[12] *Sermo in Synodo Cameracensi*, TS, 4. 'Sed hic diligenter advertat charitas vestra quod ut digne ambuletis tria precipue vobis sunt necessaria. Primo ut ambuletis caute per clarem et circumspectam cognitionem. Secundo ut ambuletis recte per iustam et virtuosam operationem. Tertio ut ambuletis munde per sanctam et honestam conversationem.'

case of parishes run by religious orders. Those who have not entered through the proper gate, d'Ailly designates as false pastors, thieves, and bandits.[13]

In speaking of d'Ailly's condemnation of tyrannical use of power on the part of secular princes and the papacy in the selection of candidates for ecclesiastical offices, it is important to remember that by d'Ailly's time within most dioceses the vast majority of such appointments and the benefices associated with them were in the hands of secular authorities, the papacy, religious orders, and cathedral chapters. With regard to the papacy, such intervention was generally achieved through the system of papal provisions which manifested itself in terms of papal reservations and expectancies. While a reservation gave its recipient a right to a specific vacant benefice, an expectancy was more indefinite in that it conveyed only the right to apply for the next benefice within the diocese that might become free. Regardless of the different forms of provision, specific fees were exacted for their conferral by the papal curia.[14]

Appointments made in the above context related to such offices as parish vicariates, cathedral chapters, deaneries, archdeaconries, and the episcopacy. Within d'Ailly's own diocese of Cambrai, there were six archdeaconries. The archdeaconry of Cambrai alone comprised some one hundred and sixty five parishes, yet only in two parishes did the bishop have the right to select the pastors for those parishes. Appointments in thirty three other parishes were made by the cathedral chapter and the remainder by secular and other religious institutions. Of the twelve bishops who occupied the see of Cambrai in the fourteenth century practically all but one were nominated by the pope

---

[13] *Homelia facta in Synodo Cameracensi*, TS, 2. 'Unde ergo illi qui vel symoniaca pravitate vel tyrannica potestate honores ecclesiasticos usupare praesumunt quia qui non intrant per ostium in ovile sed ascendunt aliunde, illi profecto non sunt veri pastores sed veritatis testimonio fures sunt et latrones.'

[14] For a detailed description of the origins and development of papal provisions see Stump, *The Reforms of the Council of Constance*, 77–81, and E. Delaruelle et al., *L'Eglise au temps du Grand Schisme et de la crise conciliaire*, 2 vols., Histoire de l'Eglise, 14, ed. J.B. Delaruelle and Eugène Jarry (Paris: Bloud and Gay, 1962), 1:295–313. A brief but very clear description of the various forms of papal provisions and the procedures required to obtain them can be found in Howard Kaminsky, 'Provisions, Ecclesiastical,' in *DMA*, 10:193b–194a. While the term benefice technically refers to the temporal possessions and income attached to an office, it gradually became used interchangeably with the notion of office. On ecclesiastical benefices see Joseph Strayer, 'Benefice: Ecclesiastical,' *DMA*, 2:179a-b, and the more extensive treatment by Guillaume Mollat, 'Benefices écclesiastiques en occident,' *DDC*, 2:416–428.

upon the recommendation of the King of France. In the case of the one exception, the nomination was made by the cathedral chapter. D'Ailly's own appointment as bishop of Cambrai in 1397 was made by Benedict XIII.[15] Although d'Ailly himself had profited from the prevailing system of ecclesiastical appointments and benefices, he and many of his contemporaries saw that system not only as a perversion of proper ecclesiastical order but also as a diminution of episcopal authority and pastoral effectiveness, especially in the realm of diocesan visitations and fraternal correction of the clergy. As will be seen, episcopal visitations and correction were central to d'Ailly's thought regarding episcopal and priestly reform.

Closely associated with the problems created by papal provisions was that of multiple benefices. While the holding of several benefices at one time was often fostered by financial greed, it was also occasionally necessitated by the declining economic conditions of the late Middle Ages, for only by combining benefices could one secure sufficient income for a decent living. Although d'Ailly himself held multiple benefices in his early ecclesiastical career and even though, as will be seen, he showed great concern for the impoverished condition of many ecclesiastics, later in his life he strongly condemned the practice of simultaneously holding multiple benefices, a stance clearly evident in his *De reformatione*.[16] The reasons given for this condemnation, as in the case of papal reservations, are again essentially pastoral and are to be found more explicitly treated in the third part of his *De materia concilii*. Here d'Ailly cites such harmful pastoral consequences as the impoverization of churches, the absence of qualified and learned pastors, the deprivation of liturgical services, and above all the bad example they set for the laity and clergy.[17]

As d'Ailly saw the situation, the extensive authority exercised by the papacy over ecclesiastical appointments and the attached temporal benefices was not an original dimension of papal authority. In d'Ailly's view of the Church's history, the primitive church exercised no such authority since it was a purely spiritual institution and there-

---

[15] With regard to the phenomenon and consequences of the system of provisions in d'Ailly's own diocese of Cambrai see Pierre Pierrard, ed., *Les diocèses de Cambrai et Lille*, Histoire des diocèses de France, 8 (Paris: Editions Beauchesne, 1978), 74–76, 85–88.

[16] *De reformatione*, Miethke-Weinrich, 1:350. 'Item circa statum cardinalium et aliorum ecclesiasticorum providendum esset quod deinceps non tenerent illam monstrosam et multipliciter scandalosam beneficiorum multitudinem.'

[17] *De materia concilii*, Oakley, 325.

fore devoid of temporal possessions. Only with the endowment of the Church by Constantine did the problem of temporal benefices emerge since only then did the Church possess the possessions which provided the income associated with such benefices.[18] D'Ailly maintains, nevertheless, that during the early centuries of the post-Constantinian period the Church was able to maintain a proper balance between episcopal and papal authority in the realm of ecclesiastical benefices. With the passage of time, however, abuses gradually developed in the distribution and administration of such benefices. It was to correct these abuses that the papacy assumed increasing control over ecclesiastical benefices and indeed to such an extent that d'Ailly claimed that by his time prelates had lost the authority to confer even the smallest benefice.

Given his reluctance to regard the model of the primitive Church as an absolute norm for ecclesiastical reform, d'Ailly does not call for an end to papal influences in ecclesiastical appointments but rather a return to the situation that existed in the early post-Constantinian period which, as seen above, was characterized by a proper balance between papal and episcopal authority in the distribution of ecclesiastical benefices. If that earlier balance should prove to be unattainable, d'Ailly called for, at least, 'a tolerable moderation,' in papal authority over ecclesiastical benefices.[19]

As seen earlier, the practice of simony also contributed to the difficulty of appointing qualified candidates to ecclesiastical office. D'Ailly's strong attack against simony with regard to the episcopal and priestly offices manifested itself in his early years as bishop of Cambrai and was reflected in his sermon at the diocesan synod of 1398. However, in his

---

[18] For d'Ailly's views on the nature of the primitive church and the consequences of the Constantinian Donation see his *De materia concilii*, Oakley, 259–261. While d'Ailly's ideas on the primitive church are not as extensive as Gerson's, he does share many of his views on the subject. Like Gerson, he accepts the Donation of Constantine as both authentic and valid. Together with Gerson, he also holds that while the primitive church represented a privileged period in the Church's history, its example should not become an absolute norm for the post-Constantinian Church, thereby prohibiting subsequent and valid developments in the Church's structure and government. Such attitudes towards the Donation placed Gerson and d'Ailly at odds with some reformers of the high and late medieval Church, especially reformers such as Wyclif and Hus who saw in the Donation the beginning of the Church's decline because of its excessive involvement in material and temporal matters. For a full discussion of Gerson's views on the primitive Church see Louis B. Pascoe, 'Jean Gerson: The Ecclesia Primitiva and Reform,' *Traditio*, 30 (1974), 379–409.

[19] *De materia concilii*, Oakley, 261.

De materia concilii, written in 1402/1403, d'Ailly's thinking on the subject reflects a more compromising assessment of the problem. He now recognizes that long established and deeply engrained practice of simony might necessitate some modification in canonical legislation regarding simony, especially legislation that nothing should be given or received for ordination or for the granting of the pallium in the case of archbishops.[20] He also extends his moderating views concerning financial matters related to the administration of the sacraments, burials, and other activities associated with the office of prelates.[21] In this context, he remarks that legislation regarding such matters reflects not so much evangelical precepts but rather counsels and therefore should not be enforced with legalistic rigor.

While d'Ailly was concerned with the issue of simony as related to the conferral of offices or the administration of the sacraments, he was even more concerned about the canonical status of prelates who obtained their office through simony. On this point, he was especially disturbed by the harmful pastoral consequences which resulted from the failure of such prelates to regularize their situation. Canonical legislation in such cases normally called for interdiction, suspension, or removal from office. The primary canonical argument used by d'Ailly for requesting a modification in legislation regarding such prelates was essentially the legal principle of *necessitas*.[22] In this context, he cites a decree of Nicholas II (1058–1061) who, recognizing the prevalence of simony in the Church of his day, sadly came to the conclusion that it was impossible to maintain the full rigor of canonical legislation in this area. The necessity of the times, Nicholas argued, required some

---

[20] *De materia concilii*, Oakley, 332. 'Item, si obstante consuetudine non placet servare illam rigorosam regulam contra simoniam … ut nihil pro ordinatione aut pallio detur vel accipiatur … saltem super his esset aliqua moderatio adhibenda.'

[21] *De materia concilii*, Oakley, 332. That d'Ailly was very knowledgeable regarding canonical legislation on simony is seen in his reference to Gregory I's teaching on simony as contained in the *Decretum*, C. 1, q. 1, c. 27 and subsequent canonical legislation as contained in C. 1, q. 1–3, especially C. 1, q. 1, c. 107–110.

[22] The scriptural sources upon which medieval canonists built their notion of *necessitas* were Mk. 2:25–25 and Mt. 12:1–8. In these passages the Pharisees charge that Christ's disciples were working on the sabbath since they were picking grain to eat. In response to their charge, Christ states that since his disciples were hungry and in need of food their actions did not constitute a violation of the Sabbath laws. On the notion of *necessitas* in medieval canon law see Gaines Post, *Studies in Medieval Legal Thought* (Princeton: Princeton University Press, 1964), 21, 318, and Stephan Kuttner, *Kanonistische Schuldlehre von Gratian bis auf die Dekretalen Gregors IX* (Vatican City: Vatican Press, 1935), 291–298. For Gerson's understanding and use of *necessitas*, see Pascoe, *Jean Gerson*, 73–74.

form of dispensation from existing laws which would at least permit simoniacally consecrated bishops to retain their office.[23]

D'Ailly calls for a similar form of declaration in his time to allow such prelates to continue to exercise their pastoral office. Only by such legal accommodation can peace of conscience be restored to those prelates tainted by simony. Finally, he also argues that only by some mitigation in canonical legislation can the scandal created in the laity by the difference between canonical legislation and actual practice be removed.[24] That d'Ailly's call for canonical moderation on the issue of simony remained a constant in his thought is seen in his inclusion of the same recommendations in his *De reformatione* written at the time of the Council of Constance.[25]

D'Ailly's critique of the prevailing situation regarding the appointment of ecclesiastical prelates, especially bishops, even extended to recommending the elimination of certain ranks within the ecclesiastical hierarchy which he regarded as superfluous. On this point it should be noted that the norm he uses in calling for their elimination is essentially pastoral. With regard to the episcopacy, d'Ailly calls for the elimination of titular bishops, that is, bishops created and assigned sees that no longer exist, especially sees in territories in the East which had been overrun by the Arabs. To create someone as bishop without an actual group of persons under his pastoral care is for d'Ailly not only a foolish course of action but also one that detracts from the episcopal state, for it separates what it most distinctive of the episcopal office, namely pastoral care, from the office itself.[26]

Another ecclesiastical office that d'Ailly considers for possible elimination is that of archdeacon, an office that emerged in the third century when the archdeacon appears as head of the deacons within a diocese. By the ninth century the archdeacon had assumed extensive powers in

---

[23] *De materia concilii*, Oakley, 332. While d'Ailly speaks of the decree of Pope Nicholas 'in synodo Constantianae,' Oakley has shown that the decree is that of Nicholas II as promulgated at the Lateran Synod of 1061. For the text of the decree see J.D. Mansi, *Sacrorum conciliorum nova et amplissima collectio* (Florence-Venice, 1757–1798), 19:899 and for the context of the decree, Hefele-Leclercq, *Histoire des conciles* (Paris: 1907), 4:1169.

[24] *De materia concilii*, Oakley, 332–333. '... saltem super his esset aliqua moderatio adhibenda, et pro conscientiarum sedatione, et multitudini errantium pie condescendo ... Similiter etiam eadem vel majori ratione permissio et condescensio facienda esset super pluribus aliis juribus et constitutionibus quae communiter in scandalum plurimorum non servantur ...'

[25] *De reformatione*, Miethke-Weinrich, 1:358–360.

[26] *De reformatione*, Miethke-Weinrich, 1:356.

assisting the bishop in the exercise of his pastoral duties, especially in the realms of liturgy, clerical discipline, and the administration of ecclesiastical property. As the Middle Ages progressed archdeacons became increasingly powerful within dioceses and often transgressed upon episcopal authority.[27] By the late Middle Ages many of the larger dioceses had several archdeacons with each assigned a specific geographical area within the diocese. As indicated earlier, in d'Ailly's time, the diocese of Cambrai had six archdeacons. By the end of the Middle Ages, however, archdeacons had usurped many of the bishop's pastoral functions.[28]

D'Ailly was aware of the historical evolution of the archdeacon's office and the fact that its original role was to serve as an aid to the bishop in the execution of his pastoral office. Concerned, however, with the increasing power of the archdeacon's office in the later Middle Ages, d'Ailly asserts that archdeacons should perform their duties in accordance with the guidelines established in canon law.[29] If they do not do so and thereby become a burden to the Church, then, he maintains that their office should be abolished. He finds a parallel for such a course of action in the Church's elimination of the office of the chorbishop in the twelfth century.[30] D'Ailly's highly critical attitude toward the archdiaconate may have been the result of his personal

---

[27] *De reformatione*, Miethke-Weinrich, 1:368. For the historical evolution of the archdeacon's office within the Church see A. Amanieu, 'Archdiacre,' *DDC*, 1:948–1004. See also A. Gréa, 'Essai historique sur les archdiacres,' *BEC*, 12 (1851), 39–67, 215–247, and A.H. Thompson, 'Diocesan Organization in the Middle Ages, Archdeacons and Rural Deans,' in *PBA*, 29 (1943), 153–194.

[28] Pierrard, *Cambrai et Lille*, 91. Pierraud also emphasizes that in the late Middle Ages bishops increasingly appointed vicar generals in their dioceses as a means of circumventing powerful archdeacons. While the office of archdeacon was generally a permanent benefice, that of vicar general was not necessarily such and was generally held at the will of the bishop. For the role of archdeacons and vicars general in the Diocese of Cambrai see also Maillard-Luypaert, *Paupauté, clercs et laics: Le diocese de Cambrai*, 94–95. A map of the archdeaconaries of Cambrai can also be found at the end of this work (Figure 1).

[29] *De reformatione*, Miethke-Weinrich, 1:368. In referring to D. 13 in Gratian's *Decretum* as the canonical source on the duties of archdeacons, d'Ailly appears to have erred since this distinction does not treat of the archdeaconate. It seems more likely that he intended to refer to the *Decretales* of Gregory IX, especially X, 1, 23 since all the chapters in this title deal with the archdeacon's office.

[30] *De reformatione*, Miethke-Weinrich, 1:368. Chorbishops appeared in the eastern Church around the second or third centuries and in the West about the fifth century. They served primarily as auxiliaries for the bishops in rural and missionary territories of their dioceses. Their attempts to expand their authority were increasingly seen as a threat to that of the bishops and their office was gradually abolished in the twelfth

experience as Bishop of Cambrai but there is no direct evidence to this effect. Nonetheless, he clearly reflects the increasing criticism in many areas of the Church of his time with regard to the archdeacon's office, especially its incursions upon and usurpation of episcopal authority.

While the papal prerogatives in the appointment to the office of the cardinalate were clearly recognized by d'Ailly, he nonetheless had some criticisms related to the appointment process. His first criticism related to the excessive number of cardinals appointed. On this point, his argument rested primarily upon the heavy financial burdens that such numbers placed upon the Church. D'Ailly also criticized the papacy for failing to be aware of the need for greater geographical diversity in the appointment of cardinals. Too often large numbers of cardinals have been chosen from one kingdom, nation, or province with the result that in the selection of popes they regard the papal office almost as an hereditary possession of their country. Given the high percentage of French cardinals appointed since the beginning of the Avignon papacy, especially cardinals from the Limousin area, d'Ailly is rather courageous in attacking a prevailing custom so favorable to his own country.

In his call for the selection of cardinals from more diversified geographical areas, d'Ailly goes so far as to indicate that there should be one cardinal from each ecclesiastical province. Geographical diversity in the composition of the college of cardinals, he argues, would bring to the attention of the Roman Church the diversity of cultures and customs within it and better enable it to provide for the spiritual direction of its members. While d'Ailly's recommendations concerning the selection of cardinals were first made in his *De materia concilii*, written in 1402/1403 while he was still Bishop of Cambrai, his views on the subject remained essentially unchanged after he became cardinal as can be seen in his *De reformatione* of 1416.[31]

After discussing the factors that had a negative impact on ecclesiastical appointments as well as delineating those offices to be eliminated or modified, d'Ailly next turns his attention to the type of per-

---

century. Many of their duties were assumed by the archdeacons. Cf. Jacques Leclef, 'chorévêque,' *DDC*, 3:686–695.

[31] *De materia concilii*, Oakley, 323, and *De reformatione*, Miethke-Weinrich, 1:348. The charge that the cardinals of one nation had almost come to regard the papacy as the hereditary possession of their nation was also made by d'Ailly in his first letter to John XXIII, written shortly after he had been raised to the rank of cardinal in 1411. Cf. Dupin, 2:882–883.

sons who should be appointed to ecclesiastical office, especially the episcopacy. He begins his analysis, however, by citing the type of persons who should not be selected. Too many such persons had indeed already been promoted to the office of bishop. In this context, he condemns the elevation of young persons who have not attained the proper canonical age for holding such offices. Also to be avoided are those who are carnal and devoid of spiritual sensitivity, as well as those who have been deficient in their ecclesiastical duties. On the financial and legal side, d'Ailly criticizes those candidates who would impose heavy service and financial obligations on their peoples or become overly involved in litigation. Finally, he singles out those who were notorious for their lifestyle, especially those who frequented indecent public shows and sumptuous banquets. D'Ailly also criticizes the appointment of nobles, foreigners, lawyers, and officials of both secular and ecclesiastical curias. The appointment of such persons, d'Ailly maintains, has especially characterized the policy of the Roman Curia in its distribution of ecclesiastical benefices.[32] With regard to ecclesiastical appointments, it is important to recall that d'Ailly cited the selection and promotion of unworthy persons and the bypassing of better qualified candidates as one of the apocalyptic signs associated with the persecution of the Church in its final days.[33]

To avoid the appointment of unworthy candidates such as those described above, especially for the offices of major prelates such as bishops, d'Ailly calls for a more conscientious approach toward the examination process for candidates to ecclesiastical office. This examination, he continues, must be conducted with the greatest diligence and detail. In such an examination, moreover, it is not sufficient that nothing be said against the candidate but rather that the integrity of his life and his possession of the appropriate qualifications be clearly demonstrated.[34] In appointments to all ecclesiastical benefices, emphasis must be placed on selecting the learned and the wise, those of mature age as well as those who know the customs and language of the people who have been entrusted to their pastoral care. Above all preference must be given to those whose personal lives are not only beyond reproach but

---

[32] *De reformatione*, Miethke-Weinrich, 1:366.
[33] *Epistola ad Johannem XXIII, I*, Dupin 2:878. Speaking of the signs prefiguring the arrival of the Antichrist, d'Ailly says: 'Sextum signum est promotio indignorum et vilipensio meliorum.'
[34] *De reformatione*, Miethke-Weinrich, 1:356.

also reflect full conformity with the ideals of the *vita apostolica*. D'Ailly's strong conviction as to the need to appoint qualified personnel to ecclesiastical offices is seen in his call for the Council of Constance to establish stricter guidelines for the conferral of ecclesiastical benefices.[35]

D'Ailly concludes his analysis of the first specific area related to the reform of the office of ecclesiastical prelates by discussing the issue of their financial and material needs. In this context, one of the greatest obstacles was that of the heavy papal taxation associated with their respective offices. While all forms of papal taxation had become more burdensome in the late Middle Ages, the ones that generated the most criticism, especially among late medieval reformers, were annates and services. Annates were taxes that were levied upon lesser benefices and were generally calculated in terms equal to the first full year's taxable revenue. Services were fees paid on the occasion of nomination, confirmation, or translation to major appointments such as abbacies and bishoprics and were generally equivalent to one third of the first year's taxable revenue.

Other forms of papal taxation included tenths, procurations, spoils, and vacancies. Tenths was a form of clerical income tax paid to the papacy at times of great financial need such as the organization of a crusade or the defense of the papal states. Procurations were related to taxes levied by bishops and lesser prelates on the occasion of visitations. Papal dispensations from the obligation to perform such visitations while still collecting the associated taxes could be obtained by payment of established fees. Spoils related to the right to seize the personal property of a deceased bishop. Finally, vacancies involved the right of the papacy to collect income from vacant benefices under papal jurisdiction.[36]

Many reformers saw the payment of annates and services as well as the other forms of papal taxation as thinly disguised forms of simony.[37] D'Ailly, however, did not share this opinion. While, as seen earlier,

---

[35] *De reformatione*, Miethke-Weinrich, 1:366.

[36] For a brief but very clear analysis of the various forms of papal taxation and the general reaction to such taxation in the late Middle Ages see George Mollat, *The Popes at Avignon*, 9th ed. (London: Thomas Nelson, 1963), 319–334. A more detailed analysis of papal income in the late Middle Ages can be found in Jean Favier, *Les finances pontificales à l'époque du Grand Schisme d'Occident* (Paris: E. de Boccard, 1966).

[37] On the association of papal annates, services, and fees with simony see Stump, *The Reforms of the Council of Constance*, 72–75; 121; 131–132; 188–205. In this context, the authority of Aquinas was frequently invoked, especially *ST*, 2, 2, q. 100, a. 1, ad 7. This entire question is dedicated to the issue of simony.

he recognized the biblical injunction against simony, he also believed that the legal opinion which saw many forms of papal taxation as a subtle form of simony did not have a foundation in divine law but rather only in positive law and therefore capable of moderation.[38] His reaction may also have involved an element of personal concern due to the fact that curial cardinals received some of their income from such forms of papal taxation. In his *De potestate ecclesiastica*, written for the Council of Constance and publicized on October 1, 1416 while he was still a member of the first reform commission, d'Ailly urges the council fathers to recognize that the cardinals had the right to receive their portion of the papal taxes levied against ecclesiastics of lower rank.[39] Finally, it must be said that d'Ailly's views with regard to papal and other forms of ecclesiastical taxation were due to the biblically inspired belief that the laborer deserved his keep and on the application of this belief to the realm of papal taxation, he cites the authority of Aquinas. As seen earlier, provision for the material needs of ecclesiastical prelates was also an integral part of d'Ailly's interpretation of the *vita apostolica*.[40]

While d'Ailly refuses to regard the various forms of papal taxation as simoniacal transactions, he does recognize that the issue of excessive taxation was one of the major complaints against the papacy and the Roman Curia. To mitigate the burdens of excessive papal taxation, d'Ailly does present a series of reform proposals.[41] In his first proposal, he stresses that the pope and curial cardinals should adopt a more moderate lifestyle. Such a course of action, he maintains, would not only lessen the financial burdens of the clergy and laity, but would also set an excellent example of modesty. Secondly, in what appears to be a rather drastic overhaul of the prevailing system of papal finances, d'Ailly recommends the establishment of a fixed but reasonable budget for the operation of the papal and curial offices. The funds for such a budget would be obtained by a system of taxation imposed on dioceses

---

[38] In both the *De materia concilii*, Oakley, 332, and the *De reformatione*, Miethke-Weinrich, 1:358, d'Ailly refers to the rigorous interpretation of the law against simony as 'a jure humano imposita,' and therefore capable of some moderation.

[39] *De potestate ecclesiastica*, Dupin, 2:946–947.

[40] For the biblical sources of d'Ailly's thought on this issue see Mt. 10:10, Lk. 10:7, and 1 Tim. 5:18. The reference to Aquinas is to *ST*, 2, 2, q. 87, a. 4, ad 3.

[41] D'Ailly's recommendations for reducing the burdens of papal taxation can be found in his *De materia concilii*, Oakley, 324–325, and in his *De reformatione*, Miethke-Weinrich, 1:350.

in proportion to their size and wealth. Requests for money beyond the fixed terms would, however, require the approval of a General Council. The third recommendation made by d'Ailly as a means to lessen the burdens of papal and curial taxation was that of reducing the number of cardinals, a favorite theme of d'Ailly even after he himself became a cardinal.

Having seen the extensive nature of d'Ailly's reform proposals with regard to the proper selection, examination, and taxation of prelates, the question naturally arises as to what extent those proposals were received and acted on by the Council of Constance. While certainly only one of the many proponents for reform at the Council, d'Ailly ranked among the more important ones not only because of his ecclesiastical rank and theological expertise but also because he served on the first reform commission appointed by the Council. D'Ailly's reform proposals with regard to papal provisions met with some success in the deliberations of the Council of Constance and in the concordats with the German, French, English and Spanish nations.[42] His call for a 'tolerable moderation' in papal control over appointments to ecclesiastical benefices met with greater success than his more radical proposal for the overhaul of papal and curial finances. While the existing system of reservations and expectancies was left essentially intact, the number of offices subject to papal reservations was limited. Exemptions from expectancies were granted in the case of major offices related to cathedral and collegiate churches, priories, and deaneries. As for offices still subject to expectancies, the bishops acquired the right of appointing to major offices on an alternating basis with the papacy (*jus alternativum*).

---

[42] For the reform decrees of the Council of Constance see the decrees of the thirty ninth and forty third sessions, ratified on October 9, 1417 and March 21, 1418 respectively in Norman Tanner, ed., *Decrees of the Ecumenical Councils* (Washington, D.C.: Sheed and Ward and Georgetown University Presses, 1990), 1:438–443, 447–450. Hereafter cited as *DEC*. The Latin texts on the pages opposite the English translations are those from the edition of Giuseppe Alberigo et al., *Conciliorum Oecumenicorum Decreta*, 3rd. ed., (Bologna: Istituto per le Scienze Religiose, 1973). The texts of the concordats with the English, German, French, and Spanish nations can be found in Angelo Mercati, ed., *Raccolta di concordati su materie ecclesiastiche tra la Santa Sede e le autorità civili*, 2 vols. (Vatican City: Vatican Press, [1954], 1:144–168. The concordats for the German, French, and English Nations can also be found in Miethke-Weinrich, *Quellen zur Kirchenreform*, 1:516–545. The most comprehensive study of the reforms of Constance remains that of Stump, *The Reforms of Constance*. The following survey of the reforms of Constance as they relate to papal provisions and fiscal demands relies heavily on the

In the realm of fiscal reforms, the Council certainly did not envision the radical reforms proposed by d'Ailly but it did abolish papal fiscal impositions in such areas as procurations, spoils, and vacancies. The more controversial issues of annates and services were left for the concordats and greatest success in these areas was achieved in the French Concordat where services for major offices were reduced by one half. In the case of minor offices, annates were abolished for low income benefices. Annates were also abolished for benefices subject to papal expectancies. On the issue of simony, the Council appears not to have adopted d'Ailly's policy of 'tolerable moderation,' for it decreed that persons involved in future simoniacal ordinations would be punished by immediate suspension from all orders. Simoniacal provisions, elections, postulations, and confirmations were declared null and void and the parties involved excommunicated. To avoid the taint of simony, the French Concordat provided that annates were to be paid only after the peaceful possession of an office.

The concordats also addressed the problem of holding multiple benefices. Agreement was reached on the issue of pluralism primarily with regard to major prelates, especially cardinals who, through holding benefices *in commendam*, i.e., receiving the income from a benefice without actually holding the title, escaped existing legislative prohibitions on plurality of benefices. In the various concordats, major prelates agreed to give up *in commendam* holdings in exchange for adequate compensation. For the future, benefices which could be held *in commendam* were considerably restricted and their pastoral obligations more clearly defined.

With regard to the reduction in the number of cardinals and the need for diversity in their selection, d'Ailly's proposals were probably more influential than the other aspects of his reform program. The following stipulations were common to most concordats. First the number of cardinals was to be normally restricted to twenty four, and secondly, this number was to be distributed proportionately among the different parts of Christendom. This latter stipulation was appended not only out of a desire for equality but also for pastoral reasons, namely, that

---

third and fourth chapters of this work. Shorter but still incisive analysis of the reforms of Constance can be found in Walter Brandmüller's magisterial history of that Council: *Das Konzil von Konstanz, 1414–1418*. 2 vols. (Paderborn: Ferdinand Schöningh, 1991–1997), 2:67–95, 335–358, 388–397.

the needs and concerns of all areas of Christendom might be made known to the pope and the Roman Curia.[43]

As will be recalled, the second specific area of d'Ailly's critique and reform proposals with regard to ecclesiastical prelates related to their education and learning. Given d'Ailly's own educational background and administrative experience at the University of Paris, it is not surprising that the question of learning would be of great importance to him in his reflections on ecclesiastical office. Early in his career, in a sermon delivered before the Parisian synod of 1375, d'Ailly strongly criticized the prelates of his day for their overall lack of learning. Despite this deficiency, he maintained, many do not hesitate to assume pastoral office and to teach what they themselves have not learned. They underestimate the weighty obligations of their pastoral office, precisely because they know so little about the very nature of that office.[44]

Looked at more closely, it is the lack of learning in the realm of scripture and theology that d'Ailly so strongly criticizes in the prelates of his day.[45] As will be seen in a later chapter, the terms 'scripture' (*scriptura*), 'theology' (*theologia*), and 'divine wisdom' (*sapientia divina*) are often used interchangeably by d'Ailly. In a Septuagesima Sunday sermon delivered in 1388, d'Ailly restates his critique of prelates' ignorance of scripture and theology. Not only have prelates neglected such studies, he contends, but they also often despise them. *Divina sapientia* is often described by such prelates as *stultitia*, and *sacra theologia* as *stultilogia*.[46] If there is any discussion about scripture and theology among such prelates at Paris, it is between drinks at banquets. Such prelates belch

---

[43] Concordat agreements on the number and geographical diversification of cardinals are most clearly seen in the case of the French Concordat. The Spanish and German Concordats contained practically similar texts. The text on these issues in the English Concordat was considerably truncated but contained the essential reform goals. Cf. Mercati, *Raccolta di Concordati*, 1:145, 151, 158, and 165.

[44] *Sermo in Synodo in Ecclesia Parisiensi*, Tschackert, 6. 'Sunt enim hodie plurimi ignorantes penitus et ignari, qui pastorale magisterium temere suscipere non verentur ... Sunt etiam plerique qui, dum metiri se nesciunt, quae non didiscerunt docere concupiscunt et pondus magisterii tanto levius aestimant quanto vim magnitudinis illius non agnoscunt.' The fact that d'Ailly would be called upon to address a Parisian synod at such an early stage in his career, indeed, six years before he received the doctorate in theology, is an indication of the high respect he enjoyed in Parisian circles. A year earlier, he had spoken to the bishop and clergy at Amiens, also gathered in synod.

[45] *Invectiva Ezechielis contra pseudopastores*, Tschackert, 14. 'Nullum iis sacrae scripturae studium, nullum divinae sapientiae colloquium.' Almost identical phrases are expressed in d'Ailly other works. Cf. his *Sermo de beato Bernardo*, Tschackert, 22.

[46] *Sermo in Dominica Septuagesima*, TS, 12.

out their words on these subjects more from a full stomach rather than from a mind disciplined by fasting.[47] These are harsh words indeed but ones which can be partially explained by the fact that they were written about the time that d'Ailly received his doctorate in theology (1381) and so represent his youthful ardor. The main point of d'Ailly's message, however, the neglect and indeed depreciation of scriptural and theological learning among prelates, remained a constant complaint throughout his life.

In d'Ailly's mind, an important consequence of the neglect of theological studies among ecclesiastical prelates was the low esteem that so many prelates had of theologians. Many prelates, he argued, even had contempt for theologians, regarding them as useless workers in the Lord's vineyards. As a result of this attitude, prelates were often reluctant to support the appointment of theologians to ecclesiastical benefices.[48] Lawyers, curial officials, and secretaries of temporal lords were often preferred to doctors of theology. This attitude and policy, d'Ailly maintained, was especially characteristic of the Roman Curia. Because of its contempt for theologians, the Roman Curia in the distribution of ecclesiastical benefices has consistently preferred clerics trained in canon law to those trained in theology. The Roman Curia, d'Ailly argues, has again and again shown its preference for the 'lucrative sciences' (*scientiae lucrativae*), the derisive phrase coined by university theologians to describe the fields of medicine and law.[49]

D'Ailly's views on the above matters reflect the long standing professional tensions between theologians and canon lawyers that often characterized medieval university life, especially since the time of the Avignon papacy when the distribution of ecclesiastical benefices became increasingly concentrated in papal hands. In d'Ailly's view, curial preference for university candidates with legal training has resulted in the matriculation of an increasing number of the secular clergy in the law faculties rather than in the faculty of theology. As a consequence of

---

[47] *Invectiva Ezechielis contra pseudopastores*, Tschackert, 14. '… quia si forte de sacris theologicis scripturis Parisii aliquid murmurabant, hoc inter epulas, hoc inter poculas, hoc inter coenas et prandia, hoc non jejuna mente sed ventre saturo ructabant …' The highly critical imagery used by d'Ailly is borrowed from the Roman satirist, Persius (34–62 A.D.), Satire 1:30–31.

[48] *Sermo in Dominica Septuagesima*, TS, 12. '… quia sacrae scripturae doctores nec fovent nec promovent sed deprimunt potius et contemnunt, ipsosque tamquam vineae domini penitus inutiles otiosos relinquunt.'

[49] *De reformatione*, Miethke-Weinrich, 1:366–368.

this trend, the number of secular masters in the faculty of theology had become considerably less than the number from the mendicant orders.[50] As will be seen in subsequent chapters, these tensions between theologians and lawyers in the medieval universities also generated considerable debate as to the nature and value of their respective disciplines. Much speculative effort was often spent in analyzing the respective contributions of these disciplines to the life and well-being of the Church. Quodlibetal disputations in the universities often centered on the question of whether the Church would be better governed by a theologian or by a canon lawyer.

For the present, however, suffice it to say that d'Ailly saw theological studies as central to the apostolic mission of ecclesiastical prelates, especially bishops. Indeed, he identified the principle obligation of the bishop's office with that of teaching and preaching the Gospel and for him the most effective way to prepare oneself for the exercise of these duties was that of theological study.[51] He strongly asserts, moreover, that this endeavor entails the study of both the Old and New Testaments. He illustrates this need to study both testaments by reference to that part of the liturgical ceremony for the consecration of bishops where the consecrating bishop asks the bishop-to-be whether he knows both testaments and as a symbol of that knowledge and the apostolic obligation to teach and preach it, the book of the Scriptures is placed on the new bishop's neck and shoulders.[52] Should the new bishop give a false response to this most important question, he is,

---

[50] *De reformatione*, Miethke-Weinrich, 1:364. '... cum nimis multi seculares hodie studeant in litium facultate. Ipsa quoque theologia in statu secularium paucos habeat sectores propter abusum Romanae Curiae, quae theologos contempsit et in omni ecclesiastico gradu lucrativarum scientiarum studiosos praeposuit ... .'

[51] *Utrum indoctus in jure divino*, Dupin, 2:654. '... praelati ex officio specialiter tenentur Evangelium praedicare et fidem docere atque defendere, quod non possunt sine doctrina theologicae scientiae.' A few lines earlier in this work, D'Ailly asserts, 'Patet ex hoc quod prelatus debet esse doctus in sacra scriptura cum ejus praecipuum officium sit sacram Scripturam docere et praedicare.' The scriptural sources upon which d'Ailly relies for his position are Mk. 16:15 where Christ commands the apostles to go into the world and proclaim the Gospel to every creature, and 1 Pet. 3:15 where the apostle urges Christians to be always ready to give an explanation of their belief to anyone who asks. Interestingly, while the Vulgate talks of rendering a reason for one's hope (spes), d'Ailly's text speaks of rendering a reason for one's faith (fides).

[52] *Utrum indoctus in jure divino*, Dupin, 2:654. For a brief description of the history of ordination rites in the Church see the article by Roger Reynolds, 'Ordination: Clerical,' *DMA*, 9:263–269.

according to d'Ailly, guilty of sin and indeed continues to sin in the exercise of his pastoral office as long as he fails to attain the knowledge of scripture required by that office.[53]

In order to insure that the Church be provided with bishops who possess the required knowledge of Scripture, d'Ailly clearly stipulates that preference in the nomination and appointment of bishops be given to those who have studied theology. In this context he returns to his constant theme that in the past too many episcopal appointments have been given to graduates of canon law faculties. D'Ailly's critique of the appointment of canon lawyers to episcopal sees does not mean that he is radically opposed to canonical learning, nor that he does not realize its importance in the administration of a diocese. Indeed, as will be seen in a later chapter, his own writings demonstrate a highly respectable knowledge and use of canon law. His criticism is directed more towards that type of a bishop whose total training, basic mindset, and approach to his pastoral duties is essentially legalistic.[54]

With regard to priests and the need for theological training, d'Ailly also showed considerable concern since, as successors of the disciples, they shared in the same apostolic mission as the bishops. As in the case of the bishops, d'Ailly maintains that in the appointment of priests to the more important ecclesiastical benefices preference be given to university graduates in the field of theology over those with degrees in law. Similar to his views on episcopal appointments, d'Ailly's position, however, was not an uncompromising one. While consistently urging bishops to appoint graduates from the faculty of theology to ecclesiastical benefices, he does not demand that such appointments be made exclusively from the ranks of theologians but also allows some to be made from graduates in canon law. As in the case of bishops, his opposition to candidates trained in the law, therefore, would depend on the degree to which an excessively legal mind might negatively affect their pastoral ministrations. By restricting the bishops' field of choice to theologians and pastorally orientated canonists, d'Ailly allows them

---

[53] *Utrum indoctus in jure divino*, Dupin, 2:653–654. '... non potest sine peccato praesidendi officium exercere.' It is clear, however, from the general context of d'Ailly's thought that such sin does not invalidate the bishop's sacramental actions.

[54] *De reformatione*, Miethke-Weinrich, 1:356. In his reform proposals for the episcopacy stressing that preference be given to those 'qui divinis scripturis studeant, et non scientiis practicis et litigiosis totaliter inhaereant,' the operative phrase is 'totaliter inhaereant.'

to more effectively counter the incessant requests of temporal authorities that benefices be granted to favorite but often unworthy candidates.[55]

In his emphasis upon the need to appoint university graduates, especially those trained in theology, to major ecclesiastical benefices, d'Ailly, like many of the ecclesiastical reformers of his time, seems not to be aware of the fact that the number of university graduates appointed to major ecclesiastical benefices was actually on the rise throughout Europe. During the reign of John XXII (1316–1334), twenty five percent of all papal appointments in France and Burgundy involved university graduates. In England the percentage was probably higher. Within the ranks of cathedral and collegiate chapters the percentages occasionally went over the fifty percent mark as was the case in Laon. In general, however, the majority of these appointees were still graduates in civil and canon law, a point which continues to support d'Ailly's arguments regarding ecclesiastical appointments.[56]

Despite d'Ailly's emphasis on the need to appoint university graduates, especially theologians, to higher ecclesiastical benefices, the educational needs of priests who would not be attending a university were not overlooked in his plan of educational reform for the clergy. In his *De reformatione*, he proposed a series of educational measures to ameliorate their situation and thereby render such priests more pastorally effective. First among these measures was the call for the establishment of a lectorship in theology in all cathedral and collegiate churches. This call was in effect an extension of the legislation of the Fourth Lateran Council in 1215 which mandated the appointment of a lector in theology only for metropolitan churches as a way of instructing priests in the Scriptures and other matters related to the *cura animarum*.[57]

---

[55] *De reformatione*, Miethke-Weinrich, 1:366.

[56] For a general analysis of the trend towards university appointees to ecclesiastical benefices see Peter Moraw, 'Careers of Graduates,' in *Universities in the Middle Ages*, ed. H. de Ridder-Symoens, 244–279. For the situation in England and Germany see Guy F. Lytle, 'The Careers of Oxford Students in the Later Middle Ages,' and James H. Overfield, 'University Studies and the Clergy in Pre-Reformation Germany,' in *Rebirth, Reform, and Resilience: Universities in Transition, 1300–1700*, ed. James M. Kittelson and Pamela J. Transue (Columbus: Ohio State University Press, 1984), 213–253 and 254–292. For England see also T.H. Aston et al., 'The Medieval Alumni of the University of Cambridge,' *PP*, 86 (1980), 9–86.

[57] *De reformatione*, Miethke-Weinrich, 1:368–370. The legislation of Lateran IV regarding lectureships in theology can be found in its eleventh canon. Cf. *DEC*, 1:240.

In addition to calling for an extension of Fourth Lateran's legislation with regard to lectureships in theology, d'Ailly also stressed the need for such lectors and their students to have suitable libraries at their disposal. Such libraries, he insisted, should be especially strong in theology, canon law, and ethics.[58] Long before he presented this proposal to the Council of Constance, d'Ailly, aided by a considerable financial bequest from one of the cathedral canons, had already greatly expanded the cathedral library at Cambrai.[59] His continued concern for the amelioration of library resources for the education of ecclesiastics is also seen in his bequest to his beloved College of Navarre, where he had lived and studied while a student at the University of Paris and where he had served as rector from 1383 to 1389. In a special will directed to that College, d'Ailly, after establishing funds in perpetuity to be used for the support of students in arts and theology, stipulated that whatever yearly surplus remained after such bequests was to be used for the maintenance and expansion of the College's library.[60]

In his guidelines for those teaching theology in metropolitan, cathedral, and collegiate churches, d'Ailly makes specific recommendations as to how they were to use Peter Lombard's *Sentences* in their teaching. After the Bible, the standard text for the teaching of theology throughout much of the Middle Ages was Lombard's *Sentences*. In this context, d'Ailly recommends that greater emphasis be placed on the second, third and fourth books of the *Sentences* than on the first book.[61] The first book concentrated primarily upon highly abstract issues related to the nature of God and the Trinity while the remaining books dealt with

---

[58] *De reformatione*, Miethke-Weinrich, 1:370. With regard to canon law, d'Ailly calls upon metropolitan churches to purchase a copy of what he designates as the '*magnus liber conciliorum generalium*,' a text which he describes as difficult to find yet of great value for the pastoral work of clerics. In his edition of d'Ailly's *De materia concilii*, Oakley, 266, n. 1, identifies this work as the *Pseudo-Isidorian Decretals*. Miethke-Weinrich suggest the possibility of its being William Durandus, the Younger's *Tractatus de modo celebrandi concilii generalis*.

[59] Salembier, *Le cardinal Pierre d'Ailly*, 125.

[60] Salembier, *Le cardinal Pierre d'Ailly*, 361.

[61] *De reformatione*, Miethke-Weinrich, 1:368–370. Contrary to general belief, it was the Bible that remained the basic text of medieval theological education. On this point see H. Denifle, 'Quel libre servait de base à l'enseignement des maîtres en théologie?' *RT*, 2 (1894), 149–161, and P. Mandonnet, 'Chronologie des écrits scriptuaires de Saint Thomas Aquin, 3: L'enseignement de la Bible "selon l'usage de Paris,"' *RT*, 34 (1929), 489–519. For a magisterial study of the teaching of theology at Paris in the thirteenth century see Palémon Glorieux, 'Enseignement au moyen âge: Techniques et méthodes en usage à la faculté de théologie de Paris au xiiie siècle,' *AHDL*, 35 (1968), 65–186.

the more concrete drama of salvation history with the emphasis upon creation, the fall, incarnation, redemption, sacraments, and the moral virtues. The reason for d'Ailly's recommendations was the fact that too often teachers of theology spent an excessive amount of time on the first book of the *Sentences* and thereby neglected the remaining books, which d'Ailly regarded as more directly applicable to the pastoral needs of the clergy.[62]

D'Ailly demanded more from the lectors of theology than the teaching of theology to priests. In the *De reformatione*, he indicates that he also expected them to produce several types of handbooks which would further aid in the education the clergy and facilitate their pastoral work. First of all, he requested that the lectors extract from the various books of Lombard's *Sentences* theological materials which would help priests in better understanding and preaching those Gospels and Epistles which were read in the churches throughout the liturgical year. He also called for the composition in both Latin and the vernacular of short treatises dealing with the articles of the faith, the sacraments, the manner of hearing confessions, and the vices and the virtues. These treatises, he hoped, would be at the service of priests and better help them in carrying out their pastoral duties.[63] Since many such treatises were already in existence, it is surprising that d'Ailly did not call for the adoption of some of these. Indeed, his close friend, Jean Gerson, was himself the author of several such treatises.[64]

D'Ailly's reform proposals for improving the educational level of bishops and priests had far less of an impact upon conciliar and concordat legislation at Constance than his proposals regarding ecclesiastical appointments, examinations and taxation. The question of whether or not to give preference to university graduates in appointments to major offices and benefices was extensively debated.[65] Much of the opposition

---

[62] Similar complaints were made later on with regard to the use of Aquinas' *Summa Theologiae*. Too much time, it was argued was spent on the first part of that work, with its emphasis upon the nature of God and the Trinity, and not enough time on the remaining parts dealing with the issues of Christology and the virtues involved in Christian living.

[63] *De reformatione*, Miethke-Weinrich, 1:368.

[64] For the extensive production of such manuals in late medieval England see J.C. Dickinson, *An Ecclesiastical History of England: The Later Middle Ages* (London: Adam & Charles Black, 1979), 273–278, and W.A. Pantin, *The English Church in the Fourteenth Century* (Notre Dame: University of Notre Dame Press, 1962), 189–243. For Gerson's contribution to this type of pastoral literature see Brown, *Pastor and Laity*, 50–51.

[65] For a full treatment of the movement at Constance to secure greater consideration

to such legislation came from secular rulers who saw it as a threat to their power to appoint members of the nobility to such positions who frequently did not enjoy university status. Major prelates, especially bishops, were also reluctant to espouse legislation which would guarantee the appointment of university trained persons. The opposition of bishops did not so much reflect an antagonism towards learning as such but was more the result of tensions between them and the universities over the issues of reservations and expectancies. Episcopal attempts to lessen papal control over appointments to ecclesiastical benefices in their dioceses rarely received the support of the universities who generally felt that greater opportunities for their graduates could be gained through papal provisions and expectancies than through episcopal appointments. In the end, it was only in the German Concordat that a fixed quota was established for university graduates. That concordat stipulated that one sixth of all canonries and prebends in metropolitan, cathedral and collegiate churches be set aside for university graduates. The term 'graduates,' however, included not only those who had received the doctorate but also holders of the licentiate, and even those in their final years of study.[66]

The one area where d'Ailly's preference for university graduates in appointments to ecclesiastical office did achieve a clear success was in appointments to the cardinalate. Most concordats stipulated that persons elevated to the rank of cardinal be university graduates trained in either theology or law, whether canon or civil law. Even here, however, limited exceptions could be made for nobles who were not university trained yet possessed a sufficient level of learning.[67] The long standing campaign of theological faculties, especially at Paris, to secure preferences for graduates in theology over those in law in appointment to ecclesiastical office, a campaign in which d'Ailly himself was a major force, failed to achieve any success in the deliberations and decisions leading to the final versions of the concordats. Even in the

---

of university graduates in the appointment to ecclesiastical benefices see Stump, *The Reforms of the Council of Constance*, 91–95.

[66] Mercati, *Raccolta di Concordati*, 1:159–160. The stipulation with regard to collegiate churches affected only those with over two thousand members. The reference to those who had reached the final years of their studies most likely refers to those who had reached the rank of *baccalarius formatus*.

[67] For such provisions in the Concordats for the German, French, and Spanish nations see Mercati, *Raccolta di Concordati*, 1:145, 151, 158. No such provisions were made in the English Concordat.

German Concordat which provided fixed quotas for university graduates in appointments to canonries and prebends in metropolitan, cathedral, and collegiate churches, no special preference was given to graduates in theology. Equal consideration was to be given to graduates from canon or civil law faculties. Finally, mention should be made that d'Ailly's attempts to establish minimal educational requirements for the various levels of ecclesiastical offices also proved futile as well as did his efforts to correct the negligence of examiners of candidates for ordination.

As indicated earlier, the third specific area of d'Ailly's critique and reform proposals related to ecclesiastical prelates and was primarily concerned with their pastoral ministry. In this context, one of his major concerns was that of preaching. In discussing his views on the role of teaching in the pastoral realm, d'Ailly makes clear first of all that preaching is central to the very office of a prelate.[68] This centrality, no doubt, rests on the fact that preaching was an integral dimension of the apostolic mission which Christ entrusted to his apostles and disciples and consequently to their successors, the bishops and priests. D'Ailly describes the content of this preaching in the Pauline context of 'sound doctrine' (*doctrina sana*) which he understands in the sense of doctrine which contributes to the spiritual well-being and growth of those who hear and accept it. Finally, of the highest importance is the fact that d'Ailly identifies this doctrine with the content of the Scriptures.[69] As a result of his understanding of the content of preaching, it is easy to see why d'Ailly frequently referred to the preaching of prelates as salvific in nature.[70]

D'Ailly's strongly criticizes those prelates, especially bishops, who neglect this aspect of their apostolic office. He sharply criticizes them for failing to feed their flock through preaching, especially in the realm of faith and morals. He singles out those bishops and priests who,

---

[68] *De reformatione*, Miethke-Weinrich, 1:362. '… praedicatio quae propter sui reverentiam ad prelatos pertinet … .'

[69] *De ecclesiastica potestate*, Dupin 2:925. '… doctrina sana, id est ad sanitatem animae spiritualem scilicet ad virtutem et salutem aedificativam qualis est doctrina scripturae sacrae in qua super omnem aliam doctrinam singulariter consistet vitae spiritualis virtus et salutaris sanitas animae.' The Pauline reference to 'doctrina sana,' can be found in Tit. 1:9. It should also be noted that this reference in Paul relates to the office of both bishops and priests since at this early stage the terms bishops and priests were used interchangeably.

[70] *Invectiva Ezechielis contra pseudopastores*, Tschackert, 14. The specific phrase used by d'Ailly is '*salutifera praedicatio*.'

fearing the loss of human respect, do not have the courage to speak the truth or to correct the vices of their people. He calls such bishops and priests 'pseudopastors' (*pseudopastores*) and he describes them in terms of the harsh words that the prophet Isaiah used of the spiritual leaders of Israel, 'Dumb watchdogs all, unable to bark.'[71] Like many of his contemporaries, d'Ailly is also highly critical of indulgence preachers. By their lies, he asserts, they destroy the credibility of the Church and make it a laughing stock. Moreover, they render the preaching office contemptible in the eyes of the faithful.[72]

Despite the great emphasis that d'Ailly places on preaching in the pastoral ministry of bishops and priests, it is surprising that, in his writings and in his reform proposals for Constance, he presents very few concrete proposals for its amelioration. This surprise is compounded by the fact that among the secular clergy, d'Ailly himself was one of the most outstanding preachers of his time. While constantly emphasizing that preaching concerns itself with matters of faith and morals, he has little concrete to say about the particular beliefs and moral principles that need to be emphasized in the Church of his day. Even less is said about improving the techniques of preaching, some of which, like the excessive use of exempla, allegories, metaphors, scholastic subtleties and the excessive desire to entertain, had come in for much contemporary criticism.[73] He does, however, call for a reduction in the number of indulgence preachers.[74] In the final analysis then it appears that d'Ailly is sufficiently confident that if more bishops and priests were exposed to

---

[71] *Sermo in synodo in Ecclesia Parisiensi*, Tschackert, 6. '… quique vanam mundi gloriam appetentes et laudem humanam perdere formidantes recta loqui, vera dicere, et vitia corrigere pertimescunt; quorum taciturnitatem per prophetam dominus increpat dicens: canes muti non valentes latrare,' The biblical reference is to Isa. 56:10 which from the time of Gregory the Great was often used to describe bishops and priests deficient in their duties of rooting out doctrinal error and immorality. See Gregory's *Regula Pastoralis*, 15, c. 4. This passage was incorporated into Gratian's *Decretum*, D. 43, c. 1.

[72] *De reformatione*, Miethke-Weinrich, 1:362 . 'Qui suis mendaciis et immundiciis maculant Ecclesiam et eam irrisibilem reddunt et officium praedicationis maxime honorandum jam contemtibile efficiunt.'

[73] For an excellent analysis of late medieval preaching, especially with regard to northern France, see Hervé Martin, *Le métier de prédicateur à la fin du moyen âge, 1350–1520* (Paris: Editions du Cerf, 1988). For his treatment of the positive and negative dimensions of late medieval preaching see pp. 613–627. While not equal to the quality of the mendicants, the preaching of the secular clergy is described by Martin in more positive context than is generally acknowledged by scholars. Cf. pp. 131–143.

[74] *De reformatione*, Miethke-Weinrich, 1:362.

a scripturally inspired program of theological studies at the university and cathedral school levels, the quality of preaching within the Church would vastly improve.

Although preaching enjoyed the highest priority in d'Ailly's thought on the duties of bishops and priests, there were other important activities related to their offices that were also in need of reform. In the case of bishops, especially those of metropolitan sees, regular holding of synods and conduct of visitations within their dioceses were regarded by d'Ailly as of central importance. While d'Ailly felt strongly that matters of common concern on the issue of church reform would better be left to a general council, he maintained that until such a council was convoked the reform of the Church on the local level could readily progress through the agency of provincial and diocesan synods.[75] The stress upon the need and importance of such synods further emphasizes the pastoral ideal of episcopal reform that was central to d'Ailly's thought.

In his call for the regular holding of provincial synods, d'Ailly shows himself cognizant of all the pertinent canonical legislation in Gratian's *Decretum*, especially D. 18. He notes that the canonical obligation to hold provincial synods twice a year was established by the Council of Nicaea in 325 and reemphasized by the Council of Chalcedon in 451. He is aware that this obligation was reduced to once a year by the Second Council of Nicaea in 787 because of the physical and financial difficulties occasioned by semi-annual synods. Recognizing such difficulties as still operative in his own time, d'Ailly would require that such synods be held only every three years.[76]

In support of his call for regular provincial and diocesan synods, d'Ailly used the model of the primitive Church with its frequent gatherings of the apostles, disciples, and others to resolve the more serious problems facing the Church of their day.[77] After his conversion to the

---

[75] *De materia concilii*, Oakley, 256. 'Sed ad hoc agendum sufficerent concilia provincialia et ad quaedam satis essent concilia diocesana et synodalia ...'

[76] *De reformatione*, Miethke-Weinrich, 1:340–342. The legislation of the Council of Nicaea on this point can be found in canon 5; that of the Council of Chalcedon in canon 19, and for the legislation of the Second Council of Nicea see canon 6. These canons can be found respectively in *DEC*, 1:8, 96, and 143–144.

[77] The conciliar tradition generally regarded four such gatherings of the apostles and disciples as early examples of councils. These gatherings were frequently identified as those in *Acts* 1:13–26 where the apostles gathered to select a successor to Judas, *Acts* 6:1–6, the creation of the first deacons, and *Acts* 15:1–29 and 21:17–25 which were concerned with the circumcision of the Gentiles and their observance of the Judaic

conciliar cause, d'Ailly, in an address before the fifth National Council of Paris in 1406, used the practice of the primitive church not only to call for the holding of synods on the provincial and diocesan levels but also to support his arguments for the convocation of a general council to end the Schism.[78] At the time of the Council of Constance, the use of the primitive Church as a model for the convocation of general councils had been challenged by the papal curia which claimed that it could best handle many of the more serious problems facing the Church. In response to this claim, d'Ailly reaffirmed the validity of the example of the primitive Church and reasserted his strong conviction that the failure to hold regular councils at all levels of the Church's structure explains the presence and persistence of so many of the problems facing the Church of his day.[79]

Within d'Ailly's own diocese of Cambrai, the tradition of regular diocesan synods was much more alive than general surveys of the Church in the late Middle Ages would lead one to believe. Diocesan synods in Cambrai during the first half of the fourteenth century were held with remarkable regularity. Records indicate no less than twenty nine such synods during this period. In d'Ailly's time as bishop of Cambrai, that is, from 1397 to 1411, at least three diocesan synods were held and, as seen earlier, there are three extant sermons which he delivered on these occasions.[80] During the fourteenth and early fifteenth centuries there is also considerable evidence that provincial synods were

---

law. Cf. Conrad of Gelnhausen, *Epistola concordiae*, 1, ed. E. Martène and U. Durand, *Thesaurus novus anecdotorum* (Paris, 1717), 2:1204 B-E. Conrad's position was adopted verbatim by Henry of Langenstein in his *Epistola concilii pacis*, 13, Dupin, 2:822. Gerson also borrowed from Gelnhausen and Langenstein with regard to this dimension of the primitive Church. Cf. *Propositio facta coram Anglicis*, G, 6:133.

[78] *Pax Dei*, Salembier, 'Les oeuvres francaises du Cardinal Pierre d'Ailly,' *RL*, 7 (1906–1907), 871. While retaining the quadriform number of councils in the primitive Church, d'Ailly in this address cites a somewhat different series of apostolic gatherings in Acts. He retains 1:13–26 and 21:17–25 but identifies the other two gatherings as those described in 2:1–4, the gathering at the first Pentecost, and 17:1–15, which describes Paul's journeys in Thessalonica, Beroea, and Athens. In this latter passage, however, it is hard to find an example of an apostolic gathering.

[79] *De reformatione*, Miethke-Weinrich, 1:342. In this passage d'Ailly identifies the four apostolic councils in the more common pattern of Acts used by conciliarists as described earlier. The variations among conciliarists as to which apostolic gatherings in Acts were to be identified as early councils indicate that they were more interested in the general phenomena of such gatherings than in identifying the precise gatherings. Such is clearly the case with d'Ailly.

[80] Pierrard, *Cambrai et Lille*, 89–90.

held in the Archdiocese of Rheims, of which Cambrai at that time was a suffragan see. It was at one such provincial synod in Rheims in 1408 that Gerson, at the invitation of the Archbishop, Guy de Roye, delivered his famous sermon on the nature of the pastoral office within the Church.[81]

Compared with his comments on the importance of regular synods in the pastoral life of the Church, d'Ailly's statements on episcopal visitations are few. In those statements, moreover, he does not display a knowledge of canon law comparable to that manifested with regard to provincial and diocesan synods. There is some evidence, however, that he did conduct some visitations in his own diocese, especially of religious houses. It must be remembered, however, that in the late Middle Ages pastoral visitations of dioceses were generally carried out by the archdeacons of their respective geographical areas. D'Ailly certainly reacted against this tradition in his *De reformatione* where, it will be recalled, he called for the abolition of the archdeacon's office and stressed the need for bishops to visit the parishes of their dioceses on a yearly basis. While he affirms that these visitations should be conducted with such dedication as to bear solid pastoral results, he gives no specific guidelines for their conduct, such as Gerson did earlier in his *De visitatione praelatorum*.[82] D'Ailly's writings also call for archiepiscopal visitations of suffragan dioceses primarily to evaluate the pastoral effectiveness of their respective bishops. Bishops who are found to be negligent in their pastoral duties are to be brought before provincial synods and, if necessary, even before a General Council and if they refuse to correct their pastoral deficiencies, they are to receive appropriate punishments and even removed from their sees.[83]

---

[81] For the importance of his '*Bonus Pastor*' sermon in Gerson's program of episcopal reform see Pascoe, *Jean Gerson*, 110–145. The sermon is to be found in G. 5:123–144.

[82] *De reformatione*, Miethke-Weinrich, 1:356. '… qui per singulos annos parochias suas fructuoso affectu visitent …' The canonical obligation for episcopal visitations can be found in Gratian's *Decretum*, C. 10, q. 1, c. 9–12. For the great emphasis Gerson placed on episcopal visitations as an instrument of church reform see Pascoe, *Jean Gerson*, 139–145.

[83] *De reformatione*, Miethke-Weinrich, 1:356. Referring to such bishops, d'Ailly states: ' … ut talium vita et fama in provincialibus conciliis vel si opus sit quandoque in generali concilio summo pontifice referantur et ad eorum depositionem seu aliam condignam correctionem procedatur.' D'Ailly recognizes that according to contemporary canon law only the pope can depose a bishop but he expresses a desire to return to the spirit of earlier canonical legislation which gave general councils much more authority over such cases.

When he turns to the persistent problem of clerical residence, d'Ailly gives clear evidence of recognizing the extensive nature of the problem as well as its harmful pastoral consequences, especially on the episcopal level. While medieval canon law strongly emphasized the obligation of residency for bishops, it also provided a myriad of legal reasons whereby that obligation could be mitigated or circumvented. Among the principal reasons given by bishops for absence from their dioceses was that of service at the papal and royal curias. Although canon law limited the time of such service, the personal preference of some bishops resulted in the neglect of those restrictions and prolonged absences from their diocese.[84]

Though d'Ailly is clearly aware of existing canonical legislation on episcopal residency, he is not optimistic that that legislation can be more strictly implemented. In brief, he holds that the problem can best be resolved by demanding that bishops present a reasonable cause for absences beyond the time allotted by canonical legislation.[85] D'Ailly's position on episcopal residence may also have been compromised by his own example. He himself never took up residence in the first episcopal see to which he was appointed, namely the diocese of Le Puy, of which he was bishop from 1395 to 1397. His extreme involvement with efforts to settle the Schism also necessitated considerable absences from Cambrai, absences which, given the problems created by the Great Schism and the need to resolve them, were indeed understandable. As a former member of the theological faculty at the University of Paris and former chancellor of that university, he would also be aware of and supportive of existing canonical legislation regulating absenteeism from their pastoral duties for clerics studying or teaching theology or canon law. This legislation involved privileges granted by Honorius III in 1219 and Clement VI in 1346 which were known as *quinquennia* and *septennia* because they allowed absences of five to seven years for the purpose of studying theology or canon law at a university.[86] All of the above factors may well explain d'Ailly's reluctance to deal more forcefully with the problem of clerical absenteeism in the Church.

---

[84] On the issue of episcopal residency in the late Middle Ages, see Paul Ourliac, 'La résidence des évêques dans le droit canonique du xve siècle,' *AC*, 17 (1973), 707–715.

[85] *De reformatione*, Miethke-Weinrich, 1:358. On this point, he cites Gratian's *Decretum* as his canonical source, C. 7, q. 1, c. 29. Actually this canon relates specifically to deacons and priests but the fact that in citing the canon d'Ailly also adds the phrase 'cum suis similibus,' indicates that he would apply the same stipulations to bishops.

[86] *CUP*, I, 10, II, 574.

Closely associated with d'Ailly's thought on the renewal of the pastoral office of bishops and priests were matters related to the liturgy, the sacraments, and devotional practices. His treatment of these issues in the *De reformatione* is relatively brief and little related data is to be found in his other writings. In the realm of liturgical matters, d'Ailly emphasizes the reformation of the liturgy should be of special concern to the bishops. First of all, bishops should be sure that those who are to be advanced to the priesthood have the knowledge necessary for the proper fulfillment of their liturgical obligations. Another area of liturgical concern to d'Ailly relates to the excessive length of ceremonies. He gives no specific indications as to what factors contributed towards this burdensome phenomenon but does urge a return to what he calls a devout but integral brevity.[87] Also of concern to d'Ailly in the realm of liturgy was the use of apocryphal readings in ceremonies, and the employment of many new hymns and prayers unknown to the laity. His major argument against such liturgical novelties rests not so much on the issue of novelty itself but on the fact that these unauthorized readings, hymns, and prayers often replaced ancient and authentic ones, thereby weakening liturgical integrity and continuity. The liturgy, therefore, should be purged of all novelty or excessive variety and returned to a more simple and purified state.[88]

Liturgical reform in d'Ailly's mind should also be concerned with the ever-increasing number of new liturgical feast days. His complaint in this domain rests not so much on the increased number of feast days but more on the fact that rather than promoting piety, they have given rise to increased drunkenness, revelry, and debauchery among the laity. In the same vein, d'Ailly also proposes that, with the exception of Sundays and major liturgical holidays, people be permitted to work on all other feast days. The reason for his position on this matter rests not only on the problems described above but also on the fact that the increased number of liturgical feast days has reduced the number of work days to the point that the poor are unable to provide

---

[87] *De reformatione*, Miethke-Weinrich, 1:360. 'Item, quia praelatis de divino culto specialis cura esse debet, circa huiusmodi reformationem, quae necessaria est, providendum esset quod in divino servitio non tamen onerosa prolixitas quam devota et integra brevitas servaretur ... .'

[88] *De reformatione*, Miethke-Weinrich, 1:360–362. 'Et quod in huiusmodi festis scripturae apocrifae aut hymni novi vel orationes seu aliae voluntariae novitiates non legerentur, omissis antiquis et authenticis et iam in ecclesia consuetis.'

for the basic necessities of life.[89] It is interesting to note that while many contemporary scholars see the large number of feast days in the medieval Church as mitigating the heavy labor burdens of ordinary people, d'Ailly sees them more as inflicting economic hardship upon them.

With regard to the renewal of the pastoral office in terms of the administration of the sacraments and the fostering of the sacramental life, surprisingly little emerges in d'Ailly's *De reformatione*. The same conclusion holds true for his earlier writings. His primary recommendations in this area, as seen earlier, were that those to be promoted to the priesthood should have sufficient knowledge of confessional practices and that among the small manuals which he urged be composed and distributed for the use of the clergy in carrying out their pastoral duties, one such manual be reserved for the administration of the sacraments.[90]

While it is true that d'Ailly most probably took for granted the sacramental activity of the clergy and felt that the composition of an instructional manual would suffice for their needs, the minimal references in his reform treatises to the role of the sacraments, especially Penance and the Eucharist, is striking. On this point there is a considerable difference between d'Ailly and Gerson, for whom the priestly activities of confession and counseling played such an important role in his concept of pastoral reform and renewal.[91] Despite his strong affinity for the Brethren of the Common Life and their spirituality, especially their emphasis on the study and preaching of the Scriptures, d'Ailly displays little evidence of their eucharistic spirituality.[92]

Moving beyond the realm of the sacraments to other devotional aspects of the Christian life, d'Ailly complains about the increasing

---

[89] *De reformatione*, Miethke-Weinrich, 1:360–362. 'Quod praeterquam diebus dominicis et in maioribus festis ab ecclesia institutis, liceret operari post auditum officium, cum quia in festis saepe magis multiplicantur peccata, in tabernis, choreis et aliis lasciviis, quas docet otiositas, tum quia dies operabiles vix sufficiunt pauperibus ad vitae necessaria procuranda.'

[90] *De reformatione*, Miethke-Weinrich, 1:368. For a brief survey of medieval practices on the sacramental and devotional levels see the fine analysis of André Vauchez in *Un temps d'épreuves (1274–1449)*, Histoire du Christianisme, 6, ed. Michel Mollat du Jourdin et al. (Paris: Desclée-Fayard, 1990), 414–447.

[91] For Gerson's views on the administration of the sacraments, especially that of penance, see the excellent analysis of Brown, *Pastor and Laity*, 55–72.

[92] For a brief survey of the spirituality of the Brethren of the Common Life, see John Van Engen, ed., *Devotio Moderna: Basic Writings*, 7–35, and Jean Leclercq et al., eds. *The Spirituality of the Middle Ages*, vol. 2 of *A History of Christian Spirituality*, ed. Louis Bouyer et al. (London: Burns & Oates, 1968), 428–439.

number of newly canonized saints, the increased building of new churches, and, reminiscent of Bernard of Clairvaux, the excessive number of paintings and statues in the churches.[93] While not mentioned in the *De reformatione*, there were also deviations in popular piety within his diocese that he strenuously tried to correct. Among these are to be numbered the penitential excesses of the Flagellants, and the exaggerated mystical, apocalyptic, and sexual teachings and practices of the sect commonly known as the 'Men of Intelligence,' (*homines intelligentiae*), a sect which has been generally associated with the heresy of the Free Spirit. The teaching of William of Hildernissen with its highly apocalyptic, penitential, and pantheistic emphasis also commanded the pastoral attention of d'Ailly. While it can no longer be maintained that William belonged to the 'Men of Intelligence,' his teaching does reflect much that was common to that movement.[94] With regard to the phenomenon of 'bleeding hosts,' d'Ailly proved himself more sympathetic. After a thorough investigation of such incidents at Brussels and Bois-Seigneur-Isaac, d'Ailly confirmed the devotional practices that had grown up around these instances.[95]

A final area of major concern to d'Ailly with regard to the reform and renewal of the pastoral office of both bishops and priests relates to the juridical and financial realms. In the juridical realm, it has already been seen that d'Ailly frequently complained about the preference given to graduates from law faculties over those from the theological faculties in the realm of ecclesiastical appointments. In his *De reformatione* d'Ailly was also concerned with the proliferation of human legislation within the Church and its negative impact on pastoral life.

---

[93] *De reformatione*, Miethke-Weinrich, 1:360.

[94] D'Ailly's letter to the Dominican Vincent Ferrer was essentially written in support of Gerson's attacks against the Flagellants. The letter of d'Ailly can be found in Dupin, 2:659 and that of Gerson in Glorieux, 2:200. For a critical analysis of charges that William of Hildernissen was associated with the Men of Intelligence and with the Brethren of the Free Spirit, see Robert E. Lerner, *The Heresy of the Free Spirit in the Later Middle Ages* (Berkeley: University of California Press, 1972), 157–163. For the notarial evidence related to the trial of William of Hildernissen drawn up in d'Ailly's own episcopal court and in his presence, see Baluze, *Miscellanea novo ordine digesta*, 2:288–293.

[95] Salembier, *Le Cardinal Pierre d'Ailly*, 139–140. For a more negative reaction to the phenomenon of bleeding hosts in the late Middle Ages see the views of Nicholas of Cusa as papal legate to Germany in Morimichi Watanabe, 'The German Church Shortly Before the Reformation: Nicholas of Cusa and the Veneration of the Bleeding Hosts at Wilsnack,' in *Reform and Renewal in the Middle Ages and Renaissance: Studies in Honor of Louis B. Pascoe, S.J.*, ed. Thomas M. Izbicki and Christopher M. Bellitto, Studies in the History of Christian Thought, 96 (Leiden: E.J. Brill, 2000), 210–213.

In this context, d'Ailly strongly censures the Church for the creation of excessive and indeed oppressive legislation in the form of statutes, canons, and decretals, especially those that relate to matters of ecclesiastical discipline. Provincial and diocesan synods are also censored by d'Ailly for the same reasons. The proliferation of so much legislation, he argued, has placed a considerable burden on bishops and priests in the exercise of their pastoral office to say nothing of the burden placed on those under their care. As a result of the imposition of such heavy legal obligations upon those under their care, such prelates run the risk of having applied to them the rebuke given by Christ to the Scribes and Pharisees, namely that they place heavy burdens on their people and do little to ease those burdens.[96]

D'Ailly's attitude toward the imposition of excessive legal obligations upon the faithful was also clearly evident in his earlier *De materia concilii*, written while Bishop of Cambrai. Here he cites the admonition of Peter the Chanter (†1197) to the members of the Third Lateran Council (1179), namely that they create little new legislation related to ecclesiastical discipline and that they even refrain from renewing much of the older legislation of this type since excessive legislation even of a useful nature can become intolerably burdensome. Peter concludes that in general it would be much better for more people to strive to obey the prescriptions of the Gospel than to be weighed down by excessive human legislation. D'Ailly's reference to the views of Peter the Chanter also serves to emphasize the highly pastoral and evangelical nature of his views of the episcopal and priestly offices.[97]

When d'Ailly comes to specific areas in which legislation related to ecclesiastical discipline should be mitigated he singles out all disciplinary legislation which binds under the pain of serious sin. Such legislation, he argues, places excessive burdens upon people's consciences. Also on his list are laws that too readily inflict excommunication upon their transgressors. He also complains of disciplinary legislation whose violation results in financial exactions. As a final example, he cites legislation prohibiting the reception of stipends for pastoral duties such as

---

[96] *De reformatione*, Miethke-Weinrich, 1:352. The biblical reference to the Scribes and Pharisees can be found in Mt. 23:4.

[97] *De materia concilii*, Oakley, 255. 'Ex quibus patet quod multiplicatio humanorum constitutionum restringenda esset potius quam amplianda.' The reference to Peter the Chanter is taken from his *Verbum abbreviatum*, 72. The most recent study on Peter the Chanter is that of John W. Baldwin, *Masters, Princes, and Merchants: The Social Views of Peter the Chanter and His Circle*. 2 vols. (Princeton: Princeton University Press, 1970).

the administration of sacraments, burials, and similar spiritual activities. Such prohibitory legislation, he asserts, is rarely observed and as a result creates scandal among the people. As seen earlier, what he favors more is some form of legal accommodation to the prevailing reality.[98] Also to be remembered with regard to stipends for pastoral services was d'Ailly's firm belief in the statement of Christ that the laborer is worthy of his keep.[99]

Another juridical area designated by d'Ailly in which the pastoral activity of bishops and priests is negatively affected and which stands in need of reform relates to the problem of prolonged litigation. Even after a case is adjudicated, there is the incessant round of appeals from one ecclesiastical court to another. As a result of such appeals not only is the legal procedure interminably extended but the authority of the prelate under whose jurisdiction the case originated is considerably compromised. People involved in such cases become impoverished by the cost of such lengthy litigation and many despair of ever seeing justice given them. To alleviate all these problems, d'Ailly calls upon the Roman Curia and metropolitans to show moderation in accepting appeals from episcopal courts.[100]

While d'Ailly's reform proposals in the realm of pastoral ministry represent a rich segment of his views on church reform, relatively little legislation was passed at Constance related to this area of his thought.[101] At Constance, reforms in the area of preaching were not discussed and no legislation on this important area of pastoral ministry emerged from the Council. While there was some discussion on the regular holding of synods and visitations, no legislation resulted from such discussions.

---

[98] *De reformatione*, Miethke-Weinrich, 1:352. Similar reservations as to the excessive amount of disciplinary legislation can be found in d'Ailly's *De materia concilii*, Oakley, 255.

[99] Cf. Mt. 10:10, Lk. 10:7, and 1 Tim. 5:18.

[100] *De reformatione*, Miethke-Weinrich, 1:370. On the issue of excessive appeals to the Roman Curia, d'Ailly makes a clear reference to Bernard of Clairvaux's *De consideratione*, 3, 2, Leclercq, *Opera*, 3:435–439. This work was written on behalf of Pope Eugene III (1145–1153), Bernard's fellow Cistercian, friend, and former student. Bernard's *De consideratione* had an important influence on many areas of d'Ailly's reform thought and in the passage cited above, he refers to Bernard's work in the following laudatory manner: 'Qui liber in hoc et aliis multis pro reformatione ecclesiae non mediocriter utilis, sicut et plures ejus libri et epistolae.' As seen in the previous chapter, d'Ailly had made an earlier reference to *De consideratione*, 3, 2 in his *Contra Johannem de Montesonno*, d'Argentré, 79, when discussing John of Monzón's appeal from the Bishop of Paris to the Pope in Avignon.

[101] For an excellent and highly detailed analysis of the deliberations of the reform

Legislation on residency also failed to materialize in the Council. The issue of residency was taken up only in the English Concordat where dispensations from residency requirements were banned. The Council did pass a decree establishing stricter norms for the holding of multiple benefices. Even stricter guidelines were established in the English Concordat. The English Concordat also stipulated that each parish was to have one vicar whose material needs were to be adequately provided for from endowed revenues. Reform proposals related to liturgical celebrations, administration of the sacraments, and devotional practices did not materialize in conciliar or concordat legislation. Equally untreated were the issues of excessive ecclesiastical legislation and litigation.

In his analysis of the reasons why so little legislation was passed at Constance or treated in its concordats on many of the issues discussed above, Stump rightly judges that the primary reason was the Council's overriding concern for reforms related to the papacy and the cardinalate, that is, the *reformatio in capite*. Such reforms were seen as prerequisite for and integrally related to the reform of other segments of the Church, namely, the *reformatio in membris*.[102] This belief naturally flowed from the prevailing hierarchical view of society in general and in the Church in particular. As a consequence of the above, belief in a 'trickle down' reform theory is indeed understandable.

Additional reasons given by Stump include problems of enforcement, differing regional situations, and the failure of previous legislation. Existing legislation on such issues, especially the legislation of Lateran IV (1215), was often evaded or ignored. Even if penalties for such evasions or ignorals were increased, the problem of enforcement still remained. The Council also seemed to lack the will to back up many of its concerns on pastoral matters with legislation, or to strengthen existing legislation with stricter measures and penalties for enforcement. This hesitation may have flowed from a reluctance to increase legislation beyond that already contained in canon law and to increase the grounds for excommunication beyond those already in existence. As seen above, d'Ailly and many other reformers had complained about the excessive use of such coercive legislation. There is no clear evidence, however, that the Council as a whole espoused d'Ailly's views on this point.

---

committees at Constance as well as conciliar and concordat legislation dealing with matters discussed above see Stump, *The Reforms of the Council of Constance*, 138–169.
[102] Stump, *The Reforms of the Council of Constance*, 138, 164–169.

The phenomenon of different regional situations was also a considerable hindrance to common legislation since pastoral needs differed considerably from country to country. It was indeed because of these differences that whatever reforms were achieved were for the most part effected through the national concordats. The failure to effect conciliar or concordat legislation in most of the above-discussed areas of pastoral ministry, however, does not detract from the broad, detailed, and highly apostolic dimensions of d'Ailly's vision and program for pastoral reform in the Church of his day.

CHAPTER FOUR

BISHOPS: PERSONAL REFORM, AND THE APOSTOLIC LIFE

As indicated early in the last chapter, d'Ailly's call for ecclesiastical prelates to reform their lives in accordance with the apostolic ideal, extended not only to the pastoral but also to the personal dimensions of their lives. While this chapter will be concentrating on the reform of the personal dimensions of the bishops' lives, it is important to remember that these dimensions also interact with and indeed enhance the pastoral qualities studied in the previous chapter.

1. *Personal Reform: Nature and Goals*

The principle term that d'Ailly used to express this personal aspect of episcopal reform was that of '*conversatio*'. This term has its roots in the classical tradition where in both its Greek and Latin formulation it essentially expressed the action of turning or moving in place. The term then took on the sense of dwelling in a place, habitual association, community or society resulting from that dwelling. Finally, it came to connote conduct, behavior, or way of life within a community or society.[1] In the Judaic and Christian scriptures the term was generally used in the latter context.[2] As a result of Benedict's use of the term in his Rule, it became increasingly but not exclusively associated in the Middle Ages with the monastic life. In this latter sense it implied an adoption of a monastic lifestyle in accordance with the Rule.[3]

---

[1] For the original Greek sense of the term see *A Greek-English Lexicon*, ed. Henry G. Liddell and Robert Scott, 9th ed., (Oxford: Clarendon Press, 1940), s.v. αναστροφή. The Latin translation and use of the term can be found in the *Oxford Latin Dictionary*, ed., P.G.W. Glare (Oxford: Clarendon Press, 1982), s.v. 'conversatio,'

[2] For scriptural uses of the term see among other references, Wis. 13:11–12; Tob. 14:17; 2 Macc. 6:23; Eph. 4:22; Gal. 1:13; 1 Tim. 4:12; 1 Pet. 1:15, 18; 2 Pet. 2:7; and Jas. 3:13.

[3] While the term '*conversatio*' was used ten times in Benedict's Rule, it is at times used in conjunction with the words '*morum suorum*.' Cf. RB, 58:17. For an excellent analysis of the various schools of thought on the meaning of the phrase '*conversatio morum*

Given this general use of the term, it is surprising to see that d'Ailly applies it to the life of an ecclesiastical prelate and does so in the context of the *vita apostolica*. In a sermon given at Cambrai on the occasion of one of the three synods held during his tenure as bishop there from 1397 to 1411, d'Ailly eloquently maintains that if the clergy are to be true successors of the apostles and disciples then they must also imitate their virtues in their personal lives. If they succeed the apostles and disciples in office then they must succeed them in merit; if in dignity then in virtue.[4] In that sermon, he also censures the ecclesiastical prelates of his day for having fallen far short of the apostolic ideal in their personal lives. Instead of cultivating the virtues of apostles, they have adopted the vices of apostates.[5]

The importance that d'Ailly places on the need for prelates to lead a life of virtue is especially seen in a sermon delivered on Septuagesima Sunday, 1388, and therefore some nine years before he became bishop of Cambrai. Using the terminology of Gregory I, he stresses the fact that by the example of their personal lives prelates, whether bishops or priests, exercise a *magisterium virtutis*, that is, they teach by the example of their lives.[6] The prelate, therefore, exercises a twofold teaching office: the *magisterium doctrinae* and the *magisterium virtutis*. While the *magisterium doctrinae* involves the teaching of both faith and morals, the *magisterium virtutis* serves to strengthen and confirm that teaching by personal example. Similar concepts were expressed by d'Ailly in one of his synodal sermons delivered at Cambrai cited earlier when he stressed

---

suorum,' see *The Rule of Saint Benedict*, ed. Timothy Fry et al. (Collegeville, Minn.: The Liturgical Press, 1980), 458–466. After analyzing the various scholarly translations and interpretations of the phrase, the editors essentially opt for 'way of life,' 'behavior,' and more specifically, 'the monastic life'.

[4] *Homelia facta in Synodo Cameracensi*, TS, 9. 'Ecce ergo qui quales et quanti fuerunt predecessores nostri apostoli scilicet et discipuli Christi. Quorum virtutes si veri successores sumus debemus imitari ut quibus succedimus in officio succedamus in merito, quibus succedimus in dignitate, succedamus etiam in virtute.'

[5] *Homelia facta in Synodo Cameracensi*, TS, 9. 'Sed prochpudor hodie plures sunt ecclesiae ministri qui non apostolicas virtutes sed magis apostaticas priorum viciorum sordes tam publice et notorie sectantur.'

[6] *Sermo in Dominca Septuagesima*, TS, 5. Referring to prelates whose lives are such that they are unable to exercise their pastoral office worthily, d'Ailly states that such persons have assumed the *magisterium virtutis* not because of virtuous living but solely because they were elected to it: 'quia ad virtutis magisterium ex sola elatione pervenerunt. Dudum siquidem homines soliciti erant per virtutem ad dignitates ecclesiasticas pervenire.'

that priests should teach their parishioners by means of both sound doctrine and the example of a holy life.[7] In d'Ailly's thought, however, it is not sufficient that bishops and priests merely teach by the example of their lives; they must also strive to insure that their example actually contributes to the spiritual growth of their flocks, especially in terms of the virtues.[8]

According to d'Ailly, the failure of ecclesiastical prelates to exercise a *magisterium virtutis* can have disastrous consequences for the Church. Relying on what he regarded as a work of John Chrysostom (c. 347–407) but which was in reality a work of Pseudo-Chrysostom, d'Ailly cites that author's interpretation of Mt. 21:12–17, the cleansing of the Temple by Jesus. In this interpretation, the Temple symbolizes the Church, and just as both good and evil can proceed from the Temple, so too with the Church. In the Church it is the priesthood which determines the moral quality of the members. If the priesthood is morally sound then so will be the Church, but the reverse is also true, for a morally weakened priesthood will result in both a morally and doctrinally undisciplined laity.[9] Finally, as will be seen in greater detail, there is a close interrelationship between the two *magisteria* and the effective exercise of the prelate's pastoral office.

---

[7] *Homelia facta in Synodo Cameracensi, TS*, 3. 'Quia certe opus sacerdotalis est per sanam doctrinam et sanctam vitam verbo et opere Christianum populum erudire.' For earlier evidence of the importance d'Ailly places upon the relationship of sound doctrine and virtuous living see his *Sermo in synodo in Ecclesia Parisiensi*, delivered in 1375, Tschackert, 5–6 and his *Invectiva Ezechielis contra pseudo-pastores*, written between 1381–1384, Tschackert, 12–15.

[8] *Sermo in Domenica Septuagesima, TS*, 4. 'Qui a domino missi sunt debent esse laborosi ad spiritualium virtutem fructificationem.'

[9] *De reformatione*, Miethke-Weinrich, 1:374–376. 'Si enim sacerdotium integrum fuerit, tota ecclesia floret. Si autem corruptum fuerit, omnium fides et virtus marcida est. Sicut cum vides arborem pallentibus foliis, intelligas quod vitium habeat in radice. Cum videris populum indisciplinatum, sine dubio cognosce quod sacerdotium eius non sit sanum.' For the identification of Pseudo-Chrysostom's work as the *Opus imperfectum in Matthaeum* and its influence in the thought of conciliarists such as Henry of Langenstein and Jean Gerson see Oakley, *De materia concilii generalis*, 341 n. 3. As will be recalled, much of the third part of d'Ailly's *De materia* was later incoporated in his *De reformatione*. The Latin text of the *Opus imperfectum* can be found in *PG*, 56:611–948. On the question of its authorship, see G. Morin, 'Quelques apercus nouveaux sur l'Opus Imperfectum in Matthaeum, *RB*, 37 (1925), 230–262, and P. Nautin, 'L'Opus Imperfectum in Matthaeum et les Ariens de Constantinople,' *RHE*, 67 (1972), 380–408; 715–766. For the corpus of the Pseudo-Chrysostom writings see J.A. de Aldama, ed. *Repertorium pseudochrysostomicum* (Paris:CNRS, 1965), and H.J. Sieben, *DSAM*, 8:355–369.

2. *Specific Aspects of Personal Reform*

Before beginning the detailed analysis of the personal life of virtue to which d'Ailly summons all prelates, it must be remembered that he expresses his thought on this subject not in the context of a systematized philosophy or theology of the virtues such as one would ordinarily find in scholastic treatises. While certainly knowing the traditional division of the virtues in terms of the theological, intellectual, and moral virtues, d'Ailly does not attempt any specific analysis of this division as such, nor of the relationship among the virtues within each division. In dealing with the virtues, moreover, d'Ailly does not treat the virtues comprehensively. His is, therefore, a much more general and practical approach towards the topic, an approach understandably dictated by the pastoral needs of his day and the specific virtues required to meet those needs.

Central to d'Ailly's call for prelates to foster a life of personal virtue was his emphasis upon the theological virtues, especially that of charity. This emphasis upon charity, however, should not lessen the importance of the virtues of faith and hope in his thought, as can be seen in the strength of his attacks against heretics and heretical ideals in the Church of his day and the centrality he attributes to the episcopal office in the maintenance of theological orthodoxy at the diocesan level. The emphasis on charity in d'Ailly's thought, moreover, is hardly surprising given the traditional biblical, patristic, and medieval emphasis on this virtue as the basis of all the other virtues. Aquinas, indeed, designates the virtue of charity as the *mater*, *radix*, and *forma* of all the virtues, theological, intellectual, and moral.[10]

The ecclesiological context of d'Ailly's views on charity is especially seen in his second sermon delivered before the diocesan synod of Cambrai. The central theme of this sermon was taken from Eph. 4:1–6 wherein Paul describes the Christian vocation in terms of living and promoting unity within the Church. In that passage, Paul also enumerates a sevenfold basis for that unity, namely, one God, one Lord, one Spirit, one Body, one Hope, one Faith, and one Baptism. For d'Ailly too it is this sevenfold basis that ultimately contributes to the

---

[10] *ST*, 1, 2, q. 63, a. 4, c. For Aquinas' systematic treatment of the virtues see *ST*, 1, 2, qq. 56–67. For his detailed analysis of the virtue of charity see *ST*, 1, 2, qq. 23–27. A brief but very clear analysis of Aquinas' teaching on the virtues can be found in Brian Davies, *The Thought of Thomas Aquinas* (Oxford: Clarendon Press, 1992), 239–244.

buildup of the unity of the Mystical Body. Following in the Pauline tradition, d'Ailly also emphasizes that that unity is best maintained through the bond of peace which he understands as primarily rooted in charity.[11] Although the vocation of all Christians involves the call to promote the growth of the Mystical Body in terms of charity, d'Ailly sees that call as specially directed to ecclesiastical prelates. In one of his Pentecost sermons delivered in 1417 at Constance, d'Ailly especially singles out charity as an essential virtue for all prelates. What is to be especially noted in his comments on this point is the close association of the virtue of charity with the apostolic ideal, which, as seen in the previous chapter, he held up as the model for prelates in the exercise of their pastoral duties.[12]

Despite this strong emphasis upon charity in the lives of ecclesiastical prelates, d'Ailly makes few concrete recommendations as to precisely how this virtue is to be fostered and exercised in their lives, but the few he does make are rather interesting. In emphasizing the universal call for charity towards God and neighbor embodied in the first two commandments, d'Ailly, following in the tradition of Gregory the Great, indicates that any bishop or priest who does not have such charity should not assume the office of preaching.[13] A high degree of charity is also required by the prelate in exercising the evangelical obligation of fraternal correction towards those under his pastoral care who are delinquent in the fulfillment of their religious obligations. Fraternal correction, according to d'Ailly, should be rooted in charity and exercised in a spirit of humility and gentility.

---

[11] *Sermo in Synodo Cameracensi*, II, TS, 2–3. While it is generally maintained that from the mid-twelfth century the term *corpus mysticum* gradually lost its liturgical and sacramental context and assumed a more sociological and canonical dimension, this does not seem to be the case for d'Ailly who reflects here a more charity centered understanding of the term. Gerson's stress on the eucharistic context of the Mystical Body also marks him as an exception to the prevailing thesis. For the history of the gradual transformation in the understanding of the Mystical Body see Henri de Lubac, *Corpus Mysticum* (Paris: Aubier, 1949). For Gerson's views on the Mystical Body see Pascoe, *Jean Gerson*, 34, n. 73.

[12] *Sermo in die Pentecostes*, II, TS, 4. '... ut sicut praedictum est, in vobis quemadmodum in apostolis luceat et exterius appareat triplex illa virtutum perfectio. Videlicet in corde ardens caritatis dilectio, in ore fervens veritatis praedicatio, in opere vehemens virtutis operatio.'

[13] *Homelia facta in Synodo Cameracensi*, TS, 2. 'Nam ut ait Gregorius per hoc tacite innuitur quod qui erga alterum caritatem non habet predicationis officium nullatenus suscipere debet.'

Also of special interest in d'Ailly's reflections on the role of charity in the lives of ecclesiastical prelates is its importance in providing a spirit of mutual and fraternal support among prelates themselves. The need for such support was especially signified, according to d'Ailly, in the fact that when Christ commissioned the apostles and disciples to go into the world to preach his gospel he sent them out in pairs.[14] Finally, the prevailing Schism within the Church presents prelates, especially bishops, with an opportunity to restore the bond of charity which is so central to maintaining the unity of the Mystical Body. D'Ailly indeed roundly castigates those prelates who rupture that bond by promoting or by failing to extirpate schism and division within the Church.

The other virtues that d'Ailly stresses as central to the personal renewal of ecclesiastical prelates, again with special emphasis upon bishops, are fortitude and temperance. While fortitude and temperance and their various subdivisions are generally included among the cardinal and moral virtues, they are in the fullest Christian sense to be numbered among the traditionally designated gifts and fruits of the Holy Spirit.[15] This is also the sense in which d'Ailly uses them. With regard to fortitude, it must be admitted that d'Ailly rarely uses that term. In many of his sermons, however, especially those before synods, he does use terms which in effect are equivalent to fortitude or at least are closely associated with that virtue. In this context, he especially specifies the need for courage, vigilance, perseverance, and diligence on the part of pastors in the exercise of their office.[16] Accordingly, d'Ailly strongly criticizes those prelates who are unwilling to risk the loss of human favor by exercising the difficult duties of their pastoral office, especially the obligation to proclaim doctrinal truth, to enunciate proper moral principles and to correct those guilty of doctrinal and moral error.[17]

---

[14] *Homelia facta in Synodo Cameracensi*, TS, 2. 'Ideo ergo specialiter missi sunt bini. In signum quod ministri ecclesiastici sibi invicem et aliis debent charitative dilectionis vinculo copulari.' and 'Nec immerito eos ante se binos misit ... Primo propter mutuam consolationem et fraternii auxilii confortationem.'

[15] For the traditional medieval teaching on the gifts and fruits of the Holy Spirit see Aquinas, *ST*, 1, 2, q. 69, a. 1–8, and 1, 2, q. 70, a. 1–4.

[16] *Sermo de Nativitate, I*, TS, 3–4; *Sermo in Domenica Septuagesima*, TS, 5; *Homelia facta in Synodo Cameracensi*, TS, 4.

[17] *Sermo in Synodo in Ecclesia Parisiensi*, Tschackert, 6. '... quique vanam mundi gloriam appetentes et laudem humanam perdere formidantes recta loqui, vera dicere, et vita corrigere pertimescunt.' In this context, d'Ailly again has reference to the classical text of Isa. 56:10–11 wherein the leaders of Israel are compared to dumb dogs that cannot bark.

In dealing with the role of temperance in the lives of prelates, d'Ailly presents that virtue in the general context of restraint or moderation. He sees the concrete manifestation and exercise of these qualities primarily in the realm of evangelical poverty, celibacy, and humility. In discussing evangelical poverty, d'Ailly asserts that when Christ described the mission entrusted to the apostles and disciples primarily in terms of preaching the Gospel, the question of providing for their material needs emerged as an issue of central importance.[18] Christ's admonition that the disciples were to carry no purse for money nor sack for food and to wear no sandals but were to have their material needs provided for by the people among whom they labored, appeared to some late medieval reformers, such as the Waldensians, Spiritual Franciscans, Wycliffites, and Hussites, to have established an essential connection between ecclesiastical office and evangelical poverty, especially in the realm of preaching.[19] With the exception of the more extreme Spiritual Franciscans, the position of the mendicants on the relationship between preaching and evangelical poverty remained essentially within an orthodox context and was part of the larger complex of issues associated with the mendicant-secular controversies of the thirteenth and fourteenth centuries.[20]

In his third synodal sermon at Cambrai, d'Ailly also takes up the question of the relationship between ecclesiastical office, evangelical poverty, and preaching in greater detail. First of all, he recognizes that there are some who have taken Christ's mandate to the apostles and disciples regarding preaching and evangelical poverty quite literally and therefore maintain that prelates, especially bishops as the direct

---

[18] *Homilia facta in Synodo Cameracensi*, TS, 6. The apostolic mission given by Christ to the apostles and disciples is recounted in Mt. 10:1–15; Mk. 6:6–13, and Lk. 9:1–6 (apostles) and 10:1–11 (disciples).

[19] For the Waldensian position on evangelical poverty and preaching see the documents in Walter W. Wakefield and Austin P. Evans, eds. and trans., *Heresies of the High Middle Ages* (New York: Columbia University, 1969), 51–52; 202; 208–209, 387, 391–392; 395–396. The treatment of Wyclif's views are developed in detail in Gordon Leff, *Heresy in the Later Middle Ages*, 2 vols. (Manchester: Manchester University Press, 1967), 2:527–545. For Hus see Matthew Spinka, *John Hus' Concept of the Church* (Princeton: Princeton University Press, 1969), 48, 302–304; 316–317.

[20] On the mendicant-secular controversies of the Middle Ages, see Decima Douie, *The Conflict Between the Seculars and Mendicants at the University of Paris in the Thirteenth Century* (London: Blackfriars, 1954), Y. Congar, 'Aspects ecclésiologiques de la querelle entre mendiants et seculiers dans la second moitié du xiiie siècle et le début du xive siècle,' *AHDL*, 28 (1961), 35–151, and M.M. Dufeil, *Guillaume de Saint Amour et la polémique universitaire parisienne, 1250–1259*.

successors of the apostles, cannot licitly possess property. He does not identify who these thinkers may be but from passages in his later works where he discuses similar issues it is clear that he is referring to Waldensians, Wyclifites, and Hussites.[21]

In analyzing d'Ailly's response to the above position concerning the interrelationship of episcopal office, preaching, and evangelical poverty, it is important to note first of all that he takes his response practically verbatim from Aquinas' *Summa Theologiae*. In replying to the objection that bishops as the successors to the apostles should not possess anything as their own, Aquinas enumerates three patristic points of view. Jerome interpreted Christ's instructions to the apostles about not carrying a purse or sack or wearing sandals figuratively in the sense that they were not to rely upon worldly wisdom and eloquence. Augustine maintained that Christ's words to his apostles were to be taken more in the form of a counsel rather than a command. Finally there is the teaching of Chrysostom that Christ's words pertained only to the apostles' mission to the Jews but was in no way binding upon their successors in their subsequent missions. While Aquinas recognized the variety of patristic interpretations regarding Christ's instructions to the apostles, it was also clear to him that there was no support in the patristic tradition that would oblige bishops to evangelical poverty. Aquinas makes clear that any such commitment by a bishop would be a work of supererogation. He therefore adopts Augustine's position that Christ's mandate is to be understood more in the context of a counsel than a command.[22]

D'Ailly followed Aquinas in maintaining that Christ's mandate to the apostles, disciples, and their successors with regard to preaching and evangelical poverty was to be regarded as a counsel rather than a command. He adds to Aquinas' analysis the fact that canon law has not legislated against the possession of property by bishops and indeed

---

[21] *Homilia facta in Synodo Cameracensi*, TS, 6. 'Ex praemissis evangelii verbis ... quibus apostoli dicitur ... voluerunt aliqui concludere quod viri ecclesiastici et maxime episcopi qui in ecclesia apostolorum locum tenent, non possunt licite aliquid proprium possidere.' For specific mention by d'Ailly of the Waldensian, Wycliffite, and Hussite positions on prelacy and ecclesiastical property see his *Epistola II ad Joannem XXIII*, Dupin, 2:877–878, and the *De potestate ecclesiastica*, Dupin 2:926.

[22] *Homilia facta in Synodo Cameracensi*, TS, 6–7. The reference to Aquinas' *Summa Theologiae* is at 2, 2, q. 185, a. 6, ad2. The patristic references used by Aquinas are to Jerome's *Commentarium in Mathaeum* 10:10, PL, 26:63B-C, Augustine's *Liber de consensu evangelistarum*, 2, c. 30, n. 73, PL, 34:1114, and Chrysostom's *Homilia in Romanorum*, 16, 3, n. 2, PG, 51:197.

permits such possessions.[23] However, with regard to Christ's mandate that the apostles and disciples should have their material needs provided for by the people to whom they minister, d'Ailly's response was considerably different. In d'Ailly's view this part of Christ's mandate constitutes a command rather than a counsel and establishes a right and a consequent obligation. The preacher, therefore, has a right to have his material necessities provided for and the people for whom he works have an obligation to provide those necessities. D'Ailly regards this right and obligation as founded in both divine and human law, that is, in both the Scriptures and in canon law.[24]

Although d'Ailly maintains that ecclesiastical prelates have a right in divine and human law to have their material and temporal needs provided for and to use ecclesiastical property for the exercise of their office, he recognizes that there have been serious abuses in these areas. In speaking of these abuses, d'Ailly more or less presents the traditional list of complaints cited by late medieval moralists and preachers.[25] Foremost on his list are the charges of ostentatiousness in dress, insignia, and entourage. In this latter context, d'Ailly criticizes prelates for excessively large numbers of servants and attendants. He is even more critical of those prelates who engage military entourages for protection during in their travels. Excessive ecclesiastical pomp, he maintains, fosters the vices of pride, arrogance, and vanity. Charges of ecclesiastical excess are also raised in the realm of food, drink, and entertainment, especially in the case of elaborate banquets. In d'Ailly's view, such ban-

---

[23] Although d'Ailly does not indicate his canonical sources on this point, he is most likely referring to the *Decretum*, C. 12, q. 1, c. 19, Friedberg, 1:684.

[24] *Homilia facta in Synodo Cameracensi*, TS, 8. 'Ubi Christus ostendit quod ministri ecclesiastici qui populo christiano serviunt de jure divino et humano debent ab eo in corporalibus seu temporalibus sustinari.' D'Ailly asserted a similar claim earlier in 1381/1382 in his *Invectiva Ezechielis contra pseudopastores*, Tschackert., 13. In his *De potestate ecclesiastica*, written in 1416, he enumerated this right as one of the six ecclesiological powers established by Christ and granted by him to the apostles and their successors. Cf. Dupin 2:927–928.

[25] The highly pejorative view of the state of the late medieval Church that characterized so much of older scholarship is currently yielding to a much more balanced view which, while recognizing the weaknesses and failures of the Church in this period, also emphasizes its relative strengths as well as the movements for reform and renewal operative within it. In this context see Delaruelle, et al., *L'Eglise au temps du Grand Schisme*, 2, J.M. Mayeur et al., *Histoire du Christianisme*, 6, and R.N. Swanson, *Religion and Devotion in Europe, c. 1215–1515* (Cambridge: Cambridge University Press, 1995). Perhaps the most impressive monograph on this historiographical change as it pertains to England is Eamon Duffy, *The Stripping of the Altars: Traditional Religion in England, c. 1400–1580* (New Haven: Yale University Press, 1992).

quets only serve to foster the vices of gluttony and drunkenness. With regard to the latter vice, d'Ailly also cites the frequenting of taverns, an activity probably more characteristic of the parish clergy.[26]

Ecclesiastical prelates whose lifestyle reflects the above characteristics rightly deserve, according to d'Ailly, the designation of pseudo-pastors, that is, they are pastors who are more concerned with caring for themselves rather than for those under their care.[27] Such pastors, d'Ailly asserts, not only give serious scandal to their flocks but by their ostentatiousness use up ecclesiastical resources which should be applied to the needs of the poor. On this latter point, d'Ailly is referring to the medieval canonical teaching on ecclesiastical property as essentially the patrimony of the poor. According to this teaching, after provision has been made for the physical maintenance of a particular church and the temporal needs of its clergy, whatever income remained was to be given to the poor. As d'Ailly saw it, therefore, whenever a prelate retains or spends more than is necessary for his basic sustenance, he deprives the poor of their needs and is, in a sense, guilty of theft.[28]

While always maintaining the rights of prelates to material and temporal support, d'Ailly was sensitive to the above charges with regard to the lifestyle of ecclesiastical prelates. As in most other cases related to church reform, his response was essentially a call to moderation. In this particular case, it was a call for moderation in the use of material and temporal goods. Just as his critique of the lifestyle of prelates was consistent throughout his career, so too was his call for moderation in the lifestyle of prelates. This call for moderation was characteristic of many of his works related to episcopal reform. In these

---

[26] These charges were constants in d'Ailly's critique since his earliest days at Paris and continued through his years as bishop and cardinal. They can be found in his *Sermo in synodo ambianis* given in Amiens in 1375, Tschackert, 4, the *Invectiva Ezechielis contra pseudopastores* of 1381/1382, Tschackert, 13, his *Sermo de Sancto Bernardo*, Tschackert, 22, given between 1372 and 1395, the *De materia concilii*, Oakley, 331, written in 1411, and his *De reformatione*, Miethke-Weinrich, 1:354–362, 366–370, published in 1416 at the Council of Constance.

[27] *Invectiva Ezechialis contra pseudopastores*, Tschackert, 13. '... ut pseudopastores se ipsos pascentes.'

[28] *De reformatione*, Miethke-Weinrich, 1:358. On the topic of 'the patrimony of the poor,' see Gratian's *Decretum*, C. 12, q. 2, c. 28 and C. 16, q. 2, c. 68; Friedberg, 1:697 and 1:784–785. For a full historical treatment of ecclesiastical property as the 'patrimony of the poor,' see Brian Tierney, *Medieval Poor Law* (Berkeley: University of California Press, 1959), D'Ailly's most extensive treatment of the issue of ecclesiastical property can be found in the second part of his *De potestate ecclesiastica*, Dupin 2:942–944, wherein he shows great dependence upon the teaching of John of Paris.

works, d'Ailly argued that Christ's mandate to the apostles and disciples regarding dress and possessions essentially indicated that the preacher of the Gospel should not display an excessive desire to possess material goods, should not accumulate such goods to the point of superfluity and should not show inordinate solicitude for the possessions he already has. Contrary attitudes only serve to inhibit the prelate in the effective preaching of the Gospel.[29]

D'Ailly further argues that this return to a spirit of moderation, in addition to fulfilling Christ's mandate to the apostles and disciples, would also help to alleviate the burdens of poor prelates. In his writings, d'Ailly often emphasized the extreme variations of poverty and wealth found in the lives of prelates. While never advocating equality in the realm of material possessions, d'Ailly does call at least for a 'moderate inequality' among prelates in the realm of temporal and material possessions.[30] Finally, returning to a familiar theme, d'Ailly asserts that only by the application of such moderation will the Church's possessions as the patrimony of the poor be sufficiently protected from diminution, the flock not burdened, and the faithful not scandalized.[31]

A survey of synodal legislation in d'Ailly's own diocese of Cambrai reveals a long-standing concern with the issue of clerical lifestyle. The earliest extant synodal legislation of 1238 dealt in detail on such matters as clerical dress, especially during liturgical ceremonies, and improper forms of clerical recreation and occupations. The recodification of synodal legislation in 1307 which remained in force with some modifications until 1550, and which therefore was operative during d'Ailly's episcopal tenure from 1397 to 1411, continued fairly much the same legislation.[32] By its very nature, such synodal legislation most probably

---

[29] *Homelia facta in synodo Cameracensi*, TS, 6. 'In his autem verbis nihil aliud ostenditur nisi quod predicator debet esse absolutus a cupiditate, superfluitate et solicitudine temporali; ne in his impediatur aut quomodolibet retardetur a predicatione verbi.' *Invectiva Ezechielis contra pseudopastores*, Tschackert, 13, '... non ad superabundantiam sed ad sufficientiam, non ad superfluitatem sed ad necessitatem, non ad ostentationem sed ad sustentationem.'

[30] *Epistola II in Joannem XXIII*, Dupin 2:877.

[31] *Invectiva Ezechielis contra pseudopastores*, Tschackert, 13.

[32] For synodal legislation in Cambrai before 1307 see P.C. Boeren, 'Les plus anciens statuts du diocèse de Cambrai,' *RDC*, 3 (1953), 1–32; 131–172; 377–415; 4 (1954), 131–158. The pertinent decrees can be found in 3:151–154 and 4:145–147. The texts of the 1307 recodification of synodal legislation can be found in J.F. Schannat and J. Hartzheim, *Concilia Germaniae*, 2nd ed., 11 vols (Cologne, 1759–1790), 4:66–94. The pertinent decrees are at 4:76–77.

related to the lower clergy, especially priests, and not to the episcopal order to which many of d'Ailly's concerns were directed in his major writings.

While one would expect that the abuses emphasized by d'Ailly in relationship to clerical orders would be appropriately treated by the reform decrees of the Council of Constance, that unfortunately was not the case. The only area of d'Ailly's concerns with regard to clerical lifestyle related to the issue of clerical dress. The Council addressed this issue in its second set of reform decrees which were passed during its forty-third session in March, 1418.[33] After considerable debate, the Council issued a decree calling first for the observance of previous conciliar legislation on the issue. The decree next criticized the desire of many clerics to conform to the customs of the laity with regard to clothing. In this context, the Council dealt with the issues of color and style. While the Council said did not specify the colors to be worn by the clergy, the use of bright colors such as red and green as well as the use of brightly striped patterns were singled out. Similar prescriptions, however, had often been made in previous conciliar and synodal legislation. In the realm of style, Constance also censured the use of long sumptuous gloves, clothing slit at the sides and back, and the use of fur trimmings. Especially condemned was the wearing of such clothing under liturgical vestments during religious services. Violations in this area were to result in the loss of one's ecclesiastical income for one month. Such lost income was to be turned over not to the care of the poor, as d'Ailly most likely would have recommended, but to the maintenance of the fabric of the church in which the cleric's benefice was located.

In addition to his emphasis on poverty as integrally related to the virtue of temperance, d'Ailly also stressed the exercise of clerical celibacy as another manifestation of that virtue. Like poverty, celibacy was also regarded as central to the realization of the apostolic ideal. Clearly the greatest obstacle to the observance of clerical celibacy during d'Ailly's time was that of concubinage. In many dioceses of Western Europe in the late Middle Ages, the problem of clerical concubinage

---

[33] For the Council's deliberations on the issue of clerical dress see Stump, *The Reforms of the Council of Constance*, 139–142. The text of the Constance decree on clerical dress and lifestyle can be found in *DEC*, 1:449–450. Stump especially singles out a similar decree of the Council of Vienne (1311–1312), c. 8, which became incorporated into the decretals of Clement V. See Clem., 3.1.2, Friedberg, 2:1157–1158.

was a serious one, although one must be cautious when dealing with the exaggerated charges of heretics, preachers, and reformers of the time. Recent research has indicated that although diocesan and provincial synods often legislated against clerical concubinage, no firm conclusion as to its extent can be deduced from their statements. Such research has also argued that from an analysis of the extant records of diocesan visitations, the number of concubinate clergy was not as extensive as previously believed.[34] A similar conclusion holds for Cambrai, although the bishops there experienced much frustration in trying to eradicate clerical concubinage.[35]

The issue of clerical celibacy was a constantly recurring theme in d'Ailly's pastoral thought from his earliest sermons before the synods of Amiens and Paris in 1375 to his *De reformatione* delivered before the Council of Constance in 1416.[36] The most extensive treatment d'Ailly gave to the subject of clerical concubinage was in his third synodal address while bishop of Cambrai from 1397 to 1411. In that address he emphasized the seriousness of the problem and his many attempts to deal with it both in his sermons and in synodal legislation. While he speaks of some success in these efforts, he also admits that that success has not been as extensive as he would have liked it to have been. D'Ailly's statement gives some indication of frustration in not being able to root out the problem of concubinage in his diocese.[37] In his *De reformatione*, d'Ailly indicates that ecclesiastical penalties such as suspension and excommunication have proved ineffective in eradicating cler-

---

[34] On the question of the actual extent of clerical concubinage in late medieval France see P. Adam, *La vie paroissiale en France au xiv*e *siècle* (Paris: Sirey, 1964), 151–163 and Michel Mollat, *La vie et la pratique religieuse au xiv*e *siècle et dans la 1*re *partie du xv*e*, principalement en France* (Paris: Centre de documentation universitaire, 1963). For an analysis of the arguments in support of clerical celibacy in the early and high Middle Ages, especially as they pertain to ritual purity see Michael Frassetto, ed., *Medieval Purity and Piety: Essays on Medieval Clerical Celibacy and Religious Reform* (New York: Garland, 1998).

[35] Cf. Pierrard, *Cambrai et Lille*, 75–76.

[36] Cf. *Sermo in Synodo Ambianis*, Tschackert, 4; *Sermo in Synodo in Ecclesia Parisiensi*, Tschackert, 5–6; *De reformatione*, Miethke-Weinrich, 1:368.

[37] *Homilia facta in Synodo Cameracensi*, TS, 9. Referring to the phenomenon of clerical concubinage, d'Ailly designates it as 'hoc horrendum et abominabile monstrum' and indicates his frustration in failing to eradicate this problem, 'Multa in sermonibus, multa in statutibus synodalibus latravimus. Nec tamen hujusmodi scandalum ab hac dyocesi effugare valuimus ut vellemus.' In his *De reformatione*, Miethke-Weinrich, 1:368. he refers to concubinage as 'illa scandalosissima consuetudo.' D'Ailly's sense of frustration in not being able to root out the problem of concubinage in his diocese would seem to corroborate the conclusions of Pierrard.

ical concubinage and he advocates the stronger punishment of deposition from office and associated benefices. It is to be noted that in his many references to the problem and his attempts to resolve it, d'Ailly's treatment of clerical celibacy, like that of many late medieval moralists and reformers, was essentially negative in content, emphasizing the harmful consequences of concubinage. Little was said with regard to the more positive and pastoral dimensions of clerical celibacy.

In addition to the immorality represented by clerical concubinage, d'Ailly stresses the negative consequences of concubinage with regard to the overall image of the priesthood. Since the personal lives of concubinate priests were held in such disdain by so many it is not surprising, he affirms, that the image of the priesthood itself has been considerably compromised. Negative consequences are also seen in the realm of pastoral effectiveness of the clergy, especially with regard to the administration of the sacraments. Sacraments administered by concubinate priests were regarded by many as having little spiritual worth or efficacy.[38]

While d'Ailly is strongly critical of concubinate priests, he is surprisingly more critical of those who are excessive in their attacks against such priests. He accuses them of fostering irreverence and disobedience towards the diocesan clergy. Thus while trying to resolve one scandal, they inadvertently create another. Such is the product of an indiscreet zeal. While d'Ailly does not identify who these persons might be, it can be reasonably assumed that they may well have been preachers from the ranks of the mendicant orders. He accuses such preachers as manifesting more a spirit of juridical rigor than evangelical sensitivity and singles out three aspects of their preaching that reflect such rigor. First among the teaching of such critics which d'Ailly censors is their argument that priests involved in concubinage are automatically suspended from their priestly office and their Masses and sacramental ministrations, therefore, are to be avoided by the laity. Secondly, they argue that parishioners who knowingly assist at Masses celebrated by such priests commit mortal sin. Thirdly, that even if concubinate priests are tolerated by their bishops, they are to be avoided by their parishioners.[39]

In support of such arguments, these critics, d'Ailly maintains, have recourse to canonical and theological sources. With regard to canonical sources, the canons frequently referred to are *Nullus*, D. 32, c. 5;

---

[38] *Homilia facta in Synodo Cameracensi, TS*, 9.
[39] *Homilia facta in Synodo Cameracensi, TS*, 10.

Preter, D. 32, c. 6, and *Tanta*, X, 5, 3, 7. The first two of these canons come respectively from the papal reigns of Nicholas II (1058–1061) and Alexander II (1061–1073), immediate predecessors of Gregory VII (1073–1085). The third canon is from the earlier pontificate of Deusdedit (615–618).[40] D'Ailly's charge of excessive juridical rigor has some validity when one analyzes the canons at issue. While strong in their condemnation of clerical concubinage and in urging the faithful not to assist at Masses of such clerics or to receive the sacraments from them, these canons do not prescribe automatic suspension of such clerics. Nor do they indicate that those who do assist at their Masses or receive the sacraments from them are guilty of mortal sin. The need for an official episcopal condemnation of concubinate clerics before such obligations are imposed upon the laity is also clearly affirmed in these canons. As Gratian indicates these restrictions were imposed out of the conviction that they would shame concubinate clergy into repentance and abandonment of their lifestyle.

Among the theological authorities used by critics in their attacks upon concubinate clerics, the principal theological authority cited was that of Aquinas, especially his *Quaestiones quotlibetales*, 11, q. 8, a. 1, where, in dealing with the question of assisting at Masses of priests guilty of fornication, he clearly stipulates that in such cases the faithful would not only sin mortally but would also suffer excommunication. They fail to admit, however, that Aquinas does stipulate that for such punishments to be operative the bishop must officially and publicly condemn the priest involved. In cases, however, where the local ordinary has not taken such action because of negligence, lack of courage, or fear, Aquinas maintains that the faithful remain nonetheless bound to canonical legislation and subject to the severe punishments described above.[41]

In his response to the position taken by Aquinas on the issue of concubinate clerics, d'Ailly essentially agrees with the first part of his analysis, namely that in the case of concubinate clergy, the faithful are to withdraw themselves from their pastoral ministrations only after such clergy have been officially judged guilty and publicly denounced

---

[40] *Homelia facta in Synodo Cameracensi*, TS, 10–11. The three canons cited are found in Friedberg, 1:117–118 and 2:750. Gratian's commentary on these canons is to be found in his *dicta post* of D. 32, c. 6.

[41] *Homilia facta in Synodo Cameracensi*, TS, 10–11. For Aquinas' *Quaestiones quodlibetales* see the edition of Raymond Spiazzi, 8th ed. rev. (Rome: Marietta, 1949).

as such by their bishop. Unlike Aquinas, however, he does not insist that where negligent or weak bishops fail to take such actions the faithful are obliged to withdraw from the pastoral ministrations of a concubinate clergy. D'Ailly strongly opposes any such obligation until the necessary episcopal actions have been formally and officially taken.

While d'Ailly could readily find support in canon law for his arguments against the obligation to withdraw from the pastoral ministrations of concubinate clerics before a formal episcopal condemnation, especially the decrees of Lucius III (1181–1185) and Gregory IX (1227–1241), he prefers to base his argument primarily on the issue of ecclesiastical order.[42] Allowing the faithful to so act, he asserts, would lead to a threefold scandal within a diocese. First, he argues, it would engender disobedience, rebellion, and rash accusations. Merely being seen with a woman could lead to such charges. Secondly, it would give rise to discord and division within the diocese, for factions would develop within the parish according to whether or not one agreed with the accusation. Some parishioners, he argues, are overly suspicious of their pastors on such matters and therefore too often prone to agree with every accusation against them. Many parishioners, moreover, lack the discretion needed in evaluating such accusations. Most parishioners, finally, do not have the legal sophistication required for interpreting and applying canon law. Thirdly, he maintains, that allowing parishioners such freedom could lead, at times, to precipitous judgements. At times, he asserts, the curate may already have secretly repented but have received permission from his confessor to gradually separate himself from the woman with whom he has associated. Such separations, he argues, are not always easy. According to d'Ailly, moral theology does not always demand that a sinner abruptly remove himself from the occasion of his sin. A gradual separation may not only be prudent but also the only possible way out of a difficult situation.[43]

In his analysis of the relationship between concubinate priests and their parishioners, d'Ailly affirms his indebtedness to the teaching of his former pupil, close friend, and successor as chancellor of the Univer-

---

[42] *Homelia facta in Synodo Cameracensi*, *TS*, 11. The legislation of Lucius III and Gregory IX on this issue is to be found respectively at X, 3, 2, 7 and 10, Friedberg, 2:455–457. This entire title deals with the problem of concubinate clergy

[43] *Homelia facta in Synodo Cameracensi*, *TS*, 11. 'Et hanc triplici radice declaramus, nam oppositum dicere est dare subditis occasionem triplicis scandali. Primo quidem inobedientiae et rebellionis. Secundo discordiae et divisionis. Tertio temerariae diudicationis.'

sity of Paris, Jean Gerson (1363–1429).[44] While both agreed that parishioners should separate themselves from the pastoral ministrations of concubinate clerics only after their bishops have judged them guilty and publicly pronounced that judgement, d'Ailly does not follow Gerson's more lenient advice that bishops proceed cautiously in issuing such judgements. Gerson's reason for adopting such a cautious policy was twofold. First, he feared that many clerics if forced to give up their concubines would turn to even more dissolute forms of life. Secondly, Gerson also argued that the removal of large numbers of concubinate priests would inflict considerable pastoral hardships upon the faithful. For Gerson, it was better that the sacraments be administered by concubinate priests than not administered at all.[45]

In view of the persistence of the problem of clerical concubinage in the late medieval Church, it is surprising that the Council of Constance did not take up the issue in the reform decrees that it eventually passed. The issue was certainly debated in the meetings of the first reform commission and specific proposals were made to deal with the problem but no final legislation was ever effected. In the proposals of the first reform commission, concubinate clerics were to be ordered to give up their concubines within one month or suffer loss of their benefices. Given the long-standing nature of the concubinage problem, it is hard to regard such a demand as realistically enforceable. Considerable debate, however, centered around the issue that so concerned d'Ailly, namely whether or not parishioners should avoid the sacramental ministrations of concubinate clerics before such clerics have been judged guilty and publicly denounced by their bishop. While recogniz-

---

[44] *Homelia facta in Synodo Cameracensi*, TS, 11. 'In hac autem et eius annexis inferius dicendis non ego solus sed venerabilis doctor Johannes cancellarius parisiensis carissimus socius meus habita simile collatione pariter concordamus.'

[45] It is very difficult to determine to which of Gerson's work d'Ailly is referring. It cannot be Gerson's *Dialogus apologeticus pro coelibatu ecclesiasticorum*, Glorieux, 10:145–163, which was written as a response to Guillaume Saignet's treatise against clerical celibacy because that work was composed in June, 1423, several years after d'Ailly's death. It may have been Gerson's *Rememoratio agendorum durante subtractione*, a work which was most likely written in July, 1408 while d'Ailly was still bishop of Cambrai. This work is essentially a list of items to be checked by bishops in their diocesan visitations and can be found in Glorieux, 6:108–114. The specific references to concubinate clerics is at 112–113. For a brief analysis of Gerson's views on clerical concubinage see Pascoe, *Jean Gerson*, 172–173, and Brown, *Pastor and Laity*, 54–55. For a fuller survey of Gerson's thought on clerical celibacy see Nicole Grévy-Pons, *Célibat et nature: une controverse médiévale* (Paris: CNRS, 1975), In this work, Grévy-Pons has also reedited Gerson's *Pro coelibatu ecclesiasticorum* as well as the treatise of Saignet.

ing the arguments on both sides of the question, the committee, using arguments similar to those of d'Ailly, who as will be recalled was one of its members, maintained that concubinate clerics should be avoided only after public denunciation by their bishop.[46]

The subsequent concordats effected by the Council with the various nations at Constance contained no direct legislation on the issue of clerical concubinage although some historians see the *Ad vitanda* provision of the German Concordat as having been influenced by the debate over clerical concubinage since it states that the sacramental administrations of a priest are not to be avoided until the priest has actually incurred ecclesiastical censure and has been officially denounced as such. The wording of this provision in the German Concordat, however, makes no specific reference to clerical concubinage but comprises all categories of ecclesiastical censures and extends not only to persons but also to groups of persons, churches, and communities.[47] Despite the failure of Constance to act on the issue of clerical concubinage, either through direct conciliar legislation or through concordats, there was clearly sufficient earlier canonical legislation on the issue which could have been invoked. The twenty fifth session of the Council of Trent in December, 1563 reaffirmed much of this legislation in its fourteenth reform decree but added stiffer penalties and clarified some procedural questions.[48]

As indicated earlier, in d'Ailly's thought the third concrete manner in which the virtue of temperance manifests itself relates to the area of humility. When we turn to the concrete manner in which humility is treated by d'Ailly, we find that it is primarily in terms of the manner in which a prelate exercises his office. His views on this point are especially evident in his first synodal sermon at Cambrai. For this sermon, he took as his scriptural text that of Eph. 4:1–6 where Paul urges the Christians at Ephesus to live a life worthy of their calling, that is a life characterized by humility, gentleness, patience, and union towards and with their fellow Christians as members of the Mystical Body of Christ. D'Ailly then applies the message that Paul addresses to the

---

[46] Stump, *The Reforms of the Council of Constance*, 140–141. The text of the commission is on 364–365.

[47] For the text of the *Ad vitandum* provision in the German Concordat see Mercati, *Raccolta di Concordati*, 1:163. On the question of the possible influence of the deliberations of Constance's reform commission on the *Ad vitandum* provision see Stump, *The Reforms of the Council of Constance*, 140–141, n. 7.

[48] For this Tridentine reform decree see *DEC*, 2:792–793.

whole Church at Ephesus more specifically to himself as bishop and to his clergy as his pastoral assistants. Consequently in the exercise of their office they are not to show themselves as proud, domineering, or austere, but as humble, patient, and understanding servants. They are, indeed, to be preeminent in these qualities.[49]

In stressing the Pauline model for the exercise of ecclesiastical office, d'Ailly demonstrates again his emphasis on the renewal of the episcopal and priestly offices in the spirit of the *vita apostolica*. The consistency of d'Ailly's views on the apostolic dimension of ecclesiastical office can be seen in the fact as early as 1375, twenty two years before assuming the leadership of the diocese of Cambrai, in a sermon delivered before the Synod of Paris in 1375, he contrasted the pastoral style of ministry found in the Scriptures with the tyrannical style characteristic of some bishops and priests.[50] Many years after Cambrai, in a Pentecost sermon delivered at the Council of Constance in 1417, just three years before his death, d'Ailly again reminded the prelates there that they were to govern not as tyrants but in the style and spirit of the apostles.[51]

While d'Ailly has much to say about the need for cultivating the various virtues needed in the exercise of an ecclesiastical office, he has surprisingly little to say about the role of ascetical practices, personal prayer, and private devotions in the lives of ecclesiastical prelates. With regard to ascetical practices, he mentions the need for fasting, abstinence, and fraternal correction but little more. In the category of prayer and private devotions, he has even less to say beyond the need for the faithful recitation of the liturgical hours which no doubt constituted the major portion of the prayer life of an ecclesiastical prelate.[52] Given the extensive but yet relatively unexplored realm of d'Ailly's ascetical and devotional thought, this judgement will certainly be modified as research in these areas of d'Ailly's thought progresses.[53]

---

[49] *Sermo in Synodo Cameracensi I*, TS, 3. '… in quo nobis pastoribus et prelatis ceterisque ministris ecclesiasticis datur imitationis exemplum ut subiectos nobis non sicut superbi domini dura et austera correctione premamus, sed sicut humiles conservi dulci mansuetudine, mansueta benignitate, benignaque monitione et obsecratione praeveniamus.'

[50] *Sermo in Synodo in Ecclesia Parisiensi*, Tschackert, 5–6. D'Ailly builds his whole sermon around 1 Cor. 4:1–5 wherein Paul describes his ministry in terms of stewardship and service.

[51] *Sermo in die Pentecostes, II*, TS, 4. 'Attendite vos pastores ad regendam hanc ecclesiam non modo tyranico sed more apostolico.'

[52] *De reformatione*, Miethke-Weinrich, 1:360.

[53] There are no extensive studies of d'Ailly's ascetical teaching. For brief surveys see

Yet the fact remains that while he expended great care on the need for pastoral and moral renewal in the lives of prelates, little attention was given by d'Ailly to the question of a distinctly priestly spirituality that was so badly needed by bishops and priests in the exercise of their pastoral office. On this point, however, d'Ailly was fairly typical of his times. Similar criticism can be made of other late medieval reformers. The closest one comes to such a spirituality was that of the *vita canonica* in the high and late Middle Ages, which as will be recalled, was characterized by a combination of the active and contemplative forms of life. This form of life, however, was adopted by only a small number of the diocesan clergy. The more dynamic elements of this canonical movement reorganized themselves into religious orders such as the Augustinians, the Victorines and the Premonstratensians.[54] The development of a distinctly priestly spirituality had to await the appearance in the sixteenth and seventeenth centuries of the Italian and French Oratorian movements respectively under Philip Neri, Pierrre de Bérulle, and the Congregation of Saint Suplice under Jean-Jacques Olier.

Regardless of this deficiency in his program for the pastoral and personal reform of the lives of ecclesiastical prelates, d'Ailly, as seen earlier, continually emphasized the important role played by clerics in setting a good example for the laity and the consequences of that example for the reform and renewal of the Church. In one of his synodal homilies at Cambrai, he pronounced a series of prophetic warnings against those bishops and priests whose lives distorted or even denied the evangelical ideal that Christ set for his apostles and disciples.[55] In his *De reformatione* presented at the Council of Constance in 1416, he employed the similes used by Christ when he challenged his apostles and disciples to become 'the salt of the earth,' and 'the light of the world.' D'Ailly indeed reminds the bishops and priests of his day that as the successors of the apostles and disciples they are called to the same high ideals.[56]

Van Steenberghen, 'Pierre d'Ailly,' *DTC*, 1:256–260, Tschackert, *Peter von Ailli*, 322–328, and Salembier, *Petrus ab Alliaco*, 326–348.

[54] For the most recent work on the canonical life in the medieval world, see Jean Châtillon, *Le movement canonial au moyen age: spiritualité et culture*.

[55] *Homelia facta in Synodo Cameracensi*, *TS*, 4.

[56] *De reformatione*, Miethke-Weinrich, 1:356. The scriptural reference is Mt. 5:13–16.

3. *Episcopal Models of the Apostolic Life*

Given the importance of personal example in d'Ailly's thought on the apostolic renewal of ecclesiastical office and lifestyle, the question can be raised as to whether he held up any particular prelates as models of the apostolic ideal, especially someone from the ranks of the saints. As seen earlier, d'Ailly shows great reverence for the towering figures of the twelfth and thirteenth centuries such as Bernard, Francis, and, to a lesser extent, Dominic. Bernard he frequently cited for his timely admonitions to prelates concerning the various difficulties encountered in the exercise of their office, especially the tendency to forget its ministerial nature. Francis and Dominic he saw as the great exponents of the evangelical ideal especially with regard to preaching and the exercise of the virtues of poverty, chastity, and humility. Despite the close association of these saints with the apostolic ideal, all were members of religious orders and as such could not ultimately serve as an overall model for the renewal of the evangelical life among bishops and priests that d'Ailly so earnestly championed.

With regard to models of the apostolic life in the fourteenth and early fifteenth centuries, the problem is even more complex. André Vauchez has pointed out that although there was no great decline in the number of saints being canonized in this period, few seem to have attracted the universal recognition attained by Bernard, Francis, and Dominic. The number of prelates canonized during this period, moreover, continued to remain relatively low. Among their number, many seem very atypical as prelates in the sense that their sanctity appears to have emerged not so much in direct relationship to the apostolic nature of their ecclesiastical office but more in a monastic and mendicant context. Many even displayed a genuine reluctance to assume their office and once having assumed office often manifested a strong desire to relinquish it in search of a more contemplative life. In fact the two prelates that Vauchez singles out as atypical are the very ones that d'Ailly holds out as model prelates, namely Louis of Anjou and Peter of Luxembourg.[57]

---

[57] On the question of late medieval saints and sainthood, especially those from the episcopal ranks, see the comments by André Vauchez in *Histoire du Christianisme*, 6:538–539, as well as his *Sainthood in the Late Middle Ages* (Cambridge: Cambridge University Press, 1997).

Born in 1274, Louis of Anjou was the second son of Charles II of Anjou, King of Naples (1285–1309). Highly ascetical in character, Louis fell under strong Franciscan influence especially during the years 1288 to 1295 when he was held as hostage for his father by the King of Aragon. This influence, primarily through confessors and teachers, continued after his return to Naples in 1296. As recent scholarship has shown, although Louis had contact with Provincale Spirituals such as Peter John Olivi and their sympathizers such as Raymond Geoffroi, who was deposed as minister general of the Franciscans by Boniface VIII in 1295, most of Louis' Franciscan confessors and teachers cannot be classified as Spirituals.[58]

After his ordination in Rome by Boniface VIII in May, 1296, Louis yielded to the urgings of the pope that he accept the bishopric of Toulouse but did so only after the pope first allowed him to join the Franciscan order. He did not take up residence in Toulouse until May, 1297 and died suddenly in August of that same year. Although he served as bishop of Toulouse but a short time he apparently did so with much enthusiasm, showing great concern for the clergy and the poor. In his relationships with his clergy, he was especially concerned with their spiritual and moral formation. He also conducted a visitation of his diocese. For the poor he showed a special preference. He increased the amount of diocesan expenditures for their care and personally distributed alms daily. His own lifestyle as bishop exemplified the simplicity and poverty of the Franciscan tradition, while yet avoiding the extremes of the Franciscan Spirituals.

In a sermon given at Constance on August 19, 1417 commemorating the anniversary of Louis of Anjou's death, d'Ailly recognized many of the above mentioned accomplishments in Louis' life, especially his simple lifestyle, his care of the poor, and his concern for the spiritual and moral reformation of the clergy. This latter point provided d'Ailly

---

[58] For the basic details of Louis of Anjou's life and spirituality see Margaret Toynbee, *St. Louis of Toulouse and the Process of Canonization in the Fourteenth Century* (Manchester: Manchester University Press, 1929), E. Pasztor, *Per la storia di San Ludovico d'Angio, 1274–1297* (Rome: Istituto storico italiano per il Medio Evo, 1955), and more recently Jacques Paul, 'Saint Louis d'Anjou, franciscain et évêque de Toulouse (1274–1297),' *CF*, 7 (1972), 59–90. On the issue of Spiritual Franciscan influences at the Angevin Court of Naples see the articles of Ronald G. Musto, 'Queen Sancia of Naples (1286–1345) and the Spiritual Franciscans,' in *Women of the Medieval World: Essays in Honor of John H. Mundy*, ed. Julius Kirshner and Suzanne F. Wemple (New York: Blackwell, 1985), 69–100, and 'Franciscan Joachimism at the Court of Naples, 1309–1345: A New Appraisal,' *AFH* 90 (1997), 419–486.

with the opportunity to criticize the reform efforts at Constance, indicating that there have been too many speeches on the topic but little accomplished in terms of legislation. He even goes so far as to accuse the members of the Council of lacking the personal conviction needed to effect such reforms.[59] D'Ailly, then, held up Louis as an example for all ecclesiastical prelates and strongly contrasted Louis' approach toward the episcopal office and its pastoral obligations with the views and actions of those whom he so critically labeled earlier as pseudo-pastors. In this regard, he again has recourse to the prophetic warnings of Ezechiel against the false prophets of Israel. He also contrasted the self-serving concept of ecclesiastical office with the evangelical ideal evoked by Christ.[60] He even recommends that the cardinals at Constance use Louis as a model in their search for a papal candidate whose election would bring an end to the prolonged schism within the Church and initiate its long-awaited reform.[61]

D'Ailly's high praise for Louis of Anjou as bishop and his promotion of him as a model for the prelates of his time does raise some questions in view of Vauchez's comments on late medieval saints and prelates. In a sense, Louis was the embodiment of the atypical prelate that Vauchez has pointed out. As seen earlier, he was very reluctant to assume the episcopal office and did so only after being allowed to become a Franciscan. Once in office, he often spoke of resigning and freeing himself from its burdens. As his emphasis upon personal poverty and care of the poor shows, his spirituality flowed more from his Franciscan commitment than from the very nature of his episcopal office. His brief reign also did not exemplify all the episcopal ideals that d'Ailly himself had so strongly championed, especially the emphasis upon preaching. Finally, while not necessarily an atypical case, his elevation to the episcopacy and his subsequent canonization were certainly facilitated by his noble lineage, especially his connection with the ruling houses of France and Naples. On this point, d'Ailly countered by emphasizing

---

[59] *Sermo de Sancto Ludovico Tolosano*, TS, 10. Speaking of the vices of the clergy, d'Ailly adds: '... et contra haec in hoc sacro concilio multa de reformatione loquimur sed pauca vel nulla exequimur. Multa in codicibus scribimus, pauca in cordibus de morum reformatione sentimus.'

[60] *Sermo de Sancto Ludovico Tolosano*, TS, 9. 'O utinam hoc exemplum imitari studeant prelati ecclesiae ut sic evitare valeant divinam maledictionem Ezechielis prophetae. Vae pastoribus Israel qui pascebant semetipsos ... qui iuxta sententiam apostoli quaerunt quae sua sunt non quae Jesu Christi.'

[61] *Sermo de Sancto Ludovico Tolosano*, TS, 5. 'O utinam sancta mater ecclesia ... talem summum pontificem ... per canonicam electionem celeriter habere mereatur.'

that Louis possessed not only nobility of birth but also a nobility of virtue which distinguished him from so many other members of the nobility who, devoid of virtue, sought and often obtained the episcopal office.[62]

While there is indeed some truth to Vauchez's thesis as applied to Louis of Anjou, there is a sense in which his case was not as atypical as it may first seem. With regard to Louis' hesitancy to assume the episcopal office and his frequently expressed desire to resign from that office, it must be remembered that medieval theologians frequently raised the question as to whether one could intentionally aspire to the episcopal office and sought to distinguish the validity of the various motives that could inspire that desire. In a sense a certain fear, hesitancy, and humility were expected in an episcopal candidate. Medieval theologians also debated whether one could resign the episcopal office in order to more effectively pursue one's own sanctification, especially by entering a religious order. The frequency with which these questions were debated in the Middle Ages would indicate that such phenomena were not quite so atypical.[63] The fact that Louis was a member of the Franciscan Order was certainly not so unusual since the elevation of members of religious orders to the episcopal rank had become increasingly common in the high Middle Ages, nor is it surprising that such bishops would remain committed to the fundamental orientation of their previous spiritual formation.

What is especially distinctive in d'Ailly's Sermon on Louis of Anjou is the apocalyptic context in which the saint is presented. As seen in the first chapter of this work, in several of his major sermons and treatises d'Ailly presented an apocalyptic interpretation of the Church's history in terms of distinctive periods of persecution. The chronological divisions of these periods, however, varied somewhat in d'Ailly's different writings but in his Sermon on St. Francis, delivered in Paris in 1380, he described the fourth period as extending from the time of the German Emperor Henry IV (1056–1106), who strongly opposed the Gregorian reformers on the issue of episcopal appointments, to the beginning of the Great Western Schism which saw the Church divided according to

---

[62] *Sermo de Sancto Ludovico Tolosano*, TS, 7. 'Unde nec in ipso magnopere aut miror aut laudo quod nobilem ortum habuit ... Miror potius ... quod hanc originis suae claritatem nequamque perversorum morum tenebris obfuscavit sed magis ac magis illustravit. Adeo ut etiam si obscurus ei ortus fuisset, nihilominus veram nobilitatem quae non nisi per virtutem unique parta est sibi ipsi contulisset.'

[63] For Aquinas' discussion of these questions see *ST*, 2, 2, q. 185, a. 1; a. 2; a. 4.

the different papal allegiances. During this period, d'Ailly, adopting the views of Hildegard of Bingen, saw the forces of persecution as coming not from forces outside the Church, as was the case for previous persecutions, but from those within the Church, namely the forces of moral, doctrinal, and spiritual decline. D'Ailly saw the cause of this decline primarily in terms of the Church's abandonment of the evangelical ideal of poverty, chastity, and humility, especially on the part of ecclesiastical prelates. He recognized, however, that even during the fourth period of persecution the Church was not deprived of saintly personalities who exemplified that ideal in their lives and served as models for reform and renewal. Among such saints, he named Bernard of Clairvaux, Thomas Becket, Hildegard of Bingen, Joachim of Fiore, Dominic, and Francis. As seen earlier, d'Ailly regarded Francis as surpassing all the others in his dedication to the evangelical ideal.

In his Sermon on Louis of Anjou, given at Constance in 1417, d'Ailly employs the same chronological periods of persecution and decline in the Church's history as given in his Sermon on St. Francis in 1380. He also continues the same Hildegardian emphasis upon the fourth period of persecution in terms of internal moral decline.[64] He even goes so far as to place Louis of Anjou among the saints of the fourth period whom he regarded as embodying the evangelical ideal, and whose example provides hope for the Church as it lives out the fifth period of its history, namely, the persecutions inflicted by the Great Western Schism.[65] Especially noteworthy in d'Ailly's sermon is the fact that Louis is presented not primarily as a Franciscan mendicant but as bishop, reformer, and model for the episcopacy during the period of the Great Schism. As seen earlier, it was upon the example of such bishops committed to the apostolic ideal in the exercise of their office that d'Ailly rested his hopes for the resolution of the Great Schism and the reform and renewal of the Church, which, if realized, would indeed postpone the arrival of the Antichrist and the End-Times. A further indication of the apocalyptic context of d'Ailly's portrayal of Louis of

---

[64] *Sermo de Sancto Ludovico Tolosano*, TS, 12. 'Hoc namque miserabile tempus beata Hyldegardis germanorum prophetessa muliebre vocat et infame ipsumque ab anno dominicae incarnationis millesimo centesimo asserit inchoasse quia tunc apostolorum doctrina et ardens justitia ... tardare et in hesitationem verti cepit. Et deinceps omnia ecclesiastica instituta in deterius descenderunt et ex quibusdam tenebris iniustitiae obtenebrata sunt.'

[65] *Sermo de Sancto Ludovico Tolosano*, TS, 13. In this passage the list of the saints enumerated is taken practically verbatim from his Sermon on St. Francis.

Anjou is seen in the fact that d'Ailly expends considerable effort in his sermon to show that the miracles performed by Louis are not deceptive works of the Antichrist but those of a saintly and model bishop.[66]

After Louis of Anjou, the other episcopal figure that d'Ailly holds up as a model of reform was Peter of Luxembourg, bishop and cardinal of Metz.[67] Peter was born in 1369 and was a member of the House of Luxembourg. In 1377 at the age of eight he was sent to Paris for his elementary studies. Noted for his piety and aided no doubt by his family status, he was made a canon at Notre Dame in Paris the following year. In 1381 he received a canonry at Cambrai as well as archdeaconates in Dreux and Brussels. In 1384, though only fifteen, he was elected as bishop of Metz and was shortly afterward elevated to the cardinalate by the Avignon Pope, Clement VII. In 1386, he renounced his bishopric and took up residence in a Carthusian monastery near Avignon where he died the following year at the age of almost eighteen. Despite his youthful age, Peter, while bishop of Metz, distinguished himself for his pastoral activities, especially the visitation of his diocese and his concern for the poor. In his personal life, he followed a highly disciplined and ascetical routine. The same concern for the poor combined with an intense ascetical life distinguished his stay at the Carthusian monastery in Avignon. Although motions for his beatification began shortly after his death in 1387, they were not realized until 1527.

D'Ailly's thoughts on Peter of Luxembourg as a model of the evangelical ideal are captured in two sermons given in 1389 at the papal court at Avignon on behalf of his beatification. The first was delivered in the presence of the pope, Clement VII, and the second in the presence of the French king, Charles VI.[68] In these sermons there is no doubt that d'Ailly sees Peter of Luxembourg as a model not only for the reform of the episcopacy but also for the lives of all Christians during the troubled period of the Great Schism.[69] As in the case of Louis of

---

[66] *Sermo de Sancto Ludovico Tolosano*, TS, 14. '... his novissimis temporibus suspecta possunt miracula propter proximum Antichristi adventum.'

[67] For the life of Peter of Luxembourg see E. Fourier de Bacourt, *Vie du Bx. Pierre de Luxembourg* (Paris: Berche et Tralin, 1882), H. François, *La vie du Bx. Pierre de Luxembourg* (Nancy, 1927).

[68] The text for these two sermons can be found in C.E. Bulaeus, *Historia Universitatis Parisiensis*, 6 vols (Paris, 1665–1673; repr., Leiden: E.J. Brill, 1966), 4:651–663 and 4:663–669. All volume and page references will be to this edition.

[69] *Collatio pro apotheosi Petri de Luxemburgo, I*, Bulaeus, 4:661. Speaking of Peter's mira-

Anjou, d'Ailly also presents Peter of Luxembourg's life and episcopal activities within an apocalyptic context. While d'Ailly does not specifically detail the various periods of the Church's persecution as he did in his sermon on Louis of Anjou, he nonetheless maintains a general apocalyptic tone in these sermons. He leaves no doubt as to the difficulties faced by the Church in his day, a Church racked by schism and serious moral decline.[70] Even the city of Avignon is not spared d'Ailly's attacks. He compares Avignon to Nineveh which was converted by the preaching of Jonas without recourse to miracles and pleads that Avignon not be found more obdurate than Nineveh. Comparisons with Tyre and Sidon are also made.[71]

This apocalyptic context is also seen in the miracles attributed to Peter. As in the case of Louis of Anjou, the case was made by some that since the Church was living in the End-Times miracles should be looked upon with suspicion. Such miracles, they argued, may well be due to the efforts of the Antichrist to deceive true believers.[72] In his response, d'Ailly argues that the miracles of Peter can be so clearly established as valid that there is little fear of deception by the forces of the Antichrist. Such authentic miracles, d'Ailly continues, clearly establish Peter of Luxembourg as an example of the type of bishop so badly needed for the reformation of the Church during the period of the Great Schism.[73]

Through his use of Louis of Anjou and Peter of Luxembourg as episcopal models for the reform of the Church and by presenting their pastoral careers in an evangelical and apocalyptic context, d'Ailly returns to one of the central themes of his reform thought, namely that

---

cles, d'Ailly adds '… ista contigisse ad emendationem pessimorum morum nostri temporis et ad reformationem ipsorum.'

[70] *Collatio pro apotheosi Petri de Luxemburgo, I*, Bulaeus, 4:661–662. In these pages, d'Ailly speaks of the '… perditissimae mores nostrae aetatis.' He describes the mores of his contemporaries as worse than their predecessors. He quotes to this effect the Roman satirist Juvenal who wrote of his times: 'Omne in praecipiti vitium stetit.' The passage in Juvenal referred to can be found in Satire 1:149.

[71] *Collatio pro apotheosi Petri de Luxemburgo, I*, Bulaeus, 4:662.

[72] *Collatio pro apotheosi Petri de Luxemburgo, I*, Bulaeus, 4:659. 'Dicunt enim quidam novissimo hoc in tempore suspectissima debere considerari miracula quoniam ultimus Christi adventus expectatur, quem multae falsorum miraculorum apparentiae praevenient.'

[73] *Collatio pro apotheosi Petri de Luxemburgo, I*, Bulaeus, 4:659. 'Sane concesso primo assumitur de suspicione miraculorum … multa miracula fieri posse ac potuisse tam aperta et taliter circonstantionata ut omnino possit et debeat merito de eis tolli suspicio.'

only through an evangelically renewed episcopacy on both the pastoral and personal levels can the Church of his day be reformed and the tribulations associated with the coming of the Antichrist and the End-Times be postponed.

CHAPTER FIVE

THEOLOGIANS: STATUS, OFFICE, AUTHORITY

As seen in the previous chapters, for d'Ailly the reform and renewal of the Church rested upon the leadership of ecclesiastical prelates, especially bishops, and their return to the apostolic and evangelical ideal both in the exercise of their pastoral ministry and in the conduct of their personal lives. The ultimate understanding of this apostolic and evangelical model for reform and renewal within the Church, however, rests naturally upon the study of the Scriptures wherein that model and norm are contained and described. While within his diocese, the bishop remains the ultimate arbiter with regard to the understanding of the Scriptures, especially as they relate to matters of faith and pastoral care, the theologian also plays an important role in determining that understanding through his study and teaching of the Scriptures.

As will be seen in greater detail in the following chapter, theology and the work of theologians in the Middle Ages were so closely associated with the study and interpretation of the Scriptures that theology was often described simply as *Sacra Pagina*. This close association of the theologian with the Scriptures naturally raises the question of the respective roles of bishops and theologians with regard to the study, understanding, and teaching of the Scriptures. Difficulties in and failures to understand these respective roles often led to heated controversies between bishops and theologians, especially on the university level. The function of the present and following chapter is to study d'Ailly's views on the status, office, and authority of theologians as well as his understanding of theology as an intellectual discipline and the methodology employed by that discipline.

1. *Status: Order, Hierarchy and Corporation*

In analyzing the status of the medieval theologian, special care must be taken to place him not only within the context of the medieval university and the medieval Church but also within the general structure of medieval society. Modern historians of medieval society have strongly emphasized that society's conception of itself in terms of specific orders, generally political, social, intellectual and religious. The manner in which these orders were structured whether in relationship to one another or within themselves varied considerably but hierarchical and corporational principles of order were clearly among the most common modes of order.[1] Accordingly, Robert Guelluy emphasizes that the theologian must be seen within the context of a triple hierarchical order which was frequently evoked in describing medieval society. Employing categories developed and used by medieval thinkers, he designates that threefold order as secular, ecclesiastical, and scientific, understanding by the latter term the world of learning.[2] The Latin formulation of this triadic social order has been traditionally described by scholars in terms of *regnum*, *sacerdotium*, and *studium*.[3] Within each of these orders, moreover, there exists additional and highly complex hierarchical gradations.

As Guelluy indicates, in the twelfth and thirteenth centuries the scientific order became increasingly identified with the universities which were gradually replacing monastic and cathedral schools as the major

---

[1] For an excellent survey of medieval society in terms of specific levels of order, see Giles Constable, 'The Orders of Medieval Society,' in his *Three Studies in Medieval Religious and Social Thought* (Cambridge: Cambridge University Press, 1995), 249–341.

[2] Robert Guelluy, 'La place des théologiens dans l'Eglise et la société médiévale,' in *Miscellanea historica in honorem Alberti de Meyer*, 2 vols (Louvain: Bibliothèque de Université, 1946), 1, 571–589. On the medieval concepts of hierarchy and order see L. Manz, *Der Ordo-Gedanke: Ein Beitrag zur Frage des mittelalterlichen Ständegedankens* (Stuttgart: W. Kohlhammer, 1937), Herman Krings, *Ordo: Philosophisch-historische Grundlegung einer abendländischen Idee*, 2nd ed. (Hamburg: F. Meiner, 1982), and Gerhard B. Ladner, 'Homo Viator: Medieval Ideas on Order and Alienation,' *Speculum*, 42 (1967), 233–259. Augustine's concept of order and hierarchy has been studied by Josef Rief, *Der Ordobegriff des jungen Augustinus* (Paderborn: F. Schöningh, 1962) while Thomas Aquinas' views have been researched by A. de Silva Tarouca, 'L'Idée d'ordre dans la philosophie de saint Thomas d'Aquin,' *RNP*, 40 (1937), 341–384. Medieval concepts of order and hierarchy rest heavily upon the thought of Plato and Plotinus as it was transmitted to the West to a great extent through the writings of Pseudo-Dionysius. For the teaching of Pseudo-Dionsyius on these concepts see René Roques, *L'univers Dionysian: structure hiearchique du monde selon le Pseudo-Denys* (Paris: Aubier, 1954). A survey of Pseudo-Dionysius' writings, thought, and influence can be found in Roques' article, 'Denys L'Aréopagite,' in the *DSAM*, 3:244–429. For the influence of Pseudo-Dionysius' writings at the University of Paris see H.F. Dondaine, *Le corpus dionysian de l'Université de Paris au xiiie siècle*, (Rome: Edizioni di Storia e Letteratura, 1953).

[3] On the triadic structure of medieval society in terms of *sacerdotium*, *regnum*, and *studium*, see H. Grundmann, 'Sacerdotium, Regnum, Studium: Zur Wertung der Wissenschaft im XIII Jahrhundert,' *AKG*, 34 (1951–1952), 5–21.

centers of learning in the medieval world.[4] Within the universities, moreover, the scientific order was characterized by further hierarchical gradations among the various academic disciplines. The prevailing order was generally that of theology, law, medicine and the liberal arts and was reflected in the respective faculties in which these disciplines were studied.[5]

With due consideration for changes and developments over the centuries, it can be said that the above mentioned hierarchy of academic disciplines remained essentially that established by Augustine in his *De doctrina christiana* with its stress on the study and preaching of the Scriptures and the subordinate and propaedeutic role of the liberal arts in that study. The Augustinian hierarchy of learning had been adopted by most medieval monastic and cathedral schools and then incorporated within the medieval universities, where, in the thirteenth century, it became modified but never essentially transformed by the introduction of Aristotelian learning. This fusion of Augustinian and Aristotelian

---

[4] Guelluy, 'La place des théologiens,' 573–575. For general studies of the growth and organization of the medieval universities see H. Denifle, *Die Entstehung der Universitäten des Mittelalters bis 1400* (Berlin: Weidmann, 1885), Stephan d'Irsay, *Histoire des universités françaises et étrangers*, 2 vols. (Paris:Picard, 1933–1935), H. Rashdall, *The Universities of Europe in the Middle Ages*, new ed. by F.M. Powicke and A.B. Emden, 3 vols. (Oxford: Oxford University Press, 1936), A.B. Cobban, *The Medieval Universities: Their Development and Organization* (London: Methuen and Co., 1975), and H. De Ridder-Symoens, ed., *Universities in the Middle Ages*. For Paris and Oxford see Gordon Leff, *Paris and Oxford in the Thirteenth and Fourteenth Centuries* (New York: Wiley, 1968), A.B. Cobban, *The Medieval English Universities: Oxford and Cambridge to c. 1500* (Berkeley: University of California Press, 1988), J.I. Catto, ed. *The Early Oxford Schools*, and J.I. Catto and T.A.R Evans, eds., *Late Medieval Oxford*, vols 1 and 2 of *The History of the University of Oxford* (Oxford: Oxford University Press, 1984–1992), and Damian Riehl Leader, *A History of the University of Cambridge*, vol 1: *The University to 1546* (Cambridge: Cambridge University Press, 1988). The most extensive studies of education and learning before the rise of the universities can be found in Pierre Riché, *Education and Culture in the Barbarian West: Sixth Through Eighth Centuries* (Columbia: University of South Carolina Press, 1976), and *Les écoles et l'enseignement dans l'occident chrétien de la fin du ve siècle au milieu du xie siècle* (Paris: Aubier Montaigne, 1979). For Paris see Stephen C. Ferruolo, *The Origins of the University: The Schools of Paris and their Critics, 1100–1225* (Stanford: Stanford University Press, 1985).

[5] 5 For general studies of the medieval *doctor*, see Gabriel Le Bras, 'Velut Splendor Firmamenti: Le docteur dans le droit de l'Eglise médiévale,' in *Mélanges offerts à Etienne Gilson* (Paris: J. Vrin, 1959), 373–388, and Astrik L. Gabriel, 'The Ideal Master of the Medieval University,' *CHR*, 60 (1974), 1–40. An extensive and most interesting series of unedited texts pertaining to the person and office of the medieval theologian has been presented by Jean Leclercq in 'L'Idéal du théologien au moyen âge,' *RSR*, 21 (1947), 121–148.

theories as to the various academic disciplines and their respective hierarchical order was best exemplified in the teaching of Thomas Aquinas and remained essentially intact in d'Ailly's time.[6]

In addition to its hierarchical dimensions, recent historians have also stressed the corporational nature of medieval society. In this respect, the medieval university, like much of medieval society, can also be seen as one large corporation comprised of smaller corporations as reflected in the diverse faculties, nations, and colleges. As in the case of the university as a whole, these smaller corporate bodies within the university were governed by the basic principles of corporational law whose goal was to secure the proper functioning and well-being of these groups as well as to protect their rights and privileges.[7]

These smaller corporations within the medieval university were also hierarchically ordered in accordance with the prevailing hierarchy of the sciences as described above. Within this context, the faculty of theology emerged as the most important of the diverse magisterial corporations that comprised the medieval university. As a result of the corporational nature and consciousness of the faculty of theology, it must be remembered that any description of the medieval theologian pertains not only to the individual theologian but also to the corporate body of theologians.

While the notions of hierarchy and order do not play as influential a role in d'Ailly's writings as they do in other medieval thinkers, especially in the case of his student, Jean Gerson, it is nonetheless safe to say that d'Ailly essentially espoused the hierarchically ordered world view so commonly attributed to the Middle Ages.[8] As recent scholarship has shown, there is even stronger evidence for the important role that

---

[6] For a most recent study on Augustine's *De doctrina christiana*, see Gerald A. Press, 'The Content and Argument of Augustine's *De doctrina christiana*,' *Augustiniana*, 31 (1981), 165–182. With regard to the organization of teaching at the University of Paris see J. Paetow, *The Arts Course at Medieval Universities* (Urbana: University of Illinois, 1910), C. Thurot, *De l'organisation de l'enseignement dans l'Université de Paris au moyen âge* (Paris: Dezobry-Magdeleine, 1850), and P. Glorieux, 'L'enseignement au moyen âge: techniques et méthodes en usage à la faculté de théologie de Paris au xiiie siècle,' *AHDL*, 35 (1968), 65–186. For the pervasive influence of Augustine's *De doctrina christiana* in the Middle Ages see Edward D. English, ed., *Reading and Wisdom: The De Doctrina Christiana of Augustine in the Middle Ages* (Notre Dame: University of Notre Dame Press, 1995).

[7] On the corporational structure of the medieval university as realized at Paris see Gaines Post, 'Parisian Masters as a Corporation, 1200–1246,' *Speculum*, 9 (1934), 421–435.

[8] For Gerson's ideas on order and hierarchy, especially within the context of church reform, see Pascoe, *Jean Gerson*, 17–48.

corporational ideology played in his thought, especially in the realm of ecclesiology.[9] In addition to the ecclesiological realm, hierarchical and corporational theories played an important role in his views on the medieval universities, especially with regard to the faculty of theology. In the hierarchy of academic disciplines that characterized the medieval university, d'Ailly unhesitatingly gave the position of prominence to that of theology and among the various corporations that comprised the university, he consistently attributed the highest dignity to the faculty of theology.

D'Ailly's views on the hierarchical and corporational status of the medieval theologian are best seen in the treatises which resulted from two controversies in which he was involved during his teaching career at the University of Paris. The first of these controversies was the Blanchard Affair of 1384–1386, and the second was the Monzón Controversy of 1387–1388. Both controversies are also most important in illustrating his view of the relationship of medieval theologians with the broader hierarchical and corporational realities represented by the Church. In a recent article, Douglass Taber, Jr. also uses these two controversies to illustrate d'Ailly's views on the teaching authority of theologians. The treatment of the topic in the present chapter, however, represents not only a more extensive study and analysis of the topic, especially with its emphasis upon the status, office, and authority of theologians, but also differs from Taber's interpretation in several important areas.[10]

The Blanchard Affair centered around John Blanchard who, after a successful ecclesiastical career in the Lowlands, was appointed chancellor of Notre Dame by the Avignon pope, Clement VII, in 1381.[11] Early in his tenure of office, however, there were clear indications of ris-

---

[9] For the influence of corporational ideology upon d'Ailly's teaching see Oakley, *Pierre d'Ailly*, 103–129, and Pascoe, 'Theological Dimensions of Pierre d'Ailly's Teaching on the Papal Plenitude of Power,' *AHC*, 11 (1979), 357–366.

[10] Douglass Taber Jr., 'Pierre d'Ailly and the Teaching Authority of the Theologian,' *CH*, 59 (1990), 163–174.

[11] The most recent and most thorough examination of the Blanchard Affair is that of Alan E. Bernstein, *Pierre d'Ailly and the Blanchard Affair*, Studies in Medieval and Reformation Thought, 24 (Leiden: E.J. Brill, 1978). The brief presentation of the Blanchard Affair that follows relies heavily upon Bernstein's description of the controversy as given on pp. 60–81. See also the article by Gabriel Astrik, 'The Conflict between the Chancellor and the University Masters and Students at Paris during the Middle Ages,' in *Die Auseinandersetzungen an der Pariser Universität im XIII Jahrhundert*, ed. A. Zimmermann, Miscellanea Mediaevalia, 10 (Berlin: de Gruyter, 1976), 106–154.

ing faculty opposition to the new chancellor. This opposition stemmed first from the fact that as a strong supporter of the Avignon papacy, Blanchard made it increasingly difficult for supporters of the Roman papacy to secure the license in theology as well as to compete for academic posts and ecclesiastical benefices. The second and perhaps more important reason for faculty opposition to Blanchard resulted from his increasing demands for financial remuneration in return for the conferral of the license. Blanchard also required that every candidate for the licentiate take an oath of obedience to the chancellor. Such requirements were not unique to Blanchard and had been made by some of his predecessors in the chancellor's office. There was, however, considerable papal legislation against such procedures and the faculty of Paris, increasingly conscious of itself as an independent and self-determining corporation, stepped up its opposition to the chancellor's policies.

Blanchard's increasing employment of such procedures, as well as his irritating personality, seems to have crystallized faculty opposition in 1384, and formal charges against him were presented to Clement VII by the Parisian faculty. D'Ailly, then regent master and rector of the College of Navarre, played a leading role in the opposition to Blanchard. After preliminary investigations in France on the part of a papally appointed commission, the case was transferred to Avignon where d'Ailly served as representative of the Parisian masters. While the case against Blanchard was pending in Avignon, the university also presented its complaints against Blanchard to the Parlement of Paris and here too d'Ailly served as its spokesman. In the course of the hearing before the Parlement of Paris early in 1386, d'Ailly composed his two treatises against Blanchard, namely, his *Radix omnium malorum est cupiditas*, and his *Super omnia vincit veritas*.[12] The Parlement issued no decision on the matter, but in September of that same year Clement VII, while refusing to condemn his protege, nevertheless, diplomatically effected his removal from Paris by appointing him archdeacon of Ghent.

In his treatises against Blanchard, d'Ailly strove to demonstrate that the chancellor's acceptance of money or other forms of remuneration for the bestowal of the license was essentially an act of simony.[13] He

---

[12] Bernstein has provided us with excellent critical editions of these two treatises in his *Pierre d'Ailly and the Blanchard Affair*, 197–236, 237–298. Subsequent references to these works will be to the Bernstein editions.

[13] The syllogistic structure of d'Ailly's arguments and their development can be found in the first of his treatises against John Blanchard, *Radix omnium malorum est cupiditas*, Bernstein, 207–209.

argues his case by stating first that the work of the theologian is essentially spiritual since it is the Holy Spirit that illuminates his intellect in study and guides him in his teaching and preaching. To substantiate his assertions, d'Ailly has recourse to the tenth chapter of Matthew's Gospel wherein Christ commissions his disciples and instructs them as to the spiritual nature of their mission and the manner in which they are to comport themselves in its fulfillment. Foremost among the spiritual duties involved in their mission, d'Ailly asserts, are those of preaching and teaching. D'Ailly also emphasizes that Christ commands his apostles to perform their spiritual duties without charge, for what they have freely received they are to give freely.

From the spiritual nature of the theologian's activities in the realms of teaching and preaching, d'Ailly argues to the spiritual nature of the chancellor's authority since that authority is closely related to the granting of the license to perform those activities. Given the spiritual nature of the chancellor's authority, d'Ailly then argues that any attempt on the part of the chancellor to demand money or other forms of remuneration for the granting of the license constitutes an act of simony. In arguing that the chancellor's demand for remuneration in return for the granting of the license constitutes an act of simony, d'Ailly does not conclude, as logic would also seem to demand, that theologians charging fees for the exercise of their spiritual authority to teach and preach would also be guilty of simony.

While d'Ailly's treatises in relationship to the Blanchard Affair provides the historian with many profitable avenues of research, they especially reveal his views as to the status of the theologian. Within this context, what is of special interest is his concern with tracing the theologian's origin back to the apostolic Church. D'Ailly attempts to illustrate this apostolic origin by stressing that since theologians are closely associated with bishops and priests in their work of teaching and preaching and since that work rests upon and continues the apostolic mission which Christ gave his early followers, namely the teaching and preaching of the Gospel, they too share in that apostolic mission. Like the bishops and clergy, therefore, theologians have a right to the honors and privileges that result from this apostolic context of their office. D'Ailly develops his line of argumentation by recourse to passages from the New Testament, canon law, and their respective glosses.

The scriptural texts which d'Ailly uses to describe the mission which Christ entrusted to his apostles and disciples are primarily Mt. 9:37, 10:5–15, and 28:18–19. While the formulation of these texts vary, the primary dimensions of that mission are described in terms of the teaching and preaching of the Gospel. D'Ailly also sees Christ's action of sending out the apostles and the disciples to teach and to preach the Gospel as the earliest form of licensing within the Church. Throughout d'Ailly's two treatises on the Blanchard Affair, the terms 'to send' (*mittere*), 'to teach' (*docere*), 'to preach' (*predicare*), and 'to license' (*licentiare*) are all closely related.[14]

D'Ailly argues, moreover, that Christ's action in so licensing the apostles and disciples is normative for the apostolic and post-apostolic Church. Following the teaching of Paul, he believes that every action of Christ serves as an example for the Church throughout its history.[15] The apostles and disciples, consequently, were empowered to license others and with the passage of time they selected bishops and priests as their successors in carrying out Christ's commission to teach and preach the Gospel.[16] As such, therefore, bishops and priests are to be regarded as continuations of the ecclesiastical hierarchy and, as seen earlier, are designated by him respectively as *prelati maiores* and *prelati minores*.

In identifying bishops and priests as the successors of the apostles and disciples in carrying out the commission of Christ to teach and preach the Gospel, d'Ailly is adhering closely to the medieval biblical, canonical, and theological tradition on this matter. As seen in a previous chapter, this tradition appears to have originated with Jerome (†420), was further developed by Caesarius of Arles (†542) and the Venerable Bede (†735). Bede's teaching, as expressed in his *Commentary on Luke*, entered the *Glossa ordinaria*, and thereby became an integral part of medieval biblical exegesis. This tradition also made its way into the Pseudo-Isidorian Decretals of the ninth century in the form of texts from Pseudo-Anacletus, Pseudo-Clement, and Pseudo-Damasus I.

---

[14] *Radix omnium*, Bernstein, 209. 'Quarta propositio est quod potestas licenciandi in theologia est potestas spiritualis, quae patet ex hoc quia Christus in Novo Testamento hanc potestatem exercuit, quando Apostolos in theologia licentiavit dicens, "Ite, docete omnes gentes," etc. Math. 28, 19, et prius Math. 10, 7 "Euntes autem predicate."'

[15] *Super omnia*, Bernstein, 243. 'Hoc autem totum plenum est misterio et doctrinali exemplo, cum omnis Christi actio nostra sit instructio.' While not directly citing Paul, d'Ailly's reference to the normative dimensions of Christ's actions is reminiscent of 2 Tim. 3:15.

[16] *Radix omnium*, Bernstein, 209. 'Unde Apostoli ibidem receperunt a Christo non solum licentiam seu potestatem docendi et predicandi, sed etiam pro se et suis successoribus receperunt potestatem alios licenciandi ad docendum theologiam et predicandum.'

The eleventh and twelfth century Gregorian Reformers incorporated these scriptural and canonical texts into their canonical collections from which they eventually found their way into Gratian's *Decretum* and thereby passed into the mainstream of medieval canonical exegesis. Theologians of the thirteenth and fourteenth centuries such as Thomas Aquinas, Bonaventure, Henry of Ghent, James of Viterbo, and John of Paris also followed in the same tradition. As one would expect, this textual tradition played a most important role in the controversy between the secular clergy and the mendicant orders in the high and late Middle Ages, and attained one of its fullest formulations in William of St. Amour, the principle spokesman for the seculars' cause, and from whom d'Ailly borrowed heavily in the development of his own thought on the subject.[17]

D'Ailly continues his analysis by asserting that as the successors of the apostles and disciples, bishops and priests are empowered to commission or license others to aid them in the fulfillment of their task of teaching and preaching the Gospel. Such was the case, he asserts, when they designated archdeacons and archpriests to assist them in carrying out their pastoral duties. As support for this position, he cites Gregory IX's decretal *Inter cetera* which enumerated in detail the various reasons for which bishops can designate others to aid them with the pastoral work within their dioceses.[18] Basing his arguments upon the canon *Episcopi vel presbyteri* from Gratian, d'Ailly also argues that pastors of parishes and rectors of other churches can commission or license special preachers for work within their areas of jurisdiction.[19]

The pope, finally, as head of the episcopal order, is essentially empowered to designate helpers for himself in the task of teaching and preaching the Gospel throughout the universal Church and one of the several ways in which he does this is through the granting of the *licentia* in theology. When, therefore, his representative, the chancellor of the university, grants the theologian the *licentia ubique docendi et praedi-*

---

[17] *Super omnia*, Bernstein, 243–244.

[18] *Super omnia*, Bernstein, 244. The canonical reference is to X, l, 31, 15. While the main emphasis in this decretal is on the work of preaching, the hearing of confessions and the imposition of penances, a wide range of pastoral duties is also included. Since the decretal speaks of the bishop's ordaining of others to carry on this work, it most likely refers not so much to the use of mendicants as to the ordination of additional priests or bishops.

[19] *Super omnia*, Bernstein, 244. The reference to Gratian can be found in C. 7 q. 1, c. 38. This canon deals primarily with the preaching and liturgical privileges enjoyed by priests or bishops in visitations to other dioceses.

candi he is essentially authorizing him to share in the apostolic mission entrusted to the ecclesiastical hierarchy in general, and, in a more specific manner, to the papacy.[20] Despite the historical evolution of the various aspects of the *licentia*, d'Ailly always saw it as the faithful embodiment of the original commission given by Christ to his apostles and disciples, and, especially, to Peter and his successors.

There is an ironical dimension to d'Ailly's argument for the apostolic dimension of the theological *licentia* in that in order to incorporate the theologians into the apostolic mission of the ecclesiastical hierarchy, d'Ailly, a secular master, had to adopt the ideological strategy used by the mendicants in their controversy with the secular clergy in the thirteenth century. Throughout that controversy, the position of the secular theologians had been that the right to participate in the pastoral care of the faithful rested not simply upon the reception of sacred orders, for this prerogative they shared with the mendicants, but upon the reception of the necessary jurisdictional authority. To exercise the right of teaching and preaching, therefore, the mere possession of sacred orders was not sufficient; one also needed the necessary jurisdiction, that is, jurisdiction over a distinct congregation or parish. One had to be, as it were, licensed or given a mission by a bishop to teach and preach the Gospel within a specific geographical area and to a specific group of the faithful. While such an argument had the effect of protecting the special prerogative of the secular clergy over the pastoral care of the faithful, it also added a more juridical character to the original nature of the apostolic mission.[21]

---

[20] *Super omnia*, Bernstein, 244. In this passage, d'Ailly utilizes as his authority the decretal *Cum ex iniuncto*, X. 5. 7. 12. This decretal was directed against lay preaching in the diocese of Metz and its tendency to denigrate the status of the diocesan clergy. While nothing is said here about the papal office, its apostolic mission, or about theologians and the *licentia*, the issue of lay preaching did raise the issue of proper apostolic mission, especially the lack of such a mission on the part of lay preachers. Drawing an analogy from the mission of the apostles and disciples and their successors, the bishops and priests, d'Ailly clearly affirms the incorporation of the theologians into that mission: 'Et hoc modo ab eo mittuntur illi qui auctoritate apostolica in theologia licentiantur.'

[21] For a detailed historical analysis of the manner in which the issue of the pastoral care of the faithful, especially with regard to the area of preaching, was transferred from the realm of sacred orders to that of jurisdiction, see the excellent series of articles by M. Peuchmaurd, 'Le prêtre ministre de la parole dans la théologie du xiie siécle: canonistes, moines et chanoines,' *RTAM*, 29 (1962), 52–76, and 'Mission canonique et prédication: le prêtre ministre de la parole dans la querelle entre mendiants et séculiers,' *RTAM*, 30 (1963), 122–144; 251–276.

Rather than challenge the manner in which the secular masters attempted to defend their teaching and preaching prerogatives with regard to the faithful on the basis of jurisdictional authority, the mendicants sought to broaden the nature of that jurisdiction by distinguishing between ordinary and extraordinary forms of jurisdiction, with the former referring to that of the bishops who received jurisdiction over a limited geographical area and the latter to the universal jurisdiction enjoyed by the papacy and from which the mendicants derived their jurisdiction. By the application of such a distinction, the mendicants through the papacy were able to claim for themselves a share in the apostolic mission given by Christ to the ecclesiastical hierarchy. D'Ailly's strategy in the Blanchard affair was similar to that of the mendicants in that he adopted their concept of an extraordinary juridical mission and applied it to the teaching activity of the corporate body of theologians. Through the reception of the *licentia* from the chancellor as the representative of the pope, the theologians were thus entitled to share in the apostolic mission of teaching and preaching the Gospel of Christ anywhere in Christendom.

D'Ailly's views on the hierarchical and corporational dimension of the theologian's status are also seen in the treatise he wrote with regard to the Monzón Controversy. As has been seen in a previous chapter, John of Monzón's teaching on the Immaculate Conception had been condemned in 1387 by both the theological faculty and the bishop of Paris. Monzón, however, appealed his case to Clement VII in Avignon and to argue its side of the controversy before the pope, the University of Paris appointed d'Ailly, then rector of the College of Navarre, as head of a commission of four theologians. The commission was successful in the presentation of its case and the views of Monzón were condemned by a papal tribunal in 1388. As head of the university delegation to Avignon, d'Ailly was expected to present the case of the theological faculty against Monzón and in doing so he composed one of the most important treatises against Monzón. As would be expected this treatise also revealed much about his views concerning theologians, especially their office and their teaching authority.

In his treatise against John of Monzón, d'Ailly extols the theologians' status within the medieval Church by affirming their apostolic origins. On this occasion, however, he does not associate the theologians with the apostolic mission of the ecclesiastical hierarchy as he did in the Blanchard Affair but he describes them more as the successors of the *doctores* in the early Church.[22] This difference in strategy may be explained by the fact that in the Blanchard Affair it was to his advantage to identify the theologians with the apostolic mission of the ecclesiastical hierarchy, for in this way he could build up a stronger case of simony against the chancellor. In the Monzón Controversy, however, it better suited his purpose to stress the differences in the teaching status of theologians and bishops and priests, for he was defending the prerogative of the theological faculty to judge the teaching of one of its members against the right of the papacy, as head of the ecclesiastical hierarchy, to receive an appeal from that faculty.

In the development of his arguments associating theologians with the early *doctores*, d'Ailly has recourse first to the New Testament where he finds the scriptural basis for his position in Eph. 4:11. In this passage, Paul states that Christ established a diversity of offices within the early Church by designating some to be apostles, some prophets and evangelists, and others pastors and doctors. By d'Ailly's time, this passage from Ephesians had become the classical text used to establish not only the diversity of the Church's offices but also their hierarchical order. There is, therefore, no doubt in d'Ailly's mind that the office of the medieval theologian is clearly identifiable with the *doctores* of the early Church as represented in Eph. 4:11.

In equating the *doctores* of Eph. 4:11 with the theologians, d'Ailly had little historical awareness of the evolution of the office of the *doctores* from the apostolic period to the high Middle Ages.[23] In the apostolic period, the *doctor* was generally the teacher within the local Christian community whose primary function was to provide the catechetical instruction necessary for those who were about to be baptized. As a

---

[22] *Contra Johannem de Montesono*, de Argentré, 77.

[23] The best general survey of the evolution of the theologian's office from the office of the *doctor* and its relationship to the ecclesiastical hierarchy is to be found in two magisterial articles by Yves Congar, 'Pour une histoire sémantique du terme "magisterium"' and 'Brief historique des formes du "magistère" et de ses relations avec les docteurs,' *RSPT*, 60 (1976), 85–98, and 99–112. A summary presentation of these articles can be found in his 'Theologians and the Magisterium in the West: From the Gregorian Reform to the Council of Trent,' *CS*, 17 (1978), 210–224. For the period before the Gregorian Reform, see John E. Lynch, 'The Magistery and Theologians from the Apostolic Fathers to the Gregorian Reform,' *CS*, 17 (1978), 188–209. See also Jean Leclercq, 'L'idéal du théologien au moyen âge,' *RSR*, 21 (1947), 121–148, M.D. Chenu, 'The Masters of the Theological Science,' in *Nature, Man, and Society in the Twelfth Century*, 270–309, and Roger Gryson, 'The Authority of the Teacher in the Ancient and Medieval Church,' *JES*, 19 (1982), 176–187.

general rule, such a person was not a member of the ecclesiastical hierarchy since he was neither bishop, priest, nor deacon. During the third century, however, for a variety of historical reasons, the teaching functions of the *doctor* as well as the exegetical duties of the *lector* became increasingly identified with the ordained ministry, especially the episcopacy. This gradual process of incorporation was essentially completed by the time of the early Middle Ages. During the patristic and early medieval periods, therefore, the terms *episcopus* and *doctor* were practically synonymous as were the two orders they represented, namely, the *ordo episcoporum* and the *ordo doctorum*.

With the development of the cathedral schools and the universities in the high Middle Ages, however, there emerged a teaching body increasingly distinct from the episcopacy with the result that the *ordo doctorum* was no longer exclusively identified with the *ordo episcoporum* but became increasingly associated with the new corporate body of teachers, especially the theologians. D'Ailly manifests the continuity of this tradition in the late Middle Ages, for he frequently equates the *ordo doctorum* with the members of the theological faculty, although within the medieval university the term applied equally to all members of its diverse faculties.

In addition to Scripture, d'Ailly also has recourse to canon law in his efforts to exalt the status of the *ordo doctorum*. The canonical texts which he utilizes are two decretals, namely, Innocent III's *Cum ex iniuncto* and Gregory IX's *Sicut in uno corpore*. In his analysis of these decretals, d'Ailly interprets the papal references to the *ordo doctorum* as *quasi praecipuus in ecclesia* as applying to the theologians. The only reason, d'Ailly asserts, that these popes qualified their high praise for the theologians by the word *quasi* was to maintain the primacy of the episcopal order within the Church. According to d'Ailly, the intention of the popes was to rank the body of theologians immediately after the episcopacy and by so doing demonstrate the high esteem that that body enjoys within the Church.[24]

A closer analysis, however, of the decretals to which d'Ailly has reference reveals that he has considerably transformed their original meaning to suit his own line of argumentation. The decretals in question were written by Innocent III and Gregory IX in an effort to stem

---

[24] *Contra Johannem de Montesono*, d'Argentré, 77. The decretals of Innocent III and Gregory IX can be found in X. 5, 7, 12 and 5, 7, 14.

the rising tide of lay preaching within the Church of their day.[25] To accomplish their goal, therefore, the popes restricted doctrinal preaching primarily to the office of the *doctores*. From the context of these decretals, however, it is clear that the popes identified the *ordo doctorum* with the bishops and the diocesan clergy who shared with the bishops in the apostolic mission of teaching and preaching within the Church. D'Ailly, however, ignores the historical context of the decretals and interprets the *ordo doctorum* as applying as well to the body of theologians.

In addition to his portrayal of the theologian within a hierarchical and corporational context, d'Ailly also uses analogies drawn from the realm of buildings and builders in order to illustrate the status of the medieval theologian. In his *Vesperies* of 1381, d'Ailly described the Church in terms of a building and its various parts. He identified the foundation with Christ and the individual stones which made up the walls with the members of the Church. The windows, finally, through which the building was illuminated by the rays of the sun, were interpreted in terms of the theologians. From the context of d'Ailly's description, there can be no doubt that the sun also represents Christ and its rays the Sacred Scriptures. Through their study and teaching of the Scriptures, therefore, the theologians transmit the meaning of Christ's Gospel within the Church.[26]

D'Ailly's description of theologians as windows transmitting the light of the Scriptures to the interior of the Church becomes more graphic when one recalls the various ways in which the different colors of medieval stained glass windows transmit the light of the sun, especially during different parts of the day. While in his teaching and preaching the medieval theologian sought to convey the meaning of Christ's Gospel, each theologian added certain nuances and emphases characteristic of his own intellectual tradition and personality. This analysis may be reading more into the text than d'Ailly himself intended, but the analogy at least reveals d'Ailly's consciousness of the important role of the theologian within the Church and establishes that this awareness was present in his earliest writings.

---

[25] For an excellent survey of the evangelical revival within the twelfth century Church which led to the increase in lay preaching, see M. Chenu, 'The Evangelical Awakening,' in his *Nature, Man, and Society*, 239–279.

[26] *Recommendatio Sacrae Scripturae*, Dupin, I, 607. 'Habet … suos lapides, singulos scilicet Christianos et fideles, fenestras, viros speculativos, praedicatores et doctores, per quos veri solis radio illustramur, et a caecitate ignorantiae liberamur.'

While the building analogy which our young theologian used in 1381 at first sight appears to be a commonplace, it nevertheless has rich scriptural and artistic antecedents. In the Gospels, Christ tells the story of the wise man who built his house on rock in contrast to the man who built his on sand. Christ also indicated that he would build his Church upon a rock which in the Middle Ages was frequently identified with both Christ himself and St. Peter. St. Paul compares his missionary work in terms of a master builder who lays the foundation of a house upon which others are to build.[27] In the patristic period, Eusebius of Caesarea, adapting 1 Pt. 2:10 wherein Christians are compared to living stones being built into a spiritual house, likens them to the stones of the Constantinian basilica of Tyre. Also to be considered is the early Christian and medieval artistic technique of portraying the Church as a building held in the hand of some prominent pope, bishop, or other saintly personality.[28]

Continuing his building analogies, d'Ailly also describes theologians as builders of the primitive Church. As is well known, the theme of the *ecclesia primitiva* was of central importance in the writing of many medieval church reformers, since the early Church, as a result of its proximity to the life and teaching of Christ, was regarded as most faithfully exemplifying what Christ intended his Church to be. What was characteristic of the primitive Church, therefore, was frequently viewed as normative for the reform and renewal of the Church in later times.[29] From his early years as a theologian, d'Ailly manifested an

---

[27] Cf. Mt. 7:24–28; 16:18; 1 Cor. 3:10–11. In Eph. 2:19–22, Paul uses a somewhat different building analogy when he describes Christians as members of the household of God with the apostles and prophets as the foundation and Christ as the cornerstone.

[28] On the symbolism of early Christian architecture see Gerhard B. Ladner, *God, Cosmos, and Humankind: The World of Early Christian Symbolism* (Berkeley: University of California, 1995), 245–253. For some of the rich medieval symbolism on church buildings see the index under 'symbolism and architecture' in Otto von Simpson's, *The Gothic Cathedral: Origins of Gothic Architecture and the Medieval Concept of Order*, 3rd ed. (Princeton: Princeton University Press, 1989), 274.

[29] For brief historical surveys of the various ways in which the theme of the *ecclesia primitiva* has been interpreted and utilized from the fifth to the thirteenth centuries, see Peter Stockmeier, 'Die Alte Kirche: Leitbild der Erneurerung,' *TTQ*, 146 (1966), 385–480, Giovanni Miccoli, *Chiesa Gregoriana* (Florence: La Nuova Italia, 1966), 225–299, and Glenn Olsen, 'The Idea of the *Ecclesia Primitiva* in the Writings of the Twelfth-Century Canonists,' *Traditio*, 25 (1969), 61–86. While the theme of the *ecclesia primitiva* in the late Middle Ages has been considerably less researched, it continued to play an important role in the ecclesiology and reform movements of the period. For the use of the primitive church ideology in the late Middle Ages see Peter Stockmeier, 'Causa Reformationis und Alte Kirche,' in *Von Konstanz nach Trient*, ed. Remigius Bäumer

interest in the idea and normative importance of the primitive Church. In his *Epistola ad novos Hebraeos*, written around 1378 while he was in the final stages of his theological studies, he described the primitive Church as the period in which the Scriptures took form, for it was then that Christ's apostles committed their experiences of Christ and his teaching to writing.[30]

D'Ailly description of the theologians as the builders of the primitive Church appears also during the latter years of his ecclesiastical career in his *De reformatione*. In that treatise, presented at the Council of Constance in November of 1416, he describes the theologians of the early Church as the *primitivi theologi* and again associates them with the building up of the primitive church.[31] In this treatise, as in his *Vesperies*, it is clear that d'Ailly understands the *primitivi theologi* as referring to the *doctores* of Eph. 4:11, whom, as seen earlier, he in turn identified with the theologians of his day. In view of his previous description of the role of the Scriptures in the primitive Church, it can be reasonably deduced that the prominence given theologians as builders of the primitive Church rests primarily upon the fact of their teaching and preaching of the Scriptures, an office which, as will be seen, is continued in the work of the theologians of his own time.

The third and last major way in which d'Ailly describes the medieval theologian is by emphasizing his apocalyptic and prophetic roles within the Church. His views on these aspects of the theological profession were developed in his *Sermon on St. Francis*, which, as will be recalled, was delivered in 1380 and represents one of his earliest efforts to interpret the Church's history in an apocalyptic context. In that sermon, d'Ailly viewed the history of the Church in terms of a sevenfold series of persecutions which were prefigured in the seven afflictions described in Rev. 8:2–10:7. These persecutions, he maintained, would terminate first in the advent of the Antichrist, and then in the second coming and judgement by Christ. What is important for our present study, however, is the fact that d'Ailly identified the seven angels who announced the various afflictions with the seven orders of doctors.[32] By their teaching

---

(Munich: Ferdinand Schöningh, 1972), 1–13, and Louis B. Pascoe, 'Jean Gerson: The *Ecclesia Primitiva* and Reform,' *Traditio*, 30 (1974), 379–409.

[30] *Epistola ad novos Hebraeos*, Salembier, 260.

[31] *De reformatione*, Miethke-Weinrich, 1:364. '... cum tamen primitivi theologi ecclesiam aedificaverunt ...'

[32] *Sermo de Sancto Francisco*, TS, 6. After citing Rev. 8:2, d'Ailly adds: 'Septem siquidem angeli septem sunt ordines doctorum. Septem vero tubae septem sunt predi-

and preaching of the Gospel, therefore, the *doctores* were to prepare the Church for its successive periods of persecution. Since d'Ailly regarded theologians as an important segment of the *ordo doctorum*, it becomes clear that in this sermon he effectively assigns them a prominent role in the apocalyptic devolution of the Church's history. It is the theologian's function to recognize as far as possible and to proclaim the signs of the final days as predicted in the Scriptures.

In carrying out his apocalyptic role within the Church, therefore, the theologian also assumes something of a prophetic office. In his *De falsis prophetis, II*, written before 1395, d'Ailly recognizes the prophetic aspects of the theologian's functions within the Church, for he clearly identifies the *doctores* with the *prophetae* within the Church and describes their functions in terms of interpreting for the Church what has been written about Christ in the Scriptures.[33] As will be recalled from the first chapter, d'Ailly, in his Advent sermon of 1385, placed great emphasis upon those outstanding personalities who would play a prophetic role in the Church's renewal by calling for its return to the spirit of the Gospel. Only by heeding their prophecies would the Church be able to postpone the arrival of the Antichrist. In the *De falsis prophetis, II*, he does not hesitate to place the body of theologians among the number of such prophets.

2. *Office: Apostolic Mission: Teaching and Preaching*

This analysis of d'Ailly's views on the status of theologians within the medieval Church and university leads naturally to the question of their office. While Glorieux, as seen earlier, has described the principle functions of the theologian as essentially those of commenting on texts (*legere*), especially the Bible, participating in disputations (*disputare*), and preaching (*praedicare*), these activities can be essentially reduced to the two principle functions of teaching and preaching, since disputation is essentially a more active form of teaching. The goal of medieval theological education, therefore, was to prepare the young student to par-

---

cationes quibus clamaturi sunt inter persecutiones septem temporum incipientium a predicatione Christi et desinentium in consumatione saeculi.'

[33] 33 *De falsis prophetis*, II, Dupin 1, 489–490. 'Prophetae dicuntur doctores ecclesiae, qui interpretantur ea quae de Christo ab antiquis fuerunt prophetata.'

ticipate and develop his skills in the areas of teaching and preaching.[34] Although d'Ailly taught at Paris a century later than the period studied by Glorieux, there can be no doubt that he followed and shared in the same educational tradition despite the considerable changes in theological methodology that had occurred by his time.[35]

D'Ailly's *Treatise Against John of Monzón* again proves to be a rich source for his ideas concerning the principle functions of the theologian's office, especially the teaching dimension. In his reflections on the teaching and preaching functions of the medieval theologian, d'Ailly emphasizes that each of these activities has a positive and negative dimension. The positive dimension relates to the teaching and preaching of the truths contained within the Scriptures while the negative dimension involves the condemnation of doctrines which are contrary to those truths.[36] D'Ailly, indeed, sees the negative aspects of the theologian's activities as a necessary consequence of his positive functions; for he argues that the approval of a truth as being in harmony with the Scriptures necessarily involves the rejection of teaching contrary to that truth. He finds scriptural support for his position in 2 Tim. 3:16 where Paul states that all Scripture is inspired and can be profitably used both for teaching the truth and for refuting error.[37]

As to the day-to-day teaching activities of medieval theologians, d'Ailly says very little in this treatise, or, indeed, in any of his writings. The very nature of the Monzón Controversy forced him to concentrate more upon the role of the theological faculty taken as a whole, especially its part in the formulation of a corporate theological determination (*determinatio*).[38] For d'Ailly and indeed for the entire scholastic tradition, a determination issued by the theological faculty as a whole

---

[34] Glorieux, 'L'Enseignement au moyen âge,' 106–107.

[35] For a study of the theological programs in the fourteenth century see William J. Courtenay, 'Programs of Study and Genres of Scholastic Theological Production in the Fourteenth Century,' in *Manuels, programmes de cours et techniques d'enseignement dans les universités médiévales*, ed. Jacqueline Hamesse (Louvain-La-Neuve: Université Catholique de Louvain, 1994), 325–350.

[36] *Contra Johannem de Montesonno*, d'Argentré, 77. 'Ad doctores theologos pertineat sacram scripturam docere ... manifestum est, cum theologia de qua loquimur, nihil aliud sit quam sacrae scripturae doctrina. Quod autem ad eosdem pertineat, ex ejusmodi doctrina sacrae scripturae, assertiones haereticas et in fide erroneas reprobare ac veritates catholicas approbare, manifeste patet ...'

[37] *Contra Johannem de Montesonno*, d'Argentré, 77. 'Approbatio autem alicujus veritatis est reprobatio vel condemnatio contrariae falsitatis, quoniam qui aliquam approbat veritatem, per consequens reprobat falsitatem ...'

[38] At times in university texts the term *definitio* is used instead of '*determinatio*'. As far

involves the approval of a particular teaching as consonant with the catholic faith or its condemnation as erroneous or heretical. As will be recalled, Monzón had challenged the right of both the theological faculty and the bishop of Paris to pass authoritative judgement on his teaching with regard to the Immaculate Conception and insisted that such judgement rested only with the pope.

As seen in an earlier chapter, a *determinatio* was also an integral part of a disputation in a medieval university, especially in the arts and theological faculties. In the first phase of the disputation, the master would first pose the question (*quaestio*) to be debated, and then two students (*opponens* and *respondens*) would debate the negative and affirmative responses to the question. In addition to presenting the affirmative response to the question, the *respondens* had the added function of summing up the respective weight of all the arguments presented and coming to a tentative conclusion as to whether the affirmative or negative arguments prevailed. In the second phase of the disputation, which occasionally took place on a different day, the master would review the arguments presented by the two students and then issue a final judgement as to the proper response to the question. The authoritative response of the master resolving the question under debate was called a *determinatio*.[39]

As indicated above, similar actions could be taken by the whole theological faculty acting as a corporation of masters concerning doctrinal matters related to the faith or disciplinary matters related to individual members of the theological faculty. Such determinations by the faculty of theology could assume two forms: the first was designated as a *determinatio scholastica* or *doctrinalis* and the second as a *determinatio auctoritativa* or *judicialis*. While the first form implies an academic judgement on the doctrinal issue under discussion, the second generally is more disciplinary in nature involving censures, teaching prohibitions, and renunciations of condemned teachings. A similar terminology was used by the ecclesiastical hierarchy in expressing judgement on matters of doctrine related to the faith or on issues concerned with the practice of the faith. No doubt much of this terminology was adopted from the university scene and applied to already existing procedures that were always an integral part of hierarchical office. Indeed, for d'Ailly the authority to issue such determinations was vested first and foremost in

---

as ascertainable, the two terms were used interchangeably. For the sake of uniformity and clarity, the term *determinatio* will be primarily employed in the present work.

[39] Weijers, *Terminologie des universités*, 338.

the ecclesiastical hierarchy in proportion to one's rank in that hierarchy and the corresponding degree of geographical jurisdiction possessed. As such, papal authority was designated as the 'highest and final (*simpliciter suprema*)' while episcopal authority was designated as 'lesser and subordinate in scope (*inferior et subordinata*)'.[40]

The different roles exercised by the ecclesiastical hierarchy and the theological faculties in the evolution of theological definitions have their historical origins in the interpretations of ecclesiastical office that originated as early as the fifth century. In analyzing the power of the keys so commonly associated with ecclesiastical office as a result of Mt. 16:18 and Mt. 18:18, writers such as Maximus of Turin (†465) and the Venerable Bede (†735), working within the context of sacramental penance, recognized that the administration of that sacrament involved a combination of knowledge and authority. They distinguished, therefore, between a 'key of knowledge (*clavis scientiae*),' and a 'key of authority or power (*clavis potestatis*)'. Within this context, *scientia* referred to the pastoral knowledge and expertise necessary for dealing with the penitent while *potestas* referred to the sacramental power required to remit sins. Gradually, however, the distinction between *scientia* and *potestas* was extended to the non-sacramental aspects of an ecclesiastical office, especially that of a bishop.[41]

The association of *scientia* and *potestas* with the episcopal office continued in the early Middle Ages where it was also incorporated into the writings of Rabanus Maurus, and later into Peter Lombard's *Sentences* and Gratian's *Decretum*. In the high Middle Ages with the emergence of the theologians as a class distinct from that of the episcopacy, and, as will be seen in the next chapter, with a significant development in the meaning of *scientia* as a result of Aristotelian and scholastic influences,

---

[40] *Contra Johannem de Montesono*, d'Argentré, 75–76. 'Circa primum principale, est haec distinctio praenotanda, quod definitio circa ea quae sunt fidei, id est approbatio alicujus veritatis tamquam catholicae, vel reprobatio aut condemnatio oppositae falsitatis, tamquam haereticae, aut in fide erroneae, potest esse duplex; uno modo, scholastice et doctrinaliter; alio modo auctoritative et judicialiter. Et hic secundus modus est duplex, secundum quod auctoritas judiciaria est bipartita; una est simpliciter suprema; alia est inferior et subordinata.'

[41] For the historical evolution and interpretation of the terms *clavis scientiae* and *clavis potestatis*, see Ludwig Hödl, *Die Geschichte der scholastischen Literatur in der Theologie der Schlüsselgewalt* (Münster: Aschendorff, 1960), 11–12, 53–54, 91–93. For the application and historical evolution of the theory of the two keys to the papal office see Brian Tierney, *Origins of Papal Infallibility, 1150–1350*, Studies in the History of Christian Thought, 6 (Leiden: E.J. Brill, 1972), 39–45.

competence in the area of *scientia* also became increasingly associated with the theologians. Such a development naturally engendered tensions and conflicts between bishops and theologians which resulted in numerous attempts to clarify their respective roles with regard to doctrinal teaching within the Church.[42]

By the time of Thomas Aquinas in the thirteenth century a reasonable degree of clarification had been achieved. Thomas himself distinguished between a *magisterium cathedrae pastoralis* which he associated with the episcopal order and a *magisterium cathedrae magistralis* which he identified with the theologians. Each magisterium in turn possessed its own respective degree of *scientia* and *potestas*. *Scientia* in its older and more pastoral context was thus identified primarily with the episcopal order while *scientia* in the more recently developed scholastic sense was linked to the body of theologians. With regard to the teaching of the Scriptures, therefore, Aquinas maintained that there were two modes. The first related to the office of the prelate in the sense of teaching and preaching in a more pastoral sense and the second to the office of the theologian in the sense of teaching in the more scholastic context of the term. Aquinas' distinction between the two types of magisterial offices was followed by other theologians of the thirteenth and early fourteenth centuries such as Henry of Ghent and Giles of Rome.[43] In the late Middle Ages, William of Ockham distinguished between a *determinatio per modum auctoritatis* associated with the episcopal order and a *determinatio per modum doctrinae* belonging to the theologians,[44]

D'Ailly continued in the medieval tradition of maintaining a distinction between *determinationes* associated with the bishops' and theologians' office and expressed that distinction respectively in terms of a *determinatio auctoritatis/judicialis* and a *determinatio scholastica/doctrinalis*. As to the right of the theological faculty to issue *determinationes scholasticae/doctrinales*, it is clear to d'Ailly that that right rests primarily upon its close association with the study of the Scriptures. Since theology, he argues, is essentially the study and elaboration of the teachings con-

---

[42] Congar, 'Brief historique des formes du "magistère,"' 102.

[43] Congar, 'Pour une histoire sémantique du terme "magisterium,"' 91–92, 'Bref historique des formes du "magistère,"' 103, and 'Theologians and the Magisterium in the West,' 218–219.

[44] Ockham's description of the two types of determinations can be found in his *Dialogus*, 1, 1, Goldast, 2:399. The text used is that in Melchoir Goldast, *Monarchia Sancti Romani Imperii*, 3 vols. (Frankfurt, 1614; repr., Graz: Akademische Druck und Verlagsanstalt, 1960), and is cited according to volume and page.

tained within the Scriptures, and since it is the theologians who are most directly involved in this study, it is they who are most capable of ascertaining the basic truths of the catholic faith as contained in the Scriptures and of rejecting those not so contained.[45]

D'Ailly illustrates the theologian's competence with regard to such determinations by an analogy with a skilled craftsman. Such an analogy is not surprising given the fact that the university and its various faculties were in a true sense another manifestation of medieval guild consciousness and activity, albeit on the intellectual level. In all areas of creative human activity, he maintains, it is the master craftsman who knows best the materials of his trade. The master craftsman, moreover, is best qualified to identify those skills and techniques which contribute most to the realization of his craft and to reject those which render it difficult or impossible. When it comes to the evaluation of the final product, he also best recognizes when the results of his work attain to the highest levels of craftsmanship.[46]

For d'Ailly, therefore, the study of the sacred scriptures is an art or professional skill (*ars*) and the theologian is its artisan or skilled craftsman (*artifex*), not in the sense that he creates the Scriptures, but in the sense that he knows best how to determine their meaning and to ascertain whether a particular teaching is or is not in accord with the Scriptures. D'Ailly finds support for his position by claiming that Gregory the Great regarded the study and teaching of the Scriptures as the foremost of the arts (*ars artium*) because these activities contribute most directly to the pastoral care of souls.[47] In claiming the support of Gregory the Great, d'Ailly has skillfully transformed Gregory's *ars artium* from the *cura pastoralis* of bishops and priests to the study and teaching of the Scriptures by theologians.

---

[45] *Contra Johannem de Montesonno*, d'Argentré, 77. 'Tertia conclusio est, quod ad doctores theologos pertinet determinatione doctrinali et scholastica, circa ea quae sunt fidei, doctrinaliter definire. Et haec probatur, quia ad eos pertinet, ea quae sunt fidei, per modum doctrinae determinare et doctrinaliter definire, ad quos pertinet sacram scripturam docere et ex ea haereticas assertiones et in fide erroneas reprobare ac veritates catholicas approbare, sed ad doctores theologos pertinet secundum; ergo et primum.'

[46] *Contra Johannem de Montesono*, d'Argentré, 79. 'Ad unumquemque artificem pertinet circa ea quae sunt artis suae cognoscere, et ea quae ejusmodi arti conveniunt, approbare, et quae disconveniunt, condemnare, sed doctores facultatis theologiae sunt artifices, seu sapientes in arte sacrae scripturae, ergo ad eos pertinet circa errores hujusmodi artem tangentes cognoscere et eos artificiose, seu doctrinaliter condemnare.'

[47] *Contra Johannem de Montesono*, d'Argentré, 80.

The *determinatio scholastica* which d'Ailly entrusts primarily to the theologians comprises not only those truths which are clearly found in the Scriptures, but also those which are not so contained but which can be reasonably deduced from the scriptural data. It was on this latter issue that d'Ailly differed with Monzón over the doctrine of the Immaculate Conception. As seen earlier, Monzón denied the doctrine of the Immaculate Conception primarily because it was not explicitly contained in the Scriptures.[48] D'Ailly admitted that the doctrine was not so contained but contended that from the scriptural data available one could reasonably and validly argue to such a doctrine.[49] In the evolution of a *determinatio scholastica*, therefore, d'Ailly, while always maintaining the predominance of Scripture, does not make that predominance absolute. D'Ailly's teaching on the *determinatio scholastica* reveals again not only the strong scriptural orientation of his thought but also the delicate balance he maintains between scripture, tradition, and human reason.

With regard to the right of a theological faculty to issue *determinationes judiciales*, that right, as will be recalled, was restricted to its own members only. In cases involving an individual theologian or a group of theologians within its own faculty, that faculty in addition to its ability to determine that a particular teaching was erroneous or heretical could also order its members to recant such teaching or at least to refrain from teaching such views because of the theological confusion or scandal that such teaching might engender. Failure to adhere to such admonitions could lead to further censures or penalties.[50]

---

[48] One of the many propositions condemned in Monzón's teaching was cited by d'Ailly as follows: 'In expositione sacrae scripturae, sive determinando per ecclesiam, sive determinando per doctores, sive excipiendo per quemcumque, de sacra scriptura et non aliunde trahenda est determinatio, declaratio, sive exceptio.' Cf. *Contra Joannem de Montesono*, d'Argentré, 112. For Monzón's application of that principle to the Immaculate Conception see 113–114.

[49] In arguing his case, d'Ailly takes as an example the teaching that Christ, although true man, did not share in Adam's sin. With regard to this case, d'Ailly argues: 'Et tamen ex sacra scriptura sola non trahitur expresse et explicite exceptio ejus a praedicta regula, sed aliunde, scilicet ex ratione et rationali deductione in Scriptura fundata ...' The application of the same principle to the doctrine of the Immaculate Conception is seen in d'Ailly's concluding statement: 'Et hoc modo trahitur etiam ex scriptura sacra exceptio de Maria.' Cf. *Contra Johannem de Montesono*, d'Argentré, 114.

[50] *Contra Johannem de Montesono*, d'Argentré, 78. 'Quinta conclusio est, quod ad dictam facultatem theologiae contra certas personas, scilicet contra singulares magistros et baccalaureos ejusdem facultatis juratos, quandoque pertinet non solum doctrinaliter sed etiam aliquo modo judicialiter assertiones haereticas aut erroneas condemnare.'

D'Ailly's main reasons for asserting the juridical authority of the theological faculty over the teaching of its individual members rest heavily upon divine and human law, corporational theory, and public utility. His argument from divine law is very cryptic and seems to be based primarily upon his previous argument concerning the close relationship of the theologian with the study and exposition of the Scriptures. The argument from human law really constitutes his major line of argumentation and rests heavily upon the corporational nature of the medieval university with its diverse faculties which were in turn corporationally structured. The corporational structure of the medieval university and its respective faculties was often recognized and approved by the papacy.

As a corporation the theological faculty, d'Ailly maintained, had specific goals and the necessary institutional and legal structures for the attainment of these goals. As d'Ailly saw it, the primary goal of the theological faculty as an academic corporation was the search for and the defense of doctrinal truth as contained primarily within the Scriptures. Whenever, therefore, any member of that faculty acts contrary to this goal by the promotion of doctrinal error or heresy, the theological faculty has both the right and the obligation to discipline that member not only *doctrinaliter* but also *judicialiter*.[51] The individual theologian's obligation to adhere to the decisions of his faculty rests, in turn, upon the oath he takes to that faculty, which, as d'Ailly makes clear, involves the pledge to adhere to the decisions made by that faculty in all its scholastic deliberations.[52]

In addition to the argument from the corporational nature of the theological faculty, d'Ailly also uses the canonical argument from utility to sustain the right of that faculty to discipline its members juridi-

---

[51] *Contra Johannem de Montesono*, d'Argentré, 78. '... ex privilegiis a sede apostolica, seu a summis pontificibus concessis, Universitas Parisiensis et quaelibet quatuor facultatum ejusdem, et non minus facultas theologiae, habet quemdam politicum ordinem ad sua singularia supposita, et per consequens per quamdam judiciariam potestatem magistros ac baccalaureos sic juratos, tanquam eis subjectos judicialiter possunt astrigere ...' The papal decrees which d'Ailly cites as recognizing the corporate nature of the University of Paris, and especially its faculty of theology, are Innocent III's *Quoties pro commune utilitate*, and Alexander IV's *Quasi lignum vitae*. Cf. *CUP*, 1:279–285.

[52] *Contra Johannem de Montesono*, d'Argentré, 81–82. '... quandocumque quis subjicit se jurisdictioni alterius, ille potest contra sic sibi subjectum, et in eo, in quo sibi subjicitur, jus et sententiam dare, tam in jurisdictione contentiosa, quam in arbitraria ... Sed quilibet magister et baccalaureus facultatis theologiae in actibus scholasticis subjicit se eidem, et profitetur ac protestatur stare sententiae magistrourm, sicut moris est.'

cally. He maintains that it would be against the common good of all Christendom if the theological faculty did not have such power over its members. As indicated earlier, the theological faculty has as its primary goal the pursuit of doctrinal truth and it is this pursuit that should animate all its scholastic activities. Given the complex nature of these activities, d'Ailly argues, it is not surprising that occasionally some faculty members will fall into doctrinal error. If, in such circumstances, theologians were immediately delated to and judged by an episcopal tribunal, many would be seriously inhibited from pursuing their scientific investigations. Such inhibitions would, moreover, have the effect of stunting theological growth and development within the whole of Christendom.[53]

Compared with his extensive reflection on the teaching activities of the theologian, d'Ailly's explicit comments or reflections on preaching, the second principle function of the theologian, are surprisingly sparse given his recognized prominence as a preacher. While there is clear recognition on his part of the importance of preaching in the life of the theologian, he has very few explicit statements as to the various styles and techniques of preaching. Indeed this dimension of his thought merits further research. This sparcity, however, should not lead us to minimize the importance of preaching in d'Ailly's concept of the theologian. As Glorieux aptly remarks, preaching represented the crowning stage of theological education during the Middle Ages. It was not sufficient, therefore, that the theologian study and teach the Scriptures; he also had to communicate the results of his efforts to others. The theologian was called upon to draw out the practical applications of his speculative activity and present them to his audience in an effort to facilitate within them the experience of spiritual conversion (*metanoia*) which is so integral to all Christian life.[54]

---

[53] *Contra Johannem de Montesono*, d'Argentré, 79. '... si magistri et baccalaurei hujusmodi, qui inquisitioni catholicae veritatis in actibus scholasticis insistunt, quandocumque eos in hujusmodo inquisitione errare contingeret, essent ad judicium ordinarium episcoporum convocandi, ... ab inquisitione et exercitatione scholastica, quae est pro fidei defensione et totius ecclesiae utilitate publica institute, retraherentur, cum tamen ad hoc debeant provocari.'

[54] Glorieux, 'L'Enseignement au moyen age,' 148–161. This part of Glorieux's magisterial article provides an excellent survey of the role of preaching in the life of the medieval university and its theoretical function within the domain of theological education. For a study of university sermons at the Universities of Paris and Oxford see M.M. Davy, *Les sermons universitaires parisiens de 1230–1231* (Paris: J. Vrin, 1931), and A.G. Little and F. Pelster, *Oxford Theology and Theologians* (Oxford:Oxford University

The preaching activity of the medieval theologian took place both within and without the university. Within the context of the university, the theologian was called upon to provide the regular fare of sermons for Sundays, feast days, saints' anniversaries, as well as sermons on special occasions in the life of the university such as the inauguration of the teaching year and the inception of new masters. The preaching of the medieval theologian outside the university would vary considerably in accordance with his reputation and influence. Theologians who were members of the mendicant orders naturally found ready outlets for their theological expertise within their own houses and within the churches under their order's jurisdiction, but the writings of many secular masters also reveal the extensive nature of their preaching activities. Both mendicant and secular masters were often called upon to preach at the royal and papal courts as well as at diocesan and provincial synods and especially at the time of ecumenical councils.

The case of Jean Gerson provides an excellent example of the preaching activities of a medieval theologian. In addition to his extensive preaching activities within the University of Paris as its chancellor, Gerson preached frequently before the papal and royal courts at Avignon and Paris. He preached before diocesan and archdiocesan synods. In this context, he gave the major sermon for the Synod of Paris in 1404, the Synod of Rheims in 1408, and the Synod of Lyons in 1421. His sermons before the Council of Constance were numerous and related to the Council's primary concerns, namely church unity and reform and the defense of the faith against heretical teachings. He also preached regularly at the parish church of St. Jean-en-Grève where he served as pastor since 1408.[55]

D'Ailly's own preaching activities were also as numerous and diverse as those of his student, Gerson. A quick perusal of d'Ailly's many extant sermons shows a fairly complete coverage of the major feasts of the liturgical year from Advent through Christmas, Lent, Easter, Pentecost

---

Press, 1934), 147–215. An interesting study of the medieval concept of a preacher, his life, methods, and goals as well as a very rich collection of texts related to the above can be found in Jean Leclercq, 'Le magistère du prédicateur au xiiie siècle,' *AHDL*, 21 (1946), 105–147. For late medieval preaching in all its diverse dimensions see the excellent study of Hervé Martin, *Le métier de prédicateur à la fin du moyen âge, 1350–1520* (Paris: Editions du Cerf, 1988).

[55] For a quick survey of the diverse audiences to which Gerson preached see the summary descriptions of his oratorical works in G, 5, ix–xvi. These descriptions list the title of each of his sermons, place, date, and to whom addressed.

and Trinity Sunday, the latter being a feast which d'Ailly himself helped to introduce into the liturgical calendar. Among his sermons on saints are those dedicated to Chrysogonos, Bernard, Francis, Dominic, Louis of France, Louis of Anjou, and Peter of Luxembourg as well as a general sermon for All Saints Day. Reference has already been made to the sermons preached by him at diocesan synods at Amiens and Paris as well as at his own synods at Cambrai. When one turns to the geographical locations at which these sermons were preached, one finds the same degree of diversity. In addition to the university and diocesan scenes, there were also those of the royal court at Paris, the papal court at Avignon, and finally the Council of Constance.[56]

The integral role that preaching played in d'Ailly's concept of the theologian's office is made evident in the first of his treatises against the chancellor of the University of Paris, Jean Blanchard. In that work, whenever d'Ailly speaks of the theologian's teaching activities he almost always stresses the corresponding need to preach. Teaching and preaching, therefore, are always closely associated in d'Ailly's mind.[57] In his treatise against John of Monzón, d'Ailly also makes clear that both the exegesis of sacred scripture as well as its preaching are of the very essence of the theologian's life.[58]

In conclusion, therefore, it can be said that just as the dual functions of *docere* and *praedicare* came to characterize the major activities of the episcopal office, so too did they gradually become associated with the office of the theologian. This evolution is especially seen in the use and application of the terms *ordo doctorum* and *ordo praedicatorum*. By the time of Gregory the Great (590–604), the episcopal body was designated not only as the *ordo doctorum* but also as the *ordo praedicatorum*. Until the twelfth and thirteenth centuries, indeed, the *ordo doctorum* and the *ordo praedicatorum* were closely associated with the bishops and

---

[56] The extensive list of d'Ailly's sermons given in Salembier's *Petrus ab Alliaco*, xxxiii–xxvi, provides clear evidence of the diverse types of audiences to which those sermons were addressed. For some revisions as to the dates and circumstances related to d'Ailly's sermons see Palémon Glorieux, 'L'Oeuvre litteraire de Pierre d'Ailly,' *MSR*, 22 (1965), 69–71. Edith Brayer has recently edited eleven French sermons of d'Ailly found in Ms 574 of the Bibliothèque Municipale at Cambrai. For these editions see *Notices et extraits des manuscrits de la Bibliothèque Nationale*, 43 (1965), 145–342.

[57] *Radix omnium malorum*, Bernstein, 208. In this passage, d'Ailly speaks of the 'doctrina seu predicatio theologiae,' as well as the 'auctoritas docendi vel predicandi theologiam.'

[58] *Contra Johannem de Montesono*, d'Argentré, 77. 'Constat autem quod officium praedicatoris est maxime praecipium theologiae, sicut et expositio scripturae sacrae.'

their priestly assistants since it was to them that the *cura animarum* was primarily entrusted.[59] As we have seen earlier, the *ordo doctorum* during those same centuries also gradually became associated with the new body of professional theologians which developed with the rise of the universities and the use of the scholastic method. The association of the theologians with the *ordo praedicatorum*, however, was never as extensive as it was with the *ordo doctorum*. Such an association was more extensively claimed by the newly emerging mendicant orders of the thirteenth century, though not without considerable controversy over the consequences of such a development.[60]

3. *Authority: Corporate and Individual*

Having seen the general nature of the theologian's office in terms of its teaching and preaching functions, it is now appropriate to take a closer look at the teaching authority of theologians and its specific applications. While the previous analysis of d'Ailly's views on the various forms of theological determinations and their respective uses has already provided considerable insight into the nature of the teaching authority of theologians, it does not exhaust d'Ailly's rich thought on this important matter. Since medieval theologians operated both on an individual and corporate level, it is best to treat these dimensions of a theologian's authority accordingly.

With regard to the corporate dimensions of the theologian's authority, the Monzón Controversy has provided us with much information as to how medieval theologians viewed and exercised this aspect of their authority in the case of one of its own members. That controversy, moreover, raised the broader issue of the relationship between the theological faculties and bishops with regard to doctrinal issues. In this context, d'Ailly emphasizes the consultative authority enjoyed by the theological faculty. While d'Ailly never challenges the right of bishops to rule definitively and authoritatively on doctrinal matters, he does

---

[59] Congar, 'Bref historique des formes de magistère,' 103–104.
[60] On the history of the controversy between diocesan and religious clergy over the issue of preaching and the ecclesiological consequences of this controversy see Decima Douie, *The Conflict between the Seculars and the Mendicants at the University of Paris in the Thirteenth Century*, Yves Congar, 'Aspects ecclésiologique de la querelle entre mendiants et séculiers,' and Michel Dufeil, *Guillaume de Saint Amour et la polémique universitaire Parisienne, 1250–1259*.

insist that in all such cases they should never proceed unilaterally but only after they have sought out the teaching of the theologians.[61]

Put more precisely, d'Ailly is, in effect, saying that no *determinatio auctoritativa* should be arrived at by a bishop until a *determinatio scholastica* has first been obtained from the proper theological circles. D'Ailly describes this need for previous theological deliberation in terms of 'counsel (*consilium*)' and not 'consent (*consensus*)'. With regard to judicial determinations by bishops on doctrinal matters, therefore, theologians have a consultative though not a deliberative authority. He also limits the consultative role of theologians to matters of faith that are uncertain or ambiguous (*opiniones dubiae in fide*) and therefore require further theological clarification, implying that in cases when a teaching is manifestly certain or heretical prelates may proceed directly to a judicial determination without previous theological consultation. In such cases, using their *scientia pastoralis*, bishops can issue *determinationes* which are both *doctrinales* and *judiciales*. In cases involving difficult and controversial theological matters, however, they are to secure the *consensus* of the theological faculties.[62]

In addition to their consultative authority, theologians in their corporate context also play, according to d'Ailly, a corrective role within the Church. Whenever, therefore, bishops or popes neglect to seek theological consultation on controversial doctrinal issues and put forth teaching that is not in full accord with Christian belief, d'Ailly maintains the right of theological faculties to *doctrinaliter condemnare* such teaching. In establishing his claim for such extensive authority on the part of theologians d'Ailly has recourse first to historical precedent. He makes reference to Nicholas of Lyra's statement that over forty theologians at the University of Paris strongly censured John XXII's controversial teaching on the beatific vision. He cites as well Ockham's opposition to John's teaching on this same issue. In addition to historical precedent,

---

[61] *Contra Johannem de Montesono*, d'Argentré 80. 'Item nec papa nec doctores juris canonici, si non sint theologi, circa ea quae sunt fidei aliquid catholice discutiunt vel authentice determinant sine theologorum doctrinali determinatione praevia.'

[62] *Contra Johannem de Montesono*, d'Argentré, 85. 'Secundo dicendum est ... quod nec episcopus Parisiensis, nec alius quicumque, non theologus nec in sacris scripturis peritus, potest aut debet, sine theologorum consilio, opiniones doctorum theologiae in fide dubias et non manifeste haereticas sententialiter seu judicialiter condemnare.' In the case of theological opinions deemed heretical, d'Ailly states, 'Dicendum est quod, non obstantibus praedictis juribus, episcopus Parisiensis, vel alius, de consilio facultatis theologiae, seu doctorum sacrae scripturae, potest tales opiniones, si ostendantur esse contra fidem, sententialiter condemnare.'

d'Ailly also invokes the teaching of canon law and cites several decretals of Gregory IX (1227–1241) which allow subordinates to reprimand ecclesiastical prelates if they deviate in their teachings from the beliefs of the Church.[63]

D'Ailly also provides scriptural justification for the corrective authority of theologians vis-a-vis members of the ecclesiastical hierarchy. Within this context, he frequently cites Gal. 2:11–14. As will be recalled, in that passage Paul opposes Peter because of his refusal at Antioch to eat with pagan converts to Christianity. By his refusal, Peter had created the impression that only converted Jews who observed the Law with regard to circumcision were to be considered as true Christians. In rebuking Peter for his actions, Paul accuses him of not acting according to the teaching of the Gospel.[64] D'Ailly cites Aquinas as his primary authority for his interpretation of Gal. 2:11–14 but a closer reading of Aquinas on this point reveals a much more nuanced analysis of this biblical text, for Aquinas sees Gal. 2:11–14 more in the context of the principle of fraternal correction as embodied in Mt. 18:15–17.[65] There is in Thomas, consequently, no attempt to view the conflict between Peter and Paul as applicable to the relationship between members of theological faculties and bishops and popes but one could advance that argument as a deduction from or application of the principle of fraternal correction as d'Ailly seems to do here.

The invocation of Gal. 2:11–14 as a norm for governing the relationships between theologians and the ecclesiastical hierarchy followed closely upon the evolution in the high Middle Ages of the theologians as a body distinct from that of the episcopacy. As seen earlier, this evolution also modified the prevailing notions of the *clavis scientiae* and the *clavis potestatis*, with the former increasingly identified with the theologians' office and the latter with the office of the bishops. The incident narrated in Gal. 2:11–14 also engendered a further modification in the understanding of those terms in that the *clavis scientiae* was associated with Paul and the *clavis potestatis* with Peter. In this context, therefore, Paul became increasingly regarded as the embodiment of *scientia* over against Peter as the symbol of *potestas*, and consequently seen as a pre-

---

[63] *Contra Johannem de Montesono*, d'Argentré, 80.
[64] *Contra Johannem de* Montesono, d'Argentré, 80. For the history of the exegesis of Gal. 2:11–14 in the Middle Ages see G.H.M. Posthumus Meyjes, *De Controverse tussen Petrus en Paulus: Galaten 2:11 in de Historie* (The Hague: Martinus Nijhoff, 1967).
[65] For Aquinas' views on the conflict between Peter and Paul see *ST*, 2, 2, q. 33, a. 4.

figuration of the theologian and his role within the Church. Modeling themselves, therefore, upon Paul, theologians frequently asserted their right to correct the popes and other ecclesiastical prelates whenever they felt that their teaching was not in accord with the spirit of the Gospel. By the late Middle Ages the passage from Galatians had indeed become a locus classicus with regard to the relationship between theologians and ecclesiastical prelates.[66]

The corrective authority which d'Ailly attributes to theologians extends not only over ecclesiastical prelates but also over individual members of their own faculty who may be guilty of espousing erroneous or heretical views. As seen earlier, in such cases the theological faculty in addition to its right to scholastically censure or condemn such teaching can also order its individual members to recant or to refrain from teaching such theological views. Only when such orders have been ignored or spurned is the theological faculty to take its case against an individual theologian or group of theologians to the episcopal tribunal.

While the question of the corporate authority of the theological faculty at Paris played an important role in the Monzón Controversy, conflict also arose during that same controversy over the teaching authority of individual theologians. Within this context, the issue was not so much the authority of contemporary individual theologians but that of earlier theologians who had written on some of the very questions raised during that controversy. More specifically, the question centered around the authority to be given to the teaching of Thomas Aquinas since Monzón had claimed that many of his own arguments against the doctrine of the Immaculate Conception were taken directly from the works of his fellow Dominican. Monzón also contended that the teaching of Aquinas had received official recognition not only from the popes but also from the bishops of Paris and the theological faculty of the University of Paris.[67]

---

[66] In the late Middle Ages, Jean Gerson also employed Gal. 2:11–14 to compare the relationship which existed between Peter and Paul in the early Church to that which should prevail in the medieval Church between pope and theologians. For Gerson's teaching on this point see Pascoe, *Jean Gerson*, 90–91, and 'Jean Gerson: The "Ecclesia Primitiva" and Reform,' 390–391.

[67] *Contra Johannem de Montesono*, d'Argentré, 82. 'Primum est, quia aliquae conclusionum suarum trahuntur ex doctrina S. Thomae, quam facultas theologiae alias expresse commendavit, et Dominus Stephanus episcopus Parisiensis per suas litteras approbavit.' With regard to papal approbation of Thomas' works d'Ailly states, 'Secundum est quod Dominus Urbanus Papa V per ejus bullam Universitati Studii Tholosani

In his confrontation with the theological faculty at Paris, therefore, Monzón contended that in attacking his position on the Immaculate Conception, the faculty was in fact attacking the views of Aquinas, one of its most illustrious members whose teaching enjoyed full ecclesiastical approval. Monzón seems to have used this line of argumentation frequently, for d'Ailly asserts that the university has repeatedly attempted to make clear that in rejecting his arguments in favor of the doctrine of the Immaculate Conception it was not condemning the teaching of Aquinas but rather the misinterpretation of that teaching by Monzón and his followers.[68]

Realizing, however, that such clarifications on the part of the university had no effect, d'Ailly decided that he would have to treat the broader question of what authority prominent theologians of the past enjoyed in contemporary theological controversies and what was exactly meant when it was said that their teaching had received the approval of the Church. D'Ailly begins his analysis of this question with a threefold distinction as to the manner in which any teaching can be said to have been approved by the Church. The first mode of approval is had when that teaching is accepted by the Church as probably true. The second mode of approval is attained when that teaching is regarded as true in every respect. The third and final mode of ecclesiastical approval is realized when that teaching is seen as in no way erroneous in faith or heretical.[69]

As is evident, the quality of assent associated with each mode of approbation varies considerably. The assent required of the first mode is only on the level of probability whereas the other two modes entail

---

scripsit, et voluit ejusdem sancti doctrinam tanquam veridicam et catholicam sequi et teneri a christicolis et studiosis, et eam pro viribus ampliari.'

[68] *Contra Johannem de Montesono*, d'Argentré, 82. The frequency with which Monzón must have made such charges can be seen in the university's exaggerated and frustration-laden statement that : 'Nos millesies diximus, et, ut vidimus, non sufficit, qualiter sancti Thomae doctrinam in dicta nostra condemnatione nequaquam reprobamus, sed hunc ejusque fautores, doctrinam ejus ad distortum fideique absonum sensum adaptantes, aut ultra quam fieri debet, contra ejusdem doctoris documentum dilatantes, condemnandos audaciter asserimus.'

[69] *Contra Johannem de Montesono*, d'Argentré, 115. 'Praemittenda est haec distinctio, quod aliquam doctrinam esse per ecclesiam approbatam, potest tripliciter intelligi; uno modo, quod talis doctrina sit per ecclesiam tanquam utilis et in fide probabilis acceptata, et tanquam talis inter scholasticos divulgata; secundo modo, quod talis doctrina sic sit approbata, ut oporteat credere quod ipsa sit in omni sui parte vera; tertia modo, quod sic sit approbata, ut oporteat credere quod ipsa in nulla sui parte sit in fide erronea vel haeretica.'

various degrees of certitude. In the case of the second mode, the assent required involves the highest level of certitude since that mode of approbation completely excludes the possibility of error. The assent associated with the third mode involves a lesser degree of certitude since although that mode affirms that no doctrinal error or heresy is to be found in that teaching, it does allow for errors in the non-doctrinal dimensions of that teaching, especially as they relate to the realm of human knowledge and action. The second and third modes of approval are extended respectively to the teachings of the Scriptures and the universal Church, while the first mode is applied more commonly to the teachings of the saints and doctors.[70]

As to the manner of assent to be given to the teachings of prominent theologians, d'Ailly states that such assent can be expressed or tacit. Expressed assent generally takes place through some written document such as a papal decretal or a conciliar proclamation. Through such documents, the Church has expressed its approval of teachings contained in the Scriptures, the Fathers of the Church, decrees of general councils, previous papal decretals, and writings of an individual or groups of individuals having the requisite authority within the Church, such as theologians or faculties of theology. An early example of this form of ecclesiastical acceptance, and one which d'Ailly cites frequently, is the decree *Sancta Romana Ecclesia*, issued by Gelasius I (492–496). In this decree the pope, beginning with the Scriptures lists the various books, letters, and decrees which the Church accepts as an authentic expression of its beliefs.[71]

---

[70] *Contra Johannem de Montesono*, d'Argentré, 115–116. 'Secundus autem modus differt a tertio, quia stat, quod aliqua doctrina in magna sui parte sit falsa, absque eo, quod sit in fide erronea vel haeretica. Nam multa sunt falsa, quae non pertinent ad fidem, vel, si pertinerent ad fidem, tamen non inducunt errorem damnabilem … Unde primus modus approbationis, communis est multis doctrinis, seu libris vel tractatibus sanctorum et doctorum. Sed secundus et tertius valde paucis scripturis conveniunt, videlicet soli doctrinae scripturae sacrae ac universalis ecclesiae …'

[71] *Contra Johannem de Montesono*, d'Argentré, 116. 'Quilibet autem praedictorum modorum potest subdividi, quia talis approbatio alicujus doctrinae potest esse expressa vel tacita; expressa quidem per scripturam authenticam, sicut per auctoritatem scripturae divinae vel constitutionem Ecclesiae, seu per bullam apostolicam, aut aliam litteram authenticam alicujus personae vel collegii in hoc potestatem habentis, et sic expresse approbata est doctrina scripturae sacrae novi et veteris testamenti, generalium conciliorum, epistolarum decretalium et quorundam opusculorum sanctorum patrum, sicut patet ex decreto Gelasii Papae.' For the decree of Gelasius see Gratian's *Decretum*, D. 15. c. 3, Friedberg: 1:36–42.

Tacit assent, according to d'Ailly, is given by the Church when, without recourse to any written expression, it permits or tolerates the teachings of certain writers of the early Church as well as those of some later medieval theologians, even though such teachings may at times conflict with one another, provided that they are not in opposition to the accepted teaching of the Church. Such a mode of approval, d'Ailly also finds implicitly contained in Gelasius' decree where the pope states that the Church accepts the works of all those early writers whose teaching is in full accord with its own. While Gelasius naturally speaks only of the writers of the early Church, d'Ailly extends the meaning of that text to include the theologians of the medieval universities, especially those of the University of Paris.[72]

Having presented his analysis of the various ways in which theological teaching can be said to enjoy ecclesiastical approval, d'Ailly next raises the question of what mode of approval was enjoyed by the writings of Thomas Aquinas. His reflections upon this point are interesting not only because they shed light upon the diverse attitudes towards the teaching of Aquinas in the late Middle Ages, but also because they reveal d'Ailly's own views on the teaching authority of individual theologians within the Church. In his response to the above question, d'Ailly firmly states that the teaching of Aquinas clearly does not enjoy the second mode of ecclesiastical approval, for in no way can the writings of Aquinas be said to be true in every aspect of their teaching. Only the Sacred Scriptures enjoy such approval. To attribute this mode of ecclesiastical approval to Aquinas, therefore, would be tantamount to placing his writings on a level equal to that of the Scriptures.[73]

As further proof that the writings of Aquinas do not enjoy the second mode of ecclesiastical approval, d'Ailly argues that many theologians, including many of Aquinas' fellow Dominicans, have openly disagreed with him on different theological issues.[74] Among the ranks of those

---

[72] *Contra Johannem de Montesono*, d'Argentré, 116. 'Tacita vero potest esse alicujus doctrinae approbatio, per tolerantiam seu permissionem ecclesiae, et sic multae sunt doctrinae approbatae non solum sanctorum patrum sed etiam quorundam doctorum et magistrorum qui scripserunt summas et lecturas diversas et in quibusdam inter se adversas, tam in theologia quam in jure canonico ...'

[73] *Contra Johannem de Montesono*, d'Argentré, 116. 'Secunda conclusio est quod S. Thomae doctrina non est secundo modo per ecclesiam approbata, sic videlicet, ut oporteat credere quod ipsa in omni sui parti sit vera.'

[74] *Contra Johannem de Montesono*, 116. 'Multi etiam magistri et doctores sui ordinis ... in multis passibus praefatae doctrinae contradicunt, ut notum est, et ideo, secundum ipsosmet, non oportet credere quod ejusmodi doctrina in omni sui parte sit vera.'

theologians who differed with Aquinas, d'Ailly enumerates William of Paris (†1249), William of Auxerre (†1231), Alexander of Hales (†1245), Durandus of Saint-Pourçain (†1334), Duns Scotus (†1308), Giles of Rome (†1316), and Gregory of Rimini (†1358). To attribute the second mode of ecclesiastical approval to Aquinas' teaching would be, in effect, to repudiate the teachings of this distinguished array of theologians. These theologians, moreover, did not even regard the teaching of the four principle fathers of the Western Church, namely, Ambrose, Jerome, Augustine, and Gregory the Great, as enjoying the second mode of ecclesiastical approval.[75]

D'Ailly also denies that Aquinas' teaching enjoyed the third mode of ecclesiastical approval, namely, that it was in no way erroneous or heretical in matters of faith.[76] The first argument that d'Ailly uses to support this contention is that in the first question of his *Summa* Aquinas himself makes clear that the threefold authorities upon which the theologian depends in the exercise of his office are Scripture, the *doctores*, and human reason.[77] Since, d'Ailly argues, so many of Aquinas' teachings depend upon the authority of human reason and the teachings of the *doctores*, they cannot possibly command the same firmness of assent as those based principally upon the Scriptures.[78] The basis for d'Ailly's line of argumentation rests upon his belief that while theological arguments based principally upon the Scriptures constitute *argumenta ex necessitate*, those built primarily upon the teaching of the *doctores* or upon human reason result only in *argumenta probabilia*, which by their

---

[75] *Contra Johannem de Montesono*, d'Argentré, 116–117. After listing the numerous theologians whose differences with Aquinas on certain theological issues lent added weight to d'Ailly's position that Aquinas' works did not enjoy the second mode of ecclesiastical approval, d'Ailly concludes, 'Et ideo hanc doctrinam hoc modo extollere et approbare esset doctrinam aliorum doctorum evidenter reprobare.'

[76] *Contra Johannem de Montesono*, d'Argentré, 117. 'Tertia conclusio est quod praefata S. Thomae doctrina non est tertio modo praedicto per ecclesiam approbata, sic scilicet quod oporteat credere quod ipsa in nulla sui parte sit in fide erronea vel haeretica.'

[77] *Contra Johannem de Montesono*, d'Argentré, 117. 'Et haec conclusio probatur. Prima quod ex dictis ejusdem S. Thomae in prima parte suae Summae ... et postea distinguit triplicem modum auctoritatum quibus utitur sacra doctrina.' Cf. *ST*, 1, q. 1, a. 8, ad 2.

[78] *Contra Johannem de Montesono*, d'Argentré, 117–118. 'Primo sequitur quod cum auctoritas vel doctrina sancti Thomae in multis fundetur in ratione humana, saltem in illis non oportet credere quod sit ita firma quin possit esse in fide erronea.' With regard to the authority to be accorded to the *doctores*, d'Ailly states, 'Secundo ex ejus dictis sequitur quod ... auctoritas divinae seu canonicae scripturae praecellat auctoritatem aliorum doctorum ecclesiae.'

very nature do not exclude the fear of error.[79] As will be seen in the following chapter, D'Ailly's views on the nature of theological argumentation are essentially the logical consequences of his theological method which in turn is considerably influenced by his epistemological thought.

As further support for his first argument, d'Ailly maintains that since Thomas, on his own admission, was not the recipient of a special revelation such as that enjoyed by the apostles or the prophets, his teaching cannot be regarded as free from all error or heresy. To maintain, therefore, that Aquinas' writings enjoyed the third mode of ecclesiastical approval would, indeed, be repugnant to that illustrious theologian himself, for it would arrogantly affirm that his teaching did not share in the intellectual limitations common to all his fellow *doctores*.[80]

In his second argument against attributing the third mode of ecclesiastical approval to the teachings of Aquinas, d'Ailly moves from the possibility of error established in his first argument to the assertion that Aquinas had in fact erred in some of his teachings. He contends that on some theological issues Aquinas expressed contrary and inconsistent views.[81] Examples of such positions, he asserts, can be found in his ideas on the Trinity, creation, original sin, and the nature of monastic vows. While it would be of little value to the present study to elaborate on these aspects of Aquinas' teaching, it should be noted that what d'Ailly regards as contrarieties in Aquinas' thought are frequently but developments or modifications in his teaching from the earlier *Commentary on the Sentences* to the more mature *Summa Theologiae*.[82]

---

[79] *Contra Johannem de Montesono*, d'Argentré, 117. 'Sed tamen sacra doctrina hujusmodi auctoritatibus utitur quasi extraneis argumentis et probabilibus, auctoritatibus autem canonicae Scripturae utitur tamquam argumentis propriis et ex eis proprie ex necessitate arguendo. Auctoritatibus vero aliorum doctorum Ecclesiae utitur quasi arguendo ex propriis, sed probabiliter.'

[80] *Contra Johannem de Montesono*, d'Argentré, 118. '... sequitur ex praeallegatis S. Thomae verbis, quod, cum ipse nec fuerit apostolus nec propheta, nec ei, sicut nec aliis doctoribus, facta fuerit talis revelatio, cui innitatur fides nostra, ut ipsemet dicit, consequens est, quod ejus doctrina potest esse in fide erronea ...'

[81] *Contra Johannem de Montesono*, d'Argentré, 118. 'Secundo principaliter eadem conclusio sic probatur, quia de illa doctrina non oportet credere quod ipsa in nulla sui parte sit in fide erronea vel haeretica, in qua quidem continentur multae contrarietates et repugnantiae, etiam in materia ad fidem pertinente. Sed multae ejusmodi contrarietates et repugnantiae continentur in doctrina S. Thomae.'

[82] The later medieval scholastics were aware of these differences and sought to apply to Thomas' works the same principles used by Abelard and Gratian in harmonizing discordant texts in the writings of the fathers and in canonical collections. See M. Grabmann, 'Hilfsmittel des Thomas-studiums aus alter Zeit: Abbreviationes, Concordantiae, Tabulae,' *Mittelalterliches Geistesleben*, 2 vols. (Munich:Huebner, 1939), 2:424–

In his final argument against attributing the third mode of ecclesiastical approval to the teachings of Aquinas, d'Ailly maintains that other theologians throughout the Church's history have enjoyed greater ecclesiastical approval than Aquinas and yet their works have been shown to contain doctrinal error.[83] The first concrete example that d'Ailly provides to substantiate his assertion is that of Peter the Apostle. In this context, he cites the famous incident in Gal. 2:11–14 where Peter is reprimanded by Paul for appearing to espouse the position of the Judaizers with regard to the obligation of circumcision for the Gentiles. Moving to the patristic period, he narrates how the teaching of Cyprian, the first of the approved *doctores* listed in Gelasius' *Sancta Romana Ecclesia*, was strongly attacked by Augustine for his views on the validity of baptism administered by heretics. Augustine also differed considerably with Jerome over the issue of episcopal marriages.

Turning next to the medieval period, d'Ailly affirms that Peter Lombard, whose *Liber sententiarum* was, after the Bible, the most important theological textbook used in the medieval university, also erred on several questions related to the death and resurrection of Christ. In the realm of canon law, d'Ailly continues, no one can be said to have received greater ecclesiastical approval, at least tacitly, than Gratian, yet his commentaries on the canons are not immune from error. D'Ailly concludes his argumentation with the example of two outstanding scholastics of the twelfth century, Anselm of Canterbury (†1109) and Hugh of St. Victor (†1142), who, he contends, erred in some of their theological conclusions.

From his arguments rejecting the second and third mode of ecclesiastical approval for the teaching of Aquinas, it is clear that for d'Ailly the only mode of ecclesiastical approval accorded to Aquinas by the Church was the first, namely that his teaching was *utilis* and *probabilis* with regard to matters of faith.[84] In describing the precise sense

---

489, and P. Mandonnet, 'Premiers travaux de polémique thomiste: Les Concordantiae,' *RSPT*, 7 (1913), 244–262.

[83] *Contra Johannem de Montesono*, d'Argentré, 120. 'Sed aliqua est doctrina multo magis approbata quam doctrina S. Thomae quae tamen in aliqua sui parte est haeretica vel erronea in fide. Igitur hoc etiam sine ulla temeritate dici poterit de doctrina S. Thomae nonobstante ejus approbatione.' The concrete examples cited by d'Ailly in sustaining his third argument follow immediately after this text.

[84] *Contra Johannem de Montesono*, d'Argentré, 116. 'Prima ergo conclusio est, quod doctrina S. Thomae in opusculis suis theologicis contenta, primo modo est per ecclesiam approbata, id est, tamquam utilis et probabilis divulgata.'

in which Aquinas' works are to be regarded as useful to the Church, d'Ailly has recourse to Paul's statement in 2 Tim. 3:16–17, where he says that all scripture is useful for teaching, refuting error, facilitating personal correction, and providing moral guidance. While by the term '*scriptura*' Paul was most likely referring to the writings of the Old Testament, and, perhaps, even to some early Christian works, d'Ailly, as was his custom, extended the meaning of the passage to include the writings of the patristic and medieval theologians. The works of Aquinas, according to d'Ailly, have clearly met the Pauline norm for usefulness, for they have been most helpful to the Church in the elaboration of catholic doctrine, the refutation of heretical beliefs, the correction of bad morals, and the fostering of virtue.[85]

The last major issue that d'Ailly had to treat in his controversy with Monzón related to the latter's assertion that the writings of Aquinas enjoyed not only the tacit approval but also the expressed approval of the Church. The claim to expressed approval was based upon two documents, the first of which was a letter of Urban V (1362–1370) directed to the University of Toulouse in 1368 and related to the transfer of Aquinas' relics from the Cistercian monastery at Fossanuova to the Dominican priory at Toulouse. In his letter, Urban urged, indeed, ordered the masters at Toulouse to follow the teaching of Aquinas which he described as 'true and catholic (*veridica et catholica*).' They were also urged to develop that teaching through their own intellectual efforts. The second document was a letter of Etienne Bourret, bishop of Paris, dated Feb. 14, 1325. This letter, with the consent of the theological faculty at Paris, revoked the condemnation and excommunication attached to the alleged teaching of Aquinas on certain theological issues by the Condemnation of 1277 promulgated by Etienne Tempier, then bishop of Paris. This exoneration came less than two years after Aquinas' canonization at Avignon in 1323.[86]

---

[85] *Contra Johannem de Montesono*, d'Argentré, 116. After discussing Paul's words to Timothy with regard to the uses of Scripture, d'Ailly concludes, 'Sed in pluribus talis est hujusmodi doctrina sancti Thomae, nam ipsa in multis est utilis ad docendum catholicam veritatem, et ad arguendam hereticam falsitatem, et increpandum in malis moribus, et ad erudiendum in virtutibus ut notum est.'

[86] *Contra Johannem de Montesono*, d'Argentré, 122. Urban's letter can be found in Marcel Fournier, *Les status et privileges des universités françaises depuis leur fondation jusqu'en 1789*. 4 vols. (Paris: LaRose et Forcel Editeurs, 1890–1894), 1:620. The pertinent text in the letter reads: 'Volumus insuper et tenore presentium vobis injungimus, ut dicti beati Thome doctrinam tanquam veridicam et catholicam sectemini, eamque studeatis totis viribus ampliare.' For Bourret's letter see *CUP*, 2:280–282.

In his treatment of the letter of Urban V, Ailly contends that Monzón and his followers never presented that document as evidence in the controversy.[87] He asserts, however, that even if the papal document contained an expressed approbation of Aquinas' teaching, that approval would in no way have differed from the approval granted to theologians by Galesius and subsequent popes, namely, the first mode of ecclesiastical approval.[88] D'Ailly spent considerably more time in analyzing the letter of Etienne Bourret, and his analysis is a fine example of his capacities as an exegete. Monzón had charged that the present bishop of Paris, Pierre d'Orgemont, by his condemnation of Monzón and, in an implied manner, of Aquinas, was in fact contradicting the position of his predecessor, Etienne Bourret. D'Ailly responded to this charge by a skillful recourse to several important canonical principles. Canon law, he asserted, had always recognized that in the application of existing legislation, the legislator must always have due regard for changing circumstances related to persons, place, and time. He argued that Bourret himself was aware of this canonical principle and cited it as his reason for reversing the condemnation of Thomas proclaimed in 1277 by his predecessor, Etienne Tempier.[89] Another canonical principle to which d'Ailly had recourse was that which maintained that in the exercise of an ecclesiastical office one is not bound by the decisions of one's predecessors. He argued, therefore, that just as Bourret had reversed the actions of Tempier, so too the present bishop of Paris, d'Orgemont, was free to reverse the actions of Bourret.[90]

---

[87] *Contra Johannem de Montesono*, d'Argentré, 122. 'Prima est quod in dicto processu nunquam fuerit exhibita aliqua bulla papae, nec ipsius copia super confirmatione vel approbatione dictae doctrinae.'

[88] *Contra Johannem de Montesono*, d'Argentré, 122. 'Quod esto, de quo tamen non constat, quod doctrina S. Thomae esset expresse approbata per bullam papae, haec tamen approbatio per hujusmodi bullam non esset maior quam approbatio doctrinae B. Cypriani aut B. Hieronymi, aut aliorum sanctorum doctorum Ecclesiae.'

[89] *Contra Johannem de Montesono*, d'Argentré, 122. Here d'Ailly quotes the prologue of Etienne Bourret's letter: 'Magistra rerum experientia certis indiciis evidenter demonstrat, multa quibusdam temporibus ordinata consulte, novis emergentibus causis succedentibus temporibus, in contrarium debere consultius immutari.'

[90] *Contra Johannem de Montesono*, d'Argentré, 122. 'Ex quo patet, quod, si iste episcopus praedecessorum suorum ordinationem consulte potuit immutare, ita et praedecessoris illius successores episcopi possunt ordinationem suam per dictam litteram factam consulte et rationabiliter immutare, quia etiam ordinatio sua non plus ligavit successores, quam praedecessorum suorum ordinatio ipsum ligaverat, cum par in parem non habeat imperium ut jura dicunt.'

D'Ailly argued, moreover, that Bourret's exoneration of Aquinas' teaching did not totally remove the suspicion cast upon it by Tempier's condemnation. In support of this contention, he analyzes the statement of the theological faculty contained in Bourret's letter to the effect that its investigation of Thomas' writings revealed that he had never entertained nor expressed in writing any teaching that was contrary to catholic belief or morality. In his analysis of this statement, d'Ailly accuses his own faculty of a display of theological rhetoric, for it obviously could not have investigated all of Aquinas' writings at that time but only those aspects of his thought involved in the Condemnation of 1277. Fearful, perhaps, of appearing to criticize his fellow theologians excessively, d'Ailly, without much intrinsic evidence, suggests that the statement attributed to the faculty may well have been inserted by an overly zealous scribe.[91]

The main thrust of Bourret's letter, d'Ailly concludes, was not to express a general approval of Thomas's teaching, but to annul the specific charges brought against him. Bourret, as d'Ailly saw it, neither approved nor disapproved of Aquinas' teaching but, in effect, turned the question of that teaching over to the theological faculty at Paris for further scholastic discussion. By this action, d'Ailly contended, Bourret was implying that Aquinas' teaching was still capable of being found to be in error, for the whole purpose of theological discussion has always been either the approbation of a particular teaching as true or its condemnation as false.[92]

D'Ailly's treatise against John of Monzón concludes with a detailed analysis of specific theological issues on which the teaching of Aquinas has been, at least from d'Ailly's viewpoint, false or erroneous. The whole purpose of this final segment of his treatise was to illustrate in a more concrete manner, that Aquinas' teaching enjoyed only the first mode of ecclesiastical approval and not the second or third modes. While an analysis of this final section of this treatise might be of some interest, it would really not advance very much our understanding of d'Ailly's views on the status, office, and authority of the theologian

---

[91] *Contra Johannem de Montesono*, d'Argentré, 123. 'Et hoc forte continere potuit ex ignorantia vel inadvertentia notarii dictam litteram componentis.'

[92] *Contra Johannem de Montesono*, d'Argentré, 124. 'Ex quo patet manifeste propositum quia quidquid in doctrina theologica discussioni scholasticae sic liberum relinquitur, si per hujusmodi discussionem inveniatur erroneum, potest rationabiliter condemnari, aliter enim frustra esset hujusmodi discussio, nam theologicae discussionis finis debet esse veritatis approbatio et condemnatio falsitatis.'

in the Church of his time. From what has been seen in this chapter, then, it is clear that the Blanchard and Monzón controversies presented d'Ailly with excellent opportunities to develop his teaching on the status, office, and authority of theologians and the specific manner in which these dimensions of their profession differed from and yet interacted with those of bishops and even popes.

The complexity of such interactions also gives lie to any simplistic or dichotomous interpretation of d'Ailly concerning the relationship between *scientia* and *potestas* in theological determinations. For him, *scientia* is not conceived simply as resting with theologians and *potestas* with bishops and popes. In his teaching on *scientia* and *potestas*, d'Ailly makes clear that theologians, bishops, and popes, in varying degrees, all share in both of these dimensions. While the primary function of theologians, at least those belonging to university faculties, is the promotion of theological learning, they also enjoy a certain degree of jurisdictional authority over the members of their faculty. In the case of bishops, their theological knowledge is exercised primarily in a pastoral context, especially with regard to maintaining doctrinal orthodoxy in their dioceses. Their judicial authority, however, is exercised more extensively than that of theologians since it extends over their entire dioceses. Finally, the papacy is seen as exercising the fullest degree of *scientia* and *potestas* with regard to doctrinal matters, but, as seen above, the exercise of that *scientia* should depend heavily on the consultative input of theologians and the use of its *potestas*, while supreme, must respect that of the territorial bishops. What emerges from d'Ailly's thought, then, is a delicately balanced theory which provides for the cooperative interaction of theologians, bishops, and popes in the evaluation, formulation, and promulgation of theological doctrine within the Church. The respective roles of theologians, bishops, and popes in that evaluation and promulgation are clearly defined, delineated, and respected, thereby facilitating, at least in theory, the harmonious interaction of all participants.

CHAPTER SIX

THEOLOGIANS: THEOLOGY, SCIENCE, METHOD

After the analysis of the status, office, and authority of theologians in d'Ailly's thought, the question of his views on the nature of theology, its method, unity, and subject naturally arises. With the exception of Bernhard Meller's work, little attention has been given to these aspects of d'Ailly's thought, and even in Meller's work the emphasis is more on the general epistemological dimensions of d'Ailly's thought than on his views on the above questions[1]

1. *The Question of Influences*

Before beginning our analysis of d'Ailly's views on these questions, it will be helpful to place his teaching on the nature, method, unity, and subject of theology within the broader context of the major schools of late medieval thought that so influenced his thought. Considerable debate has emerged on this issue and limited studies have been published but a final judgement is not yet at hand. Until recently the nominalistic influence of William of Ockham (c. 1285–1347) was seen as all pervasive in d'Ailly's thought. The research of Louis Saint-Blançat, however, began to uncover the strong influence of the Augustinian Gregory of Rimini (c. 1300–1358), even to the point of verbatim citations from Gregory. As a result of this research, d'Ailly has also become increasingly associated with the late medieval Augustinian tradition.[2]

Heiko Oberman has qualified Saint-Blançat's research by asserting that while d'Ailly at times used the exact formulations of Gregory, the thought expressed therein is often essentially that of Ockham because

---

[1] Bernhard Meller, *Studien zur Erkenntnislehre des Peter von Ailly* (Freiburg: Herder, 1954). A brief but much more recent analysis of d'Ailly's views on theology and theological method can be found in Onorato Grassi, 'La riforma della teologia in Francia,' in *Storia della teologia nel medioevo*, ed. Giulio d'Onofrio, 3 vols (Casale Monferrato: Edizioni Piemme, 1996), 3:692–702.
[2] Louis Saint-Blancat, 'La théologie de Luther et un nouveau plagiat de Pierre d'Ailly,' *PLut*, 4 (1956), 61–81.

Gregory himself was also greatly influenced by Ockham's thought. Yet Oberman openly admitted the many differences between Rimini and Ockham and regarded Rimini as belonging to what he designated as a 'right wing division' of late medieval nominalism which was characterized primarily by its strong Augustinian emphasis on grace as contrasted with the more pelagian tendencies of a 'left wing division' of nominalism represented by Adam of Wodham.[3] More recently, the interpretation of Saint-Blancat has been reasserted and further developed by Manfred Schulze.[4]

Using strong and, at times, anachronistic language, both Saint Blancat and Schulze have gone so far as to call d'Ailly a 'plagiarist,' and have designated his *Commentary on the Sentences* a vast mosaic of borrowed theological texts.[5] Since there is no doubt that d'Ailly borrowed frequently and at times verbatim from the writings of William of Ockham and Gregory of Rimini, the question arises as to whether d'Ailly slavishly adopted the teaching of these authors or did he exercise some degree of independence towards them? Only after a more complete study of d'Ailly's teaching on the topics under discussion in this chapter will we be able to offer a more substantial response to this question.

2. *Theology: Definition, Unity, and Subject*

In dealing with d'Ailly's views on theology, its method, unity, and subject, it must be noted first of all that, as was the case with most medieval theologians, d'Ailly presents his views on these issues early in his *Commentary on the Sentences*. In raising the question of what is theology, d'Ailly responds that in its broadest sense theology is identified with the Scriptures.[6] This definition reflects one of the more general ways in which

---

[3] Heiko A. Oberman's opinion can be found in his *The Harvest of Medieval Theology*, 196–206. For Oberman's delineation of the various schools within late medieval nominalism see his 'Some Notes on the Theology of Nominalism with Attention to its Relation to the Renaissance,' *HTR*, 53 (1960), 47–76 as well as his 'Nominalism and Late Medieval Religion,' in *The Pursuit of Holiness in Late Medieval and Renaissance Religion*, 593–615.

[4] Manfred Schulze's position is presented in his '"Via Gregorii" in Forschung und Quellen,' in *Gregor von Rimini: Werk und Wirkung bis zur Reformation*, ed. Heiko A. Oberman (Berlin: Walter de Gruyter, 1981), 64–75.

[5] Saint-Blancat, 'La théologie de Luther,' 76; Schulze, 'Via Gregorii,' 70.

[6] *Sent.*, 1, q. 1, a. 3, DD. 'Primo ergo declarandum est quid sit theologia. Unde dico

theology was commonly understood in the patristic and medieval traditions wherein theology was simply designated as '*sacra pagina*' or '*divina pagina*'.[7] In a more restricted sense, however, d'Ailly regards theology as an act or habit of the mind concerning the truths of Scripture. Theology thus understood can involve a single act or habit of the mind with regard to a particular truth of Scripture or a series of such acts or habits with regard to the many different truths contained in the Scriptures.[8]

The emphasis upon theology in terms of acts or habits of the mind with regard to the truths contained in the Scriptures leads naturally to the question of theological method. In this context, d'Ailly specifies that such acts or habits can be twofold in nature. First, they can involve a careful analysis of a scriptural text in itself as well as in comparison with another scriptural text within the same book or with other related texts within the other books of Old or New Testaments in order to clarify its meaning. Secondly, such acts or habits can involve the application of reason to truths contained in the scriptures in order to deduce truths not formally contained therein.[9] The first type of activity was very characteristic of patristic and early medieval theology which concentrated heavily upon commentary and comparative analysis of texts. The second form of activity, deducing truths not formally contained in the Scriptures, became, as will be later seen in greater detail, one of

---

quod multipliciter potest capi. Uno modo pro scriptura sacri canonis.' The text used for the Commentary is that found in the reprint of the Strassburg edition of 1490 under the title: *Quaestiones super libros sententiarum* (Frankfurt: Minerva, 1968). Although the text in this reprint is unpaginated, the sections of this work are divided alphabetically and will be cited accordingly. Despite its lack of pagination, this edition was chosen because it is more readily available in most research libraries.

[7] For an excellent survey of the many ways in which theology was described by the ancient Christian, patristic and medieval thinkers see Yves M.J. Congar, *A History of Theology* (New York: Doubleday, 1968), 25–68, and Henri de Lubac, *Exégèse médiévale*, 4 vols. (Paris: Aubier, 1959), 1:43–94. A recent analysis of Bonaventure's understanding of theology can be found in Henri Donneaud, 'Le sens du mot *theologia* chez Bonaventure,' *RT*, 102 (2002), 271–295.

[8] *Sent.*, 1, q. a. 3, DD. 'Alio modo pro actu vel habitu mentis respectu illorum, quae in sacra scriptura continentur. Et hoc modo iterum dupliciter potest sumi: Uno modo pro aliquo uno actu vel habitu respectu alcuius veritatis sacrae scripturae. Alio modo pro multis actibus vel habitibus respectu plurium talium veritatum ...'

[9] *Sent.*, 1, q. 1, a. 3, DD. 'Et hoc modo iterum dupliciter potest sumi. Uno modo pro actibus vel habitibus, quibus quis notat sensum sacrae scripturae et scit unum dictum eius per aliud exponere et probare et alia, quae non formaliter continentur in ipsa, ex his quae in ea continentur deducere et inferre.'

the major characteristics of theology in the high Middle Ages with the introduction of Aristotle and the rise of scholasticism and it is in this later sense that d'Ailly primarily understands theology.

In his definition of theology and its activities, d'Ailly was deeply indebted to the late medieval nominalistic tradition, especially that as represented by Gregory of Rimini. He, indeed, took his definition of theology and its associated activities directly from Gregory of Rimini.[10] Although d'Ailly and Rimini maintained a close relationship between theology and Scripture, d'Ailly placed a greater emphasis upon the role of Scripture in theology than did Rimini. As de Vooght has indicated, d'Ailly defined theology more directly and more explicitly in terms of the Scriptures.[11]

With regard to theology as a *habitus*, d'Ailly's teaching also manifested nominalistic influences, especially the influence of Ockham and Rimini. Among these two, it is upon Rimini that he draws more frequently. These influences are especially seen in the last chapter of d'Ailly's *De anima*, which was written between 1377 and 1381 and contains his most extensive treatment of the topic, at least in its philosophical context. More specifically, d'Ailly deals in detail with the topic of habits in relationship to the sensitive, intellectual, and volitional powers of the soul. D'Ailly's *De anima* also shows the strong influence of Aristotle whose thought on the nature of habits provided the springboard for much medieval speculation on the subject. While some of this Aristotelian influence in d'Ailly's work may have come indirectly through Ockham and Rimini, d'Ailly's text also shows a surprising number of direct references to Aristotle.[12]

---

[10] For Gregory of Rimini's definition of theology see his *Sent.*, 1, Prol., q. 2, a. 2, Trapp, 1:68:1–8. The edition of Gregory's *Lectura super primum et secundum Sententiarum* cited is that of A. Damasus Trapp and Vinicio Marcolino, 7 vols. (Berlin: Walter de Gruyter, 1981–1987). References to this edition will be made according to volume, page, and line numbers.

[11] Paul de Vooght, *Les sources de la doctrine chrétienne* (Bruges: Desclée DeBrouwer, 1954), 104, 238.

[12] The first critical edition of d'Ailly's *De anima* is that of Olaf Pluta and can be found in his *Die philosophische Psychologie des Peter von Ailly* (Amsterdam: B.R. Grüner, 1987), pt. 2:1–107. The predominant influence of Rimini and Aristotle upon d'Ailly's teaching on habits is noted by Pluta throughout the footnotes to the fifteenth chapter of the *De anima*. For a succinct analysis of key texts in Ockham's writings related to the notion of *habitus*, see Léon Baudry, *Lexique philosophique de Guillaume d'Ockham* (Paris: Lethielleux, 1958). A detailed study of Ockham's views on *habitus* can be found in Oswald Fuchs, *The Psychology of Habit According to William of Ockham* (St. Bonaventure, N.Y.: The Franciscan Institute, 1952). For key Aristotelian texts related to the concept of

After his analysis of theological method in terms of acts and habits, d'Ailly divided the habits which emerge from individual acts of theological speculation into two categories: acquired and infused. Just as the repetition of individual acts results in an acquired habit which in turn facilitates subsequent acts, so too do the individual acts of theological speculation result in an acquired habit in theology and facilitate further theological activity. For d'Ailly, theology understood primarily as an acquired habit does not necessarily require faith in the teaching of the Scriptures and as such can be employed by non-believers. He argues in this context that, with the exception of faith, any act or habit which Catholic theologians can perform or acquire can be equally performed or acquired by non-Catholics and even by infidels, provided that they were raised and educated in an essentially Christian society and were trained in theology.[13]

When individual acts of theological speculation take place within the context of faith in the teaching of the Scriptures, they involve an infused as well as an acquired habit. The infused habit results from a direct and immediate supernatural intervention by God whereas the acquired habit results from repeated acts of faith. Infused habits, moreover, can be *informis* or *formatus* depending upon whether or not they coexist with charity in the soul of the believer.[14] Since theology understood in the above sense involves a faith dimension, it obviously transcends the potential of non-believers.[15] Both in his *Commentary on the Sentences* and

---

habitus see: *Nicomachean Ethics*, 1103a, 14–1103b, 26, *Eudemian Ethics*, 1220a, 38–1220b, 20, and *Politics*, 1332a, 39–1332b, 11. Aquinas' extensive treatment on habits both in their philosophical and theological context is contained in his *ST*, 1, 2, qq. 49–54.

[13] *Sent.*, 1, q. 1, a. 3, DD. 'Prima est quod sumendo theologia primo istorum duorum modorum possibile est aliquem esse infidelem seu non catholicum et tamen esse theologum. Patet quia omnem actum vel habitum praeter fidem quem acquirit theologus fidelis posset etiam acquirere infidelis si esset nutritus inter Christianos et eruditus in studio theologico.' See also Ockham, *Sent.*, 1, Prologue, q. 7, I, Gál, 190:13–22. The edition of Ockham's *Scriptum in librum primum sententiarum (ordinatio)* used in the present study is that found in his *Opera theologica*, 10 vols (St. Bonaventure, N.Y.: Franciscan Institute, 1967–1986), vol 1, ed. Gedeon Gál and Stephen Brown, and will be cited according to page and line numbers.

[14] *Sent.*, 1, q. 1, a. 3, DD. For Gregory of Rimini's views on the same topic see his *Sent*, 1, q. 1, a. 4, Trapp-Marcolino, 1:55:28–56:10. On faith as an infused and acquired habit in Scotus, Ockham, and Biel see Giuseppe Barbaglio, *Fede acquista e fede infusa secondo Duns Scoto, Occam, e Biel* (Brescia: Morcelliana, 1968).

[15] *Sent.*, 1, q. 1, a. 3, DD. 'Secunda est quod sumendo theologiam secundo illorum duorum modorum impossibile est aliquem esse infidelem seu non catholicum et esse theologum.'

in one of his treatises against the chancellor of the University of Paris, d'Ailly described theology as a '*cognitio adhesiva*,' and a '*quaedam fides*,', and it is in this faith context that he primarily understands theology.[16]

In addition to acts and habits, theological method for d'Ailly also involves theological discourse (*discursus theologicus*). The use of the term 'discourse' to describe the process of human learning has a long and venerable tradition extending from the Greco-Roman tradition to the medieval period. Aquinas used the term primarily to distinguish human knowledge or modes of knowing from those of God and the angels. God, in one and the same act, not only knows himself but in knowing himself knows all creation because creation is essentially a reflection of his own essence. Although on a lesser level, angelic knowledge, because of its purely spiritual nature, also proceeds in a complete and instantaneous manner. In comprehending an object, angelic knowledge immediately understands all that is knowable about that object. The human intellect, however, as Aquinas explains, being a more limited faculty, gains knowledge of an object gradually by a series of successive actions. Through these actions it proceeds from the known to the unknown through a variety of intellectual operations such as deduction, induction, and experience.[17] This process Aquinas describes as an intellectual motion or in a more graphic sense an intellectual 'running' (*discursus*) from one degree of knowledge to another.[18]

With regard to d'Ailly's understanding of theology as discourse, it can be described as discourse involving infused acts or habits relating to words or propositions drawn directly from the Scriptures or deduced from scriptural texts or at least from one such text.[19] It is in

---

[16] *Sent.*, 1, q. 1, a. 3, LL. 'Prima igitur conclusio erit quod theologia ... est in animo fidelis quaedam adhesio sive cognitio adhesiva.' In his *Super omnia vincit veritas*, Bernstein, 239, d'Ailly also describes theology as a 'quaedam fides seu habitus creditivus.'

[17] For Aquinas' analysis of the differences between divine, angelic, and human knowledge see *ST*, 1, q. 14, a. 7, c.; 1, q. 58, a. 3 c, ad 1; 1, q. 79, a. 8 c., and *In Post. Anal.*, 1, lect. 1, n. 4.

[18] The term *discursus* comes from the verb *discurrere* which in turn is a qualified form of *currere*, meaning to run, to hasten, or to travel quickly. In classical Latin, *discurrere* signified to run from one place or object to another or to run successively through experiences or processes. In addition to physical activity the term was also used of intellectual activity. In post-classical Latin the term gradually took on the meaning of a conversation or discourse. Understood in this sense, *discursus* is most likely related to the Greek and Roman notions of dialogue as exemplified in the writings of Plato and Cicero.

[19] *Sent.*, 1, q. 1, a. 3, EE. 'Dico igitur quod discursus proprie theologicus est quod constat ex dictis seu propositionibus in sacra scriptura contentis vel ex his quae dedu-

such theological discourse or series of discourses that d'Ailly finds the definition of theological method most properly realized.[20] In its strictest sense, then, a proposition is said to be theologically proven only when it validly results from such type of discourse.[21]

Among the sources d'Ailly drew upon for his understanding of theological discourse, it is Gregory of Rimini who uses the phrase *discursus theologicus* most frequently. Indeed, the whole first question of the Prologue to Rimini's *Commentary on the Sentences* deals with the different dimensions of theological discourse. Ockham uses this term with much less frequency in his *Commentary*, preferring instead the term *habitus theologicus*. D'Ailly, however, draws his definition of theological discourse practically verbatim from Gregory.[22]

Theological discourse, as described by d'Ailly, moreover, stands midway between demonstrative discourse (*discursus demonstrativus*) and dialectical discourse (*discursus dialecticus*). In describing the distinction between these two types of discourse, d'Ailly follows Aristotle's teaching very closely.[23] Demonstrative discourse, according to Aristotle, begins with self-evident propositions which are accepted as true in and by themselves without recourse to other propositions, or with propositions which follow immediately and necessarily from such self-evident propositions. Other terms used by d'Ailly to describe demonstrative discourse are 'demonstrative reasoning (*ratio demonstrativa*),' 'demonstrative syllogism (*syllogismus demonstrativus*)', or 'syllogistic discourse (*discursus syllogisticus*)'. Since the truths of Scripture are not self-evident but are accepted

---

cuntur ex eis vel ex altera huiusmodi.' A similar definition can be found in *Super omnia vincit veritas*, Bernstein, 238.

[20] *Sent.*, 1, q. 1, a. 3, DD. 'Et licet quodlibet istorum modorum quandoque sumatur theolgia, tamen magis proprie sumitur ultimo modo.' For a similar description of theology in the proper sense of the term see d'Ailly's *Super omnia vincit veritas*, Bernstein, 238.

[21] *Sent.*, 1, q. 1, a. 3, EE. 'Item tunc solum dicimus aliquid theologice probari quando ex dictis sacrae scripturae concluditur.' Among the authorities d'Ailly cites for his position are Pseudo-Dionysius, *De divinis nominibus*, 2, and Augustine, *De Trinitate*, 1, c. 4, n. 7, *PL*, 42:824.

[22] For Rimini's description and use of the term *discursus* to describe theological method see especially his *Sent.*, 1, Prol., q. 1, a. 2, Trapp-Marcolino, 1:13–23, especially his response at 1:18–20.

[23] For Aristotle's understanding of the difference between demonstrative and dialectical reasoning see his *Topics*, 1, 100a:25–100b, 30, and his *Posterior Analytics*, 1, 71b:17–72a:11. A brief but excellent analysis of Aristotle's views on demonstrative and dialectical argumentation can be found in Jonathan Barnes, *The Cambridge Companion to Aristotle* (Cambridge: Cambridge University Press, 1995), 47–65.

in faith as true, d'Ailly does not allow any role for demonstrative discourse in his description of theological method.

Dialectical discourse, according to Aristotle, on the other hand, is based on propositions which are opinions generally accepted by everyone, by the majority of the people, or by the learned. D'Ailly alternately describes this form of discourse as 'dialectical reasoning (*ratio dialectica*)', or 'dialectical syllogizing (*syllogismus dialecticus*)'.[24] Since dialectical discourse rests on probable opinion, it too lies outside the realm of true theological discourse.[25] Working within the certainty of faith and basing itself on propositions drawn from the Scriptures, theological discourse, for d'Ailly, clearly transcends dialectical discourse.

D'Ailly's description of theological method as he understands it reveals clearly his awareness of the evolution of theological method from its early Christian, patristic and monastic roots to the prevailing forms of high and late medieval scholasticism. Theology, therefore, following in the tradition of Anselm, Abelard, Aquinas, Scotus, Ockham, and Rimini is no longer mere commentary on the text of the Scriptures, nor the elucidation of one scriptural passage in terms of another, as was often the case with patristic and early medieval theologians, but much more the drawing out of conclusions formally contained within the Scriptures and the organization of these conclusions in a coherent and systematic manner.[26] As will be seen, the difference, between the scholastic theologians of the high and late Middle Ages lies in the degree of confidence they had in reason's ability to attain such conclusions and the degree of certitude they consequently assigned to them.

Closely associated with theological method in terms of acts, habits, and discourse in the thought of most medieval theologians was the issue of the unity of theology as an intellectual discipline. On this issue, however, there were considerable differences among theologians as to the nature of that unity, namely, whether theology comprised one or a multiplicity of habits. While Aquinas saw theology as a simple habit

---

[24] For the diverse vocabulary used by d'Ailly to explain demonstrative and dialectical discourse see *Sent.*, 1, q. 1, a. 2, S and Z.

[25] *Sent.*, 1, q. 1, a. 3, EE. 'Nullus discursus qui est ex propositionibus probabilibus vel ex altera huiusmodi est proprie theologicus.'

[26] A detailed study of the evolution of theological method in the Middle Ages can be found in Joseph de Ghellinck, *Le mouvement théologique du xiie siècle*, 2nd ed., (Bruges: Culture et Civilisation, 1948); Congar, *A History of Theology*, 69–143; M.D. Chenu, *La théologie au douzième siècle* (Paris: J. Vrin, 1957), 323–350; Henri de Lubac, *Exégèse médiévale*, 1:95–118, and G.R. Evans, *Old Arts and New Theology* (Oxford: Clarendon Press, 1980).

resulting from a multiplicity of acts, late medieval thinkers such as Ockham and Rimini saw it as a synthesis of many habits of the soul.[27] D'Ailly clearly followed in the tradition of Ockham and especially Rimini. While d'Ailly agrees with Ockham and Rimini that theology essentially comprises a multiplicity of habits and in no way is ultimately reducible to one all comprising habit as maintained by Aquinas, he devotes relatively little time to this complex issue. For d'Ailly, the unity of a discipline is sufficiently maintained if the truths of that discipline relate essentially to the same object or objects under study. In support of this argument, D'Ailly cites the authority of Aristotle. Theological truths, therefore, share a common unity in that they are ordered to God and this order is sufficient in itself to guarantee the unity of theology as an intellectual discipline.[28]

D'Ailly also devotes little attention to the question of the subject of theology, another perennial topic medieval theologians treated in their *Commentaries on the Sentences*. For Augustine and Peter Lombard, the subject of theology was God, creatures, and the sacraments. Aquinas and Scotus held it to be God under the aspect of his divinity and in relationship to his creatures. Grosseteste and Bonaventure saw the subject of theology in terms of Christ. Giles of Rome and Gregory of Rimini formulated their response in terms of God as glorificator. Ockham reviewed, critiqued, and attempted to harmonize the diverse opinions on this topic but concluded by opting for a diversity of subjects according to the different persons within the Trinity and the relationship of creatures thereto.[29]

While d'Ailly says little about the subject of theology, it seems safe to conclude, as does Congar, that for him the subject of theology is

---

[27] For Aquinas's views on the unity of theology as a science see his *ST*, 1, q. 1, a. 3. The contrary views of Ockham can be found in his *Sent.*, 1, Prol., q. 3, a. 1–3, Gál, 129–142. For an excellent survey of the views of Aquinas, Ockham, and Rimini as to whether a science involved one or many habits see Armand Mauer, 'The Unity of a Science: St. Thomas and the Nominalists,' in *St. Thomas Aquinas, 1274–1974: Commemorative Studies*, 2 vols. (Toronto: Pontifical Institute of Medieval Studies, 1974), 2:269–291, as well as his 'Ockham's Conception of the Unity of a Science,' *MS*, 20 (1958), 98–112.

[28] *Sent.*, 1, q. 1, a. 2, FF. 'Nam licet tam veritates scientiarum particularium quam veritates theologicae sint de eisdem rebus, tamen veritates theologicae sunt secundum aliam attributionem ad Deum, quae attributio vel ordo est sufficiens ad unitatem talis scientiae modo quo loquitur philosophus.' The Aristotelian reference is to his *Metaphysics*, 4, 2, 1003b:1–23.

[29] For a general survey and outline of the various positions by different theologians throughout the Middle Ages with regard to the subject of theology, see Yves Congar, *A*

Christ as revealed in the Scriptures. This conclusion is corroborated by the central role played by Scripture in d'Ailly's definition of theology, and his Christocentric interpretation of the structure, division, and goal of Lombard's *Sentences*. By declaring Christ as revealed in the Scriptures as the subject of theology, d'Ailly follows neither Aquinas, Scotus, Ockham nor Rimini but adheres more to the tradition of Grosseteste and Bonaventure.[30]

3. *The Scientific Status of Theology*

In addition to describing theology in terms of its nature, method, unity, and subject, d'Ailly also raised the question of its scientific status. Ever since the introduction into the West of the Aristotelian notion of *scientia* in the mid-twelfth century, the question of whether or not theology was a science preoccupied all scholastic theologians in the Middle Ages and was generally treated in the prologue of their *Commentaries on the Sentences*.[31] As will be seen in greater detail, the Aristotelian notion of a science involved the systematization of a body of knowledge in terms of self-evident principles and necessary conclusions resulting from demonstrative reasoning upon those principles. During the twelfth and thirteenth centuries, the question whether theology was a science was increasingly answered in the affirmative, and the classical formulation of the argument on behalf of theology's scientific status was that of Thomas Aquinas.[32] The later Middle Ages, however, witnessed a reaction against the position of Aquinas, and theologians such as Godfrey of Fontaines (c. 1250–1306), Duns Scotus (c. 1265–1308), Durandus of St. Pourçain (c. 1275–1334), Peter Aureoli (c. 1280–1322), William of Ockham (1285–1347), and Gregory of Rimini (c. 1302–1358) denied the scientific status of theology.[33] Although d'Ailly showed himself aware of

---

History of Theology, 124–125. Ockham's views can be found in *Sent.*, 1, Prol., q. 9, Gál, 226–276, especially 271–276. Gregory of Rimini treated the same topic in *Sent.*, 1, Prol., q. 4, a. 1–2, Trapp-Marcolino, 1:121–146.

[30] Congar, *A History of Theology*, 124–126.

[31] Fernand Van Steenberghen's *Aristotle in the West: The Origins of Latin Aristotelianism* (New York: Humanities Press, 1970) remains among the best treatments of this topic.

[32] The question of the scientific status of theology in the high Middle Ages is treated extensively by Congar, *History of Theology*, 37–143. See also Chenu, *La théologie comme science au xiiie siècle*, 3rd. ed. (Paris: J. Vrin, 1957), and Jean Leclercq, 'La théologie comme science d'après la litterature quodlibetique,' *RTAM*, 9 (1939), 351–374.

[33] For a general survey of late medieval views on this subject see Meller, *Studien*

the long controversy over the question of the scientific status of theology, he followed in the mainstream of late medieval thought and rejected the idea of theology as a science.[34]

As is the case with all theologians involved in the controversy over the scientific status of theology, it is necessary to understand first of all what d'Ailly meant by the term '*scientia*' if we are to fully comprehend the reason for his position. D'Ailly defines '*scientia*' as evident knowledge of a necessary truth capable of being arrived at through syllogistic discourse.[35] As seen earlier, syllogistic discourse, according to d'Ailly, is essentially an alternative term for demonstrative discourse. He identifies Aristotle as the source for his definition of *scientia*, and specifically cites the *Nicomachean Ethics* wherein Aristotle distinguishes '*scientia*' from other modes of knowing such as art, practical wisdom, philosophical wisdom, and intuitive reason.[36] D'Ailly fails to acknowledge, however, that the verbal formulation of his definition was taken directly from Ockham who cites the same Aristotelian sources.[37]

In order to fully understand d'Ailly's definition of *scientia*, it is necessary first of all to describe briefly the general epistemological dimen-

---

zur Erkenntnislehre, 244–260, Robert Guelluy, *Philosophie et théologie chez Guillaume d'Ockham* (Louvain: Nauwelaerts, 1947), 131–258, Onorato Grassi, 'La questione della teologia come scienza in Gregorio da Rimini,' *RFN*, 68 (1976), 610–644, and Richard A. Lee, Jr., *Science, the Singular, and the Question of Theology*, The New Middle Ages (New York: Palgrave, 2002).

[34] *Sent.*, 1, q. 1, a. 3, JJ.

[35] *Sent.*, 1, q. 1, a. 3, GG. 'Unde dico quod scientia proprie dicta est noticia evidens veri necesarii nata causari per praemissas applicatas ad ipsam per discursum syllogisticum.'

[36] *Sent.*, 1, q. 1, a. 3, GG. For Aristotle's understanding of a science and scientific knowledge see his *Nicomachean Ethics*, 6, 3, 1139b: 14–35; 6, 6, 1140b: 31–35–1141a: 1–8, and his *Posterior Analytics*, 1, 2, 71b: 9–33; 1, 4, 73a: 21–25. A detailed study of Aristotle's views on *scientia* can be found in John I. Jenkins, *Knowledge and Faith in Thomas Aquinas* (Cambridge: Cambridge University Press, 1997), 11–50. See also Joseph Owens, 'The Aristotelian Conception of the Sciences,' *IPQ*, 4 (1964), 200–216 and Dunstan Hayden, 'Notes on Aristotelian Dialectic in Theological Method,' *The Thomist*, 20 (1957), 383–418. For a brief survey of the major medieval theories with regard to demonstrative science see Eileen Serene, 'Demonstrative Science,' in *The Cambridge History of Later Medieval Philosophy*, ed. Norman Kretzman et al., (Cambridge: Cambridge University Press, 1982) 496–517. The application of the term *scientia* to the other disciplines taught in the medieval university as well as the use of the contrasting notion of *ars* can be found in Ingrid Craemer-Ruegenberg and Andreas Speer, eds., *Scientia und Ars in Hoch-und Spätmittelalter*, 2 vols. Miscellanea Medievalia, 22. (Berlin: Walter de Gruyter, 1994).

[37] The passages from Ockham are to be found in his *Sent.*, 1, Prol., q. 2, a. 2, Gál, 1:87:19–88:2. See also *Sent.*, Prol., q. 2, a. 1, Gál, 1:76:13–16.

sions of his thought. Given the complexity of his epistemological thought as well as the continuing research on this topic, the description which follows must of necessity be incomplete. Basic to any analysis of d'Ailly's epistemological thought is his understanding of cognition (*noticia*).[38] For d'Ailly, cognition is described as an act which represents an object to the active and comprehensive powers of the soul. Cognition can also be seen as the union of the object perceived with those powers of the soul.[39] D'Ailly then distinguishes two forms of cognition, namely, sense cognition (*noticia sensualis*) and intellectual cognition (*noticia intellectualis*).[40] Both forms of cognition, moreover, can be simple (*simplex*) or complex (*complexa*) in so far as they relate to an individual object or to the object in the context of a proposition.[41] Given the nature of the present quest, our attention will focus on d'Ailly's understanding of intellectual cognition.

D'Ailly divides intellectual cognition, whether simple or complex, into intuitive cognition (*noticia intuitiva*) and abstract cognition (*noticia abstracta*). He defines intuitive cognition as 'knowledge by virtue of which the individual object is known to exist or to not exist.'[42] As such, intuitive cognition emerges as the initial and fundamental act of intellectual cognition upon which all further intellectual activity builds. Abstract cognition is essentially knowledge not directly of the individual object but of a universal abstracted from individuals. As such, this form of cognition prescinds from the existence or non-existence of individuals as well as from their accidental or contingent characteristics.[43]

---

[38] For a general survey of d'Ailly's views on *noticia* see Meller, *Die Erkenntnislehre des Peter von Ailly*, 126–135, Ludger Kaczmarek, '"Noticia" bei Peter von Ailly, Sent., 1, q. 3, Anmerkungen zu Quellen und Textgestalt,' in *Die Philosophie im 14 und 15 Jahrhundert*, Bochumer Studien zur Philosophie, 10, ed. Olaf Pluta (Amsterdam: B.R. Grüner, 1988), 385–420, and Joël Biard, 'Presence et représentation chez Pierre d'Ailly: Quelques problèmes de théorie de la connaissance au xive siècle,' *Dialogue*, 31 (1992), 459–474.

[39] *Sent.*, 1, q. 3, a. 1, B. 'Noticia est actus aliquid repraesentans potentiae vitaliter perceptivae … Noticia est actus uniens potentiam perceptivam vitaliter cum objecto.'

[40] *Sent.*, 1, q. 3, a. 1, J. 'Prima distinctio est quod noticiarum nobis possibilium quaedam est sensualis, alia intellectualis.'

[41] *Sent.*, 1, q. 3, a. 1, J. 'Harum autem noticiarum tam secundum sensualium quam intellectualium, quaedam est simplex et incomplexa, alia vero complexa.'

[42] *Sent.*, 1, q. 3, a. 1, K. 'Noticia intuitiva rei est talis noticia virtute cuius potest sciri utrum res sit vel non sit.'

[43] *Sent.*, 1, q. 3, a. 1, K. 'Dupliciter autem potest accipi noticia abstractiva. Uno modo quia est respectu alicuius abstracti a multis singularibus. Et sic cognitio abstractiva non est alius quam cognitio alicuius universalis abstrahibilis a multis singularibus. Aliter accipitur cognitio abstractiva secundum quod abstrahit ab existentia et non existentia et ab aliis condicionibus quae contingenter accidunt rei vel praedicantur de re.'

While distinguishing between intuitive and abstract cognition, d'Ailly is nonetheless insistent on the unity and interaction of both modes of knowing for the same object is known both intuitively and abstractly.[44]

D'Ailly's emphasis on the interaction between intuitive and abstract cognition reflects the late medieval trend, as exemplified by Henry of Ghent, Duns Scotus, and William of Ockham, of grounding cognition directly in the existing individual object rather than in the universal as referred back to the individual object, which was the case in much of thirteenth century scholasticism as represented by Aquinas and his followers.[45] Ockham, however, differed from Henry of Ghent and Duns Scotus in not espousing a moderate realism as the basis for his theory of abstract cognition. Thus for Ockham there are no universal natures existing outside the mind in which individuals share and which are the basis for the mind's formation of universals. Universals, consequently, are nothing more than the mind's understanding of individuals resulting from similarities among them.[46]

While it has long been maintained that d'Ailly followed Ockham on the issue of intuitive and abstract cognition as well as on the nature of universals, recent scholarship has noted that in his *De anima*, written between 1377 and 1381 and therefore shortly after the *Commentary on the Sentences*, d'Ailly views on intuitive and abstract cognition appear to show more the influence of Gregory of Rimini. Other scholars, however, while recognizing this influence, have denied any substantial change in his understanding of these two forms of cognition.[47]

---

[44] *Sent.*, 1, q. 3, a. 1, 'Non quod aliquid cognoscatur per noticiam intuitivam quod non cognoscatur per abstractivam, sed idem totaliter et sub omni eadem ratione cognoscitur per utramque.'

[45] A survey of late medieval views on intuitive and abstract cognition can be found in John F. Boler, 'Intuitive and Abstract Cognition,' in *The Cambridge History of Late Medieval Philosophy*, 460–478.

[46] For a detailed analysis of Ockham's emphasis upon the primacy of intuitive over abstract cognition as well as his differences with Aquinas, Henry of Ghent, and Duns Scotus over the issue of universals see Marilyn McCord Adams, 'Universals in the Early Fourteenth Century,' in *The Cambridge History of Later Medieval Philosophy*, 411–439, and her more recent work, *William of Ockham*, 2 vols. (Notre Dame: University of Notre Dame Press, 1987), 1:3–107. See also Gordon Leff, *William of Ockham: The Metamorphosis of Scholastic Discourse* (Manchester: Manchester University Press, 1975), 2–6, 62–77, and Frederick Copleston, *A History of Philosophy*, 3 vols (Westminster: The Newman Press, 1960–1963), 3:48–59.

[47] These varying opinions can be found in Biard, 'Présence et représentation chez Pierre d'Ailly,' 473, n. 14, L. Kaczmarek, 'Noticia bei Peter von Ailly, Sent 1, q. 3: Annerkungen zu Quellen und Textgestalt,' 385–420, and Pluta, *Die Philosophische Psychologie des Peter von Ailly*, 108–110,

Integrally related to an understanding of d'Ailly's epistemological thought in general and to his understanding of *scientia* in particular is the question of evidence (*evidentia*). Evidence grounds the quality of an assent, that is, the degree of certitude associated with that assent. In treating the question of evidence, d'Ailly distinguishes between evident and non-evident cognition (*evidens vel non-evidens noticia*). With regard to evident cognition, d'Ailly states that throughout the history of thought there have been two extreme responses. The extreme left position is best epitomized by the Academicians who claimed that no truths could be known with evident knowledge. This position, he maintained, has been effectively refuted by Augustine in his *Against the Academicians*. On the extreme right is to be found the school of thought attacked by Thomas Bradwardine for its claims that all truth can be known with evident knowledge. D'Ailly concludes his remarks by stating that his position will be midway between these both extremes.[48]

For d'Ailly there are two kinds of evident cognition: absolute (*absoluta*) and conditioned (*condicionata*). Absolute evidence relates to the evidence of first principles, especially the principle of contradiction, or to conclusions essentially reducible to first principles.[49] According to d'Ailly, absolute evidence involves a true assent, placed without fear of error, caused naturally, and such that it is impossible for the intellect to place such an assent and in so doing be deceived or err.[50] After giving his basic definition of absolute evidence, d'Ailly takes time to carefully explain the key elements of his definition. The words 'true assent' serve to distinguish this form of assent from false or erroneous assent. The phrase 'placed without fear of error' is used to distinguish such assent from opinion, suspicion, or conjecture. The phrase 'caused naturally' distinguishes this form of assent from that involved in an act of faith which, while placed without fear of error, is nonetheless not caused naturally by the evidence but flows from the interaction of grace and free will. The remaining phrases of the definition are self-explanatory.

---

[48] *Sent.*, 1, q. 1, a. 1, E. The reference in Bradwardine is to be found in his *Summa*, 1, pt. 32, c. 1.

[49] *Sent.*, 1, q. 1, a. 1, E. 'Unde dico quod duplex est evidentia. Quaedam est evidentia absoluta, qualis est evidentia primi principii vel reducibilis ad eam; alia est evidentia condicionata qualis est evidentia nostri ingenii quae est citra primam.'

[50] *Sent.*, 1, q. 1, a. 1 E. 'Evidentia absoluta simpliciter potest describi quod est assensus verus sine formidine, causatus naturaliter, quo non est possibile intellectum assentire et in sic assentiendo decipi vel errare.'

D'Ailly admits, furthermore, that within the context of absolute evidence there are varying degrees. As would be expected, the highest degree of absolute evidence is that based on the principle of contradiction. The other degrees vary according to the extent to which they are reducible to that principle.[51] Conclusions, therefore, which follow closely from the principle of contradiction rank high in the realm of absolute evidence.[52] Knowledge drawn from the sciences, especially mathematics, also falls within the realm of absolute evidence since such sciences depend heavily upon first principles in their operation and conclusions.[53] Finally, even some contingent truths can be known with absolute evidence, such as a person's knowledge that he exists or that he knows.[54]

Conditional evidence (*evidentia condicionata*) for d'Ailly involves an assent which is true, placed without fear of error, caused naturally, and such that it is impossible for the intellect to place such an assent and in so doing be deceived or err. Thus far d'Ailly's definition parallels practically verbatim his definition of absolute evidence. What really distinguishes conditional from absolute evidence, however is the qualifying statement by d'Ailly: 'provided that God's general concursus is operative and that no miracle has occurred.'[55] The latter qualification reflects d'Ailly's nominalistic concern with the distinction between God's absolute power (*potentia absoluta*) and ordinary or ordained power (*potentia ordinaria*).[56] Since conditional truths fall within the realm of

---

[51] *Sent.*, 1, q. 1, a. 1, K. 'Imo in evidenta sunt gradus. Quia primum principium est evidentissimum. Et deinde alia magis vel minus, secundum quod magis vel minus appropinquant ad primum principium.'

[52] *Sent.*, 1, q. 1, a. 1, E. '... quia quilibet experitur non solum primum principium esse sibi evidens modo predicto sed etiam multas consequentias, sicut ... si equus currit, animal currit, etc.'

[53] In his arguments on behalf of our ability to obtain absolute evidence about many truths, d'Ailly argues that unless such were the case the sciences themselves would be threatened: '... quia aliter sequitur omnes scientias perire quod est inconveniens, maxime de mathematicis quae secundum Philosophum sunt in primo gradu certitudinis.' Cf. *Sent.*, 1, q. 1, a. E.

[54] *Sent.*, 1, q. 1, a. 1, E. '... possibile est viatorem de multis veritatibus contingentibus habere evidentiam absolutam sive noticiam simpliciter evidentem, verbi gratia quod ipse est, quod ipse cognoscit, etc.'

[55] *Sent.*, 1, q. 1, a. 1, E. 'Evidentia autem secundum quid potest describi quod est assensus verus sine formidine, causatus naturaliter, quo non est possible, stante Dei influentia generali et nullo facto miraculo, intellectum assentire et in sic assentiendo decipi vel errare.'

[56] Detailed descriptions of the understanding of *potentia absoluta* and *potentia ordinata* in the high and late Middle Ages as well as the consequences of that understanding in

God's ordained power, d'Ailly asserts that there is no reasonable basis for doubting their validity, although there is always the possibility that through the use of his absolute power God could intervene and suspend the normal course of cosmic and human causality.[57]

In treating of non-evident cognition, d'Ailly deals primarily with the phenomenon of faith (*fides*), which he defines as a true and firm assent placed without fear of error.[58] That assent, however, does not flow from the natural evidence characteristic of absolute or conditional cognition but from the interaction of grace and free choice.[59] Faith, then, is a form of certain yet non-evident knowledge because its assent is based not upon knowledge acquired rationally through intuition, abstraction, or syllogistic discourse but upon trust placed in the data of Revelation. Within the context of non-evident knowledge, however, faith differs from opinion because it is marked by a firm belief and is placed without fear of error. Following traditional scholastic teaching, d'Ailly enumerates three forms of faith, namely, actual (*actualis*), habitual (*habitualis*), and objectival (*objectalis*). Actual faith is best described as a concrete act or series of acts of assent, while habitual faith connotes more the facility in placing such acts. Finally, objectival faith is essentially identified with the various truths to which a firm assent is given.[60]

Having seen the basic outline of d'Ailly's epistemological thought, we can now proceed to a more detailed analysis of his understanding of *scientia* and the reasons why he refused to attribute a scientific status

---

the realm of philosophy and theology can be found in William J. Courtenay, *Capacity and Volition: A History of the Distinction of Absolute and Ordained Power* (Bergamo: Lubrina, 1990), Irven M. Resnick, *Divine Power in St. Peter Damian's 'De divina omnipotentia'* (Leiden: E.J. Brill, 1992), Lawrence Moonan, *Divine Power: The Medieval Power Distinction up to its Adoption by Albert, Bonaventure, and Aquinas* (Oxford: Clarendon Press, 1994), and Oberman, *The Harvest of Medieval Theology*, 30–56.

[57] *Sent.*, 1, q. 1, a. 1, E. 'Loquendo de evidentia secundum quid seu conditionata vel ex suppositione scilicet stante Dei influencia generali et cursu naturae solito nullo facto miraculo talia possunt esse nobis sufficienter evidentia sic quod de ipsis non habemus rationabiliter dubitare.'

[58] *Sent.*, 1, q. 1, a. 2, S. '... Fides potest describi quod est assensus verus firmus sine formidine non evidens.'

[59] *Sent.*, 1, q. 1, a. 1, E. In describing the ways in which an assent based on evident knowledge differs from assent based on faith, d'Ailly states: 'Tertia est causatus naturaliter, id est ex causis ncessitantibus intellectum ad sic assentiendum, ad differentiam fidei que licet sit assensus sine formidine tamen non est causatus naturaliter sed libere.'

[60] For d'Ailly's use of the traditional threefold sense of faith see his *Utrum Petri Ecclesia rege gubernatur*, Dupin, 1:673. For additional examples of the use of this threefold description in the late Middle Ages see Joannes Altensteig and Joannes Tytz, eds., *Lexicon theologicum* (Cologne, 1619), 324–326.

to theology. As will be recalled, d'Ailly defined *scientia* as evident knowledge of a necessary truth capable of being arrived at though syllogistic reasoning. Evident knowledge, moreover, can result from three sources: from direct experience, from self-evident propositions, and from deductions from such propositions. In describing *scientia* as evident knowledge d'Ailly seeks to distinguish scientific knowledge from all forms of non-evident knowledge such as error, suspicion, opinion, and faith. By stating that *scientia* is evident knowledge of a necessary truth, d'Ailly further distinguishes *scientia* from evident knowledge of contingent truths. By insisting on the role of syllogistic reasoning, he distinguishes the truths of *scientia* from the self-evident truths of first principles. Finally, the phrase 'capable of being arrived at' is added to his definition because, as seen above, evident knowledge can also originate from experience. One can have evident knowledge that the moon can be eclipsed on the basis of experience and without the use of syllogistic reasoning.[61]

Given his definition of '*scientia*' as evident knowledge of a necessary truth arrived at through the means of syllogistic reasoning, d'Ailly's rejection of theology as a science is a foregone conclusion. The truths of the Scriptures, which are the principles upon which theology is constructed, originate not from human reason but from divine revelation. As such the theologian can have no evident knowledge of these truths through syllogistic reasoning but accepts them as true on the basis of faith. It follows, therefore, that the knowledge he draws from them will never qualify as a science in the strict Aristotelian sense of the term. If such were not the case, he argues, any infidel studying the Scriptures would be led automatically to assent to the truth of all conclusions drawn from them.[62]

As mentioned earlier, d'Ailly was aware of the long and controversial history associated with the question of the scientific nature of theology. While he recognized the many positions taken on this question, he treated in detail only the position of Aquinas and his followers since

---

[61] *Sent.*, 1, q. 1, a. 3, GG. 'Per primam ergo particulam excluditur error, opinio, suspicio et fides, et atque omnes noticiae quae non sunt evidentes. Per secundam excluditur notiica evidens verorum contingentium quae non est proprie scientia. Per tertiam excluditur noticia evidens primorum principiorum quia illa non habentur per discursum syllogisticum. Dico autem nata causari quia non oportet quod de facto causetur per tales praemissas. Nam potest per experientiam causari. Potest enim aliquis sine syllogismo evidenter scire quod luna est eclypsabilis per solam experientiam sine syllogismo.'

[62] *Sent.*, 1, q. 1, a. 3, DD, LL. See also *Super omnia vincit veritas*, Bernstein, 239.

he regarded the Thomistic position as presenting the more probable arguments on behalf of theology as a science.[63] Followers of that tradition, he argues, would admit that the theologian himself does not have evident knowledge of the truths of his discipline since those truths are based on revelation and are accepted on faith. In this context, therefore, even they would not claim that theology could be called a science in the strictest Aristotelian sense of the term.

Aquinas and his followers, he continues, maintained that theology was a science by arguing that the truths of Scripture with which the theologian works are known with evident knowledge by God and the blessed. They argued, moreover, that since these truths were evident to the minds of God and the blessed and had been revealed in the Scriptures, theologians can readily be assured of their scientific nature and, consequently, of the scientific status of their discipline. Theology understood in this sense was described by Thomists as a subalternate science (*scientia subalternata*), which they understood as a science which borrows its principles from a higher science. The notion of a subalternate science also had Aristotelian roots. Just as Aristotle argued that the science of perspective takes its principles from geometry, and music draws its principles ultimately from arithmetic, so too, Thomists argued that theology takes its principles from the higher knowledge of God and the blessed.[64]

In responding to the Thomistic position, d'Ailly again affirms his basic epistemological position that evident knowledge arrived at through syllogistic reasoning is essential to the meaning of *scientia*. Since the principles upon which theology is built are not arrived at through syllogistic reasoning but are revealed, theology can in no way qualify as a science. Nor does it suffice, he argues, to maintain that theology's principles are known with evident knowledge in the minds of God and the blessed, since no scientific knowledge existing in the mind of

---

[63] *Sent.*, 1, q. 1, a. 3, JJ, 'Sed nolo omnes recitare ideo unam solam quae apparet mihi probabilior volo hic breviter transire.' For the historical background to Aquinas's teaching on the scientific status of theology see Romanus Cessario, 'Towards Understanding Aquinas' Theological Method: The Early Twelfth Century Experience,' and Mark D. Jordan, 'Aquinas' Middle Thoughts on Theology as a Science,' in *Studies in Thomistic Theology*, ed. Paul Lockey (Houston: University of St.Thomas Press, 1995), 17–89 and 91–111. For a detailed study of the Thomistic position of theology as a science see Congar, *History of Theology*, 91–96, Chenu, *La théologie comme science*, 67–85, and John I. Jenkins, *Knowledge and Faith in Thomas Aquinas*, 78–98.

[64] *Sent.*, 1, q. 1, a. 3, JJ. The texts in Aristotle upon which the Thomistic school generally relied were from his *Posterior Analytics*, 1, 2, 72a:14–20, and l, 13, 78b:35–39.

one person can automatically engender evident knowledge in another.[65] While the argument used by d'Ailly in rejecting theology as a subalternate science is essentially that of Ockham, he relies heavily on the verbal formulation of Gregory of Rimini, perhaps to avoid the derogatory tenor of Ockham's refutation of Aquinas' position as 'puerile.'[66] As will be recalled, d'Ailly regarded Aquinas as the most prominent defender of the scientific nature of theology.

4. *Method: Theological Discourse and Apologetics*

Given the basic outline of d'Ailly's teaching on theology and its scientific status, his understanding of theological method in terms of theological discourse can now be more readily grasped. As seen earlier, d'Ailly described theological discourse in terms of propositions drawn from the scriptures or deduced therefrom. These propositions constitute what he designates as theological truths (*veritates theologicae*). D'Ailly describes these truths in both a broad and a strict sense. Taken in their broad sense, theological truths are those which have been formulated or are capable of being formulated about God or about creatures in so far as they have a relationship to God through creation, providence, redemption, justification, or remuneration. Strictly speaking, theological truths are those specific truths within the general body of theological truths which are necessary for the individual Christian to attain eternal salvation or for the Church in the evolution of its belief and in the defense of that belief against heretics and non-believers.[67]

---

[65] *Sent.*, 1, q. 1, a. 3, JJ. 'Sed contra istam opinionem arguitur sic, quia omnis scientia proprie dicta est noticia evidens ut patet ex dictis, sed theologia non est noticia evidens, ut patet ad experientiam, igitur etc. Confirmatur quod ad hoc quod ego habeam scientiam de aliqua conclusione non sufficit quod principia eius sint alteri nota quoniam per nullam noticiam existentem in alio causare potest immediate et naturaliter aliqua scientia in mente mea. Cum igitur principia theologiae non sint aut fuerint nobis evidenter nota ut isti concedunt, sequitur quod theologia quae acquiritur de communi lege in nobis vere non est scientia.'

[66] The passages taken from Gregory of Rimini are: *Sent.*, 1, Prol., q. 1, a. 4, Trapp-Marcolino, 1:51:1–13. For Ockham's rejection of Aquinas' position on theology as a science see, *Sent.*, 1, Prol., q. 7, Gál, 199.

[67] *Sent.*, 1, q. 1, a. 2, R. 'Unde dico quod de ipsis possumus loqui dupliciter. Uno modo stricte. Alio modo large. Stricte loquendo veritates theologicae sunt veritates necessariae viatori ad eternam beatitudinem consequendam vel veritates quas credere viatori est necessarium ad salutem. Sed magis loquendo veritates theologicae sunt illae veritates quae sunt de Deo formatae vel formabiles, vel etiam de creaturis ut habent attri-

After having given a general explanation of the nature of theological truths, d'Ailly next divides these truths into three categories. The first category he designates as theological principles (*principia theologica*) since they embody truths clearly and explicitly contained in the Scriptures.[68] Truths which are not explicitly contained in the Scriptures but which follow logically and necessarily from theological principles are designated by d'Ailly as theological conclusions (*conclusiones theologicae*). Such conclusions may subsequently become the subject of a determination (*determinatio*) of the Church.[69] Finally, the third category of theological truths are those which are in some sense related to the Scriptures but which are neither explicitly contained therein nor follow necessarily from the Scriptures.[70] D'Ailly does not give these truths any special title, but in effect they correspond to his earlier description of theological truths in the broad sense of the term.

As in the case of his description of theological discourse, d'Ailly depends heavily upon the teaching of Rimini for his understanding of theological principles and conclusions. His definition of theological principles is taken practically verbatim from Rimini as is his description of theological conclusions.[71] D'Ailly and Rimini, moreover, differed considerably from Ockham on the issue of theological truths in that Ockham does not distinguish between the broad and strict senses of theological truths. Ockham also allows conclusions drawn from natural reason, such as that God exists, that he is wise and good, to be included into the realm of theological principles and conclusions and to play a role in theological discourse. D'Ailly and Rimini, however, limit that discourse to principles and conclusions drawn from the Scriptures alone.[72]

---

butionem vel per se ordinem ad Deum, puta secundum creationem, gubernationem, reparationem, iustificationem, remunerationem et similia.'

[68] *Sent.*, 1, q. 1, a. 3, EE. 'Sunt enim ipsae sacri canonis veritates,' See also *Super omnia vincit veritas*, Bernstein, 238–239.

[69] *Sent.*, 1, q. 1, a. 3, EE. 'Sunt enim illae veritates quae non formaliter in sacra scriptura continentur sed ex contentis in ipsa de necessitate sequuntur sive sint articuli, sive sint per ecclesiam determinatae sive non, sive sint scitae sive non.' See also *Super omnia vincit veritas*, Bernstein, 239.

[70] *Sent.*, 1, q. 1, a. 3, EE. 'Multae sunt veritates tales quae nec sunt principia theologica nec conclusiones.'

[71] Rimini's descriptions of *principia theologica* and *conclusiones theologicae* are to be found in *Sent.*, 1, Prol., q. 1, a. 2, Trapp-Marcolino, 1:20.

[72] For Ockham's teaching on the nature of theological truths see *Sent.*, 1, Prol., q. 1, Gál, 7.

D'Ailly maintained, moreover, that corresponding to the different categories of theological truths were varying degrees of certitude. Theological principles, based explicitly as they are on the Scriptures and the individual's faith therein, enjoy that firm certitude which is characteristic of faith. Theological conclusions, since they follow logically and necessarily from theological principles, also enjoy a faith-based certitude. Those theological truths which are neither theological principles nor theological conclusions possess only a high degree of probability.[73]

D'Ailly's teaching on the function of theological conclusions in the process of theological discourse places him squarely in the deductive school of theology so ardently represented and defended by Gregory of Rimini, and against the declarative school traditionally represented by Peter Aureoli (c. 1280–1322).[74] While Aureoli recognized the multiple intellectual activities engaged in by theologians, even that of deductive reasoning from revealed truths, he nonetheless maintained that such actions did not represent the distinguishing characteristic of theology and theological method. The primary function of theology, Aureoli emphasized, was not to develop new theological conclusions and so extend the domain of faith, but to bring greater clarity to the articles of faith already established in the Scriptures and through the determinations of the Church. By so acting, theologians make those articles of faith more explicit and therefore more understandable to the faithful. Through such intellectual activity, theologians also help to explain and defend the Christian faith against heretics and non-believers.

To justify their concept of theology, Aureoli and his followers frequently cited 1 Pt. 3:15 wherein the writer urges believers to always 'be ready to make your defense to anyone who demands from you an accounting for the hope that is in you …' and Augustine's statement in his *De Trinitate* that the task of theology was 'to nourish, strengthen, and defend the faith.' For Aureoli, then, theology in its strictest sense was more a form of apologetics than a development and extension of the content of the faith.[75] Despite his great emphasis on the important

---

[73] *Sent.*, 1, q. 1, a. 3, EE. 'Patet ubi dictum fuit aliquae sunt probabiles precise quia nec continentur in sacro canone nec inde sequuntur de necessitate.'

[74] The clearest and most succinct description of the differences between the declarative and deductive schools of theology as they developed in the late Middle Ages can be found in the articles of Stephen Brown, 'Philosophy and Theology, Western Europe: Late Middle Ages,' *DMA*, 9:608–615, and 'Peter of Candia's Hundred Year History of the Theologian's Role,' *MPT*, 1 (1991), 156–190.

[75] Aureoli's analysis of the nature of theological method can be found in the pro-

role of declarative theology, Aureoli regards the conclusions arrived at through its methodology only on the level of opinion. According to Aureoli, therefore, theology in its most proper sense, namely, declarative theology, represents essentially the views of theologians and as such reaches only the level of probability.

As Gregory of Rimini saw it, the distinguishing characteristic of theology, over and above the emphasis of Aureoli, was to extend the content of the faith by deducing truths not formally contained in the Scriptures by the use of truths so contained. Thus his specific understanding of the role of theological principles and conclusions in theological discourse. In Rimini's view, the conclusions so evolved represent real extensions of the faith and demand the same degree of consent as truths formally contained in the Scriptures. As seen above, d'Ailly followed closely in the tradition of Rimini and criticized the position of Aureoli with a vigor almost equal to that of Rimini.[76] While d'Ailly strongly rejected Aureoli's definition of theology and theological discourse in terms of apologetics based on probable opinions, he does not deny a role for apologetics and probable knowledge in the theological endeavor. In a sense then, d'Ailly takes what Aureoli regards as the primary function of theology, namely, apologetics, and reduces it to a secondary or auxiliary role.

In order to better comprehend d'Ailly's teaching on apologetics and its limited probative value, it is important first of all to analyze his understanding of the term 'probable' (*probabilis*).[77] It is to be noted that

---

logue to his *Scriptum super primum sententiarum*. See *Sent.*, Prol., q. 1, a. 2, Buytaert, 1:154–159 and a. 3, Buytaert, 1:159–171. The edition used is that of E.M. Buytaert, 2 vols. (St. Bonaventure, N.Y.: The Franciscan Institute, 1952–1956). References to this edition will be made according to volume and page number. For detailed studies of Peter Aureoli's views on the nature of theology see S.R. Streuer, *Die theologische Einleitungslehre des Petrus Aureoli* (Werl in Westfalen: Dietrich-Coelde Verlag, 1968) and Onorato Grassi, 'Probabilismo teologico e certezza filosofica: Pietro Aureoli e il dibattito sulla conoscenza nel 1300,' in d'Onofrio, *Storia della teologia nel medioevo*, 3:515–540. A more extensive study of the various deductive schools of theology in the late Middle Ages can be found in Albert Lang, *Die theologische prinzipienlehre der mittelalterlichen Scholastik* (Freiburg: Herder, 1964). The reference to Augustine was to his *De Trinitate*, 14, c. 1, *CCL*, 50A:421–422.

[76] Rimini's analysis and rejection of Aureoli's position is found in *Sent.*, 1, Prol., q. 1, a. 2, Trapp-Marcolino, 1:13:1–23:30, and d'Ailly's shorter treatment in *Sent.*, 1, Prol., q. 1, a. 1, EE.

[77] An excellent study of the evolving meaning of the word '*probabilis*' in the medieval period up to and including Aquinas can be found in Thomas Deman, 'Notes de lexicographie philosophique médiévale,' *RSPT*, 22 (1930), 260–290. See also A. Gardeil, 'La certitude probable,' *RSPT*, 5 (1911), 237–266, 441–445.

throughout his analysis, d'Ailly depends much more on Aristotle than on Ockham.[78] According to d'Ailly, the term 'probable' can be used in a primary sense (*simpliciter*) or in a secondary sense (*secundum quid*). He explains its primary sense in terms of propositions which, although true and necessary, manifest themselves not with evident cognition (*evidens noticia*) but only with apparent cognition (*apparens notitia*) to all persons, to many, and especially to the wise.[79] As such, this definition excludes all contingent propositions, whether true or false, all theological principles and conclusions as well as necessary propositions that appear to be false to many or to all people.[80] With regard to its secondary sense (*secundum quid*), the term can be used of propositions which, whether necessary or contingent, are themselves true but which manifest themselves to a particular person or group of persons with only apparent cognition.[81]

While maintaining that not all probable theological truths are probable in the primary sense of the term, d'Ailly nonetheless maintains that many are such.[82] Some theological propositions enjoy such a high degree of probability that, for all practical purposes, they exclude any doubt or fear of error. Assent to such propositions, he maintains, is almost as firm as the assent to propositions based on evident knowledge.[83] Other probable propositions, namely, those that are probable in the secondary sense of the term, do not enjoy such a firm assent.

---

[78] Aristotle's definition can be found in his *Topics*, 1, 1, 100b:20–22. For Ockham's definition see his *Sent.*, 3, 3, c. 9, *Opera theologica*, 6, ed. Francis E. Kelly and Gerard L. Etzkorn (St. Bonaventure: The Franciscan Institute, 1982).

[79] *Sent.*, 1, q. 1, a. 2, Z. 'Ad istas rationes responditur per ordinem. Unde ad primam premittenda est una distinctio quae est quod aliquid esse probabile postest dupliciter intelligi. Uno modo simpliciter, alio modo secundum quid. Unde secundum Philosophum illud dicitur probabile simpliciter quod videtur omnibus vel pluribus vel maxime sapientibus. Quae descriptio sic intelligitur, quod probabile est quod cum sit verum et necessarium non est tamen evidens sed apparens omnibus vel pluribus vel maxime sapientibus.'

[80] *Sent.*, I, q. 1, a. 2, Z. 'Per primam clasulam excluduntur falsa et vera contingentia ... Per secundam excluduntur etiam principia et conclusiones demonstrationum ... Per tertiam excluduntur necessaria quae apparent falsa omnibus vel pluribus.'

[81] *Sent.*, I, q. 1, a. 2, Z. 'Sed alio modo et magis large aliquid dicitur probabile secundum quid, quod cum sit verum et necessarium sive contingens non est tamen evidens sed apparens alicui vel aliquibus.'

[82] *Sent.*, 1, q. 1, a. 2, Z. '... non omnes theologicae veritates sunt primo modo probabiles ... Tamen cum istis stat quod multae veritates sunt theologicae probabiles primo modo.'

[83] *Sent.*, 1, q. 1, a. 2, Z. 'Secunda est quod non omnis ratio probabilis seu dylectica facit semper dubitationem seu formidinem sed frequenter firmam adhesionem. Patet, quia quandoque adheremus ita firmiter probabilibus sicut evidenter notis.'

As seen earlier, although d'Ailly refused to assign probable propositions any formal role in the realm of theological discourse and designated all discourse based on probable propositions as dialectical discourse, he does allow probable propositions and dialectical discourse an important role in the realm of Christian apologetics, for although such propositions cannot demonstrate the truth of the faith, they can show its appropriateness or congruence within the total scheme of theological knowledge. Such propositions can also be a very persuasive force in bringing the human will to assent in faith to the Scriptures and to the many theological truths contained therein.[84]

While the above analysis of d'Ailly's thought on theology and theological method in no way pretends to represent the full extent of his views on these topics, it has emphasized its major characteristics and consequently does allow for some general conclusions. First of all, it can be said that d'Ailly's views on the subject of theology and theological method represents, within the context of late medieval nominalistic thought, a relatively unified and coherent system. Older descriptions of d'Ailly's thought in these areas as purely eclectic can no longer be sustained. Within late medieval nominalism, however, as within most schools of thought, there were, as indicated earlier, several variations or divisions and d'Ailly does draw upon these various divisions to formulate his own views on theology, its method, subject, and unity. Although the general epistemological context of his thought was essentially Ockhamistic, his definition and understanding of theology, theological truths, and theological method were drawn primarily from Gregory of Rimini. Our study, therefore, can be regarded as providing added support for Saint-Blançat's and Schultz's thesis that d'Ailly, while remaining essentially in the nominalistic tradition, belongs much more to the school of Rimini than to that of Ockham. Yet even in this context, d'Ailly maintains a respectable degree of independence. As seen earlier, he differed from Rimini concerning the subject of theology as

---

[84] *Sent*, 1, q. 1, a. 2, U, 'Naturaliter est viatorem de illis veritatibus habere opinionem ad quas probandas naturaliter potest habere rationes dyalecticas seu probabiles inducentes ad assentiendum intellectum indifferentem, sed sic est de multis veritatibus theologicis.' For further analysis of d'Ailly's attitude to and use of probable propositions see Alfonso Maierù, 'Logique et théologie trinitaire: Pierre d'Ailly,' in *Preuve et raisons à l'Université de Paris: Logique, ontologie et théologie au xive siècle*, ed. Zénon Kaluza and Paul Vignaux (Paris, 1984), 254–255, and Maurice de Gandillac, 'De l'usage et de la valeur des arguments probables dans les Questiones du Cardinal Pierre d'Ailly sur le Livre des Sentences,' *AHDL*, 8 (1932–1933), 43–91.

well as the role and significance of probable reasons in theology. Also in his use of Aristotle, d'Ailly shows a greater direct contact with the Stagirite's texts and thought than earlier realized.

D'Ailly's teaching on theology, theological truths, and theological method also reflects the increased emphasis on the role of Scripture in his thought. While this increased emphasis was indeed characteristic of much late medieval nominalistic thought which stressed the necessity of returning to the Scriptures as the primary basis for theological speculation, d'Ailly's emphasis was even more pronounced than that of his peers. This strong emphasis was seen in his restriction of theological discourse primarily to theological principles and conclusions drawn from the Scriptures. Unlike Ockham, he excluded from the realm of theological discourse all conclusions drawn from natural reason relating to God's existence and nature. A similar emphasis on Scripture was seen in his position that Christ was the subject of theology. If such be the case, then the primary source which provides knowledge of Christ is the Scriptures and what can be immediately be concluded from them. The prominence of Scripture in his theological speculation also helps to explain his popularity among the Brethren of the Common Life, who published some of his works after his death and who received his strong support at the Council of Constance when their mode of religious life came under severe attack. Finally, the strong emphasis on the Scriptures in d'Ailly's thought did not make him a 'forerunner' of the '*sola scriptura*' theories of the Protestant reformers, for he always provided a sufficient role for the determinations of the Church with regard to what theological truths were consonant with its true nature.

The tendency of d'Ailly to restrict the domain of theology and its methodology, to deny its scientific status, as well as his heavy emphasis upon Scripture have occasionally resulted in his being accused of skepticism and fideism, an accusation that has been leveled against many nominalistic thinkers of the late Middle Ages.[85] While it is not the purpose of this chapter to enter into such a highly complex and controversial issue, it should be noted that recent research on the history of late medieval nominalistic thought has done much to show that

---

[85] For the accusations leveled against d'Ailly, see Tschackert, *Peter von Ailly*, 314–315 and Salembier, *Petrus ab Alliaco*, 144–146. The charges against late medieval nominalism in general are best epitomized by Etienne Gilson in his *The History of Christian Philosophy in the Middle Ages* (New York: Random House, 1955), 471–545 passim. These charges are also reviewed by Congar, *A History of Theology*, 131–136.

this highly adverse judgement was not always merited and was more characteristic of later generations of thinkers influenced by nominalistic thought.[86] Clearly such was the case with d'Ailly. Although he did not allow conclusions drawn from natural reason regarding God's existence and nature to play a role in strict theological discourse, he firmly maintained that using natural reason, one can have evident knowledge of some theological truths such as that God exists and that he is one, good, simple, and eternal.[87] With regard to probable propositions, he maintained that the degree of probability could often be so high as to exclude all reasonable doubt or fear of error, a position that closely approaches the level of what would later be designated as moral certitude. While not allowing the use of probable propositions in the realm of theological discourse, he did assign them a prominent role in the realm of apologetics.

Without intending to contradict the above conclusions with regard to the charges of skepticism and fideism in d'Ailly's thought, it must be admitted that his views on theology and theological method tended to reduce one's confidence in the role of reason in theological speculation. His teaching on the nature of theology and theological method was certainly more circumscribed than had been the case with theologians of the High Middle Ages, especially Aquinas and his followers. This circumscription was especially seen in his desire to restrict the domain of theological truths employed in theological discourse primarily to principles and conclusions drawn from the Scriptures. Furthermore, truths that were earlier regarded as integral to the nature of theological discourse were reduced to the realm of apologetics and relegated to the realm of the probable.

Finally, it must be added that d'Ailly's emphasis on deductive theology as the principle form of theological method had the effect of reducing the other functions of theology, namely, the establishing of the preambles of the faith, the defense of the faith, and its explicative or declarative function, to more secondary roles within the theologi-

---

[86] On this point see Oberman, *The Harvest of Medieval Theology*, 51–52, Gordon Leff, *William of Ockham*, xiii, and Adams, *William of Ockham*, 1:588–601, 625–629. Even the earlier work of Frederick Copleston exhonorated late medieval nominalism from the charge of scepticism. On this point see his *A History of Philosophy*, 3:151–152.

[87] *Sent*, 1, q. 1, a. 2, X, 'Secunda conclusio quod naturaliter possibile est viatorem de multis veritatibus theologicis habere noticiam evidentem. Probatur, quia philosophi sequentes rationem naturalem devenerunt licet a posteriori ad noticiam evidentem istarum veritatum: Deus est, Deus est unus, bonus, simplex, eternus, etc.'

cal endeavor. The consequence of such an emphasis was to disturb the more or less harmonious balance among the different functions of theology that characterized much of the theology of the high Middle Ages. In this respect, d'Ailly was very much a representative product of late medieval nominalistic schools of theology.

CHAPTER SEVEN

CANON LAWYERS: LAW, CRITIQUE, AUTHORITY

After the theologians, the next major professional group within the Church upon which d'Ailly concentrated considerable attention was that of the canon lawyers. The professionalization of the lawyer class had occurred as a result of the political, social, economic and religious developments of the twelfth and thirteenth centuries. Lawyers were increasingly needed by the rising monarchies of the time. The bureaucratic centralization of the Church also increased the need for legally trained clerics. Both emperor and pope showed increasing reliance on lawyers as they became locked in heated controversies involving matters of church and state. Finally, the social and economic revival of the twelfth century created whole new categories of legal problems that required the aid of skillful lawyers. The professionalization of the lawyer class was also manifested in the creation of faculties of law and the development of legal courses of study in the rising universities of the time.[1]

As the legal profession began to prosper, it increasingly became the object of criticism from the different quarters of medieval society. Medieval literature, especially sermon and satirical literature, abounds with such criticism.[2] This critical attitude towards lawyers was also

---

[1] For a brief description of the increasing professionalization of the lawyer class see Johannes Fried, *Die Entstehung des Juristenstandes im 12 Jahrhundert*, Forschungen zur Neueren Privatsrechtsgeschichte, 21, (Cologne: Böhlau, 1974), Harold J. Berman, *Law and Revolution: The Formation of the Western Legal Tradition* (Cambridge, Mass.: Harvard University Press, 1983), 7–10, and James A. Brundage, 'Legal Aid for the Poor and the Professionalization of Law in the Middle Ages,', *Journal of Legal History*, 9 (1988) 169–179, and 'The Rise of the Professional Jurist in the Thirteenth Century,' *Syracuse Journal of International Law and Commerce*, 20 (1994), 185–190.

[2] Descriptions and analyses of the rising criticism of the lawyer class in the high Middle Ages can be found in John A. Yunck, 'Venal Tongue: Lawyers and the Medieval Satirists,' *American Bar Association Journal*, 46 (1960), 267–270, John W. Baldwin, 'Critics of the Legal Profession: Peter the Chanter and his Circle,' *Proceedings of the Second International Congress of Medieval Canon Law*, ed. Stephan Kuttner and J. Joseph Ryan (Vatican City: Vatican Press, 1965), 249–259, Jonathan Rose, 'Medieval Attitudes Towards the Legal Profession: The Past as Prologue,' *Stetson Law Review*, 28 (1998), 345–368. For Bernard of Clairvaux's attitude towards lawyers see James A. Brundage, 'St. Bernard

manifested in university circles, especially among members of the faculty of theology at Paris. Theologians such as Bonaventure and Aquinas strongly criticized canon lawyers for their involvement in issues and controversies which they regarded as primarily theological. As will later be seen, their critique also extended to the excessive confidence that canonists placed on their methodology and their failure to recognize the limitations of that methodology. Finally, the preference by the papal curia for graduates of the law faculties in the granting of ecclesiastical benefices greatly irked theologians and was often at the center of their critique.[3] While the modern reader must always be cautious in accepting fully these caricatures of the legal profession, there certainly must have been some basis for the complaints. There is a striking similarity to complaints against lawyers in most periods of history, a similarity grounded both in reality and in the human tendency to stereotype and caricature.

The criticism of the theological faculty against the lawyer class as embodied in the faculty of law did not develop to any degree in the early years of the University of Paris, for during that time the faculty of theology was much more preoccupied with problems arising from the arts faculty.[4] With the gradual rediscovery of Aristotle's writings in the twelfth and thirteenth centuries and their increasing use and eventual predominance in the arts curriculum, there was a tendency among some members of that faculty, especially the followers of Siger of Brabant (1240–1284), to overexalt the power of reason with the result that they arrived at positions contrary to Catholic belief, especially with regard to such issues as the eternity of the world, the freedom of the will, the immortality of the soul, and the nature of truth. The strong tensions between the two faculties finally resulted in the famous

---

and the Jurists,' in *The Second Crusade and the Cistercians*, ed. Michael Gervers (New York: St. Martin's Press, 1992), 25–33, and Amelia J. Uelmen, 'A View of the Legal Profession from a Mid-Twelfth-Century Monastery,' *Fordham Law Review*, 71 (2003), 1517–1541.

[3] On these latter points see Takaski Shogimen, 'The Relationship Between Theology and Canon Law: Another Context of Political Thought in the Early Fourteenth Century,' *JHI*, 60 (1999), 417–431, and G.H.M. Posthumous Meyjes, 'Exponents of Sovereignty: Canonists as Seen by Theologians in the Late Middle Ages,' in *The Church and Sovereignty, c. 590–1918: Essays in Honor of Michael Wilks*, ed. Diana Wood (Oxford: Basil Blackwell, 1991), 299–312.

[4] A very good survey of the history of law and theological faculties at medieval universities can be had in the chapters by Antonio García y García, 'The Faculties of Law,' and Monica Asztalos, 'The Faculty of Theology,' in De Ridder-Symoens, ed., *Universities in the Middle Ages*, 388–408, 409–441.

condemnations of the teaching of the Latin Averroists by the Bishop of Paris, Etienne Tempier, in 1270 and 1277.[5]

After these condemnations, the problems facing the theologians within the university came more from the faculty of law which, since the abolition of the study of civil law at Paris by Innocent III in 1209, was concerned only with the study of canon law. The reasons for this increased tension will be seen when d'Ailly's views on canon law and its practitioners are examined in his writings. His views are especially valuable not only because they manifest the traditional accusations made against lawyers, but also because they serve as a microcosm of the specific problems facing the late medieval Church and the manner in which those problems increased the tension between theologians and canonists.

1. *Attitude towards Canon Lawyers*

D'Ailly's critique of the lawyer class manifested itself early in his teaching career, more specifically with his introductory lecture (*principium*) to his second year of teaching as a *baccalarius biblicus* in 1375. In that lecture, he carefully distinguishes between good and bad lawyers. He indicates that he regards the lawyers of his day, whether civil or canon lawyers, as falling into two groups, namely, those who have betrayed the ideals of their profession and those who have remained loyal to them. It is against the former alone, especially the canon lawyers, that his criticisms are directed.[6]

One of the first charges leveled against those who have betrayed the ideals of their profession was that of financial greed. This charge enjoyed a long historical tradition throughout the Middle Ages and frequently appears in subsequent periods of history. Following in that tradition, d'Ailly asserts that canon lawyers too frequently have grown

---

[5] On the influence of Aristotle in the Middle Ages, see the excellent survey article by Leslie Brubaker in *DMA*, 1:456–469. For specific studies concerning the rise of Latin Aristotelianism see the works by Fernand van Steenberghen, *Aristotle in the West*, and *Thomas Aquinas and Radical Aristotelianism* (Washington: The Catholic University of America Press, 1980).

[6] *Quaenam doctrina haec nova*, Dupin, 1:614. 'Ipsorum igitur qui vel in civilis vel canonici juris schola aut student aut docent, bifariam divisionem reperio.'

rich on the tears of widows, the hunger of orphans, the afflictions of the simple, and the nudity of the poor.[7]

A second criticism made by d'Ailly against the canonists of his day was related to their continual quest for ecclesiastical preferment. As indicated earlier, the growth of the administrative and judicial dimensions of ecclesiastical government in the high Middle Ages and the intensification of that growth during the Avignon Papacy had created a great demand for clerics trained in canon law.[8] Given this situation, the law of supply and demand had its impact on the medieval university, for many students were increasingly attracted to the faculty of canon law, since training in that discipline more readily assured them of an ecclesiastical benefice. D'Ailly's reaction to this continued policy of preferment was especially seen in a disputed question (*quaestio disputata*) argued sometime between the University of Paris' letter to the French Crown on June 6, 1394 and the death of Clement VII in September of that same year. This letter urged the consideration of various possible solutions to the Schism, especially the resignation of both papal contenders. The opposition of the law faculty to such a policy certainly intensified d'Ailly's negative view of lawyers.[9] Like many theologians of his time, D'Ailly referred to the study of law in his disputed question as a lucrative science (*scientia lucrativa*), and bitterly complained that most ecclesiastical benefices and offices were given to graduates of the faculty of canon law. As a result of this tendency, he asserted, fewer

---

[7] *Quaenam doctrina haec nova*, Dupin 1:614. 'Nam quidem, et multi, proh dolor! linguam prostituunt, quaestum quaerunt, aequitatem solvunt, pacem confundunt, sopitarum litium cineres suscitant, pactiones violant, adulteria dissimulant, matrimonia diffamant, luxuriantur in lachrymis viduarum, in fame pupillorum, in afflictione simplicium, et in pauperum nuditate.'

[8] On the growth of the administrative and judicial aspects of the Church's government during the periods of the Avignon papacy and the Great Western Schism see Bernard Guillemain, *La cour pontificale d'Avignon, 1309–1376* (Paris: De Boccard, 1962), and Jean Favier, *Les finances pontificales à l'époque du Grand Schisme d'Occident, 1378–1409* (Paris: De Boccard, 1966).

[9] D'Ailly's disputed question in its written form was entitled: *Utrum indoctus in jure divino possit juste praeesse*. For the history and content of the University's letter see Robert N. Swanson, *Universities, Academics, and the Great Schism* (Cambridge: Cambridge University Press, 1979), 83–89. For an historical analysis of the relationship between the university and the crown as well as the tensions between the faculties of theology and canon law during this period at Paris, with special emphasis upon the role played by d'Ailly, see Douglas Taber, 'The Theologian and the Schism,' 105–155. The arguments in favor of the 1394 dating of d'Ailly's disputed question can be found in Palémon Glorieux, 'L'oeuvre litteraire de Pierre d'Ailly,' 65, and Taber's 'The Theologian and the Schism,' 169, n. 29 and 197, n. 96.

students were matriculating in the faculty of theology, especially from among the ranks of the secular clergy.[10]

A third charge made by D'Ailly against the canon lawyers of his day and manifested in his introductory lecture as a *baccalarius biblicus*, involved the area of what may be today called unprofessional conduct. D'Ailly, however, preferred to use more forceful language and accused them of prostituting their profession by making it serve goals contrary to its true nature. Getting down to concrete details, he asserted that by their deliberate manipulation of language, canon lawyers had fostered a spirit of lying and deceit. In legal controversies involving contracts, moreover, they deliberately sought to undermine the sanctity of a contract, especially that of matrimony. Such canonists, he felt, have not only destroyed individual rights but also made a mockery of equity, a cornerstone of the medieval canonical tradition.[11]

Closely associated with the above criticism was d'Ailly's fourth charge against canon lawyers, namely, that they had created a spirit of excessive litigation within the late medieval Church, thereby ignoring Paul's admonition to Christians in 2 Tim. 2:24 not to engage in legal quarrels among themselves. The overall result of such activities was that instead of harmonizing the Church's laws in order to produce order and peace, one of the major goals of canon law as envisioned by Gratian, they had created legal chaos and unrest. Such a charge was, indeed, tantamount to accusing the canonists of betraying the very spirit and ideals of their discipline.[12]

---

[10] *Utrum indoctus in jure divino*, Dupin, 1:654. 'Sedes apostolica plures hodie promovet legistas, et canonistas, quam theologos ad Ecclesiae praelaturas.' For d'Ailly's use of the term '*scientia lucrativa*' as well as his frequent complaint that too few members of the secular clergy were matriculating in the faculty of theology, see also his *De materia concilii generalis*, Oakley, 335, and his *De reformatione*, Miethke-Weinrich, 1:364. In the above references, d'Ailly refers to the attitude of the Roman Curia towards graduates trained in theology as one of contempt: 'Ipsa quoque theologia in statu secularium paucos habeat sectatores, propter abusum Romanae Curiae, quae theologos contempsit, et in omni ecclesiastico gradu lucrativarum scientiarum studiosos praeposuit ... .' The phrase *scientiae lucrativae* was used by Honorius III in his decretal *Super speculam domini*, November 16, 1219, wherein he renewed the call of the Fourth Lateran Council (1215) for the establishment of benefices in cathedral and collegiate churches for the promotion of theological studies. Cf. H. Denifle, *CUP*, 1:90–93.

[11] *Quaenam doctrina haec nova*, Dupin 1:614–615.

[12] *Quaenam doctrina haec nova*, Dupin 1:614–615. For an analysis of the spirit and methodology of medieval canon law, see Stephan Kuttner, *Harmony from Dissonance: An Interpretation of Medieval Canon Law* (Latrobe, Pa.: The Archabbey Press, 1960). This contribution to the Wimmer Lecture Series of St. Vincent's Archabbey has been reprinted with expanded notes in Kuttner's *The History of Ideas and Doctrines of Canon Law*

The fifth charge which D'Ailly levied against the canon lawyers of his day and the one which especially reflected the concerns of late medieval theologians at Paris, was that they had overemphasized the importance of their discipline and attributed to it a role in the life of the Church far greater than it deserved. Expressed in different terms, they had failed to recognize the proper rank and function of their discipline within the traditional medieval intellectual hierarchy. As a result of this neglect, he continued, they increasingly treated the canonical collections with a reverence equal to that due to the sacred scriptures. All these tendencies, he concluded, led to the denigration of scriptural studies and the theological profession.[13]

A final but most important criticism that D'Ailly hurled against the canon lawyers of his time was, in effect, really the result of all the above mentioned attitudes, namely that they had contributed to both the cause as well as the prolongation of the Great Schism. The canonical issues raised with regard to the election of 1378 had led to the outbreak of the Schism and the consequent multiplicity of popes. The legal claims of each contender in turn, had resulted in considerable legal confusion within the Church. As a result of this confusion, the Church had arrived at a legal impasse and was able to secure neither the resignation of the various papal contenders nor the convocation of a general council to resolve the controversy. Plan after plan proposed by the theologians for the resolution of the Schism was rejected as being contrary to existing canonical legislation. An example of such opposition has already been seen in the law faculty's negative reaction to the University's letter of June 6th, 1394 to the French Crown urging the consideration of broader means to secure the resolution of the Schism.

Even after the Council of Constance had been called in 1414, there were further legal controversies occasioned by the organization of the council, the flight of John XXIII from Constance, the deposition of the papal contenders, and the election of a new pope. D'Ailly especially singled out a concrete example of such opposition during the Council

---

in the Middle Ages (London: Ashgate Variorum, 1980). A more recent study of the same themes can be found in Richard Helmholz, *The Spirit of Classical Canon Law* (Athens, Ga.: University of Georgia Press, 1996).

[13] *Quaenam doctrina haec nova*, Dupin, 1:614. 'Sed reperio iterum in hac schola quosdam juris canonici professores qui etiam suas decretales epistolas, quasi scripturas accipiunt; et eas taliter venerantur, ut propter hoc eorum aliqui plerumque in divinarum prorumpant blasphemiam Scripturarum.'

of Constance, when Maurice of Prague was prevented by canonists favorable to the papal cause from presenting his views on the nature of papal authority. By seeking to extend the plentitude of power to the Council as a whole, his views naturally went contrary to those of the canonists who sought to restrict the exercise of that power to the papacy alone. D'Ailly strongly protested the use of such tactics by the canonists and defended the right of theologians to argue their case freely at the Council.[14]

As has been mentioned, d'Ailly's attitude towards canon law and its practitioners was not totally negative, for he also maintained that he had encountered many canon lawyers whom he believed had lived up to the highest ideals of their profession. Canonists who fell within this category, he asserted, direct their endeavors not towards the pursuit of wealth and office but towards the study of truth and the practice of equity. They demonstrate judicial righteousness when dealing with the guilty and canonical mercy when faced with the penitent. Lawyers of this caliber, he continued, defended the rights of orphans and widows, sought to alleviate the poverty of the needy, and worked to provide shelter for the homeless. Finally, such canonists were always solicitous to defend the freedom of the Church from all attacks.[15] To portray d'Ailly, therefore, simply as an outspoken enemy of the lawyer class is to do him a disservice and to present the scholarly world with an incomplete view of his attitude towards the legal profession of his day. Despite the positive dimensions which d'Ailly recognized in the canon lawyers of his day, it is still safe to say that, like many of his contemporaries, he concentrated more on the negative than on the positive characteristics of their profession.

2. *Law: Nature, Varieties, Relationships*

D'Ailly's critique of canon lawyers, however, caused him to analyze more deeply not only canon law but the very nature of law itself, its varieties, and their respective interrelationship. In order to better understand d'Ailly's views on the above issues, it will be of considerable

---

[14] *De potestate ecclesiastica*, Dupin 2:949–950. 'Protestatus sum quod doctoribus sacrae theologiae maxime in concilio … non debent inhiberi disputatio aut scholastica determinatio.'

[15] *Quaenam doctrina haec nova*, Dupin 1:615.

help to describe briefly the prevailing theological views on these issues for it is within this context that d'Ailly evolved and formulated his own views. In this context, therefore, it will help to briefly survey the thought of Aquinas and Ockham since they constituted the most influential thinkers at the time on these topics.

Before beginning any detailed analysis of these respective traditions, it is important to remember that in developing their views on law and its varieties medieval thinkers such as Aquinas, Ockham, and d'Ailly maintained that all forms of law enjoyed an essential unity and interrelationship. The same can be said for canonists speculating on the same topics. Given the fact that all theologians and canonists shared in the same body of revealed knowledge, which in varying ways provided the basis for their respective disciplines, and given the fact that both agreed upon the same finality for human existence and institutions, such a conclusion is readily understandable. The degree of that unity and interrelationship, however, varied according to one's metaphysical, epistemological, and even political thought. Such clearly was the case with Aquinas, Ockham, and d'Ailly whose theories on the nature of law, its varieties, and their interrelationship reflected the differences between realism and nominalism, rationalism and voluntarism, and emerged amid vastly different political contexts.

In the case of Aquinas, the nature, varieties, and interrelationships of law are explained in the context of his philosophical realism and more specifically in terms of the principles of analogy and participation.[16] He defined law generically as 'a certain rule or measure of action according to which one is led to act or to refrain from action.[17] That rule or measure was identified, moreover, with reason, or, more specifically, with practical reason (*ratio practica*) as directing the will in the selection or rejection of various courses of action in so far as they pertain or do not pertain to the common good. The rule of reason, finally, is promulgated by the person who has been charged with the care of the community.[18]

---

[16] Aquinas' magisterial treatment of law and its diverse varieties can be found in his *ST*, 1, 2, qq. 90–97.

[17] *ST*, 1, 2, q. 90, a. 1, c. 'Lex quaedam regula est et mensura actuum, secundum quam inducitur aliquis ad agendum vel ab agendo retrahitur.'

[18] *ST*, 1, 2, q. 90, a. 1, c. 'Regula autem et mensura humanorum actuum est ratio ... Unde relinquitur quod lex sit aliquid pertinens ad rationem.' For Aquinas' view of law as a matter of the *ratio practica*, see *ST*, 1, 2, q. 91, a. 3, c., and for his analysis of the differences between *ratio speculativa* and *ratio practica*, see *ST*, 1, q. 97, c. The finality of

The prime analogate for all law, according to Aquinas, is the eternal law, in the sense that it is God's reason which orders all created reality according to a divine plan.[19] Aquinas' next categories of law, namely divine and natural law, participate analogously in the divine reason which constitutes eternal law, the former as the revelation of that reason in the prescriptions of the Old and New Testaments, and the latter as a created reflection of that reason in the rational tendencies in human nature. These tendencies were implanted by God in human nature in order to direct it towards the realization of its proper good.[20] In this context, therefore, it is the function of human reason to establish norms of action which follow from human nature either as self-evident principles or as immediate conclusions therefrom.[21] The analogous and participative nature of law in Aquinas' thought is also manifested in his last category of law, namely human law. In the realm of human law, human reason seeks to further specify the dictates of divine and natural law in order to meet concrete individual human situations. These specifications occur either in the form of conclusions drawn from the principles of these laws or as further determinations of those laws with regard to matters on which they provide insufficient guidelines.[22]

The question of the nature, varieties, and interrelationships of law in Ockham's thought is much more complex and difficult than was the case for Aquinas. Unlike Aquinas, Ockham never wrote an independent treatise on the subject of law. His writings during his academic years at Oxford reveal little interest in the question of law. What

---

all law in terms of the common good is seen in *ST*, 1, 2, q. 90, a. 2, c., and the need for the promulgation of a law is evidenced in *ST*, 1, 2, q. 90, a. 4, c. Aquinas's classical definition of law as embodying all the above elements can also be found in ST, 1, 2, q. 90, a. 4, c. 'Definitio legis, quae nihil est aliud quam quaedam rationis ordinatio ad bonum commune, ab eo qui curam communitatis habet promulgata.'

[19] *ST*, 1, 2, q. 91, a. 1, c. 'Et ideo ipsa ratio gubernationis rerum in Deo sicut in principe universitatis existens, legis habet rationem. Et quia divina ratio nihil concipit ex tempore, sed habet aeternum conceptum ... inde est quod huiusmodi legem oportet dicere aeternam.'

[20] In his treatment of the various forms of law subsequent to the eternal law, Aquinas treats first of natural law in *ST*, 1, 2, q. 91, a. 2, c. After describing the manner in which the inclinations of human nature are a reflection of the eternal law, Aquinas concludes: 'Lex naturalis nihil aliud est quam participatio legis aeternae in rationali creatura.' See also *ST*, 1, 2, q. 71, a. 6, ad 4 and *ST*, 1, 2, q. 93, a. 3.

[21] For Aquinas' analysis of the manner in which specific precepts or prohibitions of the natural law are evolved see *ST*, 1, 2, q. 94, a. 2, c.

[22] *ST*, 1, 2, q. 95, a. 2, c.

later caused him to reflect more seriously on the topic was his involvement in the controversy between John XXII and the Franciscan Order over the question of poverty and in the controversy between Louis of Bavaria and John XXII over the issue of the imperial succession. Ockham's views on law, therefore, developed more within the context of the particular controversies in which he was involved rather than within an academic atmosphere.[23] As a result of these controversies, Ockham showed increased attention to the legal status of the arguments which the papacy invoked in defense of its position, especially its claim to temporal possessions and authority on the basis of the papal plentitude of power. He, therefore, began to carefully inquire as to what extent such papal claims were based in divine, natural, or human law, especially canon law.[24] As a result of the manner in which Ockham's views on law developed, his teaching does not have the systematic unity and order characteristic of Aquinas. Despite this factor, one can, through careful analysis, arrive at a fairly coherent understanding of his legal thought.[25]

Traditionally Ockham's teaching on law has been described almost exclusively in voluntaristic terms and sharply contrasted with the rationalistic approach of Aquinas. Just as the analogical and participatory dimensions of Aquinas teachings on divine, natural, and human law were based on reason, so these same aspects in Ockham's legal thought have the will as their basis.[26] To what extent one can speak of analogy and participation in a nominalistic context, however, remains a contro-

---

[23] On the controversy over the extent of the influence of Ockham's philosophical thought upon his political thought see Brian Tierney, 'Natural Law and Canon Law in Ockham's *Dialogus*,' in *Aspects of Late Medieval Government and Society: Essays Presented to J.R. Landner*, ed. J.G. Rowe (Toronto: University of Toronto Press, 1986), 3–8.

[24] *Dialogus*, 1, 6, c. 22, Goldast, 2:528:18–24, 45–56. The edition of the *Dialogus* used is that given in Melchior Goldast, *Monarchia Sancti Romani Imperii*, 3 vols. (Frankfurt, 1614, repr. Graz: Akademische Druck und Verlagsanstalt, 1960), and is cited according to volume, page, and line numbers.

[25] Gordon Leff, *William of Ockham: The Metamorphosis of Scholastic Discourse*, 614–615, and George de Lagarde, *La naissance de l'esprit laïque au déclin du moyen age*, Vol. 6: *Ockham: La morale et le droit* (Paris: Presses Universitaires, 1946), 93–101. For the study of Ockahm's views on law, the first edition of de Lagarde's work was preferred because of its more systematic treatment of the subject. In his second edition, de Lagarde dedicated two volumes to Ockham, namely, volumes four and five entitled respectively: *Guillaume d'Ockham: Defense de l'Empire* (Louvain: Editions Nauwelaerts, 1962), and *Guillaume d'Ockham: Critique des structures ecclésiales* (Louvain: Editions Nauwelaerts, 1963).

[26] For this approach see especially De Lagarde, *Ockham: La morale et le droit*, 111–124.

versial issue but one which has important consequences for a definitive judgement as to the unity and interrelationship of law in Ockham's thought.

Recent research, however, into Ockham's understanding and teaching on the nature of law has made clear that the traditional interpretation of Ockham's legal thought exclusively in voluntaristic terms is no longer sustainable. This research has shown that Ockham attributes a greater role to right reason (*recta ratio*) in his teaching on law than has been previously acknowledged.[27] While Ockham's teaching on God's absolute power (*potentia absoluta*) and ordained power (*potentia ordinata*) might be seen as diminishing the role of right reason in his thought, these notions, while prominent in his university writings, were much less referred to in his later political works.[28]

Although right reason is now generally acknowledged as playing a more important role in Ockham's legal thought than previously believed, the balance between the voluntaristic and rationalistic elements within each category of law varies accordingly, with the former more prominent in his teaching on divine law and the latter more characteristic of his views on natural law. Even though Ockham, like so many of his predecessors and contemporaries defined natural law in a variety of ways, the three definitions that Ockham presents in his *Dialogus* all emphasize the importance of reason.[29] Finally, human law remains for Ockham much more voluntaristic than it was for Aquinas.

---

[27] For a more positive view of the role of *recta ratio* and its varying meanings in Ockham's legal thought see the following articles: David W. Clark, 'Voluntarism and Rationalism in the Ethics of Ockham,' *FS*, 31 (1971), 72–87, and 'William of Ockham on Right Reason,' *Speculum*, 48 (1973), 13–36, Leff, *William of Ockham*, 480–487, L. Urban, 'William of Ockham's Theological Ethics,' *FS*, 33 (1973), 310–350, and K. McDonnell, 'Does William of Ockham Have a Theory of Natural Law,' *FS*, 34 (1974), 383–392.

[28] Arthur S. McGrade, *The Political Thought of William of Ockham* (Cambridge: Cambridge University Press, 1974), 198–199. For an historical survey of the use and understanding of the terms *potentia absoluta* and *potentia ordinata* in Ockham's thought, see Jürgen Miethke, *Ockhams Weg zur Sozialphilosophie*, 135–156, Marilyn McCord Adams, *William of Ockham*, 2:1186–1207, and Klaus Bannach, *Die Lehre von der doppelten Macht Gottes bei Wilhelm von Ockham* (Wiesbaden: Franz Steiner Verlag, 1975).

[29] For a recent analysis of the various ways in which Ockham described natural law, the role of reason in each definition, and the canonical influences on his legal thought see Brian Tierney, 'Natural Law and Canon Law in Ockham's *Dialogus*', 9–15, H.S. Offler, 'The Three Modes of Natural Law in Ockham: A Revision of the Text,' *FS*, 15 (1977), 207–218, and Francis Oakley, 'Medieval Theories of Natural Law: William of Ockham and the Significance of the Voluntarist Tradition,' *NLF*, 6 (1960), 47–76.

Before we begin our study of the varieties of law operative within d'Ailly's legal thought, we must realize that, like Ockham, d'Ailly did not write a specific treatise on law and its varieties. Again like Ockham, his views emerged more out of concrete circumstances related to his teaching obligations, his role as chancellor of the University of Paris, and his involvement in discussions and deliberations related to the Schism. Because of the circumstantial context of his views on law, d'Ailly does not begin with an abstract definition of the nature of law but more with its concrete and specific varieties. It seems best, therefore, to begin with his understanding of the latter and after an analysis of their specific characteristics to abstract, if possible, those traits common to all categories of law. Only in this way can we safely draw any conclusions as to d'Ailly's general understanding of law.[30] The general outline of his legal thought can be easily discerned in two of his early theological works. These works are his *Quaestiones super libros sententiarum*, written during the 1376–1377 academic year when he was a *baccalarius sententiarius* in the faculty of theology at the University of Paris, and his *Utrum Petri Ecclesia lege reguletur*, which was one of the questions debated in his *vesperies* on April 10, 1381.[31]

In his delineation of the specific varieties of law, d'Ailly makes clear that the highest category of law is that of uncreated law, which he also designates as first law or eternal law. In his description of this law, d'Ailly draws almost exclusively upon St. Augustine who in his *De libero arbitrio* defined eternal law as the divine reason which should always be obeyed. A fuller definition of Augustine's concept of eternal law, however, can be found in his *Contra Faustum*, where it is described as the divine mind or will commanding that the natural order be observed and forbidding that it be disturbed.[32] The use of Augustine's definition to describe eternal law may cause some confusion since it employs such diverse terms as *ratio*, *mens*, and *voluntas*. From d'Ailly's writings, however, it is clear that for him the eternal law is primarily associated with the divine will.[33]

---

[30] One of the best treatments of d'Ailly's thought on law and its various categories is that in Oakley, *The Political Thought of Pierre d'Ailly*, 163–197.

[31] The dating accepted for d'Ailly's *Vesperies* is that given by Glorieux, 'L'oeuvre litteraire de Pierre d'Ailly,' 65.

[32] *Utrum Petri ecclesia lege reguletur*, Dupin, 1:663, and *Questiones super libros sententiarum*, I, *Prin.*, M. The references to Augustine are from the *De libero arbitrio*, 1, and the *Contra Faustum*, 13.

[33] *Sent.*, II, Prin., L, '... quamvis dixerim quod voluntas divina sit prima lex ...'; *Sent.*, I, q. 14, M, 'Licet voluntas divina sit lex aeterna ...'

Since d'Ailly admits of no real distinction in God between intellect and will, one can legitimately ask why he prefers to identify the eternal law with the divine will rather than with the divine intellect.[34] He explains his preference by arguing that the concept of obligation is more appropriately predicted of the will than the intellect, for the activity of the will necessarily implies obligation while such is not the case for the activity of the intellect. It cannot be argued, he maintains, that whatever the intellect knows also involves obligation.[35]

After having described his understanding of the eternal or uncreated law, d'Ailly turns his attention to created law which he subdivides into the three traditional categories: divine, natural, and human.[36] For d'Ailly, the *lex divina* is the divinely inspired law whose prescriptions have been promulgated in the Scriptures. These prescriptions are to be found in both the Old and New Testaments and are identified respectively with the law of Moses and the law of Christ. It is the *lex Christi*, however, which holds the position of central importance in d'Ailly's teaching on divine law.

The tendency of d'Ailly to understand the Scriptures within the broader concept of law appears to be very characteristic of the medieval mindset. Although Walter Ullmann has maintained that because of their legal outlook and training medieval canonists viewed the study of the Scriptures as essentially a higher form of legal studies, the deeper reason for their outlook was probably similar to that of the theologians, namely the Judaic custom of viewing not only the first five books of the Bible (The Pentateuch) but also the whole of the Old Testament as God's law (Torah)[37] In its original context, 'Torah' had a less juridical meaning and designated teaching, instruction, or guidance. It

---

[34] *Sent.*, I, Prin., R, '... cum in deo sit idem esse, velle, et intelligere.'

[35] *Sent.*, II, Prin., L. '... quia quidquid voluntas divina vult obligari obligatur, sed non quicquid intellectus intelligit.'

[36] *Sent.*, I, Prin., M, 'Sed capiendo istum terminum lex pro lege creata adhuc quandoque sumitur generaliter pro qualibet tali naturali lege humana vel divina, scripta vel non scripta.'

[37] For Walter Ullmann's views see his *Medieval Papalism* (London:Methuen, 1949), 27. For the various ways in which 'torah' was understood in the Judaic tradition see the *Encyclopedia Judaica*, 15, s.v. 'torah,' by Warren Harvey, 1235–1246. See also *The Oxford Dictionary of the Jewish Religion*, s.v. 'torah,' by Baruch J. Schwartz. The later and more juridical sense of the term reflects the Hellenistic influence in the latter part of the Second Temple Period.

is this earlier and less juridical sense of the term which New Testament authors, early Christian writers, and medieval theologians such as d'Ailly used to designate the Scriptures as a form of law and the New Testament specifically as the *lex Christi*.[38]

Natural law is the next category of law which d'Ailly signals out in his hierarchy of created laws. In his description of this form of law, he has recourse to Cicero who defined natural law as reason (*ratio*) implanted in man by nature which commands what is to be done and prohibits the contrary.[39] Although d'Ailly adopts Cicero's use of the term reason to describe natural law, the employment of this term must not be seen as a modification of his essentially voluntaristic approach towards law. The role of reason in d'Ailly's concept of law always remains circumscribed by the predominantly voluntaristic parameter of his legal thought. In this respect, therefore, Oakley's analysis is most correct when he states that d'Ailly would certainly agree with Ockham's statement that right reason dictates what is to be willed but only because the divine will wishes it so.[40]

D'Ailly asserts that the dictates of natural law fall into two categories. The first comprises those principles which flow immediately from human nature. These principles can be further described as those to which all rational persons would assent regardless of their educational background, such as that justice should be rendered to all and that no one should injure another. Such principles are to be regarded as the first principles of morality. The second category comprises those principles that are arrived at with greater intellectual difficulty and are consequently comprehended primarily by the learned. D'Ailly asserts that Paul spoke of this category when in his description of the Gentile philosophers he said that although they do not have the law, they 'do by nature what the law requires.' These principles are called mediate

---

[38] For the use of this term in the New Testament see Gal. 6:2, Rom. 8:2, 1 Cor. 9:21, and Jas. 2:8–9. As seen in James, New Testament writers also understood the term in the richer context of love. This charity centered approach to law manifested itself in medieval theologians such as Jean Gerson. On this point see Pascoe, *Jean Gerson*, 76–79. As seen in Paul, this emphasis on the Scriptures as the law of Christ often went hand-in-hand with a highly pejorative view of Old Testament law.

[39] *Sent.*, I, Prin., M. 'Lex est ratio insita natura, que iubet quae sunt facienda, prohibetque contraria.' See also *Utrum Petri Ecclesia lege reguletur*, Dupin, 1:663. Cicero's definition can be found in his *De legibus*, 1, 6:7–10. Cf. Konrat Ziegler, ed., *M. Tullius Cicero De Legibus*, (Heidelberg: F.H. Kerle, 1950), 29.

[40] Oakley, *The Political Thought of Pierre d'Ailly*, 189.

since they are arrived at only through the further application of reason to the first principles of the natural law.[41]

When d'Ailly comes to the category of human or positive law, under which he includes both canon and civil law, his theological and philosophical reflections become more sparse. While the reasons for this sparsity will be discussed later in this chapter, it can be concluded with Oakley that the essence of human or positive law for d'Ailly is the expressed will of a properly constituted lawmaking authority. This authority can be either civil or ecclesiastical, although in the majority of cases when d'Ailly speaks of positive law he does so primarily in terms of ecclesiastical authority and with reference to canon law.[42] In support of Oakley's judgement, there is an interesting passage in his d'Ailly's *Quaestiones super libros sententiarum* where, in describing human law, he has recourse to Gratian's *Decretum* where the noted jurist states that such law is a written decree enacted by the Senate and approved by the people. Although Gratian's definition draws heavily upon Roman sources, it clearly substantiates Oakley's position that d'Ailly regards human law primarily as the expressed will of a properly constituted lawmaking authority[43]

After this brief sketch of the various forms of law as understood by d'Ailly, we can now abstract from these forms the elements common to all and thereby arrive at a general notion of d'Ailly's understanding of law. Following this procedure, it is clear that for d'Ailly the essence of all law is rooted in obligation as imposed by the will of a duly constituted authority, whether that authority be divine or human. This obligation, moreover, manifests itself analogously in divine, natural, and human law. D'Ailly, furthermore, defines obligation as being held to act or to refrain from acting in a certain manner. He then describes the phrase 'to be held' as meaning to receive a precept or prohibition from one who is in a position of superior authority. The action commanded or prohibited, however, must be within the power of the person so commanded.[44] Central to d'Ailly's concept of human law, therefore, is the

---

[41] *Sent.*, I, Prin., L. The reference to St. Paul is Rom. 2:13–15.
[42] Oakley, *The Political Thought of Pierre d'Ailly*, 175–176, 191–192.
[43] *Sent.*, I, Prin., M. 'Quandoque etiam sumitur pro lege humana scripta et sic diffinit Gratianus ... Lex est constitutio populi qua maiores natu simul cum plebibus aliquid sanxerunt.' This passage is repeated almost verbatim in *Utrum Petri Ecclesia lege reguletur*, Dupin, 1:663. Gratian's definition, drawn from the *Etymologies* of Isidore of Seville, can be found in Dist. 2, c. 1, Friedberg, 1:3.
[44] *Sent.*, I, Prin., F, 'Dico igitur quod obligari est teneri ad aliqualiter esse vel non

notion of voluntarism. This voluntaristic dimension characterized every category of law in his legal hierarchy and places him clearly within the nominalistic and more precisely Ockhamistic legal tradition. As such his teaching is clearly distinguishable from that of the Thomistic school, which saw law more as a matter of reason wherein is perceived the proper order to be followed. Obligation in the Thomistic tradition, therefore, arises more from the dictates of reason than from the direct will of the legislator.

3. *Canon Law: Characteristics and Relationships*

Having seen d'Ailly's thought on the nature of law, its varieties, and their interrelationships, we can now turn our attention more directly to his views on canon law, its principle characteristics, its distinction from other forms of law, and its relationships to those forms. As was the case with the study of d'Ailly's views on law, it will be helpful to understand the general historical context in which his views developed. It is important to note that even during the classical period of the history of medieval canon law, namely, from 1140 to 1378, canon law was still often closely associated with, and, at times, identified with divine law.[45] As indicated earlier, the fact that all medieval legal thinkers shared in the same body of revealed knowledge generally conceived of within the context of law facilitated this identification. Central in the development of this way of looking at canon law was the influence of Gratian, the father of the new science of canon law, whose teaching on this issue, with some modifications, influenced subsequent canonical thought.[46] Following in this tradition, Huguccio († 1210) equated canon

---

esse ... Sed teneri est habere a suo superiori prohibitionem vel praeceptum de aliquo existente in inferioris libera potestate.' See also *Sent.*, II, Prin., O.

[45] For an excellent survey of the history of canon law for this period see Gabriel Le Bras et al., *L'Age classique, 1140–1378: Sources et théorie du droit*, Histoire du droit et des institutions de l'Eglise en Occident, 7 (Paris: Sirey, 1965). The earlier medieval period is especially well presented in Paul Fournier and Gabriel Le Bras, *Histoire des collections canoniques en occident depuis les fausses décrétales jusqu'au Décret de Gratien*. 2 vols. (Paris: Sirey, 1931–1932, rpr. Aalen: Scientia Verlag, 1972). Walter Ullmann's, *Medieval Papalism*, 40–46 contains a rich array of canonical sources illustrating the diverse vocabulary used in the Middle Ages to designate canon law.

[46] For a study of Gratian as an historical personality see Stephan Kuttner, 'The Father of the Science of Canon Law,' *The Jurist*, 1 (1941), 2–19, and the more recent article of John Noonan, 'Gratian Slept Here: The Changing Identity of the Father of

law with divine law. The anonymous glossator of Stephen of Tournai's († 1203) *Summa* did not hesitate to describe natural, evangelical, and canon law as subdivisions of the divine law. Hostiensis († 1271) also emphasized that canon law should not be excluded from the domain of the divine law.[47]

Despite the somewhat fluid and imprecise manner in which canon law was designated during the classical period of its history, canon law was never simply equated with divine law in the strict sense of the term nor its study identified with theology. While the terms 'divine' and 'sacred' were often used to describe canon law and its study, these terms were always applied to it in a qualified sense. Canon lawyers, like their civilian counterparts, saw all forms of law as in some way related to divine law in the sense that their origins and ultimate validation were to be found in that law. Canon law was also called divine law in the sense that it was established in order that mankind might more effectively be directed to God. The study of canon law, finally, was regarded as a sacred science more in the sense that it governed the Church or because its clerical administrators exercised divinely established offices within the Church.[48]

The classical period of canonical scholarship, however, gave strong evidence of a gradual clarification in its terminology and understanding of the various laws that governed the Church. Natural law became more clearly distinguished from divine law, and canon law from both divine and natural law, and increasingly seen as a form of human law.[49] In order to emphasize the instrumentality of the human legislator in

---

the Systematic Study of Canon Law,' *Traditio*, 35 (1979), 145–172. For a detailed study of Gratian's theory of law which served as the basis for all subsequent canonical speculation on the subject see Luigi de Luca, 'La nozione della legge nel Decreto di Graziano: Legalità o assolutismo?' *SGrat*, 11 (1967), 403–430. See also Franz Arnold, 'Die Rechtslehre des Magisters Gratianus,' *SGrat*, 1 (1953), 451–482, and Jean Gaudemet, 'La doctrine des sources du droit dans le Décret de Gratien,' *RDC*, 1 (1951), 5–31.

[47] The views of Huguccio and the anonymous glossator are given in Ullmann, *Medieval Papalism*, 40–46. On the nature of canon law, Huguccio cryptically states: 'Dicitur jus divinum jus canonicum sive ecclesiasticum.' The annonymous glossator, however, is more expansive: 'Jus divinum est a Deo insitum menti, ut lex naturalis; a Deo traditum, lex Mosaica; a Deo editum, evangelium; pro Deo conditum, canones.' A similar viewpoint of Hostiensis is cited in Brian Tierney's '"Sola Scriptura" and the Canonists,' *SGrat*, 11 (1967), 351, n. 6. '... ars artium est divina lex a qua non est excludenda canonica nec humana. This text is from Hostinensis' *Lectura ad X*, 1.14.4.

[48] Brian Tierney, 'Sola Scriptura,' 351.

[49] For the detailed history of these developments see Le Bras, *L'Age classique*, 367–396. Ullmann, *Medieval Papalism*, 42–43, n. 4 cites texts from canonists before Aquinas who

the creation of human law, that law, beginning with Abelard in the twelfth century and continuing with many of the canonists of that same century, was increasingly designated as positive law (*jus positivum*).[50]

Paralleling these developments in the field of canon law were those in the realm of theology which often manifested the same ideological and terminological imprecision with regard to the different forms of law, especially canon law. Heavily influenced by the newly rediscovered works of Aristotle, Aquinas was able to distinguish more precisely the natural and supernatural orders not only in terms of metaphysics, psychology, and ethics but also with regard to legal theory. As a result of Aquinas' teaching, a sharper distinction emerged in theological circles between divine, natural, and human law.[51] Reflecting the earlier terminological changes with regard to human law, Aquinas uses the terms *jus humanum* and *jus positivum* interchangeably.[52] In his treatment of human or positive law, Aquinas tends to deal primarily with the general characteristics and properties of that law. When he does specify the various forms of human law, he speaks only of the *jus gentium* and the *jus civile*; there is no explicit mention of *jus canonicum*.[53] Although he does not employ the latter term, he does describe canon law by such terms as *leges, praecepta, statuta,* and *ordinationes Ecclesiae,* and clearly regards these forms of law as falling within the category of human or positive law.[54]

---

give some evidence of a clearer awareness of the differences between divine, natural, and human law.

[50] Etymologically the word 'positive' comes from the verb '*ponere*,' which had, among its various meanings, that of ordaining or establishing a rule of law. For an historical analysis of the origins of the term *jus positivum*, see Stephan Kuttner, 'Sur les origines du terme "Droit Positif,"' *RHDF*, 15 (1936), 728–740, reprinted with retractions in his *The History of Ideas and Doctrines of Canon Law*, and Damien Van den Eynde, 'The Terms "*Jus Positivum*" and "*Signum Positivum*" in Twelfth-Century Scholasticism,' *FS*, 9 (1949), 41–49, who shows that earlier than Abelard, Hugh of St. Victor (†1142) had employed the term *justitia positiva* in a sense very close to that of Abelard. Sten Gagnér in his *Studien zur Ideengeschichte des Gesetzgebung*, Studia Iuridica Upsaliensia, 1 (Stockholm: Almquist and Wiksell, 1960), 210–248 presents a detailed survey of the use of the term *jus positivum* in the twelfth and thirteenth centuries.

[51] Le Bras, *L'Age classique*, 382–384.

[52] See *ST*, 1, 2, q. 95, a. 2, c.; a. 3, incip.; and a. 4, c. Occasionally Aquinas will also use the phrase *lex humanitus posita*, a phraseology which illustrates clearly the etymological origins of the term *lex positiva*. For examples of such use see *ST*, 1, 2, q. 95, a. 2, c; q. 96, a. 4, c.

[53] *ST*, 1, 2, q. 95, a. 4, c.

[54] For Aquinas' use of these terms to designate canon law see *ST*, 2, 2, q. 186, a. 9, ad 2; 3, q. 72, a. 12, c; *Supp.* q. 23, a. 3, ad 2, q. 54, a. 4, ad 1–2.

The increasing delineation of canon law as a form of human law became even more evident in the thought of Ockham, especially in his writings related to the controversies with John XXII over the issue of Franciscan poverty and the imperial succession. As a result of these controversies, Ockham distinguished canon law more carefully from divine and natural law, denied it a privileged place in the hierarchy of laws, and placed it on the same human level as the civil law. Papal decrees, therefore, which were not specifically grounded in divine or natural law, enjoyed nothing more than the authority of human and positive law. As a result of Ockham's approach to and interpretation of canon law, that law lost most of its sacrality.[55]

As a form of human law, canon law, according to Ockham, was very much a creation of the human will. The prominence of the human will in the formulation of human law is seen in his emphasis upon the fact that such law arises from the agreement of human wills (*ex pactione*). This dimension of canon law is especially brought out in the early pages of his *Dialogus* where Ockham emphasizes that it is ultimately the will of the pope that is central in the making of canon law, so central, indeed, that he refers to the pope as *conditor canonum*.[56] It should be remembered that this title had been used by John XXII himself in his bull *Ad conditorem canonum* of 1322 in which he discontinued the policy of Nicholas III with regard to the Church's holding legal title to Franciscan property and rejected the Franciscan argument that the order enjoyed no right in positive law to the use of temporal goods.[57]

Although he designates the pope as *conditor canonum*, Ockham is not unaware of the diverse legal sources which are included in canon law, for in subsequent chapters he accepts the canonists' own description

---

[55] For a survey of Ockham's views on human law, especially canon law, see De Lagarde, *Ockham: Le morale et le droit*, 193–202, Leff, *William of Ockham*, 616–633, and Gabriel LeBras, *Le droit post-classique, 1378–1500*, Histoire du droit et des institutions de l'Eglise en Occident, 13 (Paris: Editions Cujas, 1971), 142.

[56] *Dialogus*, 1, 1, 4, Goldast, 2:402:54–64–403:1–17. This legal phrase was generally used to refer to the legislator as founder and interpreter of the law. On this point see Luigi De Luca, 'La nozione della legge nel Decreto di Graziano,' 425–426. For the various senses in which the word *conditor* can be used see *Mittellateinisches Wörterbuch*, 2:1260. While the sense of *legislator* appears as the meaning in which it is used in papal letters, the other meanings of *creator, fundator*, and *constitutor*, cannot be ruled out since papal approval and promulgation are also closely associated with canon law.

[57] *Bullarium Franciscanum sive Romanorum Pontificum constitutiones, epistolae, diplomata tribus ordinibus Minorum concessa*, 7 vols. Vols. 1–4, ed. Giovanni Sbaralea (Rome, 1759–1768), Vols. 4–7, ed. Conrad Eubel, (Rome, 1898–1904), 5:233–246.

of their science as a composite of biblical teachings, moral precepts of the natural law, the teaching of the saints and theologians, imperial legislation, and the decrees of the popes and general councils.[58] Despite his awareness of the biblical and theological elements in canon law, Ockham maintains that canon law deals with few theological truths as such and remains therefore very much a matter of human law.[59] The human dimension of canon law is also emphasized by Ockham in an implied contrast of the work of canonists with that of the evangelists who wrote the Gospels completely under the influence of divine not human inspiration.[60]

The increasing tendency among canonists and theologians to identify canon law with human and positive law, and to distinguish it more sharply from divine and natural law is clearly reflected in the writings of d'Ailly, especially in the vocabulary he uses to describe canon law. As seen earlier in this chapter, although d'Ailly uses the terms *jus canonicum*, *lex canonica*, *scientia canonica*, and *doctrina canonica*, he also frequently refers to canon law in the broader context of human law and employs such terms as *jus humanum*, *jus positivum*, *lex humana*, and *humanae constitutiones*.[61] On a limited number of occasions, he also describes canon law as *jus commune* or *jus commune positivum*.[62] D'Ailly's writings are devoid of references to canon law in terms of *lex divina* or *lex naturalis*.

As Oakley has pointed out, the major line of demarcation in d'Ailly's legal thought is drawn between divine and natural law, on the one hand, and human or positive law, on the other.[63] This division was

---

[58] *Dialogus*, 1, 1, 8, Goldast, 2:405:2–10.
[59] *Dialogus*, 1, 1, 2, Goldast, 2:400:36–39.
[60] *Dialogus*, 1, 1, 2, Goldast, 2:400:60–63–401:1–4. 'quia scriptores scripturae divinae nihil penitus conscripserunt ex humano ingenio sed solum ex divina inspiratione …' In referring to scriptural prophecy in this same passage, Ockham also asserts 'non enim voluntate humana allata est aliquando prophetia …'
[61] This terminology can easily be verified by referring to previously cited texts in this chapter where d'Ailly refers to law and lawyers.
[62] For references to canon law as *jus commune*, see his *De materia concilii generalis*, Oakley, 266, *De ecclesiastica potestate*, Dupin 2:941, *De reformatione*, Miethke-Weinrich, 1:354, and *Pro emendatione Ecclesiae*, Dupin 2:921. The clearest association of *jus commune* with canon law can be found in his *Propositiones utiles*, in Edmund Martène and Ursin Durand, eds., *Veterum scriptorum et monumentorum historicorum, dogmaticorum, moralium, amplissima collectio*, 9 vols (Paris: Montalant, 1724–1733), 7:912: 'Patet ex juribus communibus, quae habentur in decretis et decretalibus.' On one occasion d'Ailly did use *jus commune* in the sense of comprising divine, natural, and positive law. For this reference see Oakley, *The Political Thought of Pierre d'Ailly*, 173–176.
[63] Oakley, *The Political Thought of Pierre d'Ailly*, 176.

very much influenced by the ecclesiological problems raised by the Schism and its extended duration. Like many theologians of his day, especially those at Paris, d'Ailly felt that canon law and its practitioners posed one of the major obstacles to a resolution of these problems. The canon law faculty at Paris, especially during the early years of the Schism, frequently sided with the French crown in an effort to prohibit university discussion on the means for resolving the Schism. In subsequent years and especially during the period of the Council of Constance (1414–1418) many of the staunchest supporters of the papal cause were canonists. Given this situation it is very understandable that in opposing such canonists, d'Ailly would depend heavily upon divine and natural law. Only by relying on the higher nature of these laws could d'Ailly effectively counter the claims of the canonists. It is also very understandable that in such circumstances d'Ailly would also emphasize the human dimensions of canon law, thereby weakening the force and authority of their arguments.

D'Ailly's criticism of and opposition to canon lawyers, however, should not blind us to the fact that he was also very knowledgeable and competent in the use of canon law, as is evidenced by the great number of canonical sources used in his writings, especially those writings related to the Great Schism.[64] Like Ockham and John of Paris, d'Ailly's conciliar ecclesiology was also very much indebted to corporational theory as found in the canonical tradition.[65]

Despite his strong emphasis on the human dimensions of canon law, d'Ailly does not deny that canon law has a relationship to eternal, divine, and natural law. This relationship is clearly seen in his affirmation that all created law must be consonant with eternal law. He

---

[64] On the question of d'Ailly's knowledge and command of canon law, see Oakley, *The Political Thought of Pierre d'Ailly*, 209–211.

[65] For the classical study of the canonical contribution to medieval corporational theory see Brian Tierney, *Foundations of the Conciliar Theory: The Contribution of the Medieval Canonists from Gratian to the Great Schism*. Tierney regards John of Paris as much more influenced by the medieval canonical tradition on corporational theory than previously believed. Cf. 157–178. On Ockham's debt to corporational theory see also Tierney, *Ockham, the Conciliar Theory, and the Canonists* (Philadelphia: Fortress Press, 1971). In addition to corporational theory, the influence of Aristotle is much more extensive than realized. While Oakley, *The Political Thought of Pierre d'Ailly*, 199, has downplayed the influence of Aristotle on d'Ailly's ecclesiology, I have attempted to show that that influence was more extensive than previously believed. On this point, see Pascoe, 'Theological Dimensions of Pierre d'Ailly's Teaching on the Papal Plenitude of Power,' 357–366.

establishes this consonance by an argument from analogy, more specifically an analogy between efficient causality and legal causality. In summary form his argument affirms that just as it is necessary to seek a first cause, namely God, to explain created reality, so too is it necessary to search for a first cause as the root of all legal obligation, namely, the divine will as reflected in eternal law. Just as it is impossible to maintain that any created reality can be an efficient cause without a relationship to the first efficient cause, so it is impossible to conceive of any created law as being law unless it is somehow related to the first law.[66] Likewise, if a created cause cannot act contrary to the first cause, so too is it impossible for any created law to be contrary to the first law.[67] In like manner, just as no creature has the power to create itself, so too no created law has the power to obligate unless it is somehow rooted in the obligation resulting from eternal law.[68]

While the analogy upon which d'Ailly draws is that between eternal law and created law in general, a more specific analogy can be constructed between divine and natural law on the one hand, and human law on the other since divine and natural law are in essence created manifestations of eternal law. D'Ailly's presupposition of such an analogy and resultant legal consonance is seen in his affirmation that no edict of a prince, precept of a prelate, or statute or decree of civil or ecclesiastical government is to be regarded as just and obligatory unless it is consonant with divine law. Since in the specific types of legislation mentioned d'Ailly included forms of both of civil and ecclesiastical legislation, there can be no doubt that he sees a legal consonance between canon law and divine and human law.[69]

The consonance that d'Ailly regards as necessarily existing between canon law and divine and natural laws leads him to affirm two basic

---

[66] *Sent.*, 1, Prin., D. 'Igitur sicut est devenire ad unam primam causam, sic est devenire ad unam legem obligantem, quia consimilis est ratio in uno et in alio.' The argument as to the need to return to one ultimate efficient cause is clearly a reference to Aristotle's argument for a prime mover. On this point see his *Metaphysics*, 2:2:994a, 1–5 and Aquinas, *ST.*, q. 2, a. 1, c.

[67] *Sent.*, 1, Prin., D, 'Igitur sicut impossible est quod aliqua causa sit primae causae contraria, sic impossible est quod aliqua lex vel regula sit primae legi dissona.'

[68] *Sent.*, 1, Prin., D. 'Nulla res creata habet ex se potestatem creandi, sic nulla lex creata habet ex se potestatem obligandi.'

[69] *Sent.*, 1, Prin., E. 'Ex quo sequitur quod nullum principis edictum, prelati preceptum, politiciae statutum aut ecclesiae decretum est iustum vel iuste obligatorium, nisi sit divini legi consonum.' As his authorities on this point, d'Ailly cites Augustine's *De vera religione*, 22, and *De libero arbitrio*, 1, and John of Salisbury's *Policraticus*, 4, 6.

legal principles. The first is that if a human law is to be regarded as just, its legislation must also be just in terms of divine and natural law.[70] Secondly, what is just in the context of divine and natural law must also be just in the realm of human law and can in no way be declared unjust by that law.[71] The principle of consonance which d'Ailly sees as operative in the realm of divine, natural, and canon law had become by his time a legal commonplace.[72]

A practical application of d'Ailly's position that human law can in no way declare unjust what is just in the context of divine and natural law is seen in that aspect of his conciliar thought related to the convocation of a general council. On this point, d'Ailly concedes that as a result of the growth of the primitive Church, the right to convoke a general council gradually became restricted to the papacy. This right, he affirms is clearly established in both decretal and decretalist legislation. Divine and natural law, however, provide the universal Church with a similar authority which permits the convocation of a council without papal approval under certain circumstances such as a schism, heresy, insanity, or incapacity to carry out one's duties. In such cases, canonical legislation supportive of papal authority regarding the convocation of a council cannot be invoked against the prerogatives of the universal Church as established in divine and natural law. What is just, therefore, according to these laws cannot be nullified by canon law.[73]

4. *Relationship of Canon Law to Theology*

In addition to the question of the relationship of canon law to divine and natural law, d'Ailly was also preoccupied with the issue of the relationship between canon law and theology.[74] His most extensive treatment of this subject can be found in his disputed question, *Utrum*

---

[70] *Sent.*, 1, Prin., E. 'Quidquid est iustum lege humana est iustum lege divina.'

[71] *Sent.*, 1, Prin., E. 'Quidquid divino iure est iustum, nullo jure est inustum.'

[72] On this point see Le Bras, *L'Age classique*, 369, 381, 386 where he discusses the views of Gratian and Hostiensis on this issue.

[73] *Propositiones utiles*, 7–9, Martène-Durand, 7:910. Similar arguments can be found in his *De potestate ecclesiastica*. For an analysis of the latter work in this regard see Pascoe, 'Theological Dimensions of Pierre d'Ailly's Teaching,' 357–366.

[74] For a general but professional treatment of this topic see the recent work by G.R. Evans, *Law and Theology in the Middle Ages*. (London: Routledge, 2002).

indoctus in jure divino. As indicated earlier, this work was composed in 1394 when the canon law faculty continued its refusal to join with the theology faculty in petitioning the French king to lift the ban against university deliberations on the various ways in which the Schism might be resolved. Composed thirteen years after his last major treatment on canon law, his doctoral *vesperies*, this work demonstrates D'Ailly's continued interest in issues related to canon law.

D'Ailly's disputed question contains three articles which are essentially concerned with the different qualities needed by a prelate in the exercise of his office. The first article raises the question of whether or not a prelate must be in a state of grace. The second asks whether a prelate must be learned in theology. The third poses the question of whether a prelate must be free of scandal.[75] In asking whether the qualifications stipulated in all three articles should be manifest in a prelate for the exercise of his office, d'Ailly is not simply asking whether they should be present as desired qualifications (*desiderata*), but, rather, whether they should be there as necessary ones (*necessaria*), that is, if the prelate, to use his own words, is to properly exercise his office (*juste praeesse*).

While the term *praeesse* can generally be understood in terms of the exercise of an office, the word *juste* requires further clarification. D'Ailly recognizes this need by stating that there are two senses in which the term '*juste*' can be employed. In its first sense, it could mean that such qualities are necessary in the prelate for the valid exercise of his office, such that, if they were absent, a prelate would by that very fact lose the legitimate or valid title to his office. D'Ailly, however, makes clear that this is not the sense in which he is using the term. By making this affirmation, D'Ailly disassociates himself from a long standing heretical tradition that originated with Donatism in the fourth century and repeatedly manifested itself in the Middle Ages, primarily with the Waldensians in the eleventh century and again in d'Ailly's own era with Richard FitzRalph, John Wyclif, John Hus, and their followers. The second sense of the term *juste*, and the sense employed by D'Ailly, is that if a prelate exercised his office without the above mentioned

---

[75] *Utrum indoctus in jure divino*, Dupin 1:647. 'Ideo juxta harum trium, et circa materiam tactam supra in tribus articulis ante oppositum, quasi tres principales articulos pertractabo. Primus erit, utrum praelatus injustus possit juste praeesse. Secundus erit, utrum praelatus indoctus possit juste praeesse. Tertius erit, utrum praelatus scandalosus possit juste praeesse.' The text used for this work is that found in Dupin, 1:646–662.

qualities, he would be guilty of sin, a condition that, deplorable as it may be, does not affect the validity of his tenure in office nor the legitimate exercise of that office.[76]

While this latter sense of the term '*juste praesse*' pertains to all three articles in d'Ailly's q*uodlibet*, it is only its use in the second article that is of present concern. In its fullest formulation, this article asks whether a prelate who is not learned in the teachings of the scriptures (*doctrina sacrae scripturae*) can justly exercise his office. Given the close association between theology and the scriptures in d'Ailly's thought, the question can validly be restated in terms of whether a prelate who is untrained in theology can so exercise his office. Rephrased further the question asks whether a prelate who is not well educated in theology can exercise his office without incurring sin. Regardless of the manner in which the question is formulated, d'Ailly's response is always in the negative.[77]

As was customary in the organization of medieval disputations, d'Ailly in his treatment of the second article first carefully enumerates and describes the arguments against his position. These arguments asserted firstly that canon law, unlike theology, relates to both the spiritual and temporal dimensions of the Church's life. Secondly, that canon law enjoys a greater dignity than theology because of its composite nature. Thirdly, that canon law is of greater utility than theology in life of the Church. The fourth and final argument was based on the greater antiquity of canon law.[78] While each of these arguments will be dealt with in greater detail later in this chapter, taken as a whole they essentially affirmed the priority of canon law in the intellectual formation of an ecclesiastical prelate, and denied any negative moral consequences resulting from such a formation in the case of prelates.

---

[76] *Utrum indoctus in jure divino*, Dupin 1:649. 'Cum quaeritur utrum injustus potest juste praeesse: hoc dupliciter potest intelligi: Uno modo ... determinet jus seu authoritatem praesidendi; sic quod juste habeat praesidentiam, idest justo titulo, et non furtive, seu violenter. Alio modo ... determinet actum seu usum officiandi, sic quod juste exerceat officium praesidendi, ita quod careat culpa, officium praesidentiae exercendo.' D'Ailly's adoption of the second meaning of the term is clearly indicated by his statement that 'quod secundo modo supradicto, injustus non potest juste praeesse ... idest sine carentia culpae, praesidendi actum seu officium exercere.'

[77] *Utrum indoctus in jure divino*, Dupin, 1:653. 'Quantum ad secundum articulum, in quo quaeritur utrum prelatus indoctus possit juste praeesse. Dicendum est quod prelatus indoctus, specialiter in doctrina sacrae scripturae et in divino jure, non potest juste praeesse.'

[78] *Utrum indoctus in jure divino*, Dupin 1:654–655.

This line of argumentation, d'Ailly argued, reflected the belief of many of his contemporaries in the faculty of canon law at the University of Paris. While D'Ailly does not indicate any particular names or groups, he cites such teaching as a common error (*communis error*) in that faculty.[79] He does, however, make clear that in the elaboration of their arguments, his opponents drew heavily upon the teaching of the renowned thirteenth-century canonist, Henry of Segusia, better known as Hostiensis (†1271). Since Hostiensis' work was extensively used to defend and enhance the reputation of the legal profession, it is important to study his views on the nature of canon law before analyzing the manner in which that teaching was used by contemporary canonists.

Hostiensis, one of the most prominent canon lawyers of the high Middle Ages, was trained in both civil and canon law at Bologna. While the argument that he began his teaching career at his alma mater is only probable, there is no doubt that by 1239 he had become a regent master at the University of Paris. In 1244, he was appointed to the bishopric of Sisteron, and, in 1250, Innocent IV, his fellow student at Bologna, made him archbishop of Embrun. He was selected by Urban IV in 1262 to become cardinal of Ostia, from which see he acquired his more commonly used name. Despite an extremely active ecclesiastical career, he continued his studies and writing in the field of canon law. By 1253 he had completed his *Summa aurea*, a synthesis of Roman and Canon Law for the use of canonists, and which he had begun during his teaching days at Paris. His other major work, the *Lectura in quinque libros decretalium*, a commentary on the Decretals of Gregory IX, also begun during his Parisian years, did not see completion until about a year before his death in 1271. Of all his works, however, it was the *Summa aurea* that was the most influential in the subsequent medieval centuries and even into the seventeenth century.[80]

From an analysis of D'Ailly's statements, it is clear that it was from the prologue of Hostiensis' *Summa aurea* that many of d'Ailly's contem-

---

[79] *Utrum indoctus in jure divino*, Dupin 1:654. 'Sed contra hanc conclusionem, est hodie communis error quorundam, dicentium quod ad praelatorum officium magis pertinent doctrina juris humani civilis, scilicet et canonici, quam theologica sapientia, seu doctrina juris divini …'

[80] The best general survey of Hostiensis' life, career, and writings is to be found in Charles Lefebvre's article on him in the *DDC*, 5:1211–1227. See also the recent article by Elizabeth Vodola on Hostiensis in the *DMA*, 6:298–299. For a more detailed study of Hostiensis' views on canon law and its function within the Church see Clarence Gallagher, *Canon Law and the Christian Community: The Role of Law in the Church According to the Summa Aurea of Cardinal Hostiensis* (Rome: Gregorian University Press, 1978).

poraries drew their arguments in favor of canon law in the intellectual formation of an ecclesiastical prelate.[81] In that prologue, Hostiensis situates canon law within a multifold context of history (*historia*), law (*leges*), learning (*scientia*), and society (*genera hominum*). Each of these categories is further divided in a triadic manner. With regard to human history, Hostiensis uses a division that was very popular with medieval thinkers, namely, the division according to three temporal periods: time before the Law (*tempus ante legem*), time under the Law (*tempus sub lege*), and time after the Law (*tempus post legem*).[82]

Closely associated with each of these periods, according to Hostiensis, is a triad of laws. The time before the Law, which covers the period from the creation to the time of Moses, is characterized by the *lex naturalis communis*, the *lex naturalis rationalis*, and the *lex gentium naturalis*. The time under the Law runs from the time of Moses to the coming of Christ and is marked by the appearance of the *lex mosaica*, the *lex prophetica*, and the *lex civilis*. With the period after Christ, namely, the period after the Law, comes the appearance of a third triad of laws, namely, the *lex evangelica*, the *lex apostolica*, and the *lex canonica*.[83]

After delineating his threefold division of human history and the legal triads associated with each division, Hostiensis goes on to describe a threefold level of legal science which incorporates all the above forms of law. The first level he designates as the *scientia civilis*, which in the formulation of its laws, depends heavily upon the principles of the *lex naturalis communis*, the *lex naturalis rationalis*, and the *lex gentium naturalis*. The second level comprises the *scientia theologica*, which, while embodying the principles of the above mentioned laws, concerns itself primarily with the *lex Mosaica*, the *lex evangelica*, and the *lex apostolica*. Finally, the *scientia canonica*, as the third level of legal science, utilizes all the above laws in the formulation of its decrees.[84] Understood more generally, the *scientia civilis* can be described as primarily concerned with the *lex humana*, the *scientia theologica* with the *lex divina*, and the *scientia canonica* with both the *lex divina* and the *lex humana*.

---

[81] *Summa aurea*, 2ᵛ–5ᵛ. The edition used is that of Niccolò Soranzo (Venice: Melchior Sessa, 1574, rpr. Torino: Bottega d'Erasmo, 1963). A detailed discussion of Hostiensis' views on canon law and canon lawyers as presented in his *Summa aurea* can be found in Walter Ullmann's *Medieval Papalism*, 26–37.

[82] *Summa aurea*, 3ᵛ.

[83] *Summa aurea*, 3ᵛ.

[84] *Summa aurea*, 4ʳ. 'Sed haec omnia, lex canonica, immo et omne jus, comprehendit sive sit divinum, sive humanum, publicum vel privatum.'

Because the *scientia canonica* is a composite of all the above mentioned forms of law, Hostiensis argues that it has priority over both the *scientia civilis*, and the *scientia theologica*. Essential to his argumentation is his belief that composition is superior to simplicity. Since, therefore, *scientia canonica* is neither purely *scientia civilis* nor purely *scientia theologica*, but an amalgam of both disciplines, it is not only superior in dignity to these disciplines but also rightly deserves the title of *scientia scientiarum*.[85]

In supporting his argument for the superiority of composition over simplicity, Hostiensis has recourse to the case of man, who is neither purely spiritual, such as the angels, nor purely material, such as inanimate objects, but, rather, a composite of both spirit and matter. While man's superiority over purely material beings is obvious, his superiority over purely spiritual beings such as angels is harder to establish, but Hostiensis makes a valiant attempt to illustrate his position from Scripture, theology, and animate nature. In the realm of Scripture, he maintains that when Paul in 1 Cor. 6:3 admonishes the Corinthians for taking their disputes before civil judges, he asks them how they who were to judge angels could submit themselves to be judged by the secular courts. In Rev. 19:10, John, after hearing the heavenly songs of victory, kneels in worship at the feet of the angelic messenger but is forbidden by the angel to do so. The reason given by the angel for his reaction is that he is merely a servant like the apostle and his followers.[86]

For his theological argument on behalf of the superiority of man over the angelic realm, Hostiensis maintains that the dignity of man was especially enhanced when the second person of the Trinity took on human flesh in the person of Christ. Turning from the realms of Scripture and theology to the realm of animate nature, Hostiensis continues his line of argumentation in favor of composition over simplicity by making the startling assertion that the species of mules, being a hybrid of an ass and a horse, is greater and more noble than that of either horses or asses.[87] While Ullmann has taken Hostiensis' argument as a serious expression of his thought, Kuttner has maintained that in making such a comparison Hostiensis must indeed have been joking. Gallagher remarks that since Hostiensis' *Summa aurea* originally represented lecture notes for students, it would not be surprising that Hostiensis

---

[85] *Summa aurea*, 4^r.
[86] *Summa aurea*, 4^r.
[87] *Summa aurea*, 4^r.

might decide to poke some fun at his own discipline. Gallagher cites other instances in the work where Hostiensis demonstrates a sense of humor.[88] Even if Hostiensis were serious about his argument, he must have at least smiled upon realizing the point to which his argument from composition had brought him. One wonders, moreover, if he realized that such a hybrid is generally sterile. As Gallagher remarks, however, a much more balanced expression of Hostiensis' opinion on the relationship between canon law and theology can be found in his *Lectura* where he compares theology, civil law, and canon law to the head, feet, and hands of the human body, with the head signifying man's spiritual needs, the feet his temporal needs, and the hands as providing for both in varying degrees and circumstances.[89]

After having established his chronological, legal, and scientific triads, Hostiensis states that there is also a sociological triad within the Church. He then describes that triad and associates each part of the triad with a specific category of law and mode of life within the Church. His first sociological category corresponds to the laity in general but within this category he especially signals out civil lawyers, who by their profession are essentially associated with temporal matters and consequently with the *lex civilis*. He characterizes their lives within the context of the *vita activa*. The second sociological category comprises religious orders, such as the Carthusians, the Dominicans and the Franciscans. Because of their close relationship with spiritual matters, these orders are associated with the *lex divina* and their form of life is described in terms of the *vita contemplativa*.

The third component in Hostiensis' sociological triad is the secular clergy, especially the secular canons, in whose ranks Hostensis himself was numbered. He identifies this state with the *vita permixta* since it is concerned with both the spiritual and temporal dimensions of the Church, for it must not only provide for the pastoral needs of the Church but also care for and protect the Church's temporal possessions. In order to fulfill their spiritual and temporal obligations, the members of this triad must necessarily be trained in canon law. In view of his general principle that the composite is superior to the simple,

---

[88] For Kuttner's comments see his 'Harmony from Dissonance,' 15, n. 36. For Ullmann's position see his *Medieval Papalism*, 30–31. Gallagher's remarks on Hostiensis' argument can be found in his *Canon Law and the Christian Community*, 74–77.

[89] Gallagher, *Canon Law and the Chrisian Community*, 76–78. The reference is to Hostiensis' *Lectura*, I, 14, 14.

Hostiensis' association of the secular clergy with the *vita permixta* is, in effect, a claim for its superiority over the regular clergy, especially the mendicants.[90]

In analyzing Hostiensis' triadic categories of *tempora, leges, scientiae*, and *genera hominum* one recognizes both the traditional teaching upon which he drew as well as the skillful manner in which he transformed that tradition. As seen earlier, the triadic structuring of world history in terms of times before, under, and after the law was a common dimension of medieval historiography. This triadic formulation owed much to Augustine for its formulation and development.[91] While Hostiensis' legal triads also followed closely in the medieval legal tradition, his teaching on the scientific triads would seem to be more of his own creation. Finally, his concept of the sociological triads clearly has its origins in Gratian's famous canon, *Duo sunt genera Christianorum*, which essentially divided Christians into lay and clerical orders.[92] Hostiensis, however, broadened this twofold division into a triad of laity, religious, and secular clergy.

As seen above, Hostiensis' views on the role of canon law in universal human history, its position within the hierarchy of legal disciplines, its relationship to other intellectual disciplines, and the form of life characteristic of its practitioners constituted the main source for the opposing arguments in the second article of d'Ailly's *quodlibet* as to whether a prelate who was not well educated in theology can exercise

---

[90] *Summa aurea*, 3ᵛ. 'Ex praemissis patet fore duo genera hominum, scilicet laicorum et religiosorum. Et duo genera vitarum, scilicet contemplativae et activae. Et duo genera scientiarum, scilicet divinae et civilis … Sed sine dubio addere possumus tertium genus, ex ingenio, quasi permixtum, nos enim clerici seculares, quos oportet domino famulari et etiam curare ne pereant possessiones ecclesiasticae, in medio istorum sumus positi tanquam centrum. Aliud est enim genus religiosorum, aliud clericorum secularium … Ideo hoc tertium genus permixtum, vitam permixtam ducens, scientia permixta egebat, qua utrumque sibi commisum, scilicet spirituale et temporale, posset regere, defendere, et tueri …'

[91] The triadic division of human history in terms of *ante legem*, *sub lege*, and *post legem* had its origin in Augustine. See his *Enchiridion*, 118, *PL*, 40:287. Augustine also categorized human history in terms of seven ages. For his teaching on the seven ages of the world see Ladner, *The Idea of Reform*, 222–238. Augustine's three and sevenfold divisions of human history had a major influence on medieval historiography. For a brief but illuminating analysis of medieval concepts of history see M.D. Chenu, 'Conscience d'histoire et théologie' in his *La théologie aux douzième siécle*, 62–89. For more comprehensive surveys of medieval views of history see J.A. Burrow, *The Ages of Man: A Study in Medieval Writing and Thought* and Elizabeth Sears, *The Ages of Man: Medieval Interpretations of the Life Cycle*.

[92] For Gratian's *Duo sunt genera christianorum* see C. 12, q. 1, c. 7, Friedberg, 1:678.

his office without incurring sin. Given the strong influence of Hostiensis' thought in the formulation of these arguments, it is easy to see why in his response to these arguments, D'Ailly devotes so much attention to Hostiensis' teaching, for he realized that his real adversary was not so much his contemporaries in the canon law faculty at Paris but Hostiensis himself. This realization explains why d'Ailly's attack upon Hostiensis' views on canon law is strong, and, at times, highly emotional.

The emotional intensity of d'Ailly's response is especially seen in his reaction to Hostiensis' general thesis as to the superiority of canon law to theology, and his designation of canon law as the *scientia scientiarum*. If by that assertion, d'Ailly argues, Hostiensis meant that canon law should take precedence over theology in the intellectual formation of an ecclesiastical prelate, then his teaching must be categorically rejected as false. D'Ailly even goes so far as to designate Hostiensis' teaching on that point as heretical. His negative response to Hostiensis' views was so intense as to violate the normal professional courtesies that generally prevailed in medieval academic disputes. In such disputes, when one differed strongly with one's opponents it was customary to temper that opposition by distinguishing between the argument and its proponent. This distinction was generally maintained by the use of polite phrases such as 'with all due charity (*salva caritate*)', or 'with all due reverence (*salva reverentia*)'. In this case, however, D'Ailly firmly states that the position of Hostiensis is to be rejected 'without any reverence (*sine ulla reverentia*)'.[93] It is unfortunate that d'Ailly does not appear to be aware of Hostiensis' more balanced views on the relationship between canon law and theology as indicated earlier since he could have refuted his *quodlibet* opponents by using the very authority upon which they had build their arguments.

In responding to Hostiensis' general thesis that canon law was the *scientia scientiarum*, d'Ailly begins by making several general but important observations with regard to the differences between theology and canon law as intellectual disciplines. While he describes both theology and canon law as forms of *scientia*, he adds to theology a whole series of superlatives. Theology is thus described as the 'most perfect (*per-*

---

[93] *Utrum indoctus in jure divino*, Dupin 1:655. 'Negatur plane, et sine ulla reverentia, dictum Hostienum tanquam falsum, et haereticum, si intelligat generaliter, quod juris scientia sit dicenda scientiae scientiarum, et omnibus anteponenda; excipienda enim est theologia.'

fectissima)', 'most stable *(stabilissima)*', 'most true *(verissima)*,' and 'most harmonious *(concordantissima)*' of the sciences.[94] Canon law, on the other hand, as a form of human law is 'imperfect *(imperfecta)*,' 'unstable *(instabilis)*,' 'ever changing *(fluida)*,' and 'discordant *(discordantissima)*'.[95] While d'Ailly does not fully indicate in what context he understands the qualities attributed to theology, his constant comparison of these qualities with those of canon law would indicate that he is referring primarily to the divine law as embodied in the Scriptures and elaborated in theology. If he were referring to theology simply as an intellectual discipline, d'Ailly, as a regent master in theology at Paris, would certainly be aware of the limitations of theological knowledge, its diverse schools of thought, and its often intense controversies.

In substantiating his arguments as to the respective qualities of theology and canon law, d'Ailly uses exclusively legal sources. This approach is especially effective since, as he maintains, it is the Roman and canon lawyers who not only describe the limitations of their own sciences but also the strengths of the science of theology. D'Ailly, in effect, turns the canonical tradition against those canonists who would make greater claims for their discipline than their own tradition would justify. With regard to his argument that theology is a *scientia perfectissima* and *stabilissima*, d'Ailly draws heavily from Roman Law. In this context, he cites the classic statement of Justinian (527–565) wherein after comparing the divine and human realms and their respective laws the emperor concluded that 'divine matters are the most perfect.' Human reality, on the other hand, he maintained, is 'imperfect, unstable, and in constant flux'.[96] Although in this passage Justinian did not make explicit reference to divine law or theology as such, d'Ailly with some justification was able to make that illation. The main thrust of Justinian's statement, however, was not to contrast divine and human law as such, but to emphasize the need for recourse to imperial authority as a remedy for the insufficiencies and even contradictions within the realm of human law.

---

[94] *Utrum indoctus in jure divino*, Dupin 1:655. 'Quia theologia est scientia verissima, concordantissima, cui nihil addi potest vel minui.'

[95] *Utrum indoctus in jure divino*, Dupin 1:655. 'Jus autem humanum imperfectum est, fluidum et instabile.'

[96] *Utrum indoctus in jure divino*, Dupin 1:655 'Divinae quidem res perfectissimae sunt, humani vero juris conditio semper in infinitum decurrit; et nihil est in eo quod stare perpetuo possit.' The passage from Justinian is from the *Codex Iustinianus*, 1, 17, 2., ed. Paul Krueger, *Corpus Iuris Civilis*, 11 ed., 3 vols. (Zürich: Weidmann, 1954), 2:73.

D'Ailly also makes clear that in addition to Roman Law canon law itself recognized that theology is a *scientia verissima* and *concordantissima*. In this context, d'Ailly makes reference to the Gratian's *Decretum* and specifically to the canon *Qui sine Salvatore*, wherein it is stated that whoever seeks salvation apart from Jesus or regards himself as prudent without true wisdom is indeed nothing but a blind fool.[97] The source and content of this canon are really to be found in Augustine's *De civitate Dei*, where, treating of soothsaying, he unfavorably contrasts the knowledge gained from this activity with true knowledge (*vera scientia*), which d'Ailly interprets in terms of theology.[98] Whether the implied and unflattering association of soothsaying with canon law was consciously intended by d'Ailly is not clear.

In his description of canon law as *imperfecta*, *instabilis*, and *fluida*, d'Ailly also has recourse to Roman and Canon Law. The imperfection and instability of human law have already been indicated in the passage from Justinian cited above. In that passage, Justinian also adds that it is the nature of human law to be in a constant state of change, for, as a human creation, it lacks the permanence of divine things. The emperor Julian (361–363) is also cited as stressing the insufficiency of human law, since it cannot foresee all the various situations and circumstances which will arise with the passage of time.[99] The views of Justinian and Julian with regard to the nature of human law were, in turn, borrowed, elaborated, and applied to canon law by John XXII (1316–1334) in his preface to the edition of the *Clementina*.[100]

---

[97] *Utrum indoctus in jure divino*, Dupin 1:655. The reference to Gratian's *Decretum* is C. 26, q. 2, c. 7., Friedberg, 1:1022–1023.

[98] The passage from Augustine's *De civitate Dei* has also been cited by Rabanus Maurus, Burchard of Worms, and Ivo of Chartres. Cf. Friedberg, 1:1022, n. 92.

[99] The reference here is to the *Novellae*, 74, ed. Rudolph Schoell, *Corpus Juris Civilis*, 3:370, wherein is to found the statement of Julian, '... nulla lex neque senatusconsultus prolatum in republica Romanorum videtur ad omnia sufficienter ab initio promulgatum, sed multa indigere correctione, ut ad naturae varietatem et eius machinationes sufficiat.'

[100] *Clem. Prooemium*, Friedberg, 2:1129–1130. 'Quoniam nulla iuris sanctio, quantumcunque perpenso digesta consilio, ad humanae naturae varitatem et machinationes eius inopinales sufficit, nec ad decisionem lucidam suae nodosae ambiguitatis attingit, eo praesertim, quod vix aliquid adeo certum clarumque statuitur, quin ex causis emergentibus, quibus iura iam posita mederi non possint, in dubium revocetur; quia etiam ab adolescentia viri proclivis ad malum sensualitas humana declinat, per quod morum subversio in clero et populo frequenter obrepit: necessaria est superioris auctoritas, ut tam per determinationis opportunae suffragium tollat ambigua, lites auferat, altercationes dirimat et obscura succidat, quam per cultoris providi sarculum exstirpet vitia, virtutes inserat, corrigat excessus moresque reformet.'

268   CHAPTER SEVEN

In stressing the fact that canon law is characterized by a spirit of discordance, D'Ailly cites the very title of Gratian's work, *Concordantia discordantium canonum*, with the emphasis upon the theme of *discordantia*.[101] Although he seems aware that the main spirit behind Gratian's endeavors was that of *concordantia* since he quotes Johannes Andreae to this effect, d'Ailly affirms that the general proclivity of human institutions and laws is towards *discordantia*. Within this context, he recalls Gregory IX's (1227–1241) testimony that it was the excessive, superfluous, and contrary nature of so many existing canons that caused him to take up the codification of the papal decretals.[102] Boniface VIII (1294–1303), in his preface to the *Liber sextus*, states that a similar situation led to the corrective measures taken in his codification.[103] In his own lifetime, the many legal controversies associated with the Great Schism most likely served to impress upon d'Ailly's mind the discordant dimensions of canon law and their harmful consequences.

After his detailed refutation of the general thesis underlying the opposing arguments in his *quodlibet*, d'Ailly turns to the specific arguments made therein with regard to the superiority of canon law in the intellectual formation of an ecclesiastical prelate. As will be recalled, the first of these arguments stressed that the superiority of canon law was based on the fact that it dealt with both the spiritual and temporal aspects of the Church's life. D'Ailly responded to this claim by asserting that long before the appearance of canon law, there was a considerable body of legislation contained in the Scriptures related to temporal matters. For a considerable period of time, moreover, this legislation proved more than sufficient for the guidance of the Church's temporal affairs.[104] There was also to be found in this legislation a spirit of justice

---

[101] *Utrum indoctus in jure divino*, Dupin 1:655. 'Secunda vero pars antecedentis, scilicet quod juris scientia non sit hujusmodi, patet primo ex titulo decretorum, qui talis est: *Incipit concordia discordantium canonum*.'

[102] *Utrum indoctus in jure divino*, Dupin 1:655. '... Gratiani intentio ad hoc solum nititur, ut canones discordantes ad concordiam revocet; nec tamen plene perfecit, teste Gregorio IX in principio compilationis suae. Cujus unam causam assignat, decretalium et constitutionum aliquarum nimiam similitudinem, superfluitatem, prolixitatem, et aliquarum contrarietatem.' The reference to Gregory IX is from the introductory letter to the edition of his decretales and is to be found in Friedberg, 2:1–2.

[103] *Utrum indoctus in jure divino*, Dupin 1:655. 'Et Bonifacius, in principio libri 6, refert aliquas sibiipsis, et aliis juribus contrarias. Ideo resecat quasdam, alias abbreviat, non nullas in toto vel parte mutat, corrigit, detrahit, et addit.' Boniface IX's introductory letter to the edition of his decretals is to be found in Friedberg, 2:933–934.

[104] *Utrum indoctus in jure divino*, Dupin 1:655. 'Licet humanae constitutiones sint utiles

that served as a norm for all subsequent legislation.[105] While not denying the need for a knowledge of canon law, d'Ailly does imply that a theological education is more than sufficient for an ecclesiastical prelate in the management of the temporal affairs of his office, especially if he embodies within himself the biblical spirit of justice.[106]

The second argument in favor of canon law maintained that since that law dealt with the temporal and spiritual needs of the Church's life it was a *scientia composita* and therefore superior to a *scientia simplex* such as theology. As such, consequently, canon law was better suited for the education of a prelate. This argument was obviously taken directly from Hostiensis and d'Ailly again demonstrates considerable impatience with such thinking, for he caustically remarks that such a line of argumentation deserves more to be laughed at than to be given serious attention.[107] After having heaped ridicule upon Hostiensis' position, D'Ailly does deign to give some brief attention to the reason upon which Hostiensis based his argument, namely that the composite nature of man was superior to the simplicity characteristic of angelic nature. Taken in itself, he remarks, the argument is simply false, for in no way can the purely spiritual nature of the angels be said to be inferior to the material and spiritual composite that is man.[108] D'Ailly, however, does admit that with regard to some accidental qualities, human nature can be said to be superior to that of the angels.[109] While he does not go into specifics, he most likely is referring to the redemptive grace of Christ, which so ennobled human nature as to elevate it above that of the angels.

The third argument on behalf of the primacy of canon law was that it was more useful to a prelate because it guided him in the admin-

---

ad multa; tamen antequam forent jura, sive leges humanas, divinae leges datae erant legales et justae a legislatore Moyse. Immo verius ab Omnicreatore.'

[105] *Utrum injustus in jure divino*, Dupin 1:656. 'Antequam etiam essent decretales epistolae, datae erant leges completissimae justitiae et honestatis. Per exemplum; scilicet Christus qui est consummatio legis, ad justitiam.' On this last point, d'Ailly cites Rom. 10:4.

[106] *Utrum indoctus in jure divino*, Dupin 1:656. 'In volumine ergo novi et veteris Testamenti, ex Moysis et Christi legibus composito, omnipotentissima Dei sapientia, et justitia infinita, nullam sufficientiam praetermisit quoad bonum, immo optimum regimen universi, super quo nulli fideli haesitare licitum est.'

[107] *Utrum indoctus in jure divino*, Dupin 1:656. 'Dicendum est quod magis irridenda est quam solvenda.'

[108] *Utrum indoctus in jure divino*, Dupin 1:656. 'Hoc enim simpliciter falsum est.'

[109] *Utrum indoctus in jure divino*, Dupin 1:656. '… licet secundum quid et quoad aliquem accidentalem conditionem veritatem habere possit.'

istration and defense of the temporal possessions associated with his office. D'Ailly rejects this line of argumentation outright, because, as he asserts, even if the argument is correct, there can be no doubt that the spiritual dimensions of the Church's life have preference over the temporal.[110] While he recognizes the important role that temporal possessions play in the life of the Church, he seeks to place them more in a spiritual context, for he asserts that the study of the Church's history reveals that when it began to acquire landed property it did so primarily in order to provide for the needs of its poor. On this point, D'Ailly reflects a common medieval teaching with regard to the ownership of ecclesiastical possessions and their principal beneficiaries. What is surprising in his arguments, however, is that he uses historical chronicles as his documentary support and not the rich canonical teaching that existed with regard to this specific issue.[111]

The fourth and final argument given to support the primacy of canon law in the intellectual formation of an ecclesiastical prelate was that the historical origins of canon law considerably antedated those of theology. Supporters of this argument from antiquity generally identified the origins of canon law with Adam or Moses. Unlike the previous arguments, this argument from antiquity was not based upon the teaching of Hostiensis but on that of the canonist, Guido of Baysio (†1311), more commonly known in the late Middle Ages as the Archdeacon. Guido's thought on the question at issue was contained in the preface to his commentary on Gratian's *Decretum* and generally referred to as the *Rosarium*.[112] D'Ailly has nothing but intellectual scorn for Guido's argument and dismisses it as unworthy of any serious attention.[113] As if

---

[110] *Utrum indoctus in jure divino*, Dupin 1:656. '... quoad illud quod assumitur, doctrinam canonum utiliorem esse ad possessiones Ecclesiae diffendendas; supposito quod ita esset; hoc non probat intentum, quia spiritualia sunt temporalibus praeferenda.'

[111] *Utrum indoctus in jure divino*, Dupin 1:656. D'Ailly's reference to chronicle sources is extremely general: 'quia ecclesiae si revolvamus cronicas ...' For a brief but thorough survey of the canonical teaching on church property, its ownership, and its beneficiaries, see Brian Tierney, *Medieval Poor Law*, 39–44.

[112] *Utrum indoctus in jure divino*, Dupin 1:655. D'Ailly here cites the actual text from Guido of Baysio which concludes: 'Unde quibusdam concludendum quod juris scientia, cum sit aliis antiquior, etiam dignior est, et per consequens, magis ad praelatos pertinet.' The full title of Baysio's work is *Rosarium seu in decretorum volumen commentaria*, ed. Niccolò Soranzo (Venice: 1577). This work, published in 1300, supplemented the standard gloss on the *Decretum* and became a basic textbook in many faculties of canon law in the late Middle Ages.

[113] *Utrum indoctus in jure divino*, Dupin 1:656. 'Ad quartum dicendum, quod non est digna signari, quia clarum est divinam legem ceteras praecessisse.'

to deal the final blow to this argument, he simply cites a well-known passage from the *Digest* that states that all laws have their origins in the divine law, which, as seen earlier, d'Ailly always associates with theology.[114]

While d'Ailly's views on the relationship of canon law to theology were extensively developed in his *quodlibet* of 1394, he again takes up the discussion of that relationship in a Laetare Sunday sermon given at the Council of Constance on March 21, 1417. His treatment of the subject on this occasion, however, is much briefer and confined primarily to the question of the relationship of canonical methodology to that of theology. While his earlier writings reveal little as to his understanding of canonical methodology, it is hard to believe that he was unaware of the subject. The similarities between the methodologies of theology and canon law were too close to have escaped his attention, especially their application of reason to ascertain the underlying principles of their discipline and the conclusions which follow from those principles as well as their mutual attempt to organize those principles into one coherent system.[115] His interaction with canonists at the University of Paris, especially as chancellor of the university, and at the Council of Constance as well as the extensive use of canonical sources in his own writings would also argue in favor of a considerable knowledge about canonical methodology.

In his explicit treatment of the different methodologies employed in theology and canon law as presented in his Laetare Sunday sermon, d'Ailly does not actually use the term 'methodologies' but rather speaks in terms of a *stilus juridicus* and a *stilus theologicus* and discusses the relative merits of each with regard to determining matters of faith.[116] His understanding of the term *stilus*, moreover, closely approximates

---

[114] *Utrum indoctus in jure divino*, Dupin 1:656. The reference to the *Digest* most likely refers to the twelve canons in D. 1, Friedberg, 1:1–2, wherein Gratian treats of the various types of law and their interrelationship.

[115] For a detailed analysis of the growth of medieval canonical methodology, especially with regard to its diverse modes of reasoning, see Berman, *Law and Revolution*, 120–164, Le Bras, *L'age classique*, 352–420. For parallels between theological and canonical methodologies in the eleventh and twelfth centuries see de Ghellinck, *Le mouvement théologique du xiie siècle*, 472–499. An excellent summary presentation of the growth of scholastic theology and its methodology can be had in M.D. Chenu, 'The Masters of the Theological Science,' in his *Nature, Man, and Society in the Twelfth Century*, 270–309.

[116] *Sermo facta Constantiae in medio Quadragesimae*, TS, 8. 'Cum ergo sacra theologia sit omnium scientiarum suprema habet suum stilum sive modum appropriatum sicut scientia canonica habet suum stilum iuridicum.'

our notion of methodology, for in affirming that each *scientia* and *ars* has its proper *stilus*, he describes *stilus* as the mode of proceeding proper to each.[117] Each *stilus*, moreover, when used properly has its respective degree of legitimacy.

While d'Ailly affirms the legitimate use of canonical methodology, it is its misuse that he regards as dangerous.[118] This danger, he argues, is especially evident when canonical methodology is applied to doctrinal matters. While he does not give concrete examples of such application, he does imply that such has often been the case in conciliar deliberations at Constance. D'Ailly, therefore, urges the Council to use the *stilus theologicus* and not the *stilus juridicus* in dealing with doctrinal issues. Such issues, therefore, are to be analyzed, debated, and determined in a manner proper to theology. Not to do so would in effect force theological issues into canoncal forms of thought and would in the text of Paul, 'restrain the Word of God.'[119] As further support for his line of argumentation, d'Ailly has recourse to canon law itself when he indicates that the Pseudo-Isidorian Decretals, many of which Gratian had incorporated in his *Decretum*, clearly indicate that in their deliberations on doctrinal matters, the fathers of the early ecumenical councils employed the theological and not the juridical mode of procedure.[120]

The major failure of the canonists, according to d'Ailly, lies in their failure to recognize the limitations of their methodology. That failure, in turn, he argues, is rooted in the unwillingness of canon lawyers to recognize the subordinate status of their discipline in relationship to

---

[117] *Sermo facta Constantiae in medio Quadragesimae*, TS, 8. 'Quis enim nesciat nisi valde ignarus quod quaelibet etiam scientia imo ars quaelibet etiam mechanica habet stilum suum, id est modum procedendi sibi proprium. Quid enim est stilus nisi procedendi modus cuique scientiae appropriatus.'

[118] *Sermo facta Constantiae in medio Quadragesimae*, TS, 8. 'Iura enim bona sunt et stilus iuridicus bonus est. Ideo eis bene uti omnino bonum est. Sed ipsis sicut etiam virtutibus contingit male uti quod certe periculosissimum est, audaciter assero.'

[119] *Sermo facta Constantiae in medio Quadragesimae*, TS, 9. 'Non debet ergo sacra theologia, non debet theologicus stilus, non debet materia fidei sub regulis et ligaminibus stili iuridici coartari, non capistrari, non alligari quia secundum apostolum verbum Dei non est alligatum.' The reference to Paul can be found in 2 Tim. 2:9.

[120] *Sermo facta Constantiae in medio Quadragesimae*, TS, 9. 'Hic obsecro vobis diligenter attendamus quis stilus, quis procedendi modus in causis fidei in antiquis conciliis generalibus fuerit observatus. Legatur totus liber magnus conciliorum a quo Gratianus in suo decreto plura truncavit. Non invenietur quod antiqui patres nostri in conciliis generalibus hunc stilum sive procedendi modum iuridicum sed magis theologicum in diffiniendo causas fidei servaverint.'

theology, especially in matters of faith.[121] For d'Ailly, the subordinate status of canon law to theology rests upon the fact that canon law draws many of its conclusions from principles established in theology, especially in matters related to divine law. As a form of human law, moreover, canon law is essentially subordinate to divine law and in turn to theology. As further support of his line of argumentation, d'Ailly draws upon Scripture especially 2 Cor. 10:5 wherein Paul, reacting to the criticisms of the Corinthians with regard to certain aspects of his mission, replies that he can refute those arguments and intends to 'bring every thought into captivity and obedience to Christ.' D'Ailly broadly interpreted this passage in terms of the subjection of human reason and learning to the teaching of the faith. Since canon law and canonical methodology are much more the products of human reason than theology, they are to be subordinate to theology and its methodology.[122]

As d'Ailly saw it, failure to recognize this subordination has produced untold difficulties and confusion in the Church, especially during the period of the Great Schism which raised important and controversial issues related to the nature of the Church, papal leadership, and the proper role and authority of general councils. He firmly believed, moreover, that the insistence of the various papal contenders and their supporters on canon law and its methodology as the primary means of resolving these difficulties only served to continue the ecclesiological impasse which continued right up to the opening of the Council of Constance in late 1414. Canonists and canonistic methodology, therefore, emerged in d'Ailly's mind as the greatest obstacle to the resolution of the Schism. Only in theology and its methodology were to be found the intellectual means for resolving that impasse and for restoring unity to the universal Church.

At the time d'Ailly delivered his Laetare Sunday Sermon on March 21, 1417, however, the conciliar cause at Constance, which he had

---

[121] *Sermo facta Constantiae in medio Quadragesimae*, TS, 8. 'Et sicut scientia canonica maiori et digniori sui parte subalternata est sacrae theologiae sic stilus iuridicus stilo theologico maxime in causis fidei subalternatus est et subiectus et non econtra.'

[122] *Sermo facta Constantiae in medio Quadragesimae*, TS, 9. 'Si enim secundum apostolum captivare debemus intellectum in obsequium fidei, id est intellectualem et naturalem rationem, multo magis captivandus est et subiciendus in obsequium iuris divini et stili theologici ius humanum et stilus hominis iuridicus.' In his exegesis of 2 Cor. 10:5, d'Ailly interprets the word *intellectum* in terms of human reason and the phrase '*in obsequium Christi*' in terms of '*in obsequium juris divini*, understanding the latter phrase in terms of the *fides Christi*.'

increasingly supported and from which he gradually emerged as one of its outstanding representatives, had met with considerable success, a success which intensified even more after the date of his sermon. Two years before his sermon, the council had refused to disband and reasserted its legitimacy after the flight of the Pisan pope, John XXIII, on March 20, 1415. On April 6th of that year, the Council passed its most famous decree, *Haec sancta synodus*, which claimed conciliar superiority even over the papacy in matters relating to faith, schism, and reform. In that same year, the Council had forced John XXIII to return to Constance and declared him deposed on May 29th. On July 4th, the Council had secured the abdication of the Roman pope, Gregory XII. By the time of d'Ailly's Laetare Sunday Sermon in March, 1417, Emperor Sigismund had already attracted many of the Spanish and Portuguese followers of the Avignon pope, Benedict XIII, to the conciliar cause. Several months after d'Ailly's sermon, the Council had effected the deposition of Benedict XIII on July 26th and by November 11 the Schism was resolved by the election of Martin V. While it would be historically simplistic to attribute the Council's success in resolving the Schism solely to the influence of theologians, their discipline, and its methodology, it can be said that they contributed heavily to that success and that among these theologians d'Ailly played a major role.

In asserting d'Ailly's conviction that canon law, its methodology, and its practitioners had resisted and prolonged the resolution of the Schism, one does not thereby intend to deny the reality and importance of canonical influences in his ecclesiological thought. Nor is there the intention to deny the presence and contributions of more moderate canonists in the conciliarist ranks at Constance such as Zabarella. D'Ailly may have even been influenced by this group of canonists, especially with regard to his views on corporational theory, although that influence has occasionally been exaggerated.[123] D'Ailly's reaction against canonists and canonical methodology was not against this category of canonists but more against the larger body of canonists whose theory of papal authority in the Church was such as to result in the complete subordination of other members of the ecclesiastical hierarchy, especially bishops, to that authority. In d'Ailly's mind their application of this understanding of papal authority had long hindered the

---

[123] For an evaluation of other influences upon d'Ailly's conciliar thought, especially as they apply to his views on the papal plenitude of power see Pascoe, 'Theological Dimensions of d'Ailly's Teaching.'

resolution of the Schism. By the time of his Laetare Sunday Sermon in 1417, however, the accomplishments of the conciliarist cause at Constance had indeed given him renewed confidence in his basic conviction as to the proper relationship between canon law and theology and help to explain the more positive and joyful spirit of that sermon over and above its immediate liturgical context.

CONCLUSION

Despite the trends in recent scholarship described in the introduction to our study, d'Ailly is still regarded in many scholarly and popular circles primarily as an ecclesiastical statesman, a reputation considerably strengthened by Guenée's recent study. There can be no doubt as to d'Ailly's rightful status as an ecclesiastical statesman given his prominent role in the many deliberations and initiatives undertaken by the French Monarchy, the University of Paris, the Avignon and Pisan Papacies, their respective College of Cardinals, and the Councils of Pisa and Constance to resolve the Great Western Schism. In these efforts, d'Ailly manifested his talents as an ecclesiastical statesman through his attempts to balance the individual concerns, interests and privileges of all of the above persons, groups, and institutions against the more urgent need to achieve the common good, peace, and unity of the Church as a universal institution. In these multifold efforts, d'Ailly was joined by many other prominent ecclesiastical statesmen not only from France, but also from Italy, Germany, England, and Spain. While he shared in their many diplomatic setbacks and defeats, he also shared in their ultimate success at Constance in the resolution of the Schism and the restoration of the Church's unity.

Throughout his many years of service as an ecclesiastical statesman on behalf of the French Monarchy, the University of Paris, and the Avignon and Pisan Papacies, the sincerity of d'Ailly's motives and dedication were occasionally questioned by his contemporaries as well as by subsequent scholars. He was accused of being ambitious, opportunistic, and at times lacking the courage of his convictions. While he most likely ambitioned some of the offices he received from the above persons or institutions, there is no doubt that they also recognized his political and intellectual talents and did everything possible to gain his allegiance and support. If d'Ailly therefore received his ecclesiastical appointments from such persons and institutions, it was also because of those talents.

Given his debt to those who fostered his career, it is not surprising that throughout his long years of service he would be partial to and strive to protect their interests. Many occasions arose, however, when he was torn between the dictates of his conscience as to what would best further the resolution of the Schism and the particular interests of the individuals and institutions which helped to promote his ecclesiastical career. At such times d'Ailly generally manifested the courage to pursue a course of action which adhered more closely to his own personal convictions than to the views of those to whom he owed his appointments. On such occasions, d'Ailly proceeded with a diplomatic cautiousness that could at times be misinterpreted as a failure in courage. Always the statesman, d'Ailly realized better than most that diplomacy, like politics, is always the art of the possible.

While the image of d'Ailly as an ecclesiastical statesman remains predominant in scholarly and popular circles, many recent studies, as indicated in our introduction, have investigated and made known other dimensions of his life and thought beyond those associated with his career as an ecclesiastical statesman. Our study, it is hoped, has contributed to that trend by emphasizing aspects of his life and thought which have received little or no attention. Within this context, emphasis has been placed upon his ecclesiology, especially three major but often neglected dimensions of that ecclesiology, namely, his views on bishops, theologians, and canon lawyers. While our study of d'Ailly's thought on bishops, theologians, and canon lawyers has concentrated on their status, office, and authority, that concentration has especially brought to the fore their apocalyptic, reformative, and apostolic or pastoral dimensions.

These dimensions of d'Ailly's thought on bishops, theologians, and canon lawyers, though varying in degree of application and realization, manifested themselves early in his career at the University of Paris and continued throughout his life. They also serve to illustrate what Guenée has designated as d'Ailly's essential fidelity to the fundamental framework of his thought. While d'Ailly did make some modifications in his thought, he basically remained faithful to his earlier views. To illustrate his point, Guenée has singled out d'Ailly's consistent fidelity to his twelfth and thirteenth century authorities such as St. Bernard, the Victorines, Hugh and Richard, and William of Auvergne. Throughout his life he maintained his respect and veneration for St. Francis and the mainstream Franciscan tradition. To these areas of continuity, our study has added d'Ailly's views on the apocalyptic, reformative, and apostolic dimensions of the personal and professional lives of bishops, theologians, and canon lawyers.

In d'Ailly's case, this characteristic of fidelity and continuity is especially verifiable because, as indicated in our introduction, the codicological research of Gilbert Ouy has shown that d'Ailly was especially concerned with rereading, correcting, recopying, and republishing many of his earlier works. As a result of this concern, we are better enabled to appreciate the extent to which he modified or remained faithful to his earlier views. Where corrections or modifications did occur, they were frequently not so much rejections of former positions as developments resulting from a deeper reflection upon those positions. Gueneé speaks of such developments in terms of a 'rebirth rooted in continuity.'

As indicated earlier, our study of d'Ailly's teaching on the status, office, and authority of bishops has revealed the apocalyptic, reformative, and apostolic dimensions of his thought. As for the apocalyptic dimensions, it will be recalled that d'Ailly saw the history of the Church in terms of a series of persecutions which had reached apocalyptic dimensions with the long duration of the Schism. The Church, however, could avert the realization of these apocalyptic threats through a thorough process of reform in which the episcopacy would play a central role. As a result of our study, therefore, d'Ailly emerges with a considerably enhanced reputation not only as an apocalyptic thinker but also as an ecclesiastical reformer. While the terms ecclesiastical statesman and ecclesiastical reformer are not mutually exclusive, the extent of d'Ailly's interest in and dedication to church reform justifiably allows us to see this dimension of his life as a separate yet important component. One uses the phrase 'enhanced reputation as an apocalyptic thinker and ecclesiastical reformer' because these dimensions of his life and career have already been noted by Salembier and Oakley. Their studies, however, have been restricted primarily to a general analysis of his apocalyptic thought and an enumeration of his concrete efforts and accomplishments in the realm of reform. Our study, while building on their work has had the advantage of getting to the ideological roots which gave life and direction to his apocalyptic and reform thought.

D'Ailly's thought on the reformative role of bishops also reveals him as a much more pastorally orientated prelate than previously realized. As d'Ailly saw it, if the bishops are to be the central agents in the reform of the Church, they must rediscover the pastoral dimensions of their office. In order to do so, he called upon them to adopt the ideals of the *vita apostolica* and *evangelica*, both in the administration of their office and in their personal lives. His emphasis upon this form of life for bishops not only illustrates the strong biblical foundations of his reform thought, but also situates him in the long line of apostolic and evangelical reformers which began to emerge in the eleventh and twelfth centuries in Europe and continued throughout the remaining medieval centuries. His call upon the whole episcopal order to assume the leadership in church reform through adoption of the apostolic and evangelical ideal, especially with its stress on the notions of pastoral vocation and mission, also serves to illustrate his distinctive place within the history of late medieval evangelical reform movements and thought. It is important to note finally that d'Ailly's interest in the apostolic and evangelical ideal as especially applicable to the episcopacy began many years before his assumption of the episcopal office and continued throughout his years as a cardinal.

The model of the apostolic and evangelical life clearly influenced his critique of the pastoral failures and weaknesses of the episcopacy as well as the concrete means he proposed for its reform. As already seen, this critique was indeed a detailed one and reached into the life of the bishop on both the official and personal levels. On the official level, d'Ailly's critique covered the practical problems related to the selection, examination, appointment, and financial support of candidates to the episcopal office. Given his university background and experience, the question of the type of learning desirable in persons being considered for episcopal appointments was also of great interest to him. While the question of learning was closely related to the effectiveness of pastoral ministry, d'Ailly was also much preoccupied with the concrete and practical dimensions of that ministry such as liturgy, preaching, sacraments, devotions, visitations, synods, and residence.

As to the personal level of the bishop's life, d'Ailly paid considerable attention to the realm of moral formation and character with special emphasis upon fostering the virtue of charity as well as inculcating the proper attitudes towards the roles of poverty, chastity, and humility. He also showed much practical concern for assuring the necessary material and financial support of the bishop. While the idea of personal reform, especially as applicable to the life of a bishop, has been touched upon in our study, the whole question of d'Ailly's views on personal reform in general as well as the spirituality associated with it deserve much future attention.

In the implementation of the apostolic ideal in the official and personal lives of bishops, what especially characterized d'Ailly's reform thought was its spirit of moderation. While there is no doubt that he was greatly inspired by the Franciscan interpretation of the *vita apostolica* and *evangelica* with its emphasis upon preaching, poverty, and humility, d'Ailly carefully avoided the extreme interpretation of that ideal as espoused by the spiritual or radical Franciscans. His recourse to the spirit of moderation in this context is indeed understandable. What is to be noted, however, is that even with regard to the mainstream Franciscan interpretation of the apostolic and evangelical life, d'Ailly adopted a more moderate stance. He never called upon the bishops to adopt the Franciscan ideal of personal poverty but insisted more upon their need to be provided with a moderate amount of material and financial support to sustain them in fulfilling the duties of their office.

D'Ailly's stress on moderation in following the apostolic and evangelical life was especially manifested in his treatment of the reform of the episcopal lifestyle in such areas as personal finances, dress, and ceremony. In such areas, he counseled moderation and even spoke of the need to allow a 'moderate inequality' among members of the episcopacy according to the importance of their respective dioceses. In dealing with problems related to episcopal ministry in such areas as preaching, visitations, correction and the regulation of other dimensions of the clerical life, d'Ailly also advised recourse to the spirit of moderation. He frequently designated this spirit of moderation as one of 'tolerable moderation.' Guenée neatly summed up d'Ailly's personality and style of oratory when he wrote that d'Ailly 'stated moderate ideas with great passion.'

In defending his recourse to the spirit of moderation in the exercise of the episcopal office, d'Ailly seemed to range from an occasional sense of resignation in the face of intractable pastoral problems to the more often employed pastoral desire to strike a balance between judicial vigor and evangelical sensitivity. While he frequently invoked the Greco-Roman principles of '*mediocritas*' and '*ne quid nimis*,' in the sense of avoiding extremes, he applied those principles primarily in an apostolic and evangelical context. In situations where the practice of simony had become almost customary, he urged some degree of moderation in the strict application of laws against such practices arguing the need to avoid scandalizing the laity as well the desire not to excessively upset the consciences of those so involved, especially if they unwittingly participated in such practices. In these situations, he argued for some form of ecclesiastical dispensation.

Given the needs of the Church in d'Ailly's time, the question can be raised as to how successful can a program of reform be which stresses moderation in the achievement of its goal? While d'Ailly's call for a return to the ideals of the apostolic life was indeed radical in the sense that the Gospel itself is a radical call to conversion and reform, his emphasis upon moderation in the interpretation and implementation of that call does raise questions as to the possible effectiveness of his reform thought. D'Ailly's penchant for moderation in the implementation of the apostolic model may have been influenced by the many heretical interpretations espoused by late medieval reform movements, especially those inspired by Wyclif and Hus. He may also have been influenced by the fragmentation that occurred in the Franciscan order as it sought to implement the apostolic model in the governance of a growing and increasingly diverse membership and changing apostolic needs. It must also be remembered that d'Ailly had to adapt the apostolic ideal to the specific needs of an ecclesiastical prelate working within a specific historical context, and in doing this his sense of pastoral realism may well have been his primary guide. What seems more certain, however, is that his spirit of moderation reflected a deeply ingrained personal characteristic, no doubt considerably influenced by his experiences as university professor and administrator, bishop, and cardinal.

While there is no doubt that d'Ailly's was among the first ecclesiastical prelates of the late Middle Ages to call for episcopal reform according to the apostolic ideal, and while that call, even though moderate in its interpretation, was sincere and genuine and if realized would have represented a considerable improvement within the episcopal state, the question still remains whether that call would have been more effective if it had been promoted more intensely and with greater personal application. This question can only be fully answered after future studies have determined more clearly the degree to which d'Ailly's program of episcopal reform influenced his contemporaries. Despite his many influences on Jean Gerson, his pupil at Paris and his successor as university chancellor, Gerson's program of episcopal reform, though essentially apostolic in its roots, is framed within a Pseudo-Dionysian theory of ecclesiastical hierarchy and the hierarchical activities of purgation, illumination, and perfection, aspects which are absent in much of d'Ailly's thought. As already seen, his ideas on episcopal reform had limited influence at the Council of Constance. Perhaps the answer to our question might be realized when d'Ailly's program of episcopal reform is compared with the more successful episcopal reform model proposed and implemented by the Council of Trent.

The second area of d'Ailly's ecclesiology under study in the present work related to his teaching on the status, office, and authority of theologians as well as his views on the nature and method of theology as an intellectual discipline. What was striking about his views on theologians was the strong apostolic context in which they were presented. Theologians, according to d'Ailly, are to be seen both corporately and individually as sharing in the vocation and mission of teaching and preaching the Gospel entrusted to the ecclesiastical hierarchy, especially bishops and popes, as the successors of the apostles. Theologians shared as well in the authority associated with that vocation and mission. As seen earlier, d'Ailly's views on the apostolic dimensions of the theologian's status, office, and authority were essentially developed in two major controversies at the University of Paris, namely, the Blanchard Affair and the Monzón Controversy.

In the Blanchard Affair d'Ailly sought to establish the association of theologians with the ecclesiastical hierarchy through the *licentia ubique docendi* which was granted by the chancellor of the university to them upon the successful completion of their theological studies. Since the right to grant the *licentia ubique docendi* rested ultimately upon papal authorization, and since the pope as successor to Peter shared in the apostolic vocation and mission to teach and preach the Gospel, d'Ailly thus regarded theologians as associated with and participating in that same mission. In the Monzón Controversy, d'Ailly attempted to establish the connection between theologians and the apostolic church in a slightly different manner, namely, by describing theologians as descending from the ranks of the apostolic *doctores* mentioned in the New Testament along with other offices in the primitive church. By d'Ailly's time this association had become widely accepted in university circles. As a result of their apostolic teaching and preaching functions, d'Ailly also portrayed theologians as builders of the primitive Church. Theologians, therefore, not only share in the apostolic vocation and mission of the *doctores* by their teaching and preaching of the Gospel but also by these activities build up the Church as the Mystical Body of Christ.

In addition to associating the theologian with the ecclesiastical hierarchy in terms of apostolic vocation and mission, d'Ailly was able to articulate clearly the different levels to which each group participated in and interacted with one another in the fulfillment of that vocation and mission. Finally, d'Ailly's thought on the authority of theologians was especially distinguished by his indepth analysis of that authority in both its corporate and individual dimensions. In determining the latter dimension, d'Ailly developed to a greater degree than heretofore the different modes of approval attributable to the teaching of individual theologians as well as the varying degree of assent associated with those modes.

Having described theologians primarily in terms of their participation in the apostolic vocation and mission of teaching and preaching the Gospel, d'Ailly then logically identifies theology with the study of the Scriptures, especially the New Testament. As such there is a naturally Christocentric dimension to d'Ailly's concept of theology. This dimension is especially seen in his insistence that Christ is to be the primary subject of theology and that among the various dimensions of the divine law with which theology is to concern itself, the Law of Christ as described in the Gospel is to have predominance. The primacy of Scripture, especially the emphasis on Christ, also emerged in d'Ailly's description of theological method. As will be recalled, theological method for d'Ailly was restricted primarily to propositions taken directly from the Scriptures or those which follow immediately from such propositions. Among such propositions, those related to the Christocentric aspects of the New Testament enjoyed a special prominence.

While d'Ailly's views on the interrelationship between theology, theological method, and Scripture are not in themselves surprising since such indeed was the common tradition throughout all ages of the Church and remains so today, it is his great emphasis and insistence upon this relationship that especially distinguishes his thought. In a sense then he seems to be countering the fascination of late medieval theology and theologians with arcane and abstruse questions marginally related to the Scriptures. In so doing he joins the increasing ranks of those in the late Middle Ages who called for theology and theologians to return to the Scriptures as the main source for their professional activities of investigation, speculation, and teaching.

In addition to our study of the apostolic dimensions of d'Ailly's thought on theologians, theology and theological method, the question arises as to whether his views in these areas also reflect the apocalyptic and reformative emphasis which was so central to his teaching on bishops. While there was a strong apostolic element to d'Ailly's teaching on theologians, theology, and theological method, the apocalyptic and reformative dimensions received considerably less emphasis. In the case of theologians the apocalyptic dimension was restricted primarily to the assistance they could provide to bishops in identifying among the persecutions experienced by the contemporary Church those which truly prefigured the arrival of the Antichrist. In some sense, therefore, theirs was something of a prophetic role. As for the reformative aspect, d'Ailly docs not call for rcform in either the personal or professional lives of the theologians. Although d'Ailly's teaching on theology and theological method involved a strong return to their scriptural roots, d'Ailly does not provide any explicit critique of or call for the reform of the prevailing views on theology and theological methodology at the University of Paris during his time.

D'Ailly's failure to call for reform in relationship to theologians, theology, and theological method may be partially explained by the fact that after his episcopal appointments to Le Puy and Cambrai his contacts with the theological scene at Paris were considerably lessened and he was increasingly presented with new challenges on the diocesan level as well as with those associated with his continued involvement in the many attempts to resolve the Schism. Yet his years at Paris as student, teacher, and administrator spanned a period of thirty one years and it is surprising that he did not feel the need to call for reform in the above-mentioned areas. In this respect he differs from his close personal friends and former students, Jean Gerson and Nicolas of Clamanges, who advocated detailed programs of reform both in the personal and professional lives of theologians as well as in the realm of theology and theological method.

The third and final aspect of d'Ailly's ecclesiology that was investigated in this work related to the realm of canon lawyers and the discipline of canon law. Since d'Ailly was not a canon lawyer himself, his reflections on these topics were not as extensive as those on theologians and bishops. In discussing d'Ailly's views on canon lawyers and their discipline, it is important to remember that while many medieval theologians had a respectable knowledge of canon law, d'Ailly, as our study has shown, demonstrated a more than average knowledge of this discipline, its methodology, and its practitioners. He was also concerned that clerics studying in cathedral and metropolitan schools receive some training in canon law. As seen earlier, in his call for the buildup of libraries in these schools he stressed the need for the increased acquisition of books not only in theology, both speculative and moral, but also in canon law, especially the more important conciliar collections.

As for d'Ailly's expertise in the realm of canon law, it can be seen on the practical level in matters related to ecclesiastical appointments, offices, ordinations, sacraments, clerical celibacy, simony, episcopal residence and the conduct of synods and councils. On the more theoretical level, d'Ailly, like many medieval theologians, preferred to view canon law within the broader concept of law itself with its specific categories of eternal, divine, natural, and human law. He also realized that despite being essentially a form of human law, canon law was also a composite of all of the above laws, and the hierarchical order of the laws within that composite must be duly recognized and respected.

Essentially, then, it was primarily because of his knowledge of and respect for canon law and its methodology that d'Ailly based his critique of canon lawyers. Too often, he argued, canon lawyers acted contrary to the very principles and spirit of their discipline. In this context, d'Ailly felt that canon lawyers had lost sight of the fact that their discipline was essentially a hierarchically structured legal composite. Canonists frequently failed to acknowledge that hierarchy and treated aspects of human law as if they enjoyed the same prominence and degree of obligation accorded to divine and natural law. He often criticized canon lawyers for attempting to resolve issues which were essentially theological by the application of canonical methodology. They had also failed to realize that canon law was in the final analysis a subordinate science vis-à-vis theology since its most important legal principles were ultimately rooted in divine law which was primarily the domain of theology. As a result of this failure, canonists had too often neglected to consult with theologians in drawing up and interpreting canon law. Overconfidence in their discipline had also caused canonists to support excessive amounts of legislation in their attempts to resolve the many problems facing the Church in their time. Finally, the perennial complaint of excessive litigation within the Church was laid at the doorstep of the canonists.

It should also be recognized that professional competition between theologians and canonists played a role in d'Ailly's critique of canon law and its practitioners. On this level, d'Ailly often lamented the appointment by the papacy of so many graduates from canon law faculties to ecclesiastical offices, especially the episcopal office. While his complaint was rooted in the obvious disadvantage that such a policy created for graduates of the theological faculties, it was also based upon his strong conviction that bishops with a primarily legal mindset would be far less effective pastorally than bishops trained primarily in theology. This point brings to mind the many quodlibetal disputations at the University of Paris on the question of whether the Church would be better governed by a theologian or a canonist.

Despite his extensive critique of canon lawyers, d'Ailly did not propose a comprehensive program of reform for the personal and professional lives of the canonists. At times, however, he explicitly proposed specific areas of reform as when he associated the reform of the Church with the need to remove excessive canonical legislation on excommunication and other issues which because of variations in time, place, or local custom could not be observed. Such legislation, he argued, excessively burdened the laity and caused them to disrespect ecclesiastical legislation in general. At other times, his reform views were implied in his specific critiques, for all criticism carries within itself an implied call to reform. Essentially that call would involve a return to the classical tradition of canon law with its emphasis upon the composite nature of canon law in terms of divine, natural, and human law, as well as the hierarchical order that should prevail among these laws. Canon lawyers should also recognize that all law and obligation are somehow rooted in the divine law. From his critique of canon lawyers, one can easily deduce that d'Ailly would also recommend that, given the subordinate nature of their discipline to that of theology, canonists should have a more balanced evaluation of their discipline and its methodology.

A more comprehensive and aggressive call for reform in the realm of canon law at Paris would be taken up by d'Ailly's student, Jean Gerson. While Gerson differed from d'Ailly in calling for theological reform at Paris, they were of like mind on the need for reform in the realm of canon law. On several occasions Gerson addressed the canon law faculty at Paris on the topic and composed several treatises on the subject. The content and spirit of his critique and call for reform reflected very much that of his mentor, d'Ailly.

In addition to the reformative dimensions of d'Ailly's thought on canon law and canon lawyers, there are also some traces of the apostolic and evangelical elements which were evident in his reflections on theologians and especially in relationship to the episcopacy. While he does not call upon canonists to adopt the apostolic ideal in either their personal or professional lives, he does call upon them to be attentive to the role of the Gospel in their discipline and its practice. This role is especially seen in the prominence given to divine law within the composite of laws that make up canon law. As seen earlier, divine law in d'Ailly's theory of law is essentially the basic principles of Christian belief, action and obligation as reflected in the Gospel. As was the case with many medieval thinkers, d'Ailly conceived the Gospel primarily in terms of law, transforming and transcending Old Testament law, but nonetheless a form of law.

Also to be remembered is d'Ailly's strong criticism of canonists who ignored the evangelical roots of their discipline and thought that reform could be achieved merely by passing new legislation or by repromulgating older laws. On this point, d'Ailly was inspired by the passage in the Gospels of Matthew and Mark where Christ chastises the Pharisees whose excessive emphasis on the observance of human precepts had the effect of turning those precepts into divine law thereby heightening their degree of obligation and excessively burdening the consciences of the laity. As d'Ailly saw it, true and lasting reform, while requiring some form of legislative formulation, rests with a faithful return to the spirit of the Gospel.

The call for a return to the spirit of the Gospel permeates in varying degrees d'Ailly's thought on the status, office, and authority of bishops, theologians, and canon lawyers, especially when viewed in their apocalyptic, reformative, and apostolic contexts. In a true sense, this call can be regarded as a leitmotif in much of d'Ailly's thought, a leitmotif which flowed, in turn, from a genuinely and deeply held inner conviction. In his understanding of this call, d'Ailly was certainly influenced by lay reform movements such as the Modern Devotion, as well as by monastic and mendicant movements, especially the Franciscans, but he always sought to adapt that call to the personal and professional lives of bishops, theologians, and canon lawyers to the degree appropriate and realistically attainable within each group.

BIBLIOGRAPHY

Primary Sources: Pierre D'Ailly

Manuscripts

Brussels, Bibliothèque Royale, 1695, 1696, 1697.
Cambrai, Bibliothèque Municipale, 166, 167, 268, 514, 531, 574, 577, 926, 927, 928, 929, 940, 954.
Cambridge, Emmanuel College, 9.
Paris, Bibliothèque Nationale, Lat. 2692, 3122, 3123, 3124, 3613, 3769, 7371, 14579, 15107.
Paris, Bibliothèque de l'Arsenal, 517, 520, 521.
Paris, Bibliothèque Mazarine, 492, 615, 934, 935, 936, 940, 945, 951, 960, 969, 992, 1648, 1683.
Rome, Biblioteca Apostolica Vaticana, Vat. Lat. 4117, 4130, 4136, 4137, 4152, 4192; Reg. Lat. 689B, Ottob. Lat. 3074.

Printed

Collected Works

Petrus de Ailliaco: Tractatus et sermones. Strassburg: Jordanus de Quedlinburg, 1490; repr. Frankfurt: Minerva, 1971.
Joannis Gersonii opera omnia, ed. L. Dupin, 4 vols. Antwerp: P. de Hondt, 1706. Vols. 1 and 2 contain works of d'Ailly.
Tschackert, Paul. *Peter von Ailli*. Gotha: Perthes, 1877. Appendix, 1–53. Most of the collected works are partial editions.

Individual Works

Treatises: Academic and Ecclesiastical

———. *Ad laudem Christi*, ed. Heinrich Finke, *ACC*, 4 vols. Münster: Regensbergschen Buchhandlung, 1896–1928, 4:730–733.
———. *Contra Johannem de Montesono*, ed. Charles du Plessis d'Argentré in his *Collectio judiciorum de novis erroribus*. 3 vols. Paris: Lambert Coffin, 1724–1736; repr. Paris, 1963, 1:75–129.
———. *De anima*, ed. Olaf Pluta, *Die Philosophische Psychologie des Peter von Ailly*, Bochumer Studien zur Philosophie, 6. Amsterdam: B.R. Grüner, 1987, pp. 1–107.
———. *De falsis prophetis, I*, ed. Dupin, 1:489–510.

———. *De falsis prophetis, II*, ed. Dupin, 1:511–603.
———. *De materia concilii generalis*, ed. Francis Oakley in his *The Political Thought of Pierre d'Ailly: The Voluntarist Tradition.* New Haven: Yale University Press, 1964, 252–342.
———. *De persecutionibus ecclesiae*, ed. Noël Valois in 'Un ouvrage inédit de Pierre d'Ailly: Le De Persecutionibus Ecclesiae,' *BEC*, 55 (1904), 557–574.
———. *De potestate ecclesiastica*, ed. Dupin, 2:925–960.
———. *De reformatione*, ed. Jürgen Miethke and Lorenz Weinrich, *Quellen zur Kirchenreform im Zeitalter der grossen Konzilien des 15 Jahrhunderts.* 2 vols. Darmstadt: Wissenschaftliche Buchgesellschaft, 1995–2002, 1:338–377.
———. *Epistola ad novos Hebraeos*, ed. Louis Salembier in his 'Une page inédite de l'histoire de la Vulgate,' *RSE*, 60 (1889), 23–28, 97–108, 257–267, 369–382.
———. *Errores sectae hominum intelligentiae.* ed. Etienne Baluze, *Miscellanea novo ordine digesta.* 4 vols. Lucca: Junctinius, 1761–1764, 2:288–293.
———. *Invectiva Ezechielis contra pseudopastores.* ed. Tschackert, 12–15.
———. *Pax Dei*, ed. Salembier, 'Les oeuvres françaises du Cardinal Pierre d'Ailly,' *RL*, 7 (1906–1907), 866–882.
———. *Pro emendatione Ecclesiae*, ed. Dupin 2:917–924.
———. *Propositio facta in consistoria*, ed. Dupin, 1:702–709.
———. *Propositio prima coram papam facta*, ed. Dupin, 1:697–702.
———. *Propositiones utiles*, ed. Edmund Martène and Ursin Durand, *Veterum scriptorium et monumentorum ... amplissima collectio*, 9 vols. Paris: Delaulne, 7:909–911.
———. *Quaenam doctrina haec nova*, ed. Dupin 1:610–617.
———. *Quaestiones super libros sententiarum cum quibusdam in fine adjunctis.* Strassburg, 1490, repr. Frankfurt: Minerva, 1968.
———. *Radix omnium malorum est cupiditas*, ed. Alan E. Bernstein, *Pierre d'Ailly and the Blanchard Affair: University and Chancellor at the Beginning of the Great Schism*, Studies in Medieval and Reformation Thought, 24. Leiden: E.J. Brill, 1978, 197–236.
———. *Recommendatio Sacrae Scripturae*, ed. Dupin 1:603–610.
———. *Super omnia vincit veritas*, ed. Alan E. Bernstein, *Pierre d'Ailly and the Blanchard Affair*, 237–298.
———. *Super de Consolatione Philosophiae Boethii, Qu. 1*, ed. Marguerite Chappuis, *Le traité de Pierre d'Ailly sur la Consolation de Boèce, Qu. 1*, Bochumer Studien zur Philosophie, 20. Amsterdam: B.R. Grüner, 1993.
———. *Utrum indoctus in jure divino*, ed. Dupin, 1:646–662.
———. *Utrum Petri Ecclesia lege reguletur*, ed. Dupin, 1:662–672.
———. *Utrum Petri Ecclesia rege gubernetur*, ed. Dupin, 1:672–693.

Sermons

———. *Collatio pro apotheosi Petri de Luxemburgo, I*, ed. C.E. Bulaeus, *Historia Universitatis Parisiensis.* 6 vols. Paris: 1665–1673, repr. Leiden: E.J. Brill, 1966, 4:651–662.
———. *Collatio pro apotheosi Petri de Luxemburgo, II*, ed. C.E. Bulaeus, *Historia*

Universitatis Parisiensis, 4:663–670.
———. *Homelia facta in synodo cameracensi*, ed. *Tractatus et sermones*.
———. *Sermo de adventu Domini, III*, ed. *Tractatus et sermones*.
———. *Sermo de Nativitate, I*, ed. *Tractatus et sermones*.
———. *Sermo de Sancto Bernardo*, ed. Tschackert, 21–23.
———. *Sermo de Sancto Dominico*, ed. *Tractatus et sermones*.
———. *Sermo de Sancto Francisco*, ed. *Tractatus et sermones*.
———. *Sermo de Sancto Ludovico Tolosano*, ed. *Tractatus et sermones*.
———. *Sermo facta Constantiae in medio Quadragesimae*, ed. *Tractatus et sermones*.
———. *Sermo in die Pentecostes, I*, ed. *Tractatus et sermones*.
———. *Sermo in die Pentecostes, II*, ed. *Tractatus et sermones*
———. *Sermo in Dominica Septuagesima*, ed. *Tractatus et sermones*.
———. *Sermo in synodo ambianis*, ed. Tschackert, 3–4.
———. *Sermo in synodo cameracensi, I*, ed. *Tractatus et sermones*.
———. *Sermo in synodo cameracensi, II*, ed. *Tractatus et sermones*.
———. *Sermo in synodo in ecclesia Parisiensi*, ed. Tschackert, 5–6.

Letters

———. *Epistola I ad Joannem XXIII*, ed. Dupin, 2:876–882.
———. *Epistola II ad Joannem XXIII*, ed. Dupin, 2:882–883.

Primary Sources: Other Authors

Alberigo, Giuseppe et al. *Conciliorum oecumenicorum decreta*. 3rd ed. Bologna: Istituto per le Scienze Religiose, 1973.
Altensteig, Joannes and Tytz, Joannes, eds. *Lexicon theologicum*. Cologne, 1619.
Aquinas, Thomas. *Summa theologiae*, ed. Pietro Caramello, 3 vols. Rome: Marietti Editori, 1952–1956.
Aureoli, Pierre. *Compendium Bibliorum*, ed. Philibert Seeboeck. 4 vols. Quaracchi: Collegium Sancti Bonaventuri, 1896.
———. *Scriptum super primum sententiarum*, ed. E.M. Buytaert. 2 vols. St. Bonaventure, N.Y.: Franciscan Institute, 1952–1956.
Baluze, Etienne. *Miscellanea novo ordine digesta*. 4 vols. Lucca: Junctinius, 1761–1764.
Bernard of Clairvaux. *Sancti Bernardi opera*, ed. Jean Leclercq et al., 8 vols. Rome: Editiones Cistercienses, 1957–1977.
Biblia Sacra iuxta vulgatam versionem. 3rd. ed. Ed. Robert Weber. Stuttgart: Deutsche Bibelgesellschaft, 1983.
Boren, P.C. 'Les plus anciens statuts du diocese de Cambrai,' *RDC*, 3 (1953), 1–32, 131–172, 377–415, 4 (1954), 131–158.
Bulaeus, C.E. *Historia Universitatis Parisiensis*. 6 vols. Paris: 1665–1673, repr. Leiden: E.J. Brill, 1966.
Bullarium Franciscanum sive Romanorum Pontificum constitutiones, epistolae, diplomata tribus ordinibus Minorum concessa. 7 vols. Vols. 1–4, ed. Giovanni Sbaralia. Rome: 1759–1768; Vols. 5–7, ed. Conrad Eubel. Rome: 1898–1904.

Chartularium Universitatis Parisiensis, ed. H. Denifle and E. Chatelain. 4 vols. Paris: Delalain Frères, 1889–1897, repr. Brussels: Culture et Civilisation, 1964.
Concilia Germaniae, ed. J.F. Schannat and J. Hartzheim, 2nd ed. 11 vols. Cologne, 1759–1790, repr. Aalen: Scientia Verlag, 1970.
Corpus Iuris Canonici, ed. Aemilius Friedberg. 2 vols. Leipzig: B. Tauchnitz, 1879, repr. Graz: Akademische Druck und Verlagsanstalt, 1959.
Corpus Iuris Civilis, ed. Paul Krueger and Rudolph Schoell. 3 vols. 11th ed. Zürich: Weidmann, 1954.
D'Argentré, Charles du Plessis, ed. *Collectio judiciorum de novis erroribus*. 3 vols. Paris: Lambert Coffin, 1724–1736, repr. Brussels: Culture et Civilisation, 1963.
De Aldama, Antonio, ed. *Repertorium pseudochrysostomicum*. Paris: CNRS, 1965.
Finke, Heinrich, ed. *Acta Concilii Constanciensis*. 4 vols. Münster: Regensbergische Buchhandlung, 1896–1928.
Gerson, Jean. *Oeuvres completes*, ed Palémon Glorieux, 10 vols. Paris: Desclée, 1960–1973.
———. *Opera omnia*, ed. L. Dupin, 4 vols. Antwerp: P. de Hondt, 1706.
Glossa Ordinaria, ed. A. Rusch, *Biblia Latina cum Glossa Ordinaria*. 4 Vols. Strasbourg, 1480; repr. Turnhout: Brepols, 1992.
Goldast, Melchior, ed. *Monarchia Sancti Romani Imperii*. 3 vols. Hanover: 1611–1614, repr. Graz: Akademische Druck und Verlagsanstalt, 1960.
Gregory of Rimini. *Lectura super primum et secundum Sententiarum*, ed. A. Damasus Trapp and Vinicio Marcolino. 7 vols. Berlin: Walter de Gruyter, 1981–1987.
Guido of Baysio, *Rosarium seu in decretorum volumen commentaria*, ed. Niccolò Soranzo, et al. Venice, 1577.
Hardt, Herman van der, ed. *Magnum oecumenicum Constantiense Concilium*. 6 vols. Frankfurt: Gensius, 1692–1700.
Hefele-Leclercq. *Histoire des conciles d'après les documents origineaux*. 11 vols. Paris: Letouzey, 1907–1952.
Hildegard of Bingen. *Liber divinorum operum*, ed. A. Derolez and P. Dronke, *Corpus Christianorum: Continuatio Medievalis*, 92. Turnhout: Brepols, 1996.
———. *Epistolae*, ed. L. Van Acker and M. Klaes-Hachmoller, *Corpus Christianorum: Continuatio Medievalis*, 91, 91A, 91B. Turnhout: Brepols, 1991.
Hostiensis, *Summa aurea*, ed. Niccolò Soranzo. Venice: Melchior Sessa, 1574, repr. Turin: Bottega d'Erasmo, 1963.
John of Paris. *De potestate regia et papali*, ed. F. Bleinstein in his *Johannes Quidort von Paris: Uber königliche und päpstliche Gewalt*. Stuttgart: Ernst Klett Verlag, 1969, 69–211.
Mansi, J.D. *Sacrorum conciliorum nova et amplissima collectio*. 31 vols. Florence-Venice, 1759–1798, repr. Graz: Akademische Druck-und Verlagsanstalt, 1960.
Martène Edmund and Durand, Ursin, eds. *Thesaurus novus anecdotorum*. 5 vols. Paris: Delaulne, 1717, repr. Farnborough: Gregg, 1968–1969.
———. *Veterum scriptorum et monumentorum ... amplissima collectio*. 9 vols. Paris: Montalant, 1724–1733.

Mercati, Angelo, ed. *Raccolta di concordati su materie ecclesiastiche tra la Santa Sede e le autoritá civili*. 2 vols. Vatican City: Vatican Press, 1954.

Miethke, Jürgen and Lorenz Weinrich, eds., *Quellen zur Kirchenreform im Zeitalter der Grossen Konzilien des 15 Jahrhunderts*. 2 vols. Darmstadt: Wissenschaftliche Buchgesellschaft, 1995–2002.

Nicholas of Lyra. *Postilla litteralis super totam Bibliam*, ed. J Mentelin, 4 vols. Strasbourg, 1492, repr. Frankfurt: Minerva, 1971.

———. *Dialogus*, ed. Melchior Goldast, *Monarchia Sancti Romani Imperii*. 3 vols. Frankfurt, 1614, repr. Graz: Akademische Druck und Verlagsanstalt, 1960, 2:392–957.

Pseudo Dionysius. *The Complete Works*, trans. Colm Luibheid. Paramus: Paulist Press, 1987.

Tanner, Norman, ed. *Decrees of the Ecumenical Councils*. 2 vols. Washington, D.C.: Sheed and Ward and Georgetown University Presses, 1990.

William of Ockham, *Scriptum in Librum Primum Sententiarum, Ordinatio*, ed. Gedeon Gál. Vol. 1 of his *Opera theologica*, 10 vols. St. Bonaventure, N.Y.: Franciscan Institute, 1967–1986.

Secondary Sources

Adam, Paul. *La vie paroissiale en France au xive siècle*. Paris: Sirey, 1964.

Adams, Marilyn McCord. 'Universals in the Early Fourteenth Century,' in *The Cambridge History of Later Medieval Philosophy*, ed. Norman Kretzman et al., 411–439.

———. *William of Ockham*. 2 vols. Notre Dame: University of Notre Dame, 1987.

Alberigo, Giuseppe. *Cardinalato e collegialitá: Studi sull'ecclesiologia tra l'xi e il xiv secolo*. Florence: Vallecchi Editore, 1969.

Alphandéry, P. 'Prophètes et ministère prophétique dans le Moyen Age latin,' *RHPR*, 12 (1932), 334–359.

Arendt, Paul. *Die Predigten des Konstanzer Konzils: Ein Beitrag zur Predigt-und Kirchengeschichte des ausgehenden Mittelalters*. Freiburg: Herder, 1933.

Arnold, Franz. 'Die rechtslehre des Magisters Gratianus,' *SGrat.*, 1 (1953), 451–482.

Aston, T.H. et al. 'The Medieval Alumni of the University of Cambridge,' *PP*, 86 (1980), 9–86.

Astrik, Gabriel. 'The Conflict between the Chancellor and the University Masters and Students at Paris during the Middle Ages,' in *Die Auseinandersetzungen an der Pariser Universität im XIII Jahrhundert*, ed. A. Zimmermann, Miscellanea Mediaevalia, 10. Berlin: De Gruyter, 1976, 106–154.

Asztalos, Monica. 'The Faculty of Theology,' in *Universities in the Middle Ages*, ed. H. de Ritter-Symoens, 409–441. Vol 1 of *A History of the University in Europe*, ed. Walter Rüegg. Cambridge: Cambridge University Press, 1992.

Bakker, Paul J.J.M., ed. *Chemins de la pensée médiévale: Etudes offertes à Zénon Kaluza*. Turnhout: Brepols, 2002.

Baldwin, John W. 'Critics of the Legal Profession: Peter the Chanter and his Circle,' in *Proceedings of the Second International Congress of Medieval Canon Law*, ed. Stephan Kuttner and J. Joseph Ryan. Vatican City: Vatican Press, 1965, 249–259.

———. *Masters, Princes, and Merchants: The Social Views of Peter the Chanter and His Circle*. 2 vols. Princeton: Princeton University Press, 1970.

Bannach, Klaus. *Die Lehre von der doppelten Macht Gottes bei Wilhelm von Ockham*. Wiesbaden: Franz Steiner Verlag, 1975.

Barbaglio, Giuseppe. *Fede acquista e fede infusa secondo Duns Scoto, Occam, e Biel*. Brescia: Morcelliana, 1968.

Bardy, G. 'Saint Gregoire VII et la réforme canonial au xie siècle,' *SGreg*, 1 (1947), 47–64.

Barnes, Jonathan. *The Cambridge Companion to Aristotle*. Cambridge: Cambridge University Press, 1995.

Baudry, Léon. *Lexique philosophique de Guillaume d'Ockham*. Paris: Lethielleux, 1958.

Bäumer, Remigius, ed. *Von Konstanz nach Trient*. Munich: Ferdinand Schöningh, 1972.

Becquet, Jean. *Vie canonical en France aux xe–xiie siècles*. London: Ashgate Variorum, 1985.

Bellitto, Christopher M. 'The Early Development of Pierre d'Ailly's Conciliarism,' *CHR*, 83 (1997), 217–232.

———. *Nicolas of Clamanges: Spirituality, Personal Reform, and Pastoral Renewal on the Eve of the Reformations*. Washington, D.C.: The Catholic University of America Press, 2001.

Benson, Robert. 'Plenitudo Potestatis: Evolution of a Formula from Gregory IV to Gratian,' *SGreg*, 14 (1967), 193–217.

Berman, Harold J. *Law and Revolution: The Formation of the Western Legal Tradition*. Cambridge, Mass.: Harvard University Press, 1983.

Bernstein, Alan E. *Pierre d'Ailly and the Blanchard Affair: University and Chancellor of Paris at the Beginning of the Great Schism*. Studies in Medieval and Reformation Thought, 24. Leiden: E.J. Brill, 1978.

Biard, Joël. 'Présence et représentation chez Pierre d'Ailly: Quelques problèmes de théorie de la connaissance au xive siècle,' *Dialogue*, 31 (1992), 459–474.

Boler, John F. 'Intuitive and Abstract Cognition,' in *The Cambridge History of Late Medieval Philosophy*, ed. Norman Kretzmann et al., Cambridge: Cambridge University Press, 1982, 460–478.

Bourke, M.M. 'Reflection on Church Order in the New Testament,' *CBQ*, 30 (1968), 493–511.

Brady, Ignatius. 'The Development of the Doctrine on the Immaculate Conception in the Fourteenth Century after Aureoli,' *FS*, 15 (1955), 175–202.

Brandmüller, Walter. *Das Konzil von Konstanz*. 2 vols. Paderborn: Ferdinand Schöningh, 1991–1997.

———. *Papst und Konzil im Grossen Schisma (1378–1431): Studien und Quellen*. Paderborn: Ferdinand Schöningh, 1990.

Brown, D. Catherine. *Pastor and Laity in the Theology of Jean Gerson*. Cambridge: Cambridge University Press, 1987.

Brown, Raymond. *Priest and Bishop*. Paramus: Paulist Press, 1970.

——. et al., eds. *Peter in the New Testament*. Minneapolis: Augsburg Publishing House, 1973.
Brown, Stephen. 'Philosophy and Theology: Western Europe: Late Middle Ages,' *DMA*, 9:608–615.
——. 'Peter of Candia's Hundred Year History of the Theologian's Role,' *MPT*, 1 (1991), 156–190.
Brundage, James A. 'The Rise of the Professional Jurist in the Thirteenth Century,' *Syracuse Journal of International Law and Commerce*, 20 (1994), 185–190.
——. 'St. Bernard and the Jurists,' in *The Second Crusade and the Cistercians*, ed. Michael Gervers. New York: St. Martin's Press, 1992, 25–33.
——. 'Legal Aid for the Poor and the Professionalization of Law in the Middle Ages,' *Journal of Legal History*, 9 (1988), 169–179.
Burr, David. 'Mendicants' Reading of the Apocalypse,' in *The Apocalypse in the Middle Ages*, ed. Richard K. Emmerson and Bernard McGinn. Ithaca: Cornell University Press, 1992, 89–102.
——. *Olivi's Peaceable Kingdom: A Reading of the Apocalypse Commentary*. Philadelphia: University of Pennsylvania Press, 1993.
——. *The Spiritual Franciscans: From Protest to Persecution in the Century After Saint Francis*. University Park: Penn State University Press, 2001.
Burrow, J.A. *The Ages of Man: A Study in Medieval Writing and Thought*. Oxford: Clarendon Press, 1986.
Campenhausen, Hans von. *Ecclesial Authority and Spiritual Power in the Church of the First Three Centuries*. Stanford: Stanford University Press, 1969.
Catto, J.I., ed. *The Early Oxford Schools*. Vol 1 of *The History of the University of Oxford*. Oxford: Oxford University Press, 1984.
——and Evans, T.A.R, eds. *Late Medieval Oxford*. Vol 2 of *The History of the University of Oxford*. Oxford: Oxford University Press, 1992.
Cessario, Romanus. 'Towards Understanding Aquinas' Theological Method: The Early Twelfth Century Experience,' in *Studies in Thomistic Theology*, ed. Paul Lockey. Houston: University of St. Thomas Press, 1995, 17–89.
Chappuis, Marguerite et al. 'Die philosophischen Schriften des Peter von Ailly: Authentizität und Chronologie,' *FZPT*, 33 (1986), 593–615.
Châtillon, Jean. 'La Bible dans les écoles du xiie siècle,' in *Le Moyen Age et la Bible*, ed. Pierre Riché and Guy Lobrichon. Paris: Beauchesne, 1984, 163–197.
——. *Le movement canonical au moyen âge: Reform de l'Eglise, spiritualité et culture*. Turnhout: Brepols, 1992.
Chenu, M.D. *La théologie au douzième siècle*. Paris: J. Vrin, 1957.
——. *La théologie comme science au xiiie siècle*. 3rd. ed. Paris: J. Vrin, 1957.
——. 'Officium: théologiens et canonists,' in *Etudes d'histoire du droit canonique dediées à Gabriel Le Bras*. 2 vols. Paris: Sirey, 1965, 2:835–839.
——. *Nature, Man, and Society in the Twelfth Century*. Chicago: University of Chicago Press, 1968.
——. 'Monks, Canons, and Laymen in Search of the Apostolic Life,' in his *Nature, Man, and Society in the Twelfth Century*, 202–238.
——. 'The Evangelical Awakening,' in his *Nature, Man, and Society in the Twelfth Century*, 239–269.

———. 'The Masters of the Theological Science,' in his *Nature, Man, and Society in the Twelfth Century*, 270–309.
Clark, David W. 'Voluntarism and Rationalism in the Ethics of Ockham,' *FS*, 31 (1971), 72–87.
———. 'William of Ockham on Right Reason,' *Speculum*, 48 (1973), 13–36.
Cobban, A.B. *The Medieval Universities: Their Development and Organization*. London: Methuen, 1975.
———. *The Medieval English Universities: Oxford and Cambridge to c. 1500*. Berkeley: University of California Press, 1988.
Colson, Jean. *L'évêque dans les communautés primitives*. Paris: Editions du Cerf, 1951.
———. *Les functions ecclésiales aux deux premiers siècles*. Paris: Desclée de Brouwer, 1956.
———. *L'épiscopat catholique: collegialité et primauté dans les trois premiers siècles de l'Eglise*. Paris: Editions du Cerf, 1963.
———. *Ministre de Jésus-Christ ou le sacerdoce de l'Evangile*. Paris: Beauchesne, 1965.
Congar, Yves. 'Aspects ecclésiologiques de la querelle entre mendiants et séculiers dans la seconde moitié du xiiie siècle et le début du xive siècle,' *AHDL*, 28 (1961), 35–151.
———. 'Quelques expressions traditionnelles du service chrétien, in *L'épiscopat et l'Eglise universelle*,' ed. Yves Congar and B.D. Dupuy. Paris: Editions du Cerf, 1962, 101–132.
———, ed. *La collegialité épiscopale: histoire et théologie*. Paris: Editions du Cerf, 1965.
———. 'Notes sur le destin de l'idée de collegialité épiscopale en occident au moyen âge (viie–xvie siècles),' in *La collegialité épiscopale: histoire et théologie*, ed. Yves Congar. Paris: Editions du Cerf, 1965, 99–129.
———. *A History of Theology*. New York: Doubleday, 1968.
———. *L'Ecclesiologie du haut moyen âge*. Paris: Editions du Cerf, 1968.
———. 'Pour une histoire sémantique du terme "magisterium",' *RSPT*, 60 (1976), 85–98.
———. 'Brief historique des formes du "magistère" et de ses relations avec les docteurs,' *RSPT*, 60 (1976), 99–112.
———. 'Theologians and the Magisterium in the West: From the Gregorian Reform to the Council of Trent,' *CS*, 17 (1978), 210–224.
Constable, Giles. 'The Orders of Medieval Society,' in his *Three Studies in Medieval Religious and Social Thought*. Cambridge: Cambridge University Press, 1995, 249–341.
———. *The Reformation of the Twelfth Century*. Cambridge: Cambridge University Press, 1996.
Copleston, Frederick. *A History of Philosophy*. 3 vols. Westminster: Newman Press, 1960–1963.
Courtenay, William J. *Capacity and Volition: A History of the Distinction of Absolute and Ordained Power*. Bergamo: Lubrina, 1990.
———. 'Covenant and Causality in Pierre d'Ailly,' *Speculum*, 46 (1971), 94–119.
———. 'Programs of Study and Genres of Scholastic Theological Production in the Fourteenth Century,' in *Manuels, programmes de cours et techniques*

d'enseignement dans les universités médiévales, ed. Jacqueline Hamesse, 1994, 325–350.

———. 'The Reception of Ockham's Thought at the University of Paris,' in *Preuve et raisons à l'Université de Paris*, ed. Zénon Kaluza and Paul Vignaux, 43–64.

Craemer-Ruegenberg, Ingrid and Speer, Andreas, eds. *Scientia und Ars im Hoch- und Spätmittelalter*. 2 vols. Miscellanea medievalia, 22. Berlin: Walter de Gruyter, 1994.

Crouzel, Henri. 'Le ministère dans l'Eglise: temoignages de l'Eglise ancienne,' *NRT*, 104 (1982), 738–748.

Davies, Brian. *The Thought of Thomas Aquinas*. Oxford: Clarendon Press, 1992.

Davy, M.M. *Les sermons universitaires parisiens de 1230–1231*. Paris: J. Vrin, 1931.

DeGandillac, Maurice. 'De l'usage et de la valeur des arguments probables dans les Questiones du Cardinal Pierre d'Ailly sur le Livre des Sentences,' *AHDL*, 8 (1932–1933), 43–91.

DeGhellinck, Joseph. *Le movement théologique du xiie siècle*. Bruges: Culture et Civilisation, 1948.

DeLagarde, George. *Ockham: La morale et le droit*. Vol. 6 of his *La naissance de l'esprit laïque au decline du moyen âge*. Paris: Presses Universitaires, 1946.

Delaruelle, E. et al., eds. *L'Eglise au temps du Grand Schisme et de la crise conciliare*. 2 vols. Vol. 14 of *Histoire de l'Eglise*, ed. J.B. Duroselle and Eugène Jarry. Paris: Bloud and Gay, 1962.

De Lubac, Henri. *Corpus Mysticum*. Paris: Aubier, 1949.

———. *Exégèse médévale*. 4 vols. Paris: Aubier, 1959–1963.

De Luca, Luigi. 'La nozione della legge nel Decreto di Graziano: Legalitá o assolutismo?' *SGrat.* 11 (1967), 403–430.

Deman, Thomas. 'Notes de lexicographie philosophique médiévale,' *RSPT*, 22 (1930), 260–290.

Denifle, H. *Die Entstehung der Universitäten des Mittelalters bis 1400*. Berlin: Weidmann, 1885.

———. 'Quel libre servait de base à l'enseignement des maîtres en théologie?' *RT*, 2 (1894), 149–161.

Dereine, Charles. 'Vie commune, régle de saint Augustin et chanoines reguliers au xie siécle,' *RHE*, 41 (1947), 365–406.

DeRidder-Symoens, H., ed. *Universities in the Middle Ages*. Vol. 1 of *A History of the University in Europe*, ed. Walter Rüegg. Cambridge: Cambridge University Press, 1992.

Desharnan, R.P. 'Reassessing Nominalism: A Note on Pierre d'Ailly,' *FS*, 34 (1974), 296–305.

De Silva Tarouca, A. 'L'idée d'ordre dans la philosophie de saint Thomas d'Aquin,' *RNP*, 40 (1937), 341–384.

DeVooght, Paul. *Les sources de la doctrine chrétienne*. Bruges: Desclée de Brouwer, 1954.

Dickenson, J.C. *An Ecclesiastical History of England: The Later Middle Ages*. London: Adam & Charles Black, 1979.

D'Irsay, Stephan. *Histoire des universities françaises et étrangers*. 2 vols. Paris: Picard, 1933–1935.

Dix, Gregory. 'The Ministry in the Early Church,' in *The Apostolic Ministry: Essays on the History and Doctrine of the Episcopacy*, ed. Kenneth E. Kirk. London: Hodder and Stoughton, 1946, 185–303.

Doncoeur, Paul. 'La condemnation de Jean de Monzón par Pierre d'Orgemont, évêque de Paris, le 23 août 1387,' *RQH*, 81 (1907), 176–187.

Dondaine, H.F. *Le corpus dionysien de l'Université de Paris au xiiie siècle*. Rome: Edizione di storia e letteratura, 1953.

Donneaud, Henri. 'Le sens du mot "theologia" chez Bonaventure,' *RT*, 102 (2002), 271–295.

D'Onofrio, Giulio, ed. *Storia della teologia nel medioevo*. 3 vols. Casale Monferrato: Edizioni Piemme, 1996.

Douie, Decima. *The Conflict Between the Seculars and Mendicants at the University of Paris in the Thirteenth Century*. London: Blackfriars, 1954

Dufeil, Michel. *Guillaume de Saint Amour et la polémique universitaire parisienne, 1250–1259*. Paris: Picard, 1972.

Duffy, Eamon. *The Stripping of the Altars: Traditional Religion in England, c. 1400–1580*. New Haven: Yale University Press, 1992.

Emmerson, Richard K. and McGinn, Bernard, eds. *The Apocalypse in the Middle Ages*. Ithaca: Cornell University Press, 1992.

English, Edward D., ed. *Reading and Wisdom:The Doctrina Christiana of Augustine in the Middle Ages*. Notre Dame: University of Notre Dame Press, 1995.

Evans, G.R. *Old Arts and New Theology*. Oxford: Clarendon Press, 1980.

———. *Law and Theology in the Middle Ages*. London: Routledge, 2002.

Farrer, A.M. 'The Ministry in the New Testament,' in *The Apostolic Ministry: Essays on the History and Doctrine of the Episcopacy*, ed. Kenneth E. Kirk. London: Hodder and Stoughton, 1946, 113–182.

Fasolt, Constantin. 'Voluntarism and Conciliarism in the Work of Francis Oakley,' *History of Political Thought*, 22 (2001), 41–52.

Favier, Jean. *Les finances pontificales à l'époque du Grand Schisme d'Occident*. Paris: E. de Boccard, 1966.

Feld, H. 'Papst und Apostel in Auseinandersetzung um die rechte Lehre: Die theologische Bedeutung von Gal 2:11–14,' in *Grund und Grenzen des Dogmas*, ed. H. Feld et al. Freiburg: Herder, 1973, 9–26.

Ferruolo, Stephen C. *The Origins of the University: The Schools of Paris and their Critics, 1100–1225*. Stanford: Stanford University Press, 1985.

Fourier de Bacourt, E. *Vie de Bx Pierre de Luxembourg*. Paris: Berche and Tralin, 1882.

Fournier, Marcel. *Les statuts et privilèges des universités françaises depuis leur foundation jusqu'en 1789*. 4 vols. Paris: LaRose et Forcel Editeurs, 1890–1894.

Fournier, Paul and LeBras, Gabriel. *Histoire des collections canoniques en occident depuis les fausses decretals jusqu'au Décret de Gratien*. 2 vols. Paris, 1931–1932, repr. Aalen: Scientia Verlag, 1972.

François, H. *La vie du Bx Pierre de Luxembourg*. Nancy, 1927.

Frassetto, Michael, ed. *Medieval Purity and Piety: Essays on Medieval Clerical Celibacy and Religious Reform*. New York: Garland, 1998.

Fredriksen, Paula. 'Tyconius and Augustine on the Apocalypse,' in *The Apocalypse in the Middle Ages*, ed. Richard K. Emmersen and Bernard McGinn, 20–37.

Fried, Johannes. *Die Entstehung des Juristenstandes im 12 Jahrhundert*, Forschungen zur Neueren Privatsrechtsgeschichte, 21. Cologne: Böhlau, 1974.

Froehlich, Karlfried. 'Fallibility instead of Infallibility? A Brief History of the Interpretation of Galatians 2:11–14,' in *Teaching Authority and Infallibility in the Church*, ed., Paul C. Empie et al. Minneapolis: Augsburg Press, 1978, 259–269

Fuchs, Oswald. *The Psychology of Habit According to William of Ockham*. St. Bonaventure, N.Y.: The Franciscan Institute, 1952.

Gabriel, Astrik. 'The Ideal Master of the Medieval University,' *CHR*, 60 (1974), 1–40.

Gagnér, Stan. *Studien zur Ideengeschichte des Gesetzgebung*, Studia Iuridica Upsaliensia, 1. Stockholm: Almquist and Wiksell, 1960.

Gallagher, Clarence. *Canon Law and the Christian Community: The Role of Law in the Church According to the Summa Aurea of Cardinal Hostiensis*. Rome: Gregorian University Press, 1978.

García y García, Antonio 'The Faculties of Law,' in *Universities in the Middle Ages*, ed. H. de Ridder-Symoens, 388–408.

Gardeil, A. 'La certitude probable,' *RSPT*, 5 (1911), 237–266, 441–445.

Gaudemet, Jean. 'La doctrine des sources du droit dans le Décret de Gratien,' *RDC*, 1 (1951), 5–31.

Gilson, Etienne. *The History of Christian Philosophy in the Middle Ages*. New York: Random House, 1955.

Glorieux, Palémon. *Repertoire des maîtres en théologie de Paris aux xiiie siècle*. 2 vols. Paris: J. Vrin, 1933–1934.

——. 'Pierre d'Ailly, Jean XXIII, et Thierry de Nieheim,' *RTAM*, 31 (1964), 100–121.

——. 'L'oeuvre littéraire de Pierre d'Ailly: Remarques et precisions,' *MSR*, 22 (1965), 61–78

——. *Aux origins de la Sorbonne*. 2 vols. Paris: J. Vrin, 1966.

——. 'Pierre d'Ailly et Saint Thomas,' in *Literature et religion: Mélanges offerts à Joseph Coppin*. Lille: Facultés Catholiques, 1966, 45–54.

——. 'L'enseignement au moyen âge: Techniques et methods en usage à la faculté de théologie de Paris au xiiie siècle,' *AHDL*, 35 (1968), 65–186.

——. *La faculté des arts et ses maîtres au xiiie siècle*. Paris: J. Vrin, 1971.

——. 'Les années d'études de Pierre d'Ailly,' *RTAM*, 44 (1977), 127–149.

Gorochov, Nathalie. *Le Collège de Navarre de sa foundation (1305) au début du xve siècle (1418)*. Paris: Honoré Champion, 1997.

Grabmann, Martin. *Die Geschichte der scholastischen Methode*. 2 vols. Freiburg in Breisgau: Herder, 1909–1911.

——. 'Hilfsmittel des Thomas-studiums aus alter Zeit: Abbreviationes, Concordantiae, Tabulae,' *Mittelalterliches Geistesleben*, 2 vols. Munich: Huebner, 1939, 2:424–489.

Grassi, Onorato. 'La questione della teologia come scienza in Gregorio da Rimini,' *RFN*, 68 (1976), 610–644.

——. 'La riforma della teologia in Francia,' in *Storia della teologia nel medioevo*, ed. Giulio d'Onofrio, 3:685–720.

——. 'Probabilismo teologico e certezza filosofica: Pietro Aureoli e il dibattito sulla conoscenza nel 1300,' in *Storia della teologia nel medioevo*, ed. Giulio d'Onofrio, 3:515–540.

Gréa, A. 'Essai historique sur les archdiacres,' *BEC*, 12 (1851), 39–67, 215–247.

Grevy-Pons, Nicole. *Célebat et nature: une controverse médiévale*. Paris: CNRS, 1975.

Grundmann, H. 'Sacerdotium, Regnum, Studium: Zur Wertung der Wissenschaft im XIII Jahrhundert,' *AKG*, 34 (1951–1952), 5–21.

Gryson, Roger. 'The Authority of the Teacher in the Ancient and Medieval Church,' *JES*, 19 (1982), 176–187.

Guelluy, Robert. 'La place des théologiens dans l'Eglise et la société médiévale,' in *Miscellanea historica in honorem Alberti de Meyer*. 2 vols. Louvain: Bibliothèque de Université, 1946, 1:571–589.

———. *Philosophie et théologie chez Guillaume d'Ockham*. Louvain: Nauwelaerts, 1947.

Guenée, Bernard. *Between Church and State: The Lives of Four French Prelates in the Late Middle Ages*. Chicago: The University of Chicago Press, 1991.

Guillemain, Bernard. *La cour pontificale d'Avignon, 1309–1376*. Paris: de Boccard, 1962.

———. 'L'Exercise du pouvoir episcopal à la fin du moyen-âge,' in *L'Institution et les pourvoirs dans les églises de l'antiquité à nos jours*, Miscellanea historiae ecclesiasticae, 8, ed. Bernard Vogler. Brussels: Editions Nauwelaerts, 1987, 101–132.

Hamesse, Jacqueline, ed., *Manuels, programmes de cours et techniques d'enseignement dans les universities médiévales*. Louvain-la-Neuve, 1994.

Hayden, Dunstan. 'Notes on Aristotelian Dialectic in Theological Method,' *The Thomist*, 20 (1957), 383–418.

Helmholtz, Richard. *The Spirit of Classical Canon Law*. Athens, Ga.: University of Georgia Press, 1996.

Hödl, Ludwig. *Die Geschichte der scholastischen Literatur in der Theologie der Schlusselgewalt*. Münster: Aschendorff, 1960.

Hoenen, Marten J.F.M et al, eds. *Philosophy and Learning: Universities in the Middle Ages*, Education and Society in the Middle Ages and Renaissance, 6. Leiden: E.J. Brill, 1995.

Izbicki, Thomas M. and Bellitto, Christopher M., eds. *Reform and Renewal in the Middle Ages and Renaissance: Studies in Honor of Louis B. Pascoe, S.J.*, Studies in the History of Christian Thought, 96. Leiden: E.J. Brill, 2000.

Jenkins, John I. *Knowledge and Faith in Thomas Aquinas*. Cambridge: Cambridge University Press, 1997.

Jordan, Mark D. 'Aquinas' Middle Thoughts on Theology as a Science,' in *Studies in Thomistic Theology*, ed. Paul Lockey. Houston: University of St. Thomas Press, 1995, 91–111.

Jugie, Martin. *L'Immaculée Conception dans l'Ecriture et dans la tradition orientale*. Rome: Officium Libri Catholici, 1952.

Kaczmarek, Ludger. 'Noticia bei Peter von Ailly, Sent., 1, q. 3, Anmerkungen zu Quellen und Textgestalt,' in *Die Philosophie im 14 und 15 Jahrhundert*, Bochumer Studien zur Philosophie, 10, ed. Olaf Pluta. Amsterdam: B.R. Grüner, 1988, 385–420.

Kaluza, Zénon et al., eds. *Preuve et raisons à l'Université de Paris: logique, ontologie, et théologie au xive siècle*. Paris: J. Vrin, 1984.

———. *Les querelles doctrinales à Paris: Nominalistes et realistes aux confins du xive et du xve siècles*. Bergamo: Pierluigi Lubrina Editore, 1988.
Kerby-Fulton, Kathryn. *Reformist Apocalypticism and Piers Plowman*. Cambridge: Cambridge University Press, 1990.
———. 'Prophecy and Suspicion: Closet Radicalism, Reformist Politics, and the Vogue for Hildegardina in Riccaridan England,' *Speculum*, 75 (2002), 318–341.
Kittelson, James M. and Transue, Pamela J., eds. *Rebirth, Reform, and Resilience: Universities in Transition, 1300–1700*. Columbus: Ohio State University Press, 1984.
Kretzman, Norman, et al. eds. *The Cambridge History of Later Medieval Philosophy*. Cambridge: Cambridge University Press, 1982.
Krey, Philip D.W. 'Nicholas of Lyra: Apocalypse Commentator, Historian, and Critic,' *FS*, 52 (1992), 53–84.
——— and L. Smith, eds. *Nicholas of Lyra: The Senses of Scripture*, Studies in the History of Christian Thought, 90. Leiden: E.J. Brill, 2000.
Krings, Herman. *Ordo: Philosophisch-historische Grundlegung einer abendländischen Idee*. 2nd ed. Hamburg: Meiner, 1982.
Kuttner, Stephan. *Kanonistische Schuldlehre von Gratian bis auf die Dekretalen Gregors IX*. Vatican City: Vatican Press, 1935.
———. 'The Father of the Science of Canon Law,' *The Jurist*, 1 (1941), 2–19.
———. 'Cardinalis: The History of a Canonical Concept,' *Traditio*, 3 (1945), 129–214.
———. *Harmony from Dissonance: An Interpretation of Medieval Canon Law*. Latrobe, Pa.: The Archabbey Press, 1960.
———. *The History of Ideas and Doctrines of Canon Law in the Middle Ages*. London: Ashgate Variorum, 1980.
Ladner, Gerhart. 'The Concepts of "Ecclesia" and "Christianitas" and their Relationship to the Idea of Papal "Plenitudo Potestatis,"' in *Sacerdozio e Regno da Gregorio VII a Bonifacio VIII*, Miscellanea Historiae Pontificiae, 18 (1954), 49–77.
———. *The Idea of Reform: Its Impact on Christian Thought and Action in the Age of the Fathers*. Cambridge, Mass.: Harvard University Press, 1959.
———. 'Homo Viator: Medieval Ideas on Order and Alienation,' *Speculum*, 42 (1967), 233–259.
———. 'Terms and Ideas of Renewal in the Twelfth Century,' in *Renaissance and Renewal in the Twelfth Century*, ed. Robert Benson and Giles Constable. Cambridge, Mass.: Harvard University Press, 1982, 1–33.
Lang, Albert. 'Die conclusio theologica in der Problemstellung der Spätscholastik,' *Divus Thomas*, 22 (1944), 257–290.
———. *Die theologische prinzipienlehre der mittelalterlichen Scholastik*. Freiburg: Herder, 1964.
Lapsanski, Duane V. *Evangelical Perfection: An Historical Examination of the Concept in the Early Franciscan Sources*. St. Bonaventure, N.Y.: Franciscan Institute, 1977.
Leader, Damien Riehl. *The University to 1546*. Vol 1 of *A History of the University*

of Cambridge, ed. C.N.L. Brooke. Cambridge: Cambridge University Press, 1988.
LeBras, Gabriel. 'Velut Splendor Firmamenti: Le docteur dans le droit de l'Eglise médiévale,' in *Mélanges offerts à Etienne Gilson*, ed. Edmund J. McCorkell. Paris: J. Vrin, 1959, 373–388.
——et al. *L'Age classique, 1140–1378: Sources et théorie du droit*. Histoire du droit et des institutions de l'Eglise en Occident, 7. Paris: Sirey, 1965.
——. *Le droit post-classique, 1378–1500*, Histoire du droit et des institutions de l'Eglise en Occident, 13. Paris: Editions Cujas, 1971.
Leclercq, Jean. 'La théologie comme science d'après la literature quodlibetique,' *RTAM*, 9 (1939), 351–374.
——. 'Le magistère du prédicateur au xiiie siècle,' *AHDL*, 21 (1946), 105–147.
——. 'L'Idéal du théologien au moyen âge,' *RSR*, 21 (1947), 121–148.
——et al., eds. *The Spirituality of the Middle Ages*. Vol. 2 of *A History of Christian Spirituality*, ed. Louis Boyer et al. London: Burns & Oates, 1968.
Lee, Richard A., Jr. *Science, the Singular, and the Question of Theology*. New York: Palgrave, 2002.
Leff, Gordon. *Heresy in the Later Middle Ages*. 2 vols. Manchester: Manchester University Press, 1967.
——. *Paris and Oxford in the Thirteenth and Fourteenth Centuries*. New York: John Wiley, 1968.
——. *William of Ockham: The Metamorphosis of Scholastic Discourse*. Manchester: Manchester University Press, 1975.
Lerner, Robert E. *The Heresy of the Free Spirit in the Later Middle Ages*. Berkeley: University of California Press, 1972.
Lieberman, Max. 'Chronologie Gersonienne, VIII. Gerson et d'Ailly, III,' *Romania*, 81 (1960), 44–98.
——. 'Pierre d'Ailly, Jean Gerson et le culte de saint Joseph (I–III),' *Cahiers de Josephologie*, 13 (1965), 227–272; 14 (1966), 271–314; 15 (1967), 5–114.
Lindbeck, George. 'Nominalism and the Problem of Meaning as Illustrated by Pierre d'Ailly on Predestination and Justification,' *HTR*, 52 (1959), 43–60.
Little, A.G. and Pelster, F. *Oxford Theology and Theologians*. Oxford: Oxford University Press, 1934.
Lynch, John E. 'The Magistery and Theologians from the Apostolic Fathers to the Gregorian Reformers,' *CS*, 17 (1978), 188–209.
Lytle, Guy F. 'The Careers of Oxford Students in the Later Middle Ages,' in *Rebirth, Reform, and Resilience: Universities in Transition, 1300–1700*, ed. James M. Kittelson and Pamela J. Transue, 213–253.
Maierù, Alfonso. 'Logique et théologie trinitaire: Pierre d'Ailly,' in *Preuve et raisons à l'Université de Paris: Logique, ontologie, et théologie au xive siècle*, ed. Zénon Kaluza and Paul Vignaux. Paris: J. Vrin, 1984, 252–268.
Maillard-Luypaert, Monique. *Paupauté, clercs et laïcs: Le diocese de Cambrai à l'épreuve du Grand Schisme d'Occident (1378–1417)*. Bruxelles: Publications des Facultés Universitaires Saint Louis, 2001.
Mandonnet, P. 'Chronologie des écrits scriptuaires de Saint Thomas Aquin, 3: L'enseignement de la Bible "selon l'usage de Paris,"' *RT*, 34 (1929), 489–519.

Manz, L. *Der Ordo-Gedanke: Ein Beitrag zur Frage des mittelalterliches Ständegedankens.* Stuttgart: W. Kohlhammer, 1937.

Martin, Hervé. *Le métier de prédicateur à la fin du moyen âge, 1350–1520.* Paris: Editions du Cerf, 1988.

Masson, R. 'De Immaculata Conceptione apud Fratres Praedicatores,' *Angelicum*, 31 (1954), 358–408.

Matter, E. Ann. 'The Apocalypse in Early Medieval Exegesis,' in *The Apocalypse in the Middle Ages*, ed. Richard K. Emmersen and Bernard McGinn, 38–50.

Mauer, Armand. 'Ockham's Conception of the Unity of a Science,' *MS*, 20 (1958), 98–112.

———. 'Unity of a Science: St. Thomas and the Nominalists,' in *St. Thomas Aquinas, 1274–1974: Commemorative Studies*. 2 vols. Toronto: Pontifical Institute of Medieval Studies, 1974, 2:269–291.

McDonnell, K. 'Does William of Ockham Have a Theory of Natural Law,' *FS*, 34 (1974), 383–392.

McGinn, Bernard. *The Calabrian Abbot: Joachim of Fiore in the History of Western Thought.* New York: Macmillan, 1985.

———. *Antichrist: Two Thousand Years of the Human Fascination with Evil.* San Francisco: Harper, 1994.

McGowan, John P. *Pierre d'Ailly and the Council of Constance.* Washington: The Catholic University of America, 1936.

McGrade, Arthur S. *The Political Thought of William of Ockham.* Cambridge: Cambridge University Press, 1974.

Meller, Bernhard. *Studien zur Erkenntnislehre des Peter von Ailly.* Freiburg: Herder, 1954.

Miccoli, Giovanni. *Chiesa Gregoriana.* Florence: La Nuova Italia, 1966.

Miethke, Jürgen. *Ockhams Weg zur Socialphilosophie.* Berlin: De Gruyter, 1969.

Millet, Hèléne. 'L'Evêque à la fin du Grand Schisme d'Occident: Lucerna supra candelabrum posita,' in *L'Institution et les pouvoirs dans les églises de l'antiquité à nos jours*, ed. Bernard Vogler. Bruxelles: Nauwelaerts, 1987, 133–147.

———. 'Ecoute et usage des prophéties par les prelates pendant le Grand Schisme d'Occident,' *MEFr-MA*, 102 (1990), 425–455.

Moeller, Charles. 'La collegialité au concile de Constance,' in *La collegialité épiscopale: histoire et théologie*, ed. Yves Congar. Editions du Cerf, 1965, 131–149.

Mollat, Guillaume. 'Contribution à l'histoire du Sacré Collège de Clement V à Eugene IV,' *RHE*, 46 (1951), 22–112, 566–594.

———. *The Popes at Avignon*, 9th ed. London: Thomas Nelson, 1963.

Mollat, Michel. *La vie et la pratique religieuse au xive siècle et dans la première du xve principalment en France.* Paris: Centre de documenttation universitaire, 1963.

Moonan, Lawrence. *Divine Power: The Medieval Power Distinction up to its Adoption by Albert, Bonaventure, and Aquinas.* Oxford: Clarendon Press, 1994.

Moraw, Peter. 'Careers of Graduates,' in *Universities in the Middle Ages*, ed. H. de Ridder-Symoens, pp. 244–279.

Mortier, Daniel A. *Histoire des maîtres generaux de l'ordre des Frères Prêcheurs*, 8 vols. Paris: Picard, 1903–1920.

Moynihan, Robert. 'The Development of the Pseudo-Joachim Commentary 'Super Hieremiam:' New Manuscript Evidence,' *MEFr-MA*, 98 (1986), 109–142.

Musto, Ronald G. 'Queen Sancia of Naples (1286–1345) and the Spiritual Franciscans,' in *Women of the Medieval World: Essays in Honor of John H. Mundy*, ed. Julius Kirshner and Suzanne F. Wemple. Oxford: Blackwell, 1985, 69–100.

———. 'Franciscan Joachimism at the Court of Naples, 1309–1345: A New Appraisal,' *AFH*, 90 (1997), 419–486.

Noonan, John. 'Gratian Slept Here: The Changing Identity of the Father of the Systematic Study of Canon Law,' *Traditio*, 35 (1979), 145–172.

Oakley, Francis. 'Medieval Theories of Natural Law: William of Ockham and the Significance of the Voluntarist Tradition,' *NLF*, 6 (1960), 47–76.

———. 'Pierre d'Ailly and the Absolute Power of God: Another Note on the Theology of Nominalism,' *HTR*, 56 (1963), 59–73.

———. *The Political Thought of Pierre d'Ailly: The Voluntarist Tradition*. New Haven: Yale University Press, 1964.

———. 'Pierre d'Ailly and Papal Infallibility,' *MS*, 26 (1964) 353–358.

———. 'Gerson and d'Ailly: An Admonitions,' *Speculum*, 40 (1965), 74–83.

———. 'Pierre d'Ailly,' in *Reformers in Profile*, ed. Brian A. Gerrish. Philadelphia: Fortress Press, 1967, 40–57.

———. 'Psuedo-Zabarella's "Capitula Agendorum": An Old Case Reopened,' *AHC*, 14 (1982), 111–123.

———. *Natural Law, Conciliarism, and Consent in the Late Middle Ages: Studies in Ecclesiastical and Intellectual History*. London: Ashgate Variorum, 1984.

Oberman, Heiko A. 'Some Notes on the Theology of Nominalism with Attention to its Relation to the Renaissance,' *HTR*, 53 (1960), 47–76.

———. *The Harvest of Medieval Theology*. Cambridge, Mass.: Harvard University Press, 1963.

———. 'The Shape of Late Medieval Thought: The Birth Pangs of the Modern Era,' in *The Pursuit of Holiness in Late Medieval and Renaissance Thought*, ed. Charles Trinkaus and Heiko Oberman, 3–25.

———. 'Nominalism and Late Medieval Religion,' in *The Pursuit of Holiness in Late Medieval and Renaissance Thought*, ed. Charles Trinkaus and Heiko Oberman, 593–615.

———, ed. *Gregor von Rimini: Werk und Wirkung bis zur Reformation*, Berlin: Walter de Gruyter, 1981.

O'Connor, E.D. *The Doctrine of the Immaculate Conception: History and Significance*. Notre Dame: University of Notre Dame Press, 1958.

Offler, H.S. 'The Three Modes of Natural Law in Ockham: A Revision of the Text,' *FS*, 15 (1977), 207–218.

Olsen, Glenn. 'The Idea of the "Ecclesia Primitiva" in the Writings of the Twelfth-Century Canonists,' *Traditio*, 25 (1969), 61–86.

Ourliac, Paul. 'La residence des évêques dans le droit canonique du xve siècle,' *AC*, 17 (1973), 707–715.

Ouy, Gilbert. *Le recueil épistolaire de Pierre d'Ailly et les notes d'Italie de Jean de Montreuil*, Umbrae Codicum Occidentalium, 9. Amsterdam: North-Holland

Publishing Company, 1966.

———. 'De Pierre d'Ailly à Jean Antoine de Baïf: Un example de double orthographie à la fin du xive siècle,' *Romania*, 97 (1976), 218–248.

———. 'Autographes d'auteurs français des xive et xve siècles: Leur utilité pour l'histoire intellectuelle,' *Commentationes*, 28 (1983), 67–107.

Overfield, James H. 'University Studies and the Clergy in Pre-Reformation Germany,' in *Rebirth, Reform, and Resilience: Universities in Transition, 1300–1700*, ed. James M. Kittelson and Pamela J. Transue, 254–292.

Owens, Joseph. 'The Aristotelian Conception of the Sciences,' *IPQ*, 4 (1964), 200–216.

Paetow, L.J. *The Arts Course at Medieval Universities*. Urbana: University of Illinois Press, 1910.

Pantin, W.A. *The English Church in the Fourteenth Century*. Notre Dame: University of Notre Dame Press, 1962.

Parkes, Joseph P. 'The Epistemology of Pierre d'Ailly.' M.A. diss., University of Wisconsin, 1970.

Pascoe, Louis B. *Jean Gerson: Principles of Church Reform*, Studies in Medieval and Reformation Thought, 7. Leiden: E.J.Brill, 1973.

———. 'Jean Gerson: The Ecclesia Primitiva and Reform,' *Traditio*, 30 (1974), 379–409.

———. 'Theological Dimensions of Pierre d'Ailly's Teaching on the Papal Plenitude of Power,' *AHC*, 11 (1979), 357–366.

———. 'Pierre d'Ailly: Histoire, Schisme et Antéchrist,' in *Genèse et débuts du Grande Schisme d'Occident (1362–1394)*, ed. Michel Hayez. Paris: CNRS, 1980, 615–622.

Pasztor, E. *Per la storia di San Ludovico d'Angio, 1274–1297*. Rome: Istituto storico italiano per il Medio Evo, 1955.

Paul, Jacques. 'Saint Louis d'Anjou, franciscain et évêque de Toulouse (1274–1297),' *CF*, 7 (1972), 59–90.

Pederson, Olaf. *The First Universities: Studium Generale and the Origins of University Education in Europe*. Cambridge: Cambridge University Press, 1997.

Peuchmaurd, M. 'Le prêtre ministre de la parole dans le théologie du xiie siècle: canonists, moines et chanoines,' *RTAM*, 29 (1962), 52–76.

———. 'Mission canonique et prédication: Le prêtre ministre de la parole dans la querelle entre mendiants et seculiers,' *RTAM*, 30 (1963), 122–144, 251–276.

Phelps, Michael. 'A Study of Renewal Ideas in the Writings of the Early Franciscans.' Ph.D. diss., University of California at Los Angeles, 1972.

Pierrard, Pierre, ed. *Les dioceses de Cambrai et Lille*. Histoire des dioceses de France, 8. Paris: Editions Beauchesne, 1978.

Plongeron, Bernard. *Paris: Une histoire religieuse des origins à la Revolution*, Vol 1 of *Le Diocèse de Paris*, Histoire des dioceses de France, 20. Paris: Beauchesne, 1987.

Post, Gaines. 'Parisian Masters as a Corporation, 1200–1246,' *Speculum*, 9 (1934), 421–435.

———. *Studies in Medieval Legal Thought: Public Laws and the State, 1100–1322*. Princeton: Princeton University Press, 1964.

Post, R.R. *The Modern Devotion: Confrontation with Reformation and Humanism*,

Studies in Medieval and Reformation Thought, 3. Leiden: E.J. Brill, 1968.
Posthumus Meyjes, G.H.M. *De controverse tussen Petrus en Paulus: Galaten 2:11 in de historie*. The Hague: Martinus Nijhoff, 1967.
———. 'Exponents of Sovereignty: Canonists as Seen by Theologians in the Late Middle Ages,' in *The Church and Sovereignty, c. 590–1918: Essays in Honor of Michael Wilks*, ed. Dianna Wood. Oxford: Blackwell, 1991, 299–312.
———. *Jean Gerson-Apostle of Unity: His Church Politics and Ecclesiology*, Studies in the History of Christian Thought, 94. Leiden: E.J. Brill, 1999.
Press, Gerald A. 'The Content and Argument of Augustine's *De doctrina christiana*,' *Augustiniana*, 31 (1981) 165–182.
Rashdall, H. *The Universities of Europe in the Middle Ages*, ed. F.M. Powicke and A.B. Emden. 3 vols. Oxford: Oxford University Press, 1936.
Reeves, Marjorie. *The Influence of Prophecy in the Later Middle Ages*. Oxford: Oxford University Press, 1969.
———. *Joachim of Fiore and the Prophetic Future*. London: SPCK, 1976.
Resnick, Irven Michael. *Divine Power in St. Peter Damien's 'De divina omnipotentia.'* Leiden: E.J. Brill, 1992.
Riché, Pierre. *Education and Culture in the Barbarian West: Sixth Through Eighth Centuries*. Columbia: University of South Carolina Press, 1976.
———. *Les écoles et l'enseignement dans l'occident chrétien de la fin du ve siècle au milieu du xie siècle*. Paris: Aubier Montaigne, 1979.
Rief, Josef. *Der Ordobegriff des jungen Augustinus*. Paderborn: Ferdinand Schöningh, 1962.
Rivière, Jean. 'In Partem Sollicitudinis: Evolution d'une formule pontificale,' *RSR*, 5 (1925), 210–231.
Roberts, Agnes E. 'Pierre d'Ailly and the Council of Constance: A Study in "Ockhamite" Theory and Practice,' *Transactions of the Royal Historical Society*, 4th ser., 18 (1935), 123–142.
Robilliard, A.J. 'Sur la notion de condition (status) in St. Thomas,' *RSPT*, 29 (1936) 104–107.
Roques, René. *L'Univers Dionysian: Structure hiérarchique du monde selon le Pseudo-Denys*. Paris: Aubier, 1954.
Rose, Jonathan. 'Medieval Attitudes toward the Legal Profession: The Past as Prologue,' *Stetson Law Review*, 28 (1998), 345–368.
Rusconi, Roberto, ed. *L'Attésa dell' etá nuova nella spiritualitá della fine del medioevo*. Convegni del centro di studi sull spiritualitá medievale, 3. Todi, 1962.
———. *L'Attésa della fine: Crisi della societá, profezia et apocalisse in Italia al tempo del Grande Scisma d'Occidente (1378–1417)*. Rome: Istituto storico italiano per il Medio Evo, 1979.
———. *Profezia e profeti alla fine del Medioevo*. Rome: Viella, 1999.
Saint-Blançat, Louis. 'La théologie de Luther et un nouveau plagiat de Pierre d'Ailly,' *PLut*, 4 (1956), 61–81.
Salembier, Louis. 'Petrus ab Alliaco.' Theses Insulenses ad Magisterium in Sacra Theologia, 4. Archigymnasium Catholicum Insulense, 1886
———. 'Bibliographie des oeuvres du Cardinal Pierre d'Ailly, évêque de Cambrai (1350–1420),' *Le bibliographie moderne*, 12 (1908), 160–170.
———. *Le Cardinal Pierre d'Ailly: Chancelier de l'Université de Paris, Evêque du Puy et de*

Cambrai, 1350–1420. Tourcoing: Georges Frère, 1932.
Schulze, Manfred. 'Via Gregorii in Forschung und Quellen,' in *Gregor von Rimini: Werk und Wirkung bis zur Reformation*, ed. Heiko A. Oberman, 64–75.
Sears, Elizabeth. *The Ages of Man: Medievel Intrepretations of the Life Cycle.* Princeton: Princeton University Press, 1986.
Serene, Eileen. 'Demonstrative Science,' in *The Cambridge History of Later Medieval Philosophy*, ed. Norman Kretzman et al, 496–517.
Shogimen, Takaski. 'The Relationship Between Theology and Canon Law: Another Context of Political Thought in the Early Fourteenth Century,' *JHI*, 60 (1999), 417–431.
Smalley, Beryl. *The Study of the Bible in the Middle Ages.* Notre Dame: Notre Dame University Press, 1964.
———. 'The Bible in the Medieval Schools,' in *The Cambridge History of the Bible*, Vol. 2: *The West from the Fathers to the Reformation*, ed. G.W.H. Lampe. Cambridge: Cambridge University Press, 1969, 197–220.
Smoller, Laura Ackerman. *History, Prophecy, and the Stars: The Christian Astrology of Pierre d'Ailly, 1350–1420.* Princeton: Princeton University Press, 1994.
Spinka, Matthew. *John Hus' Concept of the Church.* Princeton: Princeton University Press, 1969.
Stockmeier, Peter. 'Die alte Kirche: Leitbild der Erneurerung,' *TTQ*, 146 (1966), 385–480.
———. 'Causa Reformationis und Alte Kirche,' in *Von Konstanz nach Trient*, ed. Remigius Bäumer. Munich: Ferdinand Schöningh, 1972, 1–13.
Streuer, S.R. *Die theologische Einleitungslehre des Petrus Aureoli.* Werl in Westfalen: Dietrich-Coelde Verlag, 1968.
Stump, Phillip H. *The Reforms of the Council of Constance, 1414–1418*, Studies in the History of Christian Thought, 53. Leiden: E.J. Brill, 1994.
Swanson, R.N. *Universities, Academics, and the Great Schism.* Cambridge: Cambridge University Press, 1979.
———. *Religion and Devotion in Europe, c. 1215–1515.* Cambridge: Cambridge University Press, 1995.
Taber, Douglass, 'The Theologian and the Schism: A Study of the Political Thought of Jean Gerson (1363–1429).' Ph.D. diss., Stanford University, 1985.
———. 'Pierre d'Ailly and the Teaching Authority of the Theologian,' *CH*, 59 (1990), 163–174.
Teeuwen, Mariken, *The Vocabulary of Intellectual Life in the Middle Ages.* Etudes sur le vocabulaire intellectuel du moyen âge, 10. Turnhout: Brepols, 2003.
Thijssen, J.M.M.H. *Censure and Heresy at the University of Paris, 1200–1400.* Philadelphia: University of Pennsylvania Press, 1998.
Thompson, A.H. 'Diocesan Organization in the Middle Ages, Archdeacons and Rural Deans,' *PBA*, 29 (1943), 153–194.
Thurot, C. *De l'organisation et de l'enseignement dans l'Université de Paris au moyen âge.* Paris: Dezobry-Magdeleine, 1850.
Tierney, Brian. *Foundations of the Conciliar Theory.* Cambridge: Cambridge University Press, 1955.
———. *Medieval Poor Law.* Berkeley: University of California Press, 1959.
———. 'Sola Scriptura and the Canonists,' *SGrat.*, 11 (1967), 345–366.

———. *Ockham, the Conciliar Theory, and the Canonists*. Philadelphia: Fortress Press, 1971.

———. *Origins of Papal Infallibility, 1150–1350*, Studies in the History of Christian Thought, 6. Leiden: E.J. Brill, 1972.

———. 'Natural Law and Canon Law in Ockham's *Dialogus*,' in *Aspects of Late Medieval Government and Society: Essays Presented to J.R. Landner*, ed. J.G. Rowe. Toronto: University of Toronto Press, 1986, 3–24.

Toynbee, Margaret. *St. Louis of Toulouse and the Process of Canonization in the Fourteenth Century*. Manchester: Manchester University Press, 1929.

Trinkaus, Charles and Heiko A. Oberman, eds. *The Pursuit of Holiness in Late Medieval and Renaissance Religion*, Studies in Medieval and Reformation Thought, 10. Leiden: E.J. Brill, 1974.

Tschackert, Paul. *Peter von Ailli: Zur Geschichte des grossen abendländischen Schisma und der Reformconcilien von Pisa und Constanz*. Gotha: Friedrich Andreas Perthes, 1877.

Uelman, Amelia. 'A View of the Legal Profession from a Mid-Twelfth-Century Monastery,' *Fordham Law Review*, 71 (2003), 1517–1541.

Ullmann, Walter. *Law and Politics in the Middle Ages: An Introduction to the Sources of Medieval Political Ideas*. Ithaca: Cornell University Press, 1975.

———. *Medieval Papalism*. London: Methuen, 1949.

Urban, L. 'William of Ockham's Theological Ethics,' *FS*, 33 (1973), 310–350.

Van den Eynde, Damien. 'The Terms "Ius Positivum" and "Signum Positivum" in Twelfth-Century Scholasticism,' *FS*, 9 (1949), 41–49.

Vanhoye, Albert. 'Le ministère dans l'Eglise: les données du Nouveau Testament,' *NRT*, 104 (1982), 722–738.

Van Steenberghen, Fernand. *Aristotle in the West: The Origins of Latin Aristotelianism*. New York: Humanities Press, 1970.

———. *Thomas Aquinas and Radical Aristotelianism*. Washington: The Catholic University of America Press, 1980.

Vauchez, André. 'Les théologiens face aux prophètes à l'époque des papes d'Avignon et du Grand Schisme,' *MEFr-MA*, 102 (1990), 577–588.

———. *Sainthood in the Late Middle Ages*. Cambridge: Cambridge University Press, 1997.

Verger, Jacques. *Les universités françaises au Moyen Age*, Education and Society in the Middle Ages and Renaissance, 7. Leiden: E.J. Brill, 1995.

Vogler, Bernard, ed. *L'Institution et les pouvoirs dans les églises de l'antiquité à nos jours*, Miscellanea Historicae Ecclesiasticae, 8. Bruxelles: Editions Nauwelaerts, 1987.

Watanabe, Morimichi. 'The German Church Shortly Before the Reformation: Nicholas of Cusa and the Veneration of the Bleeding Hosts at Wilsnack,' in *Reform and Renewal in the Middle Ages and Renaissance*, ed. Thomas M. Izbicki and Christopher M. Bellitto, 210–223.

Watt, J.A. 'The Constitutional Law of the College of Cardinals from Hostiensis to Joannes Andreae,' *MS*, 33 (1971), 127–157.

———. 'Hostiensis on *Per Venerabilem*: The Role of the College of Cardinals,' in *Authority and Power: Studies on Medieval Law and Government Presented to Walter*

Ullmann, ed. Brian Tierney and Peter Linehan. Cambridge: Cambridge University Press, 1980, 99–113.

Weijers, Olga. *Terminologie des universitiés au xiiie siècles*, Lessico Intellecttuale Europeo, 39. Rome: Edizioni dell' Ateneo, 1987.

Yunck, John A. 'Venal Tongue: Lawyers and the Medieval Satirists,' *American Bar Association Journal*, 46 (1960), 267–270.

INDEX OF SUBJECTS AND TERMS

abstinence, 155
Academicians, 220
active life *(vita activa)*, 95, 98, 263
ages of the world, 17, 20, 24, 26, 31, 38, 264
annates, 112, 115
Antichrist, 12, 16, 19, 21–42, 44–47, 50, 93, 97, 111, 161–164, 180, 285
    as *filius perditionis*, 21
    as *homo peccati*, 21
apocalypticism
    cosmological signs, 41–46
    moral decline, 14, 18–19, 161–164
    persecutions, 12–16, 20–27, 160–164, 279
    purifying effects, 49
apologetics, 225, 227–230, 232
apostles, 13, 40, 55–61, 68, 77, 84, 87–88, 95, 127, 138, 140, 154–155, 172, 174, 179, 201–202, 239, 272–273, 283
apostolic
    age, 37
    college, 55, 60, 66, 127
    ministry, 154–155
    mission, 56, 59, 69, 71, 82–84, 87–90, 105, 118–119, 124, 143, 171, 174–175, 178
    reformers, 280
    status, 60–61
    succession, 60–69, 77, 138, 143–144
    virtues, 97, 103, 138, 141, 148
    vocation, 69–72, 82, 97, 165
apostolic life *(vita apostolica)*
    abandonment of, 44–47, 95–97
    and episcopal reform, 47–48, 101–102, 112–113, 124, 138, 155, 161, 165, 281–282
    characteristics, 14–16, 19, 47–49, 71, 95–99, 101, 137, 155–156, 165, 280
    historical evolution, 98–102
    models, 98, 101, 157; *see also* Louis of Anjou and Peter of Luxemberg
appointments, 103–111; *see also* reservations, expectancies, benefices, simony
archdeacons, 108–110, 128, 170, 173
archpriests, 173
astrologers, 34, 309
astrology, 2, 11, 34–35, 45–46
astronomy, 2, 34–35, 309
auditor, 7–8
Augustinians, 156
Aulica, 9, 84

baccalarius: biblicus, sententiarius, formatus, 9, 237, 239, 246
Benedictines, *see* Benedict
benefices, 105–106, 115, 135, 237–239
bishops
    agents of reform, 51, 101, 279
    and apostolic ideal and life, *see* apostolic, evangelical life
    and *cura animarum*, 82, 120
    apostolic mission, 82–84, 87–90, 105
    apostolic succession, 60–69
    apostolic vocation, 69–72, 82, 102, 165
    as an order, *see* order *(ordo)*
    as distinguished from priests, 64–65, 67–69
    as "good shepherds", 96, 103–104
    as "new judges *(judices novi)*", 49, 51
    as "new spiritual men *(viri spirituales)*" 49

authority, *see magisterium, cathedra, clavis, par in parem*
chorbishops, 109
collegiality, 63–64
diminished reputation, 95–96
financial support, 145
reform, *see* reform: pastoral, personal
state of perfection, *see status: perfectionis*
titular bishops, 108
Blanchard Affair, 169–172, 175–176, 283

canon law
 as *scientia scientiarum*, 262, 265
 composite nature, 253–254, 259, 262, 269, 286–287
 historical evolution, 250–253
 methodology, 271–274; *see also* discourse
 qualities: negative, positive, 266–269
 subordination to theology, 272–273, 286–287
 superior to theology, 259, 262–263, 265, 268–271
canon lawyers
 criticism, 235–241, 286
 education, 285
 profession, 235
canonical life *(vita canonica)*, 15, 98–99, 156
canonizations, 131–132
canons
 regular, 54, 98–99
 secular, 54, 263
cardinals
 and *cura animarum*, 62
 apostolic origins, 62–64
 as *assessores papae,*, 58
 as *coadjutores papae,*, 58, 72–82
 as *collegium*, 57–58
 as *conciliarii papae*, 58
 as *pars apostolicae sedis*, 58, 80
 as *pars corporis papae*, 58, 80
 as *senatus*, 57

authority, *see magisterium, cathedra, clavis*
excessive numbers from one country, 110, 114–115
historical evolution, 55–62
lack of geographical diversity, 110, 115
right to financial support, 113
state of perfection, *see status: perfectionis*
university graduates, 123
Carthusians, 263
cathedra: magistralis, pastoralis, 185
causae: maiores, minores, 85–86, 91
celibacy, 15, 148–154, 285
certitude, 29, 227–229
chancellor, 1, 3, 7, 169–173, 271, 282
charity, 140–142, 280
chastity, 280
Church
 history as persecution, 2, 12–16, 20–227
 imperial (*Reichskirche*), 18, 24
 primitive, 97, 105–106, 126–127, 179–180, 257, 283
 property as patrimony of the poor, 146–147, 270
 see also Mystical Body
 six ages of history, 24–25
Cistercians, *see* Citeaux
clavis: potestatis, scientiae, 184–185, 194
clergy, 14, 18, 43–44, 96, 105, 113, 120, 125, 131
 diocesan, 15, 19, 54, 66, 101–102, 105, 116–117, 120, 122, 125, 146, 148–150, 155–156, 171, 173–174, 178, 239, 263–264
 religious, *see* monks, mendicants
 Roman, 73–75
clerical attire, 148
Cluniacs, *see* Cluny
cognition (*notitia*)
 definition, 217–219, 229
 types: *sensualis, intellectualis*, 218–219
Concordats, 6, 114–115, 123, 135–136, 154

English, 116, 123, 135
French, 115–116
German, 116, 123–124, 154
Spanish,115–116,, 123
concubinage, 18–19, 148–154
Condemnations of 1270 and 1277, 203–204, 234
contemplative life *(vita contemplativa)*, 98, 263
conversatio, 137–138
conversion, 189, 282
corporational theory, 168–169, 188, 255
correction: fraternal, 76–77, 105, 141–142, 155, 193–194, 281
Councils
 Nicaea I, 126
 Chalcedon, 126
 Nicaea II, 126
 Lateran III, 133
 Lateran IV, 101, 120–121, 135, 239
 Vienne, 148
 Pisa, 45, 83
 Constance, 1, 6, 23–24, 27, 46–51, 55, 59–60, 63–64, 71, 84, 93, 104, 108, 112–115, 121–123, 125, 127, 134–135, 141, 146, 148–149, 153–155, 158–159, 161, 180, 190–191, 240–241, 255, 271, 273–274, 282
 Trent, 154, 176, 282

definitions *(definitiones)*, see determinations
determinations *(determinationes)*
 definition, 84, 182–183, 192, 205, 226–227, 231, 243
 types: *scholastica-doctrinalis; judicialis-auctoritativa*, 84–90, 182–185, 187, 193
devotional practices
 deviations in, 132
discourse *(discursus)*
 definition, 212–213, 232
 divisions: theological, canonical, 271–274
 categories: *demonstrativus, dialecticus, theologicus*, 213–214, 230
 types of argument: *ex necessitate*, 199–200 *probabiliora* 199–200, *probabilia* 29, 196, 201, 227–232
disputations
 regular, 181
 quodlibetal, 257–259, 286
doctor, 165–168, 171–172, 176–178, 180–181, 191–192, 200, 283
Dominicans, 50, 99, 198, 263
Donation of Constantine, 106

End-Times
 knowability, 28–47
 optimistic outlook, 44–47
 postponement, 44–47
 schism as sign of, 28–29, 44, 49, 240, 268, 277
evangelical, 14–16, 19
 decline, 51
 ideal, model, 44, 47–49, 99, 156–159, 161–162, 280
 mission, vocation, 93
 origin, roots, foundation, 47, 53, 93, 288
 preaching, 99
 reformers, 48, 97, 178, 280
 rule, precept, teaching, 47, 107, 141
 spirit, sensitivity, 47–48, 82, 150, 163, 281, 287
 virtues, 47–48, 143–144
evangelical life *(vita evangelica)*
 characteristics, 280–281
 and reform, 49, 97
 and revival, 178
 see also apostolic life
evidence *(evidentia)*
 definition, 220
 types: *absoluta, conditionata*, 220–221
examinations, 111–112
excommunication, 133, 150
expectancies, 104–105, 114

faith *(fides)*, 211–213, 222, 227–228

fasting, 155
fideism, 231–232
Flagellants, 132
fortitude, 142
Franciscans
    Regular, 19, 99–100, 158–161, 244, 253, 263, 278, 281–282
    Spirituals, 19, 48–50, 100, 143, 158, 281

Gentiles, 126, 201, 248
Gospel, see Scripture
Gregorian Reform, 15, 18, 19, 173

handbooks: pastoral, 122, 131
heresy, 25, 140, 257, 282
heretics, 13, 17, 20, 140
hierarchical activities
    purgation, 282
    illumination, 282
    perfection, 282
hierarchies, 165–168
    ecclesiastical, 16, 37, 55, 64, 68, 82, 87, 102, 108, 169, 174–177, 183–184, 194, 274, 282–283
    historical (*tempora*), 261–264
    legal (*leges*), 248, 250, 253, 261–262, 264, 286–287
    learning (*scientiae*), 166–169, 216–217, 222–225, 240, 261–262, 264
    sociological (*genera*), 261, 263, 264
history
    historical periods (*tempora*), 261–264
    see also ages of the world
humility, 14–16, 47, 100, 141, 154, 157, 160–161, 280–281
Hussites, 143–144
hypocrisy, hypocrites, 17–18, 21

Immaculate Conception, 84, 175, 183, 187, 195–196
intellectus spiritualis, 36

Jews, Judaic, 13, 17, 56, 144, 194

judicialiter inhibere, 90–91
jus, see law

law
    analogies and participation, 242–243, 256
    and changing circumstances, 203
    definition, 242–243, 249
    eternal (*aeterna*), 243–244, 246, 255–256, 286
    divine (*divina*), 243–244, 246–247, 250–252, 254, 263
    natural (*naturalis*), 243–244, 247–249, 251–252, 254, 261
    human (*humana, positiva*), 243–244, 249, 251–257, 273, 286
    civil (*civilis*)252,, 261, 263
    canon (*canonica*), 252, 254, 261
    common (*communis*), 254
    nations (*gentium*), 252 261
    see also hierarchies, legal
learning, 116–124; see also scriptural studies, theology, canon law, lectureships, libraries, handbooks
lectureships: cathedral and collegiate churches, 120–121
libraries, 5, 121, 285
licentia
    licentia docendi, 8
    ubique docendi et praedicandi, 8, 172–175, 283
litigation: prolonged, 133–134, 286–287
liturgy
    excessive length of ceremonies, 130
    excessive churches, 132
    excessive feastdays, 130–131
    unknown hymns and prayers, 130
    use of apocryphal readings, 130

magister, 8, 87, 168; see also *magisterium*
magisterium, 176, 185
    doctrinae, 138–139
    virtutis, 138–139
    see also *cathedra, clavis*
mediocritas, see moderation

"Men of Intelligence" *(Homines Intelligentiae)*, 26, 132
Mendicants
    as "new spiritual men", 50–51
    conflict with secular clergy, 66–67, 143, 174–175
    see also Dominicans, Franciscans
metanoia, see conversion
methodology, *see* discourse *(discursus)*
mixed life *(vita permixta)*, 263–264
moderation
    definition, 281–282
    tolerable inequality, 106, 108, 113–115, 134, 146–147, 280–281
monastic life *(vita monastica)*
    description, 98–99, 137–138
    orders, 15, 18, 51
    see also Benedictines, Cluniacs, Cistercians, Carthusians
Monzón Controversy, *see* John of Monzón
Mystical Body, 12, 22, 80–81, 141–142, 154, 283

ne quid nimis, see moderation
necessitas, 81, 107
Nominalism, 29, 231–233, 242
notitia, see cognition

obedience, 14, 48, 90, 150, 152, 170, 273
order *(ordo)*, 165–168
    episcoporum, 177
    doctorum, 165–168, 176–178, 180–181, 191–192, 200, 283
    praedicatorum, 191–192
    see also hierarchies
ordinations, 285

paintings, 132
papacy, 1, 3, 36–37, 45, 55, 60, 63, 72, 76–78, 80–81, 86, 88, 90–91, 93–94, 99, 103–106, 110–112, 114, 117, 135, 162–163, 170, 174–176, 188, 191, 205, 238, 241, 244, 257, 274, 277, 286
par in parem, 203

Parlement of Paris, 170
Pharisees, 288
philosophy, philosophers, 2, 34
plenitudo potestatis
    types: *ordinis, jurisdictionis*, 78–79
    modes of inherence: *separabiliter, inseparabiliter, representative,*, 78–80
    see also papacy, cardinals, bishops
potentia: absoluta, ordinata, 37, 221–222, 245
poverty, 15, 95–100, 143–147, 280–281
preachers
    as an order *(ordo)*, 191–192
    indulgence, 125
    itinerant, 99, 143, 174, 178
preaching, 33, 50, 134, 167
    bishops, 71–72, 77, 82–84, 90–91, 95, 118, 124–126, 141–143, 172, 178, 280–282
    diocesan clergy, 82–83, 122, 125–126, 141–144, 178
    mendicants, 50, 98, 100, 150, 157, 159, 174
    theologians, 171–175, 178, 180–181, 189–192
prelates
    as "new judges *(judices novi)*", 49, 51
    as "new spiritual men *(viri spirituales)*", 49, 51
    authority, *see magisterium, cathedra, clavis*
    categories: *maiores, minores*, 65–69, 172
    educational formation, 258–259, 268–270
    intellectual and moral decline, 43–44
    terminological evolution, 53–54
    see also cardinals, bishops, priests
Premonstratensians, 156
priests, 21, 43
    apostolic vocation, mission, model, 72, 82, 155–156
    as pseudopastors, 21, 125

as *prelati minores*, 54, 64, 172
as successors of the disciples, 65–69, 102, 172–174
need for distinctive spirituality, 155–156
pastoral activities, 83, 96, 103, 123, 124–126, 130–131, 173, 176, 186
priestly virtues and vices, 90, 138–139, 148–155
theological education, 119–124, 130
primitive church *(ecclesia primitiva)*, see Church, primitive
probable, probability, see discourse
procurations, 112
property
 ecclesiastical, 25
 distribution of, 25, 44
prophecy, 34–41
prophets, 36, 38, 41, 181
provisions, 104–105, 114
pseudopastors *(pseudopastores)*, see bishops, priests

quinquennia, see residence
Quodlibets, 257–259, see also disputations

rationalism, 242–243
Realism, 242
reason *(ratio)*, 246, 248
 demonstrativa, 214
 dialectica, 214
 practica, 242
 recta, 245
reform
 apostolic model, see *vita apostolica/evangelica*
 episcopal: pastoral, see appointments, examinations, financial support learning, teaching, preaching, synods, visitations, residence, liturgy, sacraments, devotions, legislation and litigation
 episcopal: personal, see *conversatio*,

charity, fortitude, poverty, celibacy, humility
reformatio in capite, 135
reformatio in membris, 135
regency, 8–9
Regnum, 166
Reichskirche, see Church, imperial
reservations, 104–105, 114; see also provisions
residence, 129, 280, 285–286
 quinquennia, 129
 septennia, 129
Resumptio, 9, 84
Revelation, 33–34, 36–37, 39, 222–224, 243
 Book of Revelation, 12–18, 23–24, 26, 31–32, 50
 post-apostolic, 37–38, 200
Roman Curia, 94, 111, 113, 116–117, 134, 239

Sacerdotium, 166
Sacra Pagina, see theology
sacraments, 25, 44, 131–135, 280, 285
scepticism, 220, 231–232
Schism, Great Western, 1–3, 12, 14–16, 20–29, 36–37, 44–47, 49, 51, 60, 77, 83, 85, 95, 104, 112, 127, 129, 142, 145, 159–163, 238, 240, 246, 255–258, 268, 273–275
scientia, 184–185, 205, 216–217
 canonica, 254, 261
 civilis, 261
 composita, 269
 lucrativa, 117, 238–239
 theologica, 261–262, 265
 subalternata, 224
 see also *clavis scientiae*
Scribes, 133
Scripture
 as *Sacra Pagina*, 165, 209
 as *sapientia divina*, 116
 as *lex Christi*, 247–248
 as *vita Christi*, 100–101
 authority of, 198–199
 four senses of, 36, 42–43

INDEX OF SUBJECTS AND TERMS

sola scriptura, 231
   study of, 116–118
   uses, 202
Sedes Apostolica, 58, 87
septennia, see residence
services *(servitiae)*, 112
signs *(signa)*: *propinqua, propinquiora, propinquissima,* see apocalypticism
simony, 18–19, 25, 44, 103, 106–107, 112–115, 170–171, 176, 281, 285
spoils, 112
status, 3, 4, 53, 71
   apostolicus, 60–64
   pastoralis, 61–64
   perfectionis acquirendae, exercendae, 62–63
stilus: juridicus, theologicus, see discourse
Studium, 166
synods, 84, 126–128, 286
   Amiens, 97, 149, 191
   Cambrai, 64, 94, 96, 127, 138, 140, 143, 147, 149, 154, 156, 191
   Paris, 149
   Rheims, 96, 128, 190

teaching, 172, 181–183, 186, 191; see also *ordo doctorum*
temperance, 143
tenths, 112
theologians
   advice and counsel, 193
   apocalyptic, prophetic role, 180–181, 284
   apostolic origins, vocation, mission, 171, 175–176, 278, 283–284
   as artisans *(artifices)*, 186
   as builders of the primitive church, 179–180, 283
   as faculty, 167–170, 183–184, 187–188
   authority: individual, corporate, 192–198, 283; see also *magisterium, cathedra, clavis*
   determinations, 193
   disputations, 181, 257–259, 286
   preaching, 189–192

   preference in ecclesiastical appointments, 117–120
   reformative role,, 285
   status: hierarchical, 165–169; corporational 168–169, 188
   teaching, 181–183, 186; see also doctor
theological truths *(veritates theologicae)*
   definition, 225
   types: *principia, conclusiones, veritates*, 226–227
theology
   as acts, habits, 208–212, 284
   as an art *(ars)*, 186
   as *Divina Pagina,*, 209
   as *quaedam fides*, 212
   as *Sacra Pagina*, 165, 209
   as *scientia subalternata*, 224
   as *stultilogia*, 116
   divisions: deductive, declarative, 227–228
   method, see discourse
   qualities, 265–267
   subject, 215–216
   unity, 214–215
Torah, 271, 247

University of Paris
   corporational status, 168–170, 188
   faculties, 7–9
   officials, see chancellor
   degrees, see *baccalarius: biblicus, sententiarius, formatus; magister, licentia*
   ceremonies, see *Vesperiae, Aulica, Resumptio*
utilitas, 32, 37, 75, 81, 188–189, 201

vacancies, 112
Vesperiae, 9, 84, 246
Victorines, 156, 278
visitations, 84, 105, 128, 280–281

Waldensians, 99, 143–144, 258
Wycliffites, 19, 143–144

INDEX OF PERSONS AND PLACES

Abelard, 200, 214, 252
Adam of Wodham, 208
Alexander II, Pope, 151
Alexander of Hales, 199
Ambrose, St., 199
Ambrose Aupert, 17
Amiens, 97, 149, 191
Anacletus, Pope, 66
Angelo of Clareno, 100
Anselm of Canterbury, 201, 214
Antioch, 61, 194
Aquinas, Thomas, St., 37, 41, 53, 62–63, 67, 79, 112–113, 122, 140, 142, 144, 151–152, 160, 166, 168, 173, 185, 194–196, 198–204, 211–212, 214–217, 219, 222–225, 228, 232, 236–237, 242–245, 251–252, 256
Aristotle, 2, 8, 63, 79, 84, 167, 184, 210–211, 213–217, 223–224, 229, 231, 236–237, 252, 255–256, 262, 272
Augustine, St., 16–17, 28, 31–32, 38–39, 41, 69, 98, 144, 166–168, 199, 201, 213, 215, 220, 227–228, 246, 256, 264, 267
Augustine of Ancona, 62
Aureoli, Peter, 26, 85, 216, 227–228
Avignon, 37, 85–86, 90, 99, 134, 162–163, 170, 175, 190, 202

Babylon, 24
Basil, St., 98
Becket, Thomas, St., 14, 161
Bede, St., 17, 66–67, 172, 184
Benedict, St., 98, 137–138
Benedict XIII, Pope, 55, 64, 105, 274
Benedict of Aniane, St., 98

Bernard of Clairvaux, St., 14, 16, 21, 28, 89, 132, 134, 157, 161, 191, 235, 278
Bernard of Thirone, 99
Bérulle, Pierre de, 156
Blanchard, John, 3, 169, 170–171, 175, 191, 283
Boethius, 2
Bois-Seigneur-Isaac, 132
Bologna, 260
Bonaventure, St., 67, 173, 209, 215–216, 222, 236
Boniface VIII, Pope, 58, 75, 158, 268
Bourret, Etienne, 202–204
Bradwardine, Thomas, 220
Brethren of Common Life, 13, 48–49, 100, 131, 231
Bruno of Segni, St., 17
Brussels, 13, 132, 162
Burchard of Worms, 66, 267

Caesarius of Arles, 66, 172
Cambrai, 1–2, 4, 20, 26, 64, 69, 82, 94, 102, 104–106, 109–110, 121, 127, 129, 133, 138, 140, 143, 147, 149, 153–156, 162, 191, 285
Carthusians, 263
Cassian, John, St., 98
Champagne, County, 7
Charlemagne, King of France, 24, 73, 75
Charles II, King of France, 158
Charles VI, King of France, 162
Christ, 12–13, 16–17, 19, 22, 24, 27, 29–33, 36–44, 47, 55, 57, 65, 72, 87, 95–96, 98, 100, 102, 103, 106, 118, 124, 133–134, 139, 142–145, 156, 171–172, 175, 178–181, 231, 261, 267, 269, 273, 284, 288

Christendom, 8, 14, 43, 115–116, 175, 189
Chrysogonos, St., 191
Cicero, 212, 248
Citeaux, 99
Clement I, St., Pope, 66
Clement V, Pope, 60, 148
Clement VI, Pope, 129
Clement VII, Pope, 85–86, 162, 169–170, 175, 238
Cluny, 99
Collège de Navarre, 1, 7–8, 121, 170, 175
Conrad of Gelnhausen, 127
Constantine VI, Byzantine Emperor, 24
Cornelius, 60
Cyprian, St., 201
Cyril, St., 28

Damasus I, Pope, 66
Deusdedit, Pope, 60, 151
Dominic, St., 13–14, 28, 35, 157, 161, 191
Dreux, 162
Duns Scotus, John, 70, 199, 214–216, 219
Durandus of Saint-Pourçain, 199, 216

Embrun, 260
England, 14, 19,, 120, 122, 145, 277
Ephesus, 154
Eugene III, Pope, 89, 134
Eugene IV, Pope, 60
Eusebius of Caesarea, 179
Ezechiel, 159

Fitzralph, Richard, 258
Flagellants, 132
France, 5, 14–15, 95, 105, 120, 125, 149, 159, 170, 191, 277
Francis of Assisi, St., 13–16, 19–20, 22–23, 27–28, 35, 47–49, 51, 100, 157, 160–161, 180, 191, 278
Frederick II, Holy Roman Emperor, 60

Gelasius I, St, Pope, 197–198, 201, 203
Gerard of Borgo San Donnino, 66
Germany, 14, 99, 120, 132, 277
Gerson, Jean, 4, 35, 48–49, 68, 77, 96, 101, 106, 122, 127–128, 131–132, 139, 141, 153, 168, 190, 195, 248, 282, 285, 287
Ghent, 170
Giles of Rome, 62, 185, 199, 215
Godfrey of Fontaines, 216
Grabow, Matthew, 48–49
Grande Chartreuse, 99
Grandmont, 99
Gratian, 66–67, 73, 75, 78, 90, 125–126, 128–129, 146, 151, 173, 184, 197, 200–201, 239, 249–251, 253, 257, 264, 267–268, 270–272
Gregory I (the Great), Pope, 101, 107, 125, 138, 141, 186, 191, 199
Gregory IV, Pope, 78
Gregory VII, Pope, 19, 58, 151
Gregory IX, Pope, 60, 109, 152, 173, 177, 194, 260, 268
Gregory XII, Pope, 274
Gregory of Rimini, 70, 199, 207–208, 210–211, 213–217, 219, 225–228, 230
Grosseteste, Robert, 215–216
Guibert of Tournai, 62
Guido of Baysio, 58–59, 77, 270
Guillaume Saignet, 153
Guy de Roye, 128

Henry of Ghent, 173, 185, 219
Hostiensis, 58–59, 251, 257, 260–265, 269–270
Hugh of St. Victor, 201, 252, 278
Huguccio, 250–251
Hus, John, 83–84, 106, 143–144, 258, 282

Innocent III, Pope, 50, 58, 99, 101, 177, 188, 237
Innocent IV, Pope, 260
Isidore of Seville, St., 67–68

INDEX OF PERSONS AND PLACES

Israel, 28, 38, 40, 47, 49, 125, 142, 159
Italy, 14, 277
Ivo of Chartres, 66, 267

James of Viterbo, Bl., 173
Jeanne de Navarre, Queen Consort of France, 7
Jerome, St., 28, 41, 66–67, 69, 144, 172, 199, 201
Jerusalem, 13, 24, 29, 41, 98
Joachim of Fiore, 11, 14, 17, 20, 23, 26, 36, 38, 49–50, 161
Johannes Andreae, 58, 268
Johannes Monachus, 59
John XXII, Pope, 120, 193, 244, 253, 267
John XXIII, Pope, 24, 27, 44–45, 47, 94, 110, 240, 274
John Chrysostom, St., 139, 144
John of Monzón, 84–91, 134, 169, 175, 182–183, 187, 191–192, 195–196, 202–205, 283
John of Paris, 59, 72, 146, 173, 255
John of Salisbury, 48, 256
Jonas, 163
Judas, 126
Julian of Speyer, 90
Julian (the Apostate), Roman Emperor, 24, 267
Justinian, Roman Emperor, 266–267
Juvenal, 163

Lactantius, 41
Leo VIII, Pope, 73, 75
Le Puy, 1, 64, 129, 285
Louis of Anjou, St., 157–163, 191
Louis of Bavaria, Holy Roman Emperor, 244
Louis of France, St., 191
Lucius III, Pope, 152
Lyons, 190

Marback, 99
Martin V, Pope, 1, 6, 274
Maurice, Byzantine Emperor, 24
Maurice of Prague, 78, 241

Maximus of Turin, St., 184
Metz, 162
Moses, 269–270

Naples, 158–159
Neri, Philip, St., 156
Nicholas II, Pope, 73, 75–76, 107–108, 151, 253
Nicolas of Clamanges, 285
Nicholas of Cusa, 132
Nicholas of Lyra, 26, 50, 193
Nineveh, 163
Norbert of Xanten, St., 99

Olier, Jean-Jacques, 156
Ostia, 260
Otto I, Holy Roman Emperor, 73, 75

Pachomius, St., 98
Paris, 1–3, 7–9, 13, 18, 35, 50, 97, 99, 116, 146, 149, 162, 183, 190–191, 195–196, 202, 237, 240, 255, 265–266, 285, 287
Paul, St., 21, 23, 30, 56, 68, 70–71, 77, 79–80, 84, 88, 95, 124, 127, 140–141, 154–155, 172, 176, 179, 182, 194–195, 201–202, 239, 248–249, 262, 272–273
Persius, 117
Peter, St., 55–60, 77, 87, 96, 174, 179, 194–195, 201, 283
Peter Damian, St., 60, 222
Peter John Olivi, 100, 158
Peter Lombard, 9, 121–122, 184, 201, 215
Peter of Candia, 227
Peter of Luxembourg, St., 157, 162–163, 191
Peter the Chanter, 48, 133, 235
Peter Waldo, 99
Pharisees, 107, 288
Philip IV (The Fair), King of France, 7
Phocas, Byzantine Emperor, 24
Piero della Vigna, 60
Pierre d'Orgemont, 203

Plato, 166, 212
Plotinus, 166
Pseudo-Anacletus, 172
Pseudo-Chrysostom, 139
Pseudo-Clement, 172
Pseudo-Damasus I,, 172
Pseudo-Dionysius, 68–69, 102, 166, 213, 282
Pseudo-Isidore, 66–67, 121, 172, 272
Ptolomey, 35

Rabanus Maurus, 184, 267
Raymond Geoffroi, 158
Rheims, 67, 96, 128, 190
Richard of St. Victor, 17, 278
Robert of Arbrissel, 99
Rome, 57, 61–62, 72, 74, 99, 158, 185, 199, 215
Rottenbuch, 99
Rupert of Deutz, 17

Sibyl, 41
Sidon, 163
Siger of Brabant, 236
Sigismund, Holy Roman Emperor, 274
Sisteron, 260
Spain, 14, 277
Statius, Leonard, 94
Stephen of Tournai, 251

Tempier, Etienne, 202–204, 237
Thomas of Celano, 100
Titus, Roman Emperor, 13
Toulouse, 157–158, 163, 191, 202
Tyconius, 16
Tyre, 163, 179

Ubertino of Casale, 100
Urban II, Pope, 99
Urban IV, Pope, 260
Urban V, Pope, 202–203

Vallombrosa, 99
Vespasian, Roman Emperor, 13
Vitalis of Savigny, St., 99

William Durandus, the Younger, 121
William of Auvergne, 278
William of Auxerre, 199
William of Hildernissen, 36, 132
William of Ockham, 70, 185, 193, 207–208, 210–211, 213–217, 219, 225–226, 229–232, 242–246, 248, 250, 253–255
William of Paris, St., 199
William of St. Amour, 66, 173
Wyclif, John, 83, 106, 143–144, 258, 282

Zabarella, Franciscus, 6, 274

INDEX OF MODERN SCHOLARS

Adam, P., 149
Adams, Marilyn McCord, 219, 232, 245
Alberigo, Giuseppe, 60, 62, 114
Alphandéry, P., 37
Amanieu, A., 109
Arnold, Franz, 251
Aston, T.H., 120
Asztalos, Monica, 236

Baldwin, John H., 133, 235
Bannack, Klaus, 245
Barbaglio, Giuseppe, 211
Bardy, G., 15
Barnes, Jonathan, 213
Baudry, León, 210
Becquet, Jean, 15
Bellitto, Christopher M., 132
Benson, Robert L., 78
Berman, Harold J., 235, 271
Bernstein, Alan, 169–170
Biard, Joël, 218–219
Bishop, Jane, 19
Bleienstein, F., 72
Boler, John F., 219
Bourke, M.M., 65
Brady, Ignatius, 85
Brandmüller, Walter, 115
Brown, D. Catherine, 96, 122, 131, 153
Brown, Raymond E., 56, 65
Brown, Stephen, 227
Brubaker, Leslie, 237
Brundage, James A., 235
Burr, David, 12, 18, 50
Burrow, J.A., 17, 32, 264

Campbell, Thomas, 68
Catto, J.J., 167
Cessario, Romanus, 224

Chappuis, Marguerite, 2
Chatillon, Jean, 15, 18, 97, 156
Chenu, M.D., 48, 53, 97, 176, 178, 214, 216, 224, 264, 271
Clark, David H., 245
Cobban, A.B., 167
Colson, Jean, 65
Congar, Yves, 54, 64–67, 143, 176, 185, 192, 209, 214–216, 224, 231
Constable, Giles, 97, 166
Copleston, Frederick, 219, 232
Courtenay, William J., 182, 222
Crouzel, Henri, 65

Davies, Brian, 140
Davy, M.M., 189
De Gandillac, Maurice, 230
De Ghellinck, Joseph, 214, 271
De Lagarde, George, 244, 253
Delaruelle, E., 104, 145
De Lubac, Henri, 141, 209
De Luca, Luigi, 251, 253
Deman, Thomas, 228
Denifle, H., 121
Dereine, Charles, 15
De Ridder-Symoens, Hilde, 7, 120, 167, 236
Derolez, A., 18
De Silva, Tarouca, 166
De Vooght, Paul, 210
Dickinson, J.C., 122
D'Irsay, Stephan, 167
Dix, Gregory, 65
Doncoeur, Paul, 84
Dondaine, H.F., 68
Donneaud, Henry, 209
Douie, Decima, 143, 192
Dronke, P., 18
Dufeil, Michel, 67, 143, 192
Duffy, Eamon, 145

Emden, A.B., 7, 167
Emmerson, Richard K., 17, 22, 32
English, Edward D., 168
Evans, G.P., 214, 257

Farrer, A.M., 65
Fasolt, Constantin, 3
Favier, Jean, 105, 238
Feld, H., 77
Ferruolo, Stephen C., 167
Finke, Heinrich, 27
Fournier, Marcel, 202
Fournier, Paul, 250
François, H., 162
Frassetto, Michael, 149
Fredricksen, Paula, 17
Fried, Johannes, 236
Froehlich, Karlfried, 77
Fry, Timothy, 138
Fuchs, Oswald, 210

Gabriel, Astrik L., 167, 169
Gagnér, Sten, 252
Gallagher, Clarence, 260, 263
García y García, Antonio, 236
Gardeil, A., 228
Gaudemet, Jean, 251
Gilson, Etienne, 231
Glorieux, Palémon, 4, 7, 13, 16, 49, 121, 153, 168, 181–182, 189, 191, 238, 246
Gorochov, Nathalie, 7
Grabmann, M., 200
Grassi, Onorato, 207, 217, 228
Gréa, A., 109
Grevy-Pons, Nicole, 153
Grundmann, H., 166
Gryson, Roger, 176
Guelluy, Robert, 166–167, 217
Guenée, Bernard, 2, 84, 277–279, 281
Guillemain, Bernard, 95, 238

Hart, Columba, 19
Harvey, Warren, 247
Hayden, Dunstan, 217
Hayez, Michel, 11

Hefele, Karl J., 108
Helmholz, Richard, 240
Hödl, Ludwig, 184

Izbicki, Thomas M, 132

Jenkins, John I., 217, 224
Jordan, Mark D., 224
Jugie, Martin, 85

Kaczmarek, Ludger, 218–219
Kaminsky, Howard, 104
Kerby-Fulton, Kathryn, 19
Kirk, Kenneth, 65
Krey, Philip D.W., 26
Krings, Herman, 166
Kuttner, Stephan, 60, 107, 235, 239, 250, 252, 262–263

Ladner, Gerhart B., 17, 31–32, 78, 97, 166, 179, 264
Lampe, G.W.H., 18
Lang, Albert, 228
Lapsanski, Duane U., 97
Leader, Damien Riehl, 167
Le Bras, Gabriel, 167, 250–253, 257, 271
Leclef, Jacques, 110
Leclercq, Henri, 108
Leclercq, Jean, 72, 89, 131, 167, 176, 190, 216
Lee, Richard A., Jr., 217
Lefebvre, Charles, 260
Leff, Gordon, 143, 219, 232, 244–245
Lerner, Robert E., 132
Lieberman, Max, 20
Linehan, Peter, 59
Little, A.G., 189
Lobrichon, Guy, 18
Luibheid, Colm, 68
Lynch, John, 176
Lytle, Guy, 120

Maierù, Alfonso, 230
Maillard-Luypaert, Monique, 2, 109
Mandonnet, P., 121, 201
Manz, L., 166

Martin, Hervé, 125, 190
Masson, R., 85
Matter, E. Ann, 17
Mauer, Armand, 215
Mc Donnell, K., 245
Mc Ginn, Bernard, 17, 20, 22, 32, 36, 50
Mc Grade, Arthur S., 245
Miethke, Jürgen, 6, 59, 121, 245
Miller, Bernhard, 2, 207, 216, 218
Millet, Hèléne, 36–37, 95
Moeller, Charles, 64
Mollat, George, 112
Mollat, Guillaume, 60, 104
Mollat, Michel, 149
Moonan, Lawrence, 222
Moraw, Peter, 120
Morin, G., 139
Mortier, Daniel, 85
Moynihan, Robert, 20
Musto, Ronald, 158

Nautin, P., 139
Naz, R., 85
Newman, Barbara, 19
Noonan, John, 250

Oakley, Francis, 2–3, 6, 48, 60, 76, 78, 88, 108, 139, 245, 248–249, 254–255, 279
Oberman, Heiko A., 11, 70, 89, 207–208, 222, 232
O'Connor, E.D., 85
Offler, H.S., 245
Olsen, Glenn, 179
Ourliac, Paul, 129
Ouy, Gilbert, 5, 279
Overfield, James H., 120
Owens, Joseph, 217

Paetow, J., 168
Pantin, W.A., 122
Pascoe Louis B., 11, 49, 69, 77–78, 96, 106–107, 128, 141, 153, 168–169, 180, 195, 248, 255, 257, 274
Pasztor, E., 158

Paul, Jacques, 158
Pedersen, Olaf, 7
Pelster, F., 189
Peuchmaurd, M., 54, 174
Phelps, J. M, 97
Pierrard, Pierre, 105, 109, 127, 149
Pluta, Olaf, 2, 210, 218–219
Post, Gaines, 107, 168
Post, R.R., 49
Posthumus Meyjes, G.H.M., 77, 194, 236
Powicke, F.M., 7
Press, Gerald A., 168

Rashdall, Hastings, 7, 167
Reeves, Marjorie, 11, 20, 50
Resnick, Irven R., 222
Reynolds, Roger, 118
Riché, Pierre, 18, 167
Rief, Josef, 166
Rivière, Jean, 81
Robilliard, A.J., 53
Roques, René, 166
Rose, Jonathan, 235
Rüegg, Walter, 7
Rusch, A., 23
Rusconi, Roberto, 11

Saint-Blançat, Louis, 207–208, 230
Salembier, Louis, 1–2, 4, 58, 64, 84, 121, 127, 132, 156, 231, 279
Schulze, Manfred, 208, 230
Schwartz, Baruch, 247
Sears, Elisabeth, 17, 32, 264
Seeboeck, Philibert, 26
Serene, Eileen, 217
Shogimen, Takaski, 236
Smalley, Beryl, 18
Smith, L., 26
Smoller, Laura Ackerman, 2, 11, 16, 19–20, 23, 29, 34–35, 45–46
Spinka, Matthew, 143
Steiger, J., 85
Stockmeier, Peter, 179
Strayer, Joseph, 104
Streuer, S.R., 228

Stump, Phillip H., 53, 104, 112, 114, 123, 135, 148, 154
Swanson, R.N., 145, 238

Taber, Douglass, 83, 85–86, 169, 238
Teeuwen, Mariken, 7
Thijssen, J.M.M.H., 85
Thomson, A.H., 109
Thurot, Charles, 7, 168
Tierney, Brian, 59, 80, 146, 184, 244–245, 251, 255, 270
Toynbee, Margaret, 158
Tschackert, Paul, 2–3, 84, 156, 231

Uelmen, Amelia J., 236
Ullmann, Walter, 32, 247, 250–251, 261–263
Urban, L., 245

Valois, Noël, 23
Van Acker, L., 18
Van den Eynde, Damien, 252
Van Engen, John, 49, 97, 131
Vanhoye, Albert, 65
Van Steenberghen, Fernand, 156, 216, 237
Vauchez, André, 37, 131, 157, 159, 160
Verger, Jacques, 7
Vodola, Elizabeth, 260
Von Campenhausen, Hans, 65
Von Simpson, Otto, 179

Watanabe, Morimichi, 132
Watt, J.A., 58
Weijers, Olga, 7, 84, 183
Weinrich, Lorenz, 6, 59, 121

Yunck, John A., 235

STUDIES IN MEDIEVAL AND REFORMATION TRADITIONS

(*Formerly Studies in Medieval and Reformation Thought*)

Founded by Heiko A. Oberman†
Edited by Andrew Colin Gow

1. DOUGLASS, E.J.D. *Justification in Late Medieval Preaching.* 2nd ed. 1989
2. WILLIS, E.D. *Calvin's Catholic Christology.* 1966 *out of print*
3. POST, R.R. *The Modern Devotion.* 1968 *out of print*
4. STEINMETZ, D.C. *Misericordia Dei.* The Theology of Johannes von Staupitz. 1968 *out of print*
5. O'MALLEY, J.W. *Giles of Viterbo on Church and Reform.* 1968 *out of print*
6. OZMENT, S.E. *Homo Spiritualis.* The Anthropology of Tauler, Gerson and Luther. 1969
7. PASCOE, L.B. *Jean Gerson: Principles of Church Reform.* 1973 *out of print*
8. HENDRIX, S.H. *Ecclesia in Via.* Medieval Psalms Exegesis and the *Dictata super Psalterium* (1513-1515) of Martin Luther. 1974
9. TREXLER, R.C. *The Spiritual Power.* Republican Florence under Interdict. 1974
10. TRINKAUS, Ch. with OBERMAN, H.A. (eds.). *The Pursuit of Holiness.* 1974 *out of print*
11. SIDER, R.J. *Andreas Bodenstein von Karlstadt.* 1974
12. HAGEN, K. *A Theology of Testament in the Young Luther.* 1974
13. MOORE, Jr., W.L. *Annotatiunculae D. Iohanne Eckio Praelectore.* 1976
14. OBERMAN, H.A. with BRADY, Jr., Th.A. (eds.). *Itinerarium Italicum.* Dedicated to Paul Oskar Kristeller. 1975
15. KEMPFF, D. *A Bibliography of Calviniana.* 1959-1974. 1975 *out of print*
16. WINDHORST, C. *Täuferisches Taufverständnis.* 1976
17. KITTELSON, J.M. *Wolfgang Capito.* 1975
18. DONNELLY, J.P. *Calvinism and Scholasticism in Vermigli's Doctrine of Man and Grace.* 1976
19. LAMPING, A.J. *Ulrichus Velenus (Oldř ich Velenský) and his Treatise against the Papacy.* 1976
20. BAYLOR, M.G. *Action and Person.* Conscience in Late Scholasticism and the Young Luther. 1977
21. COURTENAY, W.J. *Adam Wodeham.* 1978
22. BRADY, Jr., Th.A. *Ruling Class, Regime and Reformation at Strasbourg, 1520-1555.* 1978
23. KLAASSEN, W. *Michael Gaismair.* 1978
24. BERNSTEIN, A.E. *Pierre d'Ailly and the Blanchard Affair.* 1978
25. BUCER, M. *Correspondance.* Tome I (Jusqu'en 1524). Publié par J. Rott. 1979
26. POSTHUMUS MEYJES, G.H.M. *Jean Gerson et l'Assemblée de Vincennes (1329).* 1978
27. VIVES, J.L. *In Pseudodialecticos.* Ed. by Ch. Fantazzi. 1979
28. BORNERT, R. *La Réforme Protestante du Culte à Strasbourg au XVIe siècle (1523-1598).* 1981
29. CASTELLIO, S. *De Arte Dubitandi.* Ed. by E. Feist Hirsch. 1981
30. BUCER, M. *Opera Latina.* Vol I. Publié par C. Augustijn, P. Fraenkel, M. Lienhard. 1982
31. BÜSSER, F. *Wurzeln der Reformation in Zürich.* 1985 *out of print*
32. FARGE, J.K. *Orthodoxy and Reform in Early Reformation France.* 1985
33. 34. BUCER, M. *Etudes sur les relations de Bucer avec les Pays-Bas.* I. Etudes; II. Documents. Par J.V. Pollet. 1985
35. HELLER, H. *The Conquest of Poverty.* The Calvinist Revolt in Sixteenth Century France. 1986

36. MEERHOFF, K. *Rhétorique et poétique au XVIᵉ siècle en France.* 1986
37. GERRITS, G. H. *Inter timorem et spem.* Gerard Zerbolt of Zutphen. 1986
38. POLIZIANO, A. *Lamia.* Ed. by A. Wesseling. 1986
39. BRAW, C. *Bücher im Staube.* Die Theologie Johann Arndts in ihrem Verhältnis zur Mystik. 1986
40. BUCER, M. *Opera Latina.* Vol. II. Enarratio in Evangelion Iohannis (1528, 1530, 1536). Publié par I. Backus. 1988
41. BUCER, M. *Opera Latina.* Vol. III. Martin Bucer and Matthew Parker: Flori-legium Patristicum. Edition critique. Publié par P. Fraenkel. 1988
42. BUCER, M. *Opera Latina.* Vol. IV. Consilium Theologicum Privatim Conscriptum. Publié par P. Fraenkel. 1988
43. BUCER, M. *Correspondance.* Tome II (1524-1526). Publié par J. Rott. 1989
44. RASMUSSEN, T. *Inimici Ecclesiae.* Das ekklesiologische Feindbild in Luthers "Dictata super Psalterium" (1513-1515) im Horizont der theologischen Tradition. 1989
45. POLLET, J. *Julius Pflug et la crise religieuse dans l'Allemagne du XVIᵉ siècle.* Essai de synthèse biographique et théologique. 1990
46. BUBENHEIMER, U. *Thomas Müntzer.* Herkunft und Bildung. 1989
47. BAUMAN, C. *The Spiritual Legacy of Hans Denck.* Interpretation and Translation of Key Texts. 1991
48. OBERMAN, H.A. and JAMES, F.A., III (eds.). in cooperation with SAAK, E.L. *Via Augustini.* Augustine in the Later Middle Ages, Renaissance and Reformation: Essays in Honor of Damasus Trapp. 1991 *out of print*
49. SEIDEL MENCHI, S. *Erasmus als Ketzer.* Reformation und Inquisition im Italien des 16. Jahrhunderts. 1993
50. SCHILLING, H. *Religion, Political Culture, and the Emergence of Early Modern Society.* Essays in German and Dutch History. 1992
51. DYKEMA, P.A. and OBERMAN, H.A. (eds.). *Anticlericalism in Late Medieval and Early Modern Europe.* 2nd ed. 1994
52. 53. KRIEGER, Chr. and LIENHARD, M. (eds.). *Martin Bucer and Sixteenth Century Europe.* Actes du colloque de Strasbourg (28-31 août 1991). 1993
54. SCREECH, M.A. *Clément Marot: A Renaissance Poet discovers the World.* Lutheranism, Fabrism and Calvinism in the Royal Courts of France and of Navarre and in the Ducal Court of Ferrara. 1994
55. GOW, A.C. *The Red Jews: Antisemitism in an Apocalyptic Age, 1200-1600.* 1995
56. BUCER, M. *Correspondance.* Tome III (1527-1529). Publié par Chr. Krieger et J. Rott. 1989
57. SPIJKER, W. VAN 'T. *The Ecclesiastical Offices in the Thought of Martin Bucer.* Translated by J. Vriend (text) and L.D. Bierma (notes). 1996
58. GRAHAM, M.F. *The Uses of Reform.* 'Godly Discipline' and Popular Behavior in Scotland and Beyond, 1560-1610. 1996
59. AUGUSTIJN, C. *Erasmus. Der Humanist als Theologe und Kirchenreformer.* 1996
60. McCOOG SJ, T.M. *The Society of Jesus in Ireland, Scotland, and England 1541-1588.* 'Our Way of Proceeding?' 1996
61. FISCHER, N. und KOBELT-GROCH, M. (Hrsg.). *Außenseiter zwischen Mittelalter und Neuzeit.* Festschrift für Hans-Jürgen Goertz zum 60. Geburtstag. 1997
62. NIEDEN, M. *Organum Deitatis.* Die Christologie des Thomas de Vio Cajetan. 1997
63. BAST, R.J. *Honor Your Fathers.* Catechisms and the Emergence of a Patriarchal Ideology in Germany, 1400-1600. 1997
64. ROBBINS, K.C. *City on the Ocean Sea: La Rochelle, 1530-1650.* Urban Society, Religion, and Politics on the French Atlantic Frontier. 1997
65. BLICKLE, P. *From the Communal Reformation to the Revolution of the Common Man.* 1998
66. FELMBERG, B.A.R. *Die Ablaßtheorie Kardinal Cajetans (1469-1534).* 1998

67. CUNEO, P.F. *Art and Politics in Early Modern Germany.* Jörg Breu the Elder and the Fashioning of Political Identity, ca. 1475-1536. 1998
68. BRADY, Jr., Th.A. *Communities, Politics, and Reformation in Early Modern Europe.* 1998
69. McKEE, E.A. *The Writings of Katharina Schütz Zell.* 1. The Life and Thought of a Sixteenth-Century Reformer. 2. A Critical Edition. 1998
70. BOSTICK, C.V. *The Antichrist and the Lollards.* Apocalyticism in Late Medieval and Reformation England. 1998
71. BOYLE, M. O'ROURKE. *Senses of Touch.* Human Dignity and Deformity from Michelangelo to Calvin. 1998
72. TYLER, J.J. *Lord of the Sacred City.* The *Episcopus Exclusus* in Late Medieval and Early Modern Germany. 1999
74. WITT, R.G. *'In the Footsteps of the Ancients'.* The Origins of Humanism from Lovato to Bruni. 2000
77. TAYLOR, L.J. *Heresy and Orthodoxy in Sixteenth-Century Paris.* François le Picart and the Beginnings of the Catholic Reformation. 1999
78. BUCER, M. *Briefwechsel/Correspondance.* Band IV (Januar-September 1530). Herausgegeben und bearbeitet von R. Friedrich, B. Hamm und A. Puchta. 2000
79. MANETSCH, S.M. *Theodore Beza and the Quest for Peace in France, 1572-1598.* 2000
80. GODMAN, P. *The Saint as Censor.* Robert Bellarmine between Inquisition and Index. 2000
81. SCRIBNER, R.W. *Religion and Culture in Germany (1400-1800).* Ed. L. Roper. 2001
82. KOOI, C. *Liberty and Religion.* Church and State in Leiden's Reformation, 1572-1620. 2000
83. BUCER, M. *Opera Latina.* Vol. V. Defensio adversus axioma catholicum id est criminationem R.P. Roberti Episcopi Abrincensis (1534). Ed. W.I.P. Hazlett. 2000
84. BOER, W. DE. *The Conquest of the Soul.* Confession, Discipline, and Public Order in Counter-Reformation Milan. 2001
85. EHRSTINE, G. *Theater, culture, and community in Reformation Bern, 1523-1555.* 2001
86. CATTERALL, D. *Community Without Borders.* Scot Migrants and the Changing Face of Power in the Dutch Republic, c. 1600-1700. 2002
87. BOWD, S.D. *Reform Before the Reformation.* Vincenzo Querini and the Religious Renaissance in Italy. 2002
88. PELC, M. *Illustrium Imagines.* Das Porträtbuch der Renaissance. 2002
89. SAAK, E.L. *High Way to Heaven.* The Augustinian Platform between Reform and Reformation, 1292-1524. 2002
90. WITTNEBEN, E.L. *Bonagratia von Bergamo*, Franziskanerjurist und Wortführer seines Ordens im Streit mit Papst Johannes XXII. 2003
91. ZIKA, C. *Exorcising our Demons,* Magic, Witchcraft and Visual Culture in Early Modern Europe. 2002
92. MATTOX, M.L. *"Defender of the Most Holy Matriarchs"*, Martin Luther's Interpretation of the Women of Genesis in the *Enarrationes in Genesin*, 1535-45. 2003
93. LANGHOLM, O. *The Merchant in the Confessional,* Trade and Price in the Pre-Reformation Penitential Handbooks. 2003
94. BACKUS, I. *Historical Method and Confessional Identity in the Era of the Reformation (1378-1615).* 2003
95. FOGGIE, J.P. *Renaissance Religion in Urban Scotland.* The Dominican Order, 1450-1560. 2003
96. LÖWE, J.A. *Richard Smyth and the Language of Orthodoxy.* Re-imagining Tudor Catholic Polemicism. 2003
97. HERWAARDEN, J. VAN. *Between Saint James and Erasmus.* Studies in Late-Medieval Religious Life: Devotion and Pilgrimage in The Netherlands. 2003
98. PETRY, Y. *Gender, Kabbalah and the Reformation.* The Mystical Theology of Guillaume Postel (1510–1581). 2004

99. EISERMANN, F., SCHLOTHEUBER, E. und HONEMANN, V. *Studien und Texte zur literarischen und materiellen Kultur der Frauenklöster im späten Mittelalter.* Ergebnisse eines Arbeitsgesprächs in der Herzog August Bibliothek Wolfenbüttel, 24.-26. Febr. 1999. 2004
100. WITCOMBE, C.L.C.E. *Copyright in the Renaissance.* Prints and the *Privilegio* in Sixteenth-Century Venice and Rome. 2004
101. BUCER, M. *Briefwechsel/Correspondance.* Band V (September 1530-Mai 1531). Herausgegeben und bearbeitet von R. Friedrich, B. Hamm, A. Puchta und R. Liebenberg. 2004
102. MALONE, C.M. *Façade as Spectacle: Ritual and Ideology at Wells Cathedral.* 2004
103. KAUFHOLD, M. (eds.) *Politische Reflexion in der Welt des späten Mittelalters / Political Thought in the Age of Scholasticism.* Essays in Honour of Jürgen Miethke. 2004
104. BLICK, S. and TEKIPPE, R. (eds.). *Art and Architecture of Late Medieval Pilgrimage in Northern Europe and England.* 2004
105. PASCOE, L.B., S.J., *Church and Reform.* Bishops, Theologians, and Canon Lawyers in the Thought of Pierre d'Ailly (1351-1420). 2005
106. SCOTT, T. *Town, Country, and Regions in Reformation Germany.* 2005